The Dynamics of Managing Diversity
A Critical Approach
Third Edition

Gill Kirton

Anne-marie Greene

Taylor & Francis Group

LONDON AND NEW YORK

First Published by Butterworth-Heinemann
This edition published 2011 by Routledge
2 Park Square, Milton Park, Abingdon, Oxon OX14 4RN
711 Third Avenue, New York, NY 10017

Notice
No responsibility is assumed by the publisher for any injury and/or damage to persons
or property as a matter of products liability, negligence or otherwise, or from any use
or operation of any methods, products, instructions or ideas contained in the material
herein. Because of rapid advances in the medical sciences, in particular, independent
verification of diagnoses and drug dosages should be made

British Library Cataloguing in Publication Data
A catalogue record for this book is available from the British Library

Library of Congress Cataloging-in-Publication Data
A catalog record for this book is available from the Library of Congress

ISBN: 978-1-85617-812-9

The Dynamics of
Managing Diversity

Contents

Acknowledgements

The authors wish to thank Hayley Salter and the team at Elsevier for their support in the writing of the third edition of *The Dynamics of Managing Diversity*. We also wish to thank the contributors – Linda Johnson and Sue Johnstone for their continued commitment to this book. The reviewers are also thanked for their feedback, encouragement and patience – we will take on board more of your comments in the fourth edition!

DEDICATIONS

This third edition is dedicated to our growing families.

About the Authors and Contributors

ABOUT THE AUTHORS

Gill Kirton, BA, MA, PhD, LicIPD, is Reader in Employment Relations at the Centre for Research in Equality and Diversity, School of Business and Management, Queen Mary, University of London. Gill teaches diversity management at undergraduate and post-graduate levels. Her current research focuses on organisational equality and diversity in a variety of different contexts. She is particularly interested in employee experiences, especially those of marginalized groups. She has published articles on gender, race and trade unionism; workplace equality and diversity management; and black and minority ethnic workers' careers, in a range of refereed journals. She has published three other books – a critical review of women's employment *Women, Employment and Organisations* (2006, Routledge) co-authored with Judith Glover; a research monograph *The Making of Women Trade Unionists* (2006, Ashgate); and a research based book *Diversity Management in the UK: Organisational and Stakeholder Experiences,* co-authored with Anne-marie Greene (2009, Routledge).

Anne-marie Greene, BA, MA, PhD, GradIPD, is Reader in Industrial Relations at Warwick Business School, University of Warwick. Her research interests include gender and workplace trade unionism, diversity and employment relations and the gender implications of the use of new information and communication technologies for collective action. She has published widely on these areas and is also author of a research monograph *Voices from the Shop Floor: Dramas of the Employment Relationship* (2001, Ashgate). Anne-marie teaches industrial relations, human resource management and equality and diversity and in addition is an active trade unionist.

ABOUT THE CONTRIBUTORS

Linda Johnson, MPhil, LLM, LLB, DipASHE, Cert Ed., is Head of Learning and Teaching at London Metropolitan Business School. Linda has been teaching employment law at undergraduate and postgraduate levels for 25 years and specialises in comparative discrimination law. Her research interests include race discrimination law and the impact of EU discrimination law on Member States.

Sue Johnstone, LLM, BA, is Editor of Equal Opportunities Review. Previously, she was a Principal Lecturer in employment law at University of North London, where she taught employment law at undergraduate and postgraduate levels for 15 years. She continues to lecture on discrimination law to HR practitioners and trade union officers and sits as a member of the Employment Tribunal. Her research interests include equal pay and age discrimination.

List of Tables and Exhibits

TABLES

EXHIBITS

Introduction – what is diversity?

Aim

To introduce the reader to the main themes of the book.

Objectives

- To outline the contexts and concepts and areas of policy and practice explored in the book.
- To provide guidance on using the book.

1.1 BACKGROUND TO THE BOOK

This is the third edition of *The Dynamics of Managing Diversity* first published in 2000. The idea for writing the first edition of this book arose from one author's experiences in planning and teaching a final year undergraduate module entitled 'Managing Diversity' in the late 1990s. That module's aim was to provide the theoretical and conceptual underpinning necessary to understand the changing British and European contexts of workforce diversity and the changing equality and diversity policies and practices of government, organisations, line-managers and human resource practitioners. Difficulties were found in identifying a suitable textbook to support the programme of teaching and learning, this despite research-based literature contained in both texts and journals and despite a range of textbooks and management guides largely originating from the US. One problem was that the management guides generally did not provide the theoretical and conceptual substance, whilst US textbooks did not provide a relevant contextual backdrop for a discussion of the UK and European approaches. Following in-depth student evaluation of the module, involving questionnaires and focus groups, the conclusion arrived at was that it was timely to write a text largely aimed at the UK market that would situate diversity and equality debates within the context of the British and European labour markets. This book explores employment patterns and outcomes of diverse social groups and the policies and practices of key actors in the labour market. It is now widely accepted that there are six main equality and diversity strands: gender, race/ethnicity, disability, sexual orientation, age and religion. At the time of writing the first and second editions, we argued that five social groups, women, black and minority ethnic people, older people, disabled people and lesbians and gay men, were widely recognized as experiencing inequalities, discrimination and disadvantage in employment. We therefore focused our analysis on these five groups. However, since then religion has increasingly been seen as a source of discrimination and disadvantage that can work independently of race/ethnicity. Whilst in this third edition we are unable to provide separate and detailed analysis of religion, it is dealt with where religion intersects with other sources of discrimination. In the fourth edition, due to be published in 2012, we plan to give more comprehensive coverage to religion. This third edition provides updated information on the labour market and legal contexts of diversity and explores some of the new developments in the theory and practice of equality and diversity policy.

This book's primary aim is to act as a teaching and learning support to modules centred on equality, diversity or discrimination in employment and to allow students to acquire the contextual, theoretical and conceptual tools necessary to access and understand the rich variety of research-based literature that now exists in the field. It is not intended as a replacement of that literature. As is the case with any text, it should be regarded as a departure point, rather than as a whole package of study and programme of learning in itself. Our aim is to stimulate students' interest in this field of study by our mapping of the territory. The further reading and references we provide should be consulted in order to deepen and broaden understanding. Feedback from the first and second editions indicates that the book has also proved a useful resource for academic readers because of its synthesis and critique of the literature in the fields of equality and diversity.

The purpose of this introductory chapter is to introduce and summarize the main themes of the book.

1.2 WHAT IS DIVERSITY?

The title of this book was chosen in the late 1990s and reflected the changes that were occurring at that time in theorizing equality, developments in organisational approaches to equality policy-making and the shift towards greater recognition of workforce diversity by employers, government, trade unions and other stakeholders. The term 'managing diversity' was popularized largely by the publication of Kandola and Fullerton's (1994) book aimed at practitioners. Since then 'diversity management' or simply 'diversity policy' has become the typical label in British organisations for policies and practices that would once have fallen under the heading of 'equal opportunities' or simply 'equality policy'. Many academic authors, including ourselves, have now settled on the label 'diversity management' and it is this that we use throughout the book when discussing policy-making and policy approaches. There is now far more academic literature addressing the theoretical and conceptual underpinning of diversity than previously and where necessary for the sake of clarity we call this 'diversity approaches'.

Unlike diversity policies, equality policies have a long history in the UK, having been part of employment policy and standard business practice (for large organisations at least) since the early 1980s following the introduction of the Sex Discrimination Act (1975) and the Race Relations Act (1976). Traditional 'equal opportunities' issues, such as race and sex discrimination, cannot be divorced from the broader issues included within diversity management such as individual and cultural differences. Where equality and diversity policies diverge is on the question of rationale. Traditionally, 'equal opportunities' reflected a moral concern for social justice, which recognized and involved implementing measures to eliminate social group-based discrimination and disadvantage. However, one of the main criticisms of 1980s-style 'equal opportunities' policies was that they were viewed by many as negative in approach. Failure to comply with the law could carry penalties, but organisations were not compelled to actually promote equality. There was also concern about focusing on the negative dimensions of social group-based difference, e.g. assuming that difference equals disadvantage. Even though advocates of diversity management do not propose abandoning the social justice principles of 'equal opportunities' altogether, it was suggested in the mid-1990s that diversity would be a new way forward (e.g. Kandola and Fullerton, 1994; IPD, 1996) for business organisations. The cornerstone of diversity management is the belief that it will deliver benefits to the organisation, in other words there is a 'business case' for work-force diversity (Cornelius et al., 2001). It is argued that organisations can gain in a number of different ways from workforce diversity. In policy terms, popular conceptions of diversity management emphasize individual difference over social group-based difference and downplay discrimination and disadvantage, while being upbeat about the positive dimensions of group-based difference. Without doubt diversity management has a certain appeal, but it was also accused fairly early on, based on the US experience, of 'upbeat naivety' (Prasad et al., 1997) because of the way it de-emphasizes the conflicts, problems and dilemmas involved in implementing meaningful initiatives and practices. These issues and ideas are explored in further detail in this book.

1.3 THE BRITISH AND EUROPEAN DIVERSITY CONTEXTS

There are salient differences in the social, economic, legal and historical contexts of different countries, which shape employment policy and practice at organisational and institutional levels, as well as impacting on the employment patterns and experiences of diverse social groups. Consequently, debates on employment policy and practice must be contextualized if the patterns and experiences are to be understood correctly. For this reason we have chosen to situate our discussion of equality and diversity largely within the British and European contexts.

In contrast, much of the diversity literature emanates from the US and whilst that literature can be useful for conceptual and theoretical debates, it is important to recognize that these debates take place within very different social, economic, legal and historical contexts. Because of contextual differences, the concerns of policy-makers in the US are not entirely transferable to the British context. For example, in the 1990s it was claimed that by 2000, white males would no longer be the dominant demographic group *entering* the US labour market (Arvey et al., 1996). This is because women and minority ethnic groups were projected to comprise a larger proportion of new entrants than formerly. US employers were urged to make adjustments to employment policy and practice to attract the new 'types' of workers. Similar arguments about increasing workforce diversity in the UK context are often put forward because of the somewhat younger age structure of some minority ethnic groups. However, the demography of the UK is markedly different from that of the US. Of particular note, when comparing the

US and UK, is the sizes of the two countries' minority ethnic populations, which are now approximately 28% and 8%, respectively. It is argued (e.g. Edwards, 1995) that these overall figures shape government policy and concerns. For instance, with a larger minority ethnic population and a history of slavery and racial segregation, US policy-makers have historically paid more attention to redressing ethnic disadvantage, partly in order to avoid widespread civil disturbance. This has been done via policies such as 'affirmative action', set against the past denial of civil rights for the black population and the perceived need to put 'right' the 'wrongs' of the past.

Within the UK the growth of a multi-racial society has more recent origins in post-war, government-sponsored immigration (Solomos, 1989) and although the minority ethnic share of the working-age population is growing, the overall size of the working-age population is decreasing. Whilst minority ethnic disadvantage is a significant feature of the UK labour market, the origins of disadvantage are rather different from the US context and the consequences and solutions are therefore not identical. For example, in the UK a more liberal, less interventionist policy approach has been taken and the legislation all but prohibits what is termed here, 'positive discrimination' (the policy equivalent of the US's 'affirmative action'). We have chosen to situate this book largely within the UK context. However, as a member of the European Union (EU), the UK context is influenced by political, social and legal developments within Europe, therefore the book also examines diversity in the European context.

Another important difference between the US and UK contexts is the circumstances surrounding the emergence of the diversity discourse. In the US, the seemingly less threatening diversity discourse has risen to the fore because of backlash and resistance to affirmative action programmes. Critics of affirmative action programmes argue that 'preferential policies' violate the rights of others to positions under the 'merit principle' (Edwards, 1995: 179). There was also concern that the 'wrong' people were paying the costs of past discriminatory practice, e.g. it is argued by some that white American men cannot get good quality jobs (*ibid*: 184). This is certainly a spurious claim, lacking empirical support, but it has nevertheless been powerful enough to cause the less threatening and less controversial diversity paradigm to emerge. With its emphasis on valuing individual difference and downplaying group-based difference, diversity approaches do not seek to engineer employment outcomes for particular social groups in the way that affirmative action does, and diversity management therefore often proves capable of winning the approval of white American males (Yakura, 1996). In the UK, whilst the less threatening nature of diversity management undoubtedly appeals to many policy-makers, it emanates more from the widespread perceived need to link equality objectives to broader business and organisational objectives. It is argued that failure to do so has been one of the key weaknesses of the traditional 'equal opportunity' approach. Therefore, diversity management was said to constitute a 'new way forward' (IPD, 1996) for beleaguered equality policies.

Our examination of the macrostructures and microstructures of inequality and the theoretical explanations is situated within debates about equality and diversity and whether recognition and celebration of workforce diversity offers a new way forward in policy terms. Our reading of the existing research-based literature leads us to a rather negative conclusion on this point. As shown in Chapters 5 and 8, most academic commentators remain sceptical about the business case for diversity and its ability to deliver equality for all. This is because of the contingent and partial nature of business case arguments and the fact that many British organisations can meet their objectives either without workforce diversity or without actually *valuing* diversity. Therefore, it is necessary to continue to recognize inequalities and to develop policies to redress discrimination and disadvantage. It also remains important for diversity management policies to grow from and onto existing equality policies, rather than replacing them.

1.4 THE SOCIAL CONSTRUCTION OF INEQUALITIES

Gender and race can be regarded as the major organizing principles of the labour market, with disability, age and sexual orientation being factors that also influence employment patterns and outcomes. Therefore we can still say that these five dimensions of diversity are main sources of employment discrimination and disadvantage, even though as stated above we recognize that religion can also be a significant factor influencing employment opportunities and experiences.

The official statistics collected by the Office for National Statistics (ONS) reveal that women are an important source of labour in the UK with 70% in employment. Women's employment is now at the highest rate ever and they comprise approximately 45% of the workforce. More than two-thirds of working-age women with dependent children are in employment. However, women are concentrated in a narrow range of sex-typed occupations and they continue to meet a 'glass ceiling' higher up the organisational ladder. Men are still far more likely than women to be managers and senior officials (ONS, 2008). Non-white minority ethnic people comprise about 6% of the British workforce and are disproportionately found in lower-skilled and lower-grade jobs. In particular, they are under-represented in senior management grades in large organisations despite increased average qualification levels. Disabled people are also over-represented in low-skilled, low-status jobs; people over 50 have more chance of being long-term unemployed and are less likely to receive training from their employers to update their skills; lesbians and gay men frequently encounter discrimination and harassment at the workplace.

Class mediates these sources of discrimination; for example, it is not the case that all men are at the top and all women are at the bottom (Cockburn, 1991). The picture is far more complex than this with educational attainment, occupation and income also playing a role in determining the work opportunities and experiences of individual men and women in the UK. However, both sexism and racism cut across class (Anthias and Yuval-Davis, 1992), such that middle-class women and minority ethnic people suffer sex and race discrimination despite their relatively privileged class position. Working-class women and minority ethnic people suffer the deprivations of their class, as well as gender and race specific deprivations. As Hall (1978) puts it '*Race is the modality in which class is lived. It is also the medium in which class relations are experienced*' (in Cockburn, 1991: 60). The same could be said of gender. We do not offer an explicit class analysis of inequalities, because of the intersection of class with the other sources of labour market disadvantage we concentrate on. We start from the position that certain groups of people enter employment and organisations already disadvantaged by wider social inequalities as reflected in, for example, the education system. The discrimination they meet in employment reinforces their disadvantaged position and militates against their progress.

Why do these patterns of inequality exist? One view drawn from neoclassical economics is that employment outcomes (e.g. pay, status or type of occupation) simply reflect a combination of individual merit, preferences and choices. So for example, this perspective would posit that women choose to go into primary school teaching or nursing knowing that the pay is relatively poor, because they prefer to work in nurturing and caring roles. Another argument is that inequalities exist because the capitalist system of production is based on the principles of market competition, which inherently creates winners and losers.

The different explanations have implications for the nature and content of equality and diversity policies. For example, should we try to ensure more diverse representation in management, or should we assume that some people (women?) prefer to stay at the lower end of the job hierarchy, perhaps so that they can balance paid work with family responsibilities? If the market creates a competition, surely the most able will win, so why should we create policies to give some groups a helping hand? The concern from an equality and diversity perspective is that people are not always able to exercise 'free' choice. For example, throughout the developed world, society does expect women to take primary responsibility for the family and this gendered ideology influences the behaviour of institutions, organisations and individual women. Further, winners and losers in the labour market 'competition' are not randomly distributed throughout the working-age population; instead they are concentrated in certain segments of the population. The five groups we identify – women, minority ethnic people, disabled people, older people and lesbians and gay men – are often the 'losers' in the competitive market and social justice would demand that we are concerned about this. An alternative, sociological explanation is that employment discrimination and patterns of inequality do not simply happen; they occur because of the actions of organisations and individuals and therefore are not inevitable or insurmountable. From this point of view, policy-making can make a difference. For example, if hospital doctors worked shorter, more family-friendly hours, perhaps more women would choose to become doctors rather than nurses? One of the problems inherent in traditional approaches to equality policy is that social group membership is usually conceptualized in juxtaposition to the dominant majority group (Roberts, 1996), which, in the UK employment context, is usually the white, non-disabled, heterosexual male. This means that, for example, men's employment and career patterns are taken as the desirable norm against which women are judged. Therefore if women are unable to work long hours because of family responsibilities, they can expect to experience career setbacks. The question is, how can organisations change to become more inclusive of diverse groups?

1.5 THE SOCIAL CONSTRUCTION OF IDENTITY

This discussion links to another major underlying theme of this book – the social construction of identity. The literature on social identity is now vast. We find Richard Jenkins' sociological framework for thinking about identity accessible and useful for addressing the questions that interest us for the purposes of this book. Jenkins acknowledges 'selfhood' – the idea that individuals are unique and variable – but he regards selfhood as socially constructed. Jenkins (2004: 17) suggests the world as constructed and experienced by humans can be best understood as three distinct 'orders':

(i) '*the individual order* is the human world as made up of embodied individuals, and what-goes-on-in-their-heads'; this 'order' helps us to think about and explain why people make the career choices they do;

(ii) '*the interactive order* is the human world as constituted in relationships between individuals, in what-goes-on-between-people'; this level of analysis focuses us on the relational, interactive aspects of working life and the way that these influence careers;

(iii) '*the institutional order* is the human world of pattern and organisation, of established-ways-of-doing-things'; this helps to shift our attention away from career decision-making at a purely individual level and highlights the wider context in which individuals operate.

Within this framework, we argue that social group membership (our gender, race, ethnicity, etc.) influences both how individuals perceive themselves and how others perceive them, which means that identity can be imposed (ascribed by others) and consciously assumed (achieved by self-identification) (Jenkins, 2004). Social identity theory states that individuals are attracted to groups that enhance their self-esteem and less attracted to groups they perceive as potentially esteem damaging. Once an individual has achieved group membership, there is a tendency to perceive groups that are different negatively and as sharing undesirable characteristics. These processes are at the root of the construction of negative stereotypes (Dick, 2003) held by dominant groups of minority groups.

Gender and race are especially salient in the construction of identity, because they fix people in an immutable and (usually) visible category. Jenkins (2004) sees gender and race as primary identities. Frequently, negative stereotypes are attached to women and minority ethnic groups. Jenkins (2004: 61) argues that '*gender is one of the most consistent identificatory themes in human history, and one of the most pervasive classificatory principles – arguably, the most pervasive – with massive consequences for the life-chances and experiences of whole categories of people*'. On the question of ethnicity, Jenkins holds that ethnic identity '*is often an important and early dimension of self-identification. Individuals often learn frameworks for classifying themselves and others by ethnicity and "race"' during childhood.... Ethnicity, when it matters to people, really matters*' (2004: 65). Other sources of identity are more fluid and often less visible, but not necessarily less salient for employment chances. For example, disability takes many different forms: it can be temporary or permanent; it can occur to anyone at any stage in the life course; and it is infinitely graduated. Similarly, sexual orientation is not necessarily fixed, and age discrimination affects people to different extents and in different ways over the life course. It can be argued that these other sources of identity and the experiences arising from them are mediated by gender and race. From this perspective, it follows that it is appropriate to accord more attention to issues of gender and race, as we do in this book. This is not to say that we do not believe that all sources of identity are important in contributing to who or what a person is and who or what others perceive a person to be.

1.6 **THE BOOK'S CONTENTS**

Reflecting the themes and issues briefly outlined above, the book is divided into two parts. Part One – *Context and concepts* – situates equality and diversity within the UK and European employment and organisational contexts. It also explores theoretical explanations for workforce diversity and labour market inequalities and presents conceptual frameworks for understanding equality and diversity policies. *Chapter 2* sets the scene for exploring and understanding equality and diversity within the context of the UK and European labour markets. It outlines the social and economic factors, which shape the labour market position and employment experiences of women, black and minority ethnic people, disabled people, lesbians and gay men and older people. The chapter draws on macro-level labour market statistics to reveal trends and patterns of inequality. *Chapter 3* presents the main theoretical explanations for employment segregation and segmentation. The strengths and weaknesses of the various conceptual frameworks are critically appraised. Importantly, the chapter also discusses social identity explanations. *Chapter 4* examines diversity, equality and discrimination issues at the level of the organisation, focusing on organisational cultures and the way in which they are infused with values constructed around an archetypal, white, non-disabled, heterosexual and masculine norm. The consequences of this are explored from the perspectives of diverse social groups. *Chapter 5* presents the chronological developments in the meaning and understanding of different approaches to equality and diversity policy. The chapter provides the conceptual and theoretical underpinning necessary to develop a critical analysis of approaches.

Part Two – *Policy and practice* – explores approaches to equality and diversity policy and practice. It considers the role of key actors in both perpetuating and seeking to challenge disadvantage and discrimination in employment. *Chapter 6* examines the nature and content of equality legislation, including developments emanating from the EU. The chapter provides a critical appraisal of the law as an instrument for overcoming inequalities and promoting diversity in employment. *Chapter 7* posits that as one of the three key industrial relations actors, trade unions have a central role to play in the challenging of discriminatory employment policy and practice and in the promotion of equality and diversity issues. Issues of equality and diversity inside trade unions are also explored. *Chapter 8* explores and critically analyses, equality and diversity policy at the level of the organisation. The main policy orientations of the social justice case and the business case are discussed and the role of key organisational actors is also considered. *Chapter 9* evaluates Human Resource Management (HRM) and what it offers to the equality and diversity project. The analysis focuses on the central tenets of HRM, namely strategic integration, employee commitment, flexibility and quality. *Chapter 10* discusses the European context of diversity. It considers examples of countries where significant developments in equality and diversity policy have occurred. The importance of social and employment policy in promoting equality and diversity is underscored. *Chapter 11*, the concluding chapter, provides a summary of the issues raised in Chapters 2–10, demonstrates how they interconnect and discusses the prospects for the diversity paradigm as a replacement of the traditional equality paradigm.

1.7 USING THE BOOK

This book aims to support a programme of teaching and learning and to provide a critical review of the literature in the field. As stated above, we seek to map the territory of equality and diversity and thereby provide a solid basis for students to progress to research-based texts and articles. With this aim in mind, we have attempted to achieve an appropriate balance between description and analysis. Description is essential to any 'mapping' exercise, whilst analysis is necessary to make sense of the landscape depicted. Our intention is to have provided relevant information and engaged critically with different arguments. What we hope to have produced is a valuable resource for students and academics, which will underpin their study in the field.

We believe that it would be wrong to claim academic writing as entirely objective and unbiased. Our choice of literature sources inevitably reflects our own beliefs and values, as is the case with any academic text or textbook. However, we consider alternative and competing perspectives and understandings of the social phenomena we describe and analyse. We do not always draw firm conclusions from our discussions and we do not make recommendations, rather we leave it to readers to make up their own minds based on the information we present. However, although we do not make explicit recommendations, clear and fairly transparent implications can be drawn from the overall contents of the book for readers with a vocational or practitioner orientation. In addition, the concluding chapter offers some reflections on the future of equality and diversity debates.

Each chapter opens with an overall aim and a set of objectives to inform the reader of the content of the chapter and to indicate what the chapter is attempting to achieve. Key learning points are provided at the end of each section within chapters. These summarize and draw out the principal messages of the section. Where appropriate, tables and diagrams are presented to reinforce the explanations and discussions contained within the text. The review and discussion questions at the end of each chapter will encourage further reading, reflection and discussion. The questions can be used by students working alone, in study groups or in seminar sessions. The suggested reading we provide for each chapter will help those discussions to be more in-depth and fruitful. As is the case with any such questions, they can be treated simply as checks on understanding of the contents of a chapter or subjected to rigorous debate and analysis. Some of the review and discussion questions lend themselves to essay questions – we leave this to tutor discretion. We also provide 'activities' within each chapter. These are intended to provide 'real life' examples and to develop students' analytical abilities by requiring that the themes of the chapter in question be reflected upon in order to understand, interpret and analyse the situations in the activity. Again, these short activities can be attempted by students working independently of classes or within seminar sessions. At the end of the book there is a glossary of terms and abbreviations of key concepts. There is also an index of authors and topics, which will assist readers in searching for information.

Although we believe the chapters are organized in a logical sequence, each one can also be read in isolation from the preceding and following chapters. Therefore, there is a high degree of flexibility in how students, tutors and other readers approach the topics covered by the book. In any subject field with a large literature, it is always necessary for authors to make decisions about what to include and what to exclude. This book is no different and doubtless there are omissions, which can be remedied by wider reading and by tutor input.

REFERENCES

Anthias, F., Yuval-Davis, N., 1992. Racialized Boundaries. Routledge, London.

Arvey, R., Azevedo, R., Ostgaard, D., Raghuram, S., 1996. The implications of a diverse labour market on human resource planning. In: Kossek, E., Lobel, S. (Eds.), Managing Diversity. Blackwell, Oxford.

Cockburn, C., 1991. In the Way of Women. Macmillan, Basingstoke.

Cornelius, N., Gooch, L., Todd, S., 2001. Managing difference fairly: an integrated partnership approach. In: Noon, M., Ogbonna, E. (Eds.), Equality, Diversity and Disadvantage in Employment. Palgrave, Basingstoke.

Dick, P., 2003. Organisational efforts to manage diversity do they really work? In: Davidson, M., Fielden, S. (Eds.), Individual Diversity and Psychology in Organisations. John Wiley, Chichester.

Edwards, J., 1995. When Race Counts. The Morality of Racial Preference in Britain and America. Routledge, London.

Hall, S., Critcher, C., Jefferson, T., Clarke, J., Roberts, B., 1978. Policing the crisis: mugging, the State and law and order. Macmillan, London.

IPD, 1996. Managing Diversity: An IPD Position Paper. IPD, London.

Jenkins, R., 2004. Social Identity, second ed. Routledge, London.

Kandola, R., Fullerton, J., 1994. Managing the Mosaic – Diversity in Action. Cromwell Press, Wiltshire.

ONS, 2008. Focus on Gender: Online Statistics.<http://www.statistics.gov.uk/cci/nugget.asp?id=1654> (accessed 26.01.08.).

Prasad, P., Mills, A., Elmes, A., Prasad, A., 1997. Managing the Organisational Melting Pot. Sage, London.

Roberts, K., 1996. Managing disability-based diversity. In: Kossek, E., Lobel, S. (Eds.), Managing Diversity. Human Resource Strategies for Transforming the Workplace. Sage, London.

Solomos, J., 1989. The politics of immigration since 1945. In: Braham, P., Rattansi, A., Skellington, R. (Eds.), Opportunities and Policies, Racism and Antiracism: Inequalities. Sage, London.

Yakura, E., 1996. EEO law and managing diversity. In: Kossek, E., Lobel, S. (Eds.), Managing Diversity. Blackwell, Oxford.

PART

1

Context
and Concepts

The UK and European diversity contexts

Aim

To examine the employment patterns and experiences of diverse social groups.

Objectives

- To examine the employment patterns and experiences of women, black and minority ethnic workers, disabled people, older people and lesbians and gay men in the UK context.
- To outline workforce diversity issues in a European context.

2.1 INTRODUCTION

This chapter presents the UK and European employment contexts for understanding the dynamics of managing diversity in the twenty-first century. It outlines the social and economic factors, which shape the labour market position and employment experiences of women, black and minority ethnic people, disabled people, lesbians and gay men and older people. This sketch of macro-level labour market trends and patterns demonstrates the existence of inequalities of outcome between and within these social groups. This chapter is a presentation of data, with some commentary, although detailed analysis and theoretical explanations are reserved for subsequent chapters.

This chapter examines the employment trends and patterns of the five social groups that are this book's focus. However, it must be noted that it is impossible to consider any of these groups entirely separately for three reasons: (i) individuals can self-evidently fall into more than one category; (ii) social group membership is not always fixed; and (iii) the groups themselves are not homogeneous. Attention is drawn, for example, to ethnic differences in women's employment to reinforce the point that the category 'women' is not a unitary one and that diversity among women exists. Similarly, diversity exists among black and minority ethnic groups' experiences of the labour market and between male and female members of these groups.

Although the data presented in this chapter are correct at the time of writing, there may have been some changes by the time of publication. However, we are concerned primarily with the *trends and patterns* revealed by the data. History shows us that change is slow and incremental rather than rapid and revolutionary, therefore the trends and patterns described and analysed below are likely to remain valid for some time to come. For the latest available information and data, details of various reliable sources are provided in the 'further reading' section at the end of this chapter.

2.2 WOMEN'S EMPLOYMENT IN THE UK – TRENDS AND PATTERNS

In the post-war period one of the major social and economic changes has been the increase in women's employment, especially married women and mothers. Women now comprise approximately 47% of the workforce. In the 1970s, 90% of men compared with 60% of women were in employment. The comparable figures now are 79% (men) and 70% (women); thus men's rate of employment has declined, whilst women's has increased. Importantly, there have been changes in the *types* of jobs that women do. One striking example is that in the 1970s just 10% of professionals were women, compared with 42% today (EOC, 2006). In the twenty-first century it is the norm for women to be in paid work, with the traditional family composition of full-time male breadwinner and full-time 'housewife' caring for the home and children now being the exception rather than the norm. The reasons behind these enormous social changes are complex and there are both demand (employer strategies and needs) and supply (employee preferences and choices) side dimensions, which we explore below and from a more theoretical perspective in Chapter 3.

Although women's labour market participation has increased rapidly and dramatically, women still tend to be concentrated in certain occupations and industries. The terms 'occupational sex segregation' or 'gender segregation' are used to describe the tendency for men and women to be employed in different occupations and sectors of the economy. It is not entirely clear whether demand or supply side factors explain gender segregation, although it is likely that both contribute (see Chapter 3).

Women form the majority of workers in three major occupational groups (EOC, 2006). These are 'administrative and secretarial' (81% women), 'personal services' (84% women) and 'sales and customer service' (69% women) and over half of all employed women work in these three occupational groups alone. Women also predominate in a raft of low-paid jobs, including receptionists (95% women), cleaners and domestics (76% women) and waiting staff (74% women). Gender segregation is particularly pronounced in part-time work, where women predominate and where many of the low-paid female jobs are located. As can be seen, women tend to be concentrated in jobs in the service sector, whereas men predominate in manual jobs in the skilled trades (92% men) and in 'process, plant and machine operatives' (87% men) (EOC, 2006).

Women and men are not simply divided along the horizontal lines described above; they are also vertically segregated. That is, men continue to be over-represented in the higher levels of organisational and occupational hierarchies including 'managers and senior officials' (66% men) and 'professional' (58% men) (EOC, 2006). Nevertheless, women have made significant gains with their overall share of managerial and professional jobs increasing from 34% to 42% over a 20 year period (1984–2005) (EOC, 2006). But, even at the higher occupational levels, we still find gender segregation. Women are more likely to be found in the professions than in management, partly because a greater number and a wider range of professional than managerial jobs are available on a part-time basis or offer flexible working arrangements. For example, women and men are almost equally represented among solicitors, lawyers, judges and coroners (47% women) (EOC, 2006). Generally though, women and men tend to be employed in different management and professional jobs, with for example, men dominating the traditionally male preserves of information communication technology (ICT) managers (79% men) and women dominating the feminised area of human resources (HR) and training managers (58% women). The general pattern is that women have increased their share of professional and managerial occupations, albeit at the lower levels, at the same time as increasing their share of low-paid, low-skill jobs. The consequence is that women as a group have become polarised, as small numbers have gained access to the higher echelons of occupational hierarchies, but the vast majority remains concentrated at the lower end. Gender segregation is a theme we return to in Chapter 3, where we consider different theoretical explanations.

Why does gender segregation matter? One important reason is that there is a strong relationship between gender segregation and lower pay for women (Blackburn et al., 2002). Millward and Woodland (1995) referred to this as the 'wage penalty' associated with working in organisations and occupations dominated by women. Women who work full-time currently earn on average 83% of the average hourly earnings of male full-time workers (EOC, 2006). This is referred to as the 'gender pay gap' – a measure of the difference between the earnings of men and women. Since 1975 (and the consolidation of equal pay legislation), the average gender pay gap has narrowed by 12% (EOC, 2006). A closer look at the available data reveals further differences between women and men and among women. Women who work part-time have much lower hourly earnings than men who work full-time: they earn 58% of men's average hourly pay. This has remained almost unchanged since the mid-1970s, so although levels of pay have improved for full-time women when compared to men, the substantial minority of women who work part-time (42%, EOC, 2006) have made very little progress towards parity with men. The corollary of this is that women who work part-time, in any industry, also earn far less (26% less) than women who work full-time. Thus, women face a higher wage penalty for working part-time. It should also be noted that the above are aggregate figures. The gender pay gap varies considerably from sector to sector as shown in Table 2.1. As can be seen from the table, the most male-dominated sectors are among the smaller gender pay gaps. Occupational groups with some of the largest gender pay gaps are skilled trades occupations (25% gap) and managers (23%). Occupational groups with some of the smallest gender pay groups include professional occupations (4%) and sales (6%) (Leaker, 2008).

2.2.1 Explaining the trends and patterns

To explain the trends and patterns in women's employment, we need to look from the perspectives of both employers and women themselves. Employers have certain requirements and preferences for labour, both in the sense of numbers and 'types' of employees sought and the skills and qualifications needed, which are shaped by industry and sector and other economic circumstances. In turn, changes, such as the restructuring of the UK economy, shape the labour market participation patterns of both men and women (Blackwell, 2001). Over the past 25 years or so, there has been a substantial decline in the manufacturing industry and in the jobs traditionally done by men and a significant growth in the service industry and jobs traditionally done

Table 2.1 Gender Pay Gap by Sector

Sector	% Women	% Men	Gender Pay Gap %
Health and social work	79	21	32
Education	73	27	12
Hotels and restaurants	56	44	17
Other community, social and personal	52	48	25
Banking, insurance and pension provision	51	49	41
Public administration and defence	51	49	20
Wholesale, retail and motor trade	50	50	22
Real estate, renting and business activities	42	58	24
Manufacturing	25	75	19
Transport, storage and communication	24	76	9
Construction	10	90	12

Source: EOC (2006).

by women. Accompanying these structural changes have been labour shortages in some industries, compelling employers to adopt new strategies to recruit and retain previously under-utilised labour sources, including women. Structural changes, combined with global competitive pressures, have also led to the increased demand for cheap, flexible labour. As discussed above, women's pay is lower than men's and they have a greater propensity to work part-time; therefore many employers have constructed jobs as part-time in order to attract women workers. Overall, men's participation in paid employment has declined (EOC, 2006), although they are presently employed in greater numbers than women. The labour market participation rates of men and women are expected to move closer together as men's rate stabilises and women's rate increases further, as a consequence of economic growth in the service sector, where women are employed in the greatest numbers. However, what this means for social and economic changes must be interpreted cautiously because the 'economic activity rate' is measured by a headcount of those participating in the formal economy, rather than by number of hours worked. Hakim (1993) argued that this can be misleading because it fails to distinguish between those in full-time and those in part-time employment. If employment participation is measured by work hours, men still dominate.

Until fairly recently, the expansion of women's employment had mainly been in part-time jobs. This can be explained partly by demand-side factors, to the extent that the expanded service industry created mainly part-time jobs. Between 1992 and 2006, the full-time employment level increased by 10% while the part-time level increased by 23%. All the evidence also points to the fact that the growth in part-time work is concentrated in certain types of work. The part-time employment rate is particularly high for women in lower level occupations (at about 71%) and lowest (20%) for women managers

(Walling, 2007). It is women with dependent children who are most likely to work part-time. Thus, as discussed below, women's labour market participation is closely associated with their childcare role. Since women often leave the workforce for a period after the birth of their first child, part-time work is an option often taken up by mothers returning to paid employment. The effect of children on women and men's employment patterns is shown in Table 2.2, from which it is clear that most women adjust their work hours to fit with the childcare needs of the family.

As we can see, economic restructuring brought with it increased job opportunities for women. But, what was going on inside the household also had an impact. Some economists argue (e.g. Joshi et al., 1985) that the dramatic fall during the post-war period in the prices of domestic, labour-saving household appliances reduced the time women spent on housework and 'released' them to take on paid employment outside the home. In other words, now that housework was no longer in itself a full-time job, the choice to enter paid work was open to women. The caveat here is that housework still needs to be done and children still need to be cared for. Evidence gathered at the European level shows that women continue to take the main responsibility for running the home and caring for the family, whether they work full- or part-time and whether or not they have children (Fagan and Burchell, 2002). Therefore, even in the contemporary period domestic work can still constrain women's availability for paid work outside the home.

Following from this, another argument is that because most women still juggle paid work with family responsibilities, especially childcare, the 'choices' open to them are in effect limited. This is why we place the word 'choice' in inverted commas to indicate that the 'choice' to work full- or part-time is constrained by the family and household circumstances that most women face. The effect of family is demonstrated by the fact that many women return to full-time work when their children are older (see Table 2.2). Only 55% of women with a child below school age (five) are in paid work, compared with 74% of women whose youngest child is over five (EOC, 2006). Having said that, many women (58%) continue to work part-time for as long as they have dependent

Table 2.2 Employment by Age of Youngest Child

	Youngest Child 0–4	Youngest Child 5 or Over	Any Dependent Children	No Dependent Children
Women				
% Full-time	36	45	42	67
% Part-time	64	56	58	33
Employment rate %	55	74	67	67
Men				
% Full-time	96	97	96	88
% Part-time	4	4	4	12
Employment rate %	90	90	90	73

Source: Adapted from EOC analysis of Labour Force Survey, Office for National Statistics (ONS) (EOC, 2006).

children (under 16), compared with a part-time working rate of 33% for women without dependent children. What do these patterns tell us? Without doubt some women actively choose to stay at home to look after their dependent children, but for others the lack of affordable childcare and lack of access to flexible working arrangements are also likely to be barriers in the UK context. Childcare is very expensive in the UK, compared to many European countries and whilst flexible work is often assumed to have increased, it is mostly part-time work that is available (usually in low-paying, low-level jobs) rather than more creative forms of flexible work (flexitime, job sharing, term-time working, etc.) that might encourage and enable women to continue working full-time through the child-rearing years (EOC, 2006). Changes in the *structure* of households also play a role in shaping women's employment patterns. Family size is important, for example, the general trend towards smaller families means that women spend a smaller proportion of their lives caring for children, again potentially 'releasing' them for paid employment. Also, marriage rates have fallen and divorce rates have risen, with the consequence of an increase in lone-parent families, the majority of which are headed by women. Potentially these changes might push women into employment out of financial need. However, perhaps counter-intuitively, until fairly recently the rise in women's paid employment has been concentrated within households in which there is a couple living in partnership. This is contrary to what might be expected given the greater financial need of lone mothers. The economic activity rate of lone mothers is relatively low at around 55%, compared to 70% for mothers in couples, although this is changing with lone mothers' employment rates on an upward trend (Walling, 2007). Even though there may be a strong financial need for paid work among lone mothers, their lower level of labour market participation is related to the constraints of caring single-handedly for young children, which prevent them from competing for jobs on an equal basis with childless women and women living with a partner.

Family responsibilities can also affect the *nature* of women's employment in the medium- to long-term. Women who take time out of employment to care for their children are at risk of 'downward occupational mobility' later on in their working lives – returning to lower paid, lower-status jobs, especially if they take part-time jobs (Blackwell, 2001). This may affect the choices some women make about returning to work: for example, in the absence of financial need some women may prefer not to engage in paid employment rather than take a lower status and possibly less satisfying job.

The rise in women's educational levels is also a significant factor in the growth of women's employment participation. The percentage of girls leaving compulsory schooling without any formal academic qualifications has fallen dramatically to around 3% (EOC, 2006). Meanwhile, the proportion of young women leaving school with at least two 'A' levels or equivalent is now 44%, compared with 35% of young men (EOC, 2006). Overall, female achievement levels in formal education are now higher than those of males. Highly educated, highly skilled women can demand higher wages, which make it more profitable to enter and stay in the labour market and make the cost of childcare more affordable. The evidence shows that women qualified above A-level have the highest economic activity rates. Eighty-five percent of this group is in paid employment compared to 46% of women without qualifications (EOR, 2001). This is a pattern particularly marked among those with children under five: of this group, 75% of highly qualified women are in paid employment, compared to 24% of women without higher-level qualifications (EOR, 2001). This highlights that the motivation to continue working throughout the child-rearing years is likely to be stronger when work is more satisfying as well as more financially rewarding. Highly qualified women are also in greater demand when compared with lower skilled women because of the growth in white-collar, non-manual and highly skilled jobs. Thus, employer strategies and choices interact with women's preferences and 'choices' to create a dynamic in which women's labour market participation is both enabled and constrained. Whichever explanation is chosen for women's increased employment participation, the fact remains that not only are women participating in greater numbers overall, but their employment rate after childbirth has changed enormously over time. Thus, having a family no longer restricts women's employment to quite the same extent as formerly. In 2002 an overwhelming 72% of women who were at work during their pregnancy returned to work, compared with only a quarter in 1979. However, 42% changed from full-time to part-time hours (Aston et al., 2004).

Key learning points

- One of the most significant features of the contemporary UK labour market is women's increased participation. This increase can be attributed to a complex combination of economic and social causes. These include the shift from an industrial to a service economy, compositional changes in the family, the rise in women's qualification levels and the availability of part-time work.
- Gender segregation operates along both horizontal and vertical dimensions. Women are heavily concentrated in a narrow range of occupations and under-represented among managers and professionals.
- On average, women earn less than do men. The gender pay gap is particularly wide between part-time women and full-time men.

Activity 2.1

Women losing jobs twice as fast as men

The government is becoming increasingly alarmed that many more women are losing their jobs than men as the recession bites. It fears they could be out of the workforce 'for a generation'. A group of senior women ministers have warned [the Prime Minister] Gordon Brown that the recession may tarnish Labour's record on equal rights. There is mounting alarm over recent figures suggesting twice as many women are being made redundant as men in some parts of the country. Ministers fear some of those being laid off are victims of discrimination by bosses seeking to avoid costs associated with the introduction of longer maternity leave and new flexible working rights... Women ministers [are] pressing for new measures to protect women:

- An inquiry by the Equality and Human Rights Commission (EHRC) into sex discrimination in the finance sector;

- New training for women to help them compete for jobs; and
- Monitoring companies to check women are not being unfairly targeted.

In a sign of how seriously the issue is being taken, Brown has agreed to dedicate a session of the G20 meeting of the world's economic powers to the impact of the recession on women. It will be the first time the G20 has held formal talks about the role of women in the economy. Harriet Harman, the women's minister, said: 'There is a major fear about women being targeted by their employers during the downturn. This is unlawful.' Another senior minister said women could be set back for 'a generation'. The latest official employment statistics show that the number of women in full-time work fell by 53,000 in the last quarter, compared with a fall of 36,000 for men. It means that women are losing full-time jobs at twice the rate of men, because men significantly outnumber women in the workplace. Women MPs are disgruntled that so much emphasis is being placed on helping male-dominated industries, such as finance and motor manufacturing, when many jobs are being lost in 'soft' sectors dominated by women, such as retail and catering. The government is to work with the EHRC to monitor businesses for evidence of discrimination over redundancies. Companies found to have unjustifiable discrepancies between male and female redundancy rates are being warned that they have to face court.

(*Source: The Times*, 25 January 2009)

Questions

1. How concerned should the government be about job losses among women workers?
2. Do you agree that measures to protect women are necessary or desirable?
3. Why do you think businesses might target women workers for redundancy?

2.3 BLACK AND MINORITY ETHNIC EMPLOYMENT IN THE UK – TRENDS AND PATTERNS

2.3.1 Defining race and ethnicity

First, it is necessary to say a few words about how race and ethnic categories are defined. This is without doubt a complex and controversial area, evidenced by the fact that the accepted categories regularly change. Plus, different definitions are used in the different data sources and literature, highlighting the difficulties of establishing universally acceptable definitions. This can make comparisons between different sources problematic. For example, in some sources the category 'black' can include people of Caribbean, African and Asian origins, whilst in others separate categories of Black Caribbean, Black African and Asian are used. The categories used by the Equality and Human Rights Commission in its publications analysing data from various official sources are now: white, mixed, Indian, Pakistani, Bangladeshi, Caribbean, Black African and Chinese. These categories capture the major ethnic groups represented in the UK labour market and at the current time reflect the generally accepted way of breaking down the black and minority ethnic group. Where appropriate, this chapter uses the original definitions employed by the data and literature sources cited to ensure that the data are not skewed by reclassification. For convenience, the term we use is 'black and minority ethnic' (BME), which encompasses people who cannot be described as white, although it is recognised that this is not an incontestable term.

2.3.2 Historical background

Writing in the early 1990s, Brown argued that we could only understand the present position and experience of BME workers if we remember that 'only one generation ago most blacks [sic] and Asians in Britain were immigrants, and if we know the causes of and conditions of their migration' (1992: 46). Today, many BME workers' parents were born in Britain and the younger groups' employment progress bears testament to the enormous social changes that have occurred over time. Nevertheless, the history surrounding the migration of different groups remains important to understanding the contemporary picture, not least how far BME people have come in improving their employment prospects. This section draws on Brown's account of BME groups' migration to Britain and the original patterns of employment among them. Most of the jobs made available to 'black and Asian' workers during the main period of immigration in the 1950s and 1960s were in public service employment, with lower wage levels than private industry, and in industrial jobs with long hours, shift work and poor conditions. Anthias and Yuval-Davis (1992) argued that these were jobs that the indigenous white population did not want. In the early phase of post-war immigration, men typically arrived in the UK without their wives and other female relatives. This was especially true of Pakistani men and this had a subsequent impact on the job opportunities available to Pakistani women who arrived in the UK later than men (Brah, 1994). It also affected other Asian women arriving in the UK in the late 1960s and early 1970s, when the economic context had altered. Ethnic differences in women's employment are further explored below.

Statistics show that by the mid-1960s, immigrant workers were concentrated in certain sectors of the economy: manufacturing, transport and communications. Thus, the early recruitment pattern laid the foundations for subsequent employment segregation by race, which proved difficult to shift. A decade later, by the mid-1970s, one of the most significant features of 'black and Asian' employment was their low representation in white-collar work and continuing high concentration in manual work (Brown, 1992: 52). This trend was partly shaped by immigrants' earlier patterns of geographical settlement and the industrial differences between the regions – i.e. immigrants settled where the available jobs were. However, employer discrimination also played a role in 'containing' BME workers in certain sectors and occupations. The role that employer discrimination played is indicated by the fact that the BME workforce also occupied *inferior positions* within the regions and industries where they were concentrated. For example, (in the mid-1970s) 24% of BME men in the South East (where the service sector was strong) had non-manual jobs compared to 47% of white men (Brown, 1992: 53). Historically, BME workers have also been disproportionately affected by unemployment as shown by Brown's charting of the period 1963–1980 (1992: 54), partly because of their concentration in the industries most affected by the economic restructuring and by the recessions of the period. But, higher unemployment levels were not just an accident of history – employer discrimination also interacted with the prevailing structural and economic forces to place BME groups in inferior and vulnerable labour market positions. In this respect, it is important to remember that race discrimination was not unlawful until 1968 and that employers did until this time openly discriminate (Brown, 1992).

2.3.3 The contemporary picture

Around half a century after the main period of immigration, where do things now stand with regard to BME employment trends and patterns in the UK? Overall, BME groups still have lower economic activity rates than do white people and all BME groups of both sexes continue to experience higher rates of unemployment than the white population (EOC, 2006). This is shown in Table 2.3. There is also evidence that BME men in particular experience longer periods of unemployment than their white peers (Platt, 2006). This has to indicate that BME groups remain disadvantaged in the UK labour market and is particularly worrying when at the time of writing the economy is in recession. However, the patterns are uneven with clear differences between and among BME groups, with significant progress being made over time by some groups whilst for others the picture is less positive.

Rates of unemployment are an indicator of labour market disadvantage and high unemployment rates among BME groups have been a long-standing concern (Heath and Cheung, 2006). Overall, in 2006 the rate of unemployment for BME men was 11%, more than twice that for the white population (5%). The unemployment rate for BME women was 9%, whilst white women's was 4% (EOC, 2006). However, Pakistani women have a far higher than average rate of female BME unemployment at 22%. Black Caribbean, Black African, Bangladeshi and Chinese men all have higher than average rates of male BME unemployment. Generally, women of all ethnic origins experience slightly lower rates of unemployment than men. The latter is partly a consequence of economic restructuring and the growth of service sector and part-time jobs which have favoured women. The conclusion is that when it comes to unemployment some BME groups appear to be more vulnerable than others, but especially men.

For those in employment, the gap between white and BME job types and levels has narrowed, but by no means disappeared, over time. BME workers are now similarly distributed among industries when compared with white workers. The four main industries that account for 85% of BME employment (public administration; education and health; distribution, hotels and catering; manufacturing; and banking, finance and insurance) are the same four main industries employing the majority of white workers. Nevertheless, BME workers remain a little under-represented in construction and manufacturing (TUC, 2008). Within BME groups, women (42%) are much more likely than men (15%) to work in public sector services. More than half of the women in work from the Black Caribbean (54%), Black African (52%) and Bangladeshi (51%) groups work in public sector services. BME workers in the public sector tend to be concentrated in lower grade jobs. In the Civil Service, for example, BME workers make up a little over 8% of the workforce, but they comprise only 3% of senior grades (CRE, 2006). Back to the broader picture and Pakistani, Bangladeshi, Black Caribbean and

Table 2.3 Employment and Unemployment by Ethnic Origin and Gender

	Employment Rate %	Unemployment Rate %
Women		
Black Caribbean	64	8
Black African	48	9
Indian	61	6
Pakistani	23	22
Bangladeshi	18	–
Chinese	55	–
Mixed	64	10
All BME	50	9
White	69	4
All ethnic groups	67	4
Men		
Black Caribbean	71	15
Black African	63	15
Indian	75	6
Pakistani	63	10
Bangladeshi	54	19
Chinese	49	14
Mixed	63	10
All BME	66	11
White	80	5
All ethnic groups	79	5

Source: Adapted from EOC analysis of Labour Force Survey, ONS (EOC, 2006).

Black African men continue to be more concentrated in routine and semi-routine jobs. Around 25% of white men are found in this category of work, whereas around 36% of Black African, 37% of Black Caribbean and 50% of Bangladeshi men hold routine or semi-routine jobs (Heath and Cheung, 2006). Heath and Cheung argue that these are long-standing disadvantages that show no sign of declining.

Nevertheless, with regard to higher-level work, there has been some improvement in the distribution of occupational attainment by ethnicity (Clark and Drinkwater, 2007). Over time most BME groups have increased their representation in professional and managerial posts, but at different rates and to different extents as shown in Table 2.4 from 1992 up to 2000. The latest evidence indicates further improvement, with 10% of BME people overall employed in the managers and administrators category (compared

Table 2.4 Percentage of Men in Professional and Managerial Posts 1992–2000

Ethnic Group	1992	1993	1994	1995	1996	1997	1998	1999	2000
White	23	24	24	25	25	25	26	26	27
Black Caribbean	8	10	11	10	11	12	13	14	14
Black African	17	11	18	18	22	17	19	27	26
Indian	25	22	21	25	27	30	28	28	28
Pakistani	13	11	12	12	12	13	14	15	14
Bangladeshi	6	7	8	7	7	7	9	13	17
Chinese	26	22	18	26	22	27	28	22	43

Source: Heath (2001) from Labour Force Surveys.

with 15% of white); 16% of BME people employed in professional occupations (compared with 13% of white); 16% of BME people employed in associate professional jobs (compared with 14% of white) (TUC, 2008). On the more negative side, there is some evidence that BME graduates find it increasingly difficult to obtain high-status jobs (Clark and Drinkwater, 2007). Again, this is particularly worrying during a recession when there will be fewer high-quality jobs to go around.

The available evidence suggests that, like women's, BME people's employment patterns are polarised between the highly qualified, where there is less objective difference between their own and the white majority group's pattern, and the low qualified, where the differences remain quite marked. However, it is important to note that some professional and managerial jobs located within low-paying sectors and industries where BME employees are concentrated, healthcare for example, will not bring the same rewards as those located in more high-paying sectors. Further, high-level work experience or qualifications will not necessarily insulate BME workers against the effects of employer discrimination in a period of recession. This is indicated by the fact that BME graduates now appear to struggle more than their white peers to obtain graduate-level employment.

2.3.4 **Ethnic pay gaps**

There has been a narrowing of pay differentials between white and BME people, but on average BME people working full-time still earn 9% less than white. However, this so-called ethnic pay gap treats all BME workers as a single group and does not consider gender separately. Disaggregating the data by gender and ethnicity produces a far more complex picture of more severe pay disadvantage for some. Bangladeshi men fare the worst, earning only 60% of white men (ethnic pay gap of 40%), and Pakistani men also do badly earning 80% of white men (ethnic pay gap of 20%). On the other hand, Indian men earn more than white men (ethnic pay gap of −6%) (TUC, 2008). BME women do not fare so badly on the earnings measure. BME women working full-time earn on average 3% less than white women. Again there are within-group differences. Indian women earn more than white women (−5% ethnic pay gap), as do Black Caribbean women (−7% ethnic pay gap). In contrast, for Pakistani women there is an ethnic pay gap of 14%. Some of the BME-white earnings disparity among men can be accounted for by differences in occupational and age structures, levels of unemployment, qualification levels and geographical residence. However, these factors do not give a full explanation, especially since there is significant diversity between BME groups. For example, the Pakistani and Bangladeshi populations are significantly less well qualified than the white and also significantly less well paid. However, the Black Caribbean and Black African populations are more highly qualified than the white, yet despite this they are more poorly paid. Generally though, being highly qualified reduces the ethnic pay gap (Platt, 2006).

2.3.5 Explaining ethnic employment gaps

What factors might cause BME employment gaps? How far can we attribute these gaps to objective circumstances such as English language fluency and qualification levels? At one time, a large proportion of Asian people had very limited English language skills on arrival in the UK, although they did usually acquire facility in English as they became settled in the country. Fluency in English is associated with age, gender and length of residence in the UK, but by the late 1990s more than three-quarters of Asian men spoke English fluently or fairly well, although for women the picture was more mixed. There was little gender difference among African Asians and the Chinese, but fewer Indian women than men and considerably fewer Pakistani and Bangladeshi women spoke English well (Modood et al., 1997). Lack of fluency in English would undoubtedly create an employment barrier and impact negatively upon the job opportunities of BME people. However, from the available evidence it is clear that since the vast majority of BME people are now fluent in English, there is little difference in this respect between them and the indigenous white population so that poorer labour market prospects cannot in most cases be explained by lack of fluency in English.

Are BME people less well qualified than their white counterparts? Among those aged 16-59, taken together, BME people are now *similarly* qualified to the white population. However, BME people are *more* likely than white people to be qualified to degree level – 24% compared to 20% although this overall pattern conceals considerable diversity between BME groups. For example, Chinese people are the most well-qualified ethnic group (Walby and Armstrong, 2008). This change in overall qualification levels of BME groups has occurred over time. Progress had been made in most groups by the second generation (those now typically aged 35-54 years who were born in Britain or migrated as children). This is especially the case for Black Caribbean men, with Bangladeshis remaining the exception. In terms of the third generation of BME workers (those now typically aged 26-34 years and born in Britain), far fewer are without qualifications. BME women in this age group have made particular progress (Modood et al., 1997). Continuing improvements in qualification levels among BME groups suggest that in the future patterns of employment and unemployment will also change, since the level of education and qualifications is linked to opportunities, prospects and attainment in employment, especially within the context of a service economy. However, there is some concern that BME people

obtain a lower return in terms of earnings on their investment in higher level qualifications when compared with white people (Clark and Drinkwater, 2007). The
overall conclusion must be that generally the employment disadvantages still experienced by some groups of BME people cannot be explained by age, education or
foreign birth. Employer discrimination undoubtedly plays a role.

2.3.6 Ethnic differences in women's employment

The earlier section examined overall patterns in women's employment. There are,
however, significant ethnic differences in women's employment, which aggregate
data on female trends and patterns do not expose. Differences exist when comparing
BME women with white women and diversity *among* BME women also exists. As
stated earlier, the economic activity rate for women and men in most BME groups is
lower than that for the white population and BME women are more likely than white
women to experience unemployment (EOC, 2006). However, overall the gap in job
levels between BME and white women is narrower than that between BME and white
men. When we compare white women with BME women, part-time work is one area
where we can uncover significant ethnic differences in women's employment
patterns. Levels of part-time working are far higher among white, Bangladeshi and
Pakistani women (at 43%, 48% and 45%, respectively). This compares with relatively
low levels of part-time working among Black Caribbean and Black African women
(27%) and Chinese women (26%) (EOC, 2006). Black Caribbean women's higher rate
of full-time employment is partly explained by the greater likelihood of their being
the sole breadwinner for the family. In addition, the ethnic pay gap means that
women's wages are often a more important source of income for BME families,
perhaps more so than in many white households. However, Holdsworth and Dale
(1997) noted that Pakistani and Bangladeshi women had the lowest levels of
economic activity despite their concentration in low-income households. This
remains true, but a note of caution is needed as home-working is commonplace
among these two groups of women (although less so in younger generations) but
official figures of economic activity do not usually include home-working. Another
area of economic activity not revealed by official data is unpaid participation in
a family business, which women from some BME groups still have a tendency
towards (Anthias and Yuval-Davis, 1992). Again, this practice can skew the data on
BME women's labour market participation.

   It is important to note intergenerational change. For example, UK-born Pakistani
and Bangladeshi women aged below 35, with no children and no partner, are almost
as likely as all other ethnic groups to be economically active. This underscores once
again the significance of the absence or presence of children in shaping women's
labour market participation, but, as shown above, we cannot assume that the
presence of children has a uniform impact on all women. This also alerts us to the
importance of avoiding explanations based on crude stereotypes, which are insen-
sitive to intergenerational social and cultural changes (Dale et al., 2002). Later
generations of BME women have begun to exhibit labour market behaviour much
more like their white counterparts than their older female relatives (Anthias and
Yuval-Davis, 1992).

Key learning points

- BME employment patterns were shaped by early employer recruitment strategies and by patterns of geographical settlement among the immigrant workers of the 1950s and 1960s, which combined to result in the concentration of BME employees in certain industries and occupations. More recently, there has been a narrowing of job types and levels between BME and white people.
- All BME groups of both sexes experience higher rates of unemployment than the white population. These disparities cannot be explained simply by qualification levels, age profiles and geographical residence.
- There is now more employment and occupational diversity than ever before among the BME population of the UK. Nevertheless, ethnic pay gaps and uneven occupational attainment remain.
- There are marked ethnic differences in women's employment patterns. Particularly notable is the tendency for certain groups of BME women to work full-time, compared to a high part-time rate among white women and other BME women. Interconnecting economic circumstances and social factors are the causes of these disparate patterns.

Activity 2.2

Race still a bar to boardroom, report says

The glass ceiling preventing talented black and minority ethnic managers from stepping up into top executive jobs is still rigidly in place despite a range of high-profile government diversity initiatives over the last few years, according to research.

Boardrooms across the public and private sectors remain stubbornly white, says a report, Race to the Top, by the charity Business in the Community (BITC). It analysed data between 2000 and 2007, and concludes that management prospects are disproportionately bleak for people from a black or minority ethnic (BME) background, and likely to worsen over the next decade unless action is taken.

Sandra Kerr, national director for the BITC's Race for Opportunity campaign, called the findings 'devastating'. Action was needed right away to 'shatter the last glass ceiling', and the government needed to lead by example. 'There is definitely a need to put this at the heart of the agenda for government and business,' she said. The report suggests that since 2000, a number of government-led legal measures and race equality initiatives designed to increase top-level opportunities for BME managers have had minimal impact. These include the strengthening of the 1976 Race Relations Act, the creation of an ethnic minority and employment taskforce, the race equality and diversity action plan, and specialist employment advisers. Kerr said that it was time for a 'rethink' in the government and in boardrooms. The report was intended 'not merely to flag up how terrible the situation is, but to start a process for improving things. Chief executives need to walk into their boardroom, take a look around, and ask themselves: "Does this represent in any way, shape or form what I see around me when I walk around streets every day?" Then they need to do something about it.'

Wilfred Emmanuel-Jones, a businessman, farmer and Conservative prospective parliamentary candidate for Chippenham at the next general election, said: 'Equality is very low down on the list of priorities in most organisations. To become a member of this elite club of senior managers and directors, it isn't simply a question of whether you are able to do the job – other things come into play: social background, how you spend your leisure time, whether other members of that club would like to spend social time with you. All too often, people of colour fail these tests.'

The report suggests that a handful of high-profile, top black and ethnic minority executives, such as Suma Chakrabarti, permanent secretary at the Ministry of Justice; Victor Adebowale, chief executive of the social care business Turning Point; and the private equity boss Damon Buffini are prominent exceptions. The gap between ethnic minority representation in senior management and numbers in the wider population is particularly worrying, the report concludes. 'Taking trend rates of the last seven years and projecting them forward shows that, if anything, the gap will widen,' the report says. 'The depressing implication is that there may still be a colour bar to management jobs 33 years after the passing of the Race Relations Act.'

(*Source: The Guardian*, 8 January 2009)

Questions

1. Discuss what measures government might take to 'lead by example' in order to increase top-level opportunities for BME people.
2. Why do you think the Race Relations Act (1976) might have had such minimal impact?
3. Why, despite BME people's increased educational attainment, is race still a bar to the boardroom?

2.4 DISABLED PEOPLE'S EMPLOYMENT IN THE UK – TRENDS AND PATTERNS

There is now much more known about disabled people's employment than formerly, but there remain many gaps in knowledge. In particular, there is still an unmet need for facts and figures to fully illuminate the labour market activity of disabled people and what policy initiatives might promote greater levels of employment. The attitudes of non-disabled people as employers and colleagues are identified as a priority area for further research. Such research would help to shed further light on some of the employment barriers encountered by disabled people. This section draws on the available data.

2.4.1 Defining disability

First, it is necessary to think about how disability is defined. The definition of disability and classification of types of disability is a complex and controversial area. The data on disabled people's labour market participation vary according to the definition of 'disability' adopted. Some studies use a broad definition, which includes 'limiting health problems' caused for example by long-term illness, whilst others use a narrower definition, which tends to exclude disabilities in this category. The consequence of the broader definition is that the disabled population of working age looks larger and the unemployment rate of disabled people lower. This is because people with limiting health problems and temporary disabilities are more likely to be in employment than people considered to be more severely and permanently disabled. Some of the latest available evidence using the broader definition states that 19% of the working-age population is disabled (Smith and Twomey, 2002).

Whichever definition of disability is used, it is generally agreed that disabled people are disadvantaged in the labour market. Organisations' negative attitudes to the recruitment of disabled people are partly responsible, although other factors, discussed below, also come into play. One study found that only 19% of organisations actively encourage job applications from disabled people, over half said that they had no policy regarding the recruitment of disabled people and 19% admitted to seeing some jobs as more suitable for disabled people than others. However, only 3% stated that they would not consider recruiting a disabled person (Goldstone and Meager, 2002). Generally employers provide paternalistic justifications and rationalisations for their discriminatory practices, claiming for example that disabled people are not suitable for jobs in their firm, especially if jobs involve shift work; the premises are not suitable for disabled people; or there are problems with access to buildings. Barnes (1992) argued that the lack of disabled applicants is also a popular explanation for the absence of disabled employees. Whilst this might provide a partial explanation, the fact remains that many disabled people encounter a hostile work environment that might discourage them from applying for jobs.

2.4.2 Employment and unemployment levels among disabled people

The employment and unemployment rates as at 2002 for disabled compared with non-disabled people are shown in Table 2.5. This table is interesting because it also shows the intersection of gender, ethnicity and age with disability and employment. The latest available evidence shows that 49% of disabled women and 52% of disabled men are in paid employment, compared to 75% and 85% of non-disabled women and men, respectively. The gender gap in disabled employment rates mirrors the situation among non-disabled people. The unemployment rate of disabled people is approximately twice that of non-disabled (EOC, 2006). It might be tempting to explain these disparities by suggesting that at least a proportion of disabled people are so severely impaired as to make paid employment impossible. Whilst this might be the case, it is also believed that there is a large group of disabled people capable of and willing to work. But, in anticipation of employer discrimination these people prefer the alternative of long-term social security benefits (Hyde, 1996). Smith (1992) referred to this group of disabled people as 'discouraged workers' – people who experience the labour market as hostile. Discouraged disabled workers are aware of the obstacles facing them in their search for employment and of the type of low-level jobs they are likely to be assigned to, when they do find employment. Research has found that 40% of disabled people aged 16–49 and 28% of disabled people over 50 are not in work, but would like to be (DWP, 2007).

Table 2.5 Employment and Unemployment Rates for Disabled and Non-disabled People of Working Age by Ethnic Group and Sex

	Employment Rates			Unemployment Rates		
	All	**Men**	**Women**	**All**	**Men**	**Women**
Disabled						
All ethnic groups	47.9	50.3	45.2	8.3	9.7	6.6
White	48.8	50.8	46.6	7.7	8.8	6.3
All minority ethnic groups	36.0	42.7	29.7	18.9	23.0	12.6
Not disabled						
All ethnic groups	81.2	86.6	75.3	4.8	5.0	4.5
White	82.7	87.8	77.0	4.4	4.5	4.2
All minority ethnic groups	63.9	71.9	55.6	10.5	11.9	8.7

Source: Smith and Twomey (2002) from Labour Force Surveys.

Thus, although economic activity rates are related to disability, with disabled people of all ages less likely to be active than non-disabled, we cannot assume that all those disabled people who are classified as inactive are neither able nor willing to work.

There is a distinctive age effect on the economic activity rate of disabled people. Younger disabled people in the age group 20–24 are the most likely to be in employment, whereas for non-disabled people it is the 35–49 age group that is most likely to be in employment (Smith and Twomey, 2002). The reasons for this are unclear, but include the greater likelihood of younger, non-disabled people being in full-time education. Disabled people generally have lower levels of education and qualification than the average. For example, 13% of disabled people are qualified to degree level, compared with 24% of non-disabled (Walby and Armstrong, 2008). Ethnicity also impacts on disabled employment patterns, with only 36% of BME disabled people being in employment, compared to around 49% of the white disabled population (Smith and Twomey, 2002).

2.4.3 Industries, occupations and pay

The likelihood of an organisation employing disabled people varies according to sector, with the public sector and manufacturing industry most likely to employ disabled people and the services sector least likely (Goldstone and Meager, 2002). The sectoral effect may be a simple reflection of the larger size of organisations in the public sector and manufacturing industry. Larger organisations experience higher staff turnover potentially creating more openings and they also have greater financial resources at their disposal to make any necessary adjustments such as disability access arrangements. Another factor, which influences the propensity of organisations to employ disabled people, is the existence of a policy on disability and employment and equality policies are more prevalent among larger employers. In terms of disabled employees' share of organisational workforces, most organisations employ very few disabled people. Two-thirds of the organisations in Goldstone and Meager's (2002) study had no more than three disabled people and only 6% had 11 or more.

Even when they are in employment, disabled people remain over-represented in low-skilled, low-status jobs (Goldstone and Meager, 2002). There are fewer than average disabled people among managers and senior officials, professional, associate professional and technical occupations and sales and customer service occupations. However, the gap between the proportions of disabled and non-disabled people in managerial and senior official positions is less than 2% (Walby and Armstrong, 2008). A higher than average number of disabled people work in administrative and secretarial, skilled trades, personal services and elementary occupations. Disabled people are also more likely to work part-time or be self-employed (Smith and Twomey, 2002). These general patterns of employment might be related to a number of objective factors including (i) the older age profile of the manual workforce and the greater incidence of disability among older people; (ii) the lower educational attainment of disabled and older people; (iii) the limiting nature of the disability itself; or (iv) individual choice. Whilst these factors without doubt have a bearing, the evidence also suggests that the labour market is discriminatory and disabled people are excluded from a broader range of work opportunities. For example, Barnes (1992) argued that in certain circumstances when 'good appearance' is deemed an important attribute for the job, disabled people, especially women, may be disadvantaged by the emphasis, placed by many male employers on physical attractiveness. Whether this negative attitude towards disability has changed over time is uncertain. This overall employment pattern of over-representation in lower-level work means that disabled people who are in employment experience an average pay gap of 6% when compared with non-disabled workers (Walby and Armstrong, 2008). Looking at the different income distributions of people living in households where disabled adults are present, Smith and Twomey (2002) found that working-age adults living in households containing at least one disabled adult were over-represented at the bottom of the income distribution and under-represented at the top end.

Key learning points

- An unknown proportion of disabled people are willing and able to work, but are discouraged by a hostile labour market.
- The economic activity rate of disabled people is related to age and gender, but the effects are different when compared with non-disabled people.
- Disabled people are far more likely to experience unemployment than are non-disabled. Disabled workers are concentrated in low-skilled, low-status jobs and they are also more likely to work part-time or be self-employed.
- Size appears to be the most significant influence on whether or not an organisation employs disabled people.

Activity 2.3

Mind over matter

For many mental illness sufferers, workplace prejudice and discrimination is commonplace. Kathryn Thomson has an illness that can be easily managed with medication. She has an enviable skillset, a strong work ethic and has proved herself in a number of different roles. But while confinement to a wheelchair or a visual impairment would be acceptable to most employers, Thomson's condition is a mental illness, which means many companies would not want to take her on. One in seven people in the UK suffers from a mental illness at some time in their lives, so why should it be such a big problem? A recent survey by the charity Shaw Trust suggested that more than half of all employers would not hire someone with a known mental disorder, while 80% thought this to be 'a risk' in a customer-facing role.

'There is a big problem between what the law states in terms of discrimination and the reality in the workplace,' says Alison Gibbs, a senior policy officer for charity Mind. 'We recently conducted a poll where a great number of people reported being discriminated against [because of] mental illness – people being demoted, refused promotion or having job offers withdrawn after having disclosed a mental health problem.' Mind is also concerned about the scope of the legislation, in terms of who qualifies for protection against discrimination. Currently people with mental health issues are covered by the Disability Discrimination Act, the scope of which was recently broadened to apply to a greater number of employers. While there has been some extra consideration of mental health, the new applications are still limited.

The law currently puts the onus on the individual to demonstrate that their illness is sufficiently severe to qualify for support under the disability act. This means they must be able to show it interferes with their life, and that it has done for at least a continuous 12-month period. Obviously some mental illnesses, such as depression, might be treated fairly quickly and never reoccur. 'If staff were discriminated against for this reason they wouldn't be covered by the act,' says Gibbs.

Struggling to cope

The experience of employees like Thomson suggests many businesses still struggle to cope with mental illness. Thomson has manic depression, for which she takes medication. The condition manifests itself as periods of mania, when she has lots of energy and bouts of hyperactivity and high enthusiasm, followed by periods of depression, when she feels low and listless. Initially diagnosed while working at an engineering company, Thomson's first experiences of tackling the subject of her mental illness in the workplace were challenging to say the least. Her manager advised her to keep the diagnosis to herself and not tell the HR department. 'It made it very difficult, and when I came back to work I was just expected to get on with it,' she says. 'There was a stage where I was changing medications and it made me very tired in the morning, but there was no option for flexible working. And when I did eventually have a conversation with my employer about my condition he actually physically recoiled from me, and communication more or less stopped from that point. It was as if by showing a vulnerability I was suddenly less respected.'

What is more, evidence suggests that modern workplaces could exacerbate or even cause mental health problems, so the 'burying the head in the sand' approach is not only short-sighted, but potentially disastrous to a productive workforce. 'The issue of mental health at work is big and it is growing,' says Cary Cooper, professor of organisational psychology and health at Lancaster University. 'In the last 10 years we have seen changes which have added to the problem. Jobs have become less secure, people are working longer hours and there is much more micromanagement – people have to work to more targets and goals, and managers tend to manage by fault-finding rather than praise. Employees don't mind hearing that they have done something wrong, but this needs to be balanced with praise for when they have done something well.'

(*Source: The Guardian*, 20 January 2009)

Questions

1. How well does the law protect people with mental health problems against discrimination?
2. Why do employers struggle to cope with and manage workers with mental health problems?

2.5 OLDER PEOPLE'S EMPLOYMENT IN THE UK – TRENDS AND PATTERNS

The UK has an ageing population. There are nearly 20 million people aged over 50 and older workers (aged between 50 and state pension age) make up around 25% of the working-age population (DWP, 2007). Therefore older people as consumers are increasingly important to the British economy and older workers are a growing proportion of the labour force. The employment rate for men and women between 50 and state pension age (SPA) (taken as 60 for women and 65 for men) is slightly lower at 71.6%, compared with 74.3% for all people of working age (DWP, 2007). There have been signs of a growth in job opportunities for older workers. From 1997 to 2003, the employment rate for the over 50s increased faster than the overall employment rate and the difference between the employment rate of people aged over 50 and all of working age has reduced to around 2.6% (DWP, 2007). However, although older people are less likely to be unemployed than the very young, those who are without work are much more likely to be long-term unemployed; 37% of unemployed older workers have been without work for a year or more; 30% of male and 22% of female older workers on state benefits and not in work would like to work (DWP, 2007). The majority of older male workers work full-time (87%), but interestingly, their rate of part-time employment increases significantly from 6% at age 50 to 21% at age 65. The reasons for this are unclear, but may be attributable to personal preferences or to structural obstacles to full-time employment. Underemployment – working in jobs of a lower skill level than previously – is something that many older workers encounter (McNair and Flynn, 2007). A large proportion (44%) of older female workers work part-time, but this is largely because women's propensity to work part-time is something that persists over the life course. Self-employment is more common among older workers (a rate of 18%, compared with 12% for the 25–49 age group) (DWP, 2007).

Table 2.6 shows occupational distribution by age and gender. As can be seen, there is no specific labour market for older workers, when compared with the 25–49 age group. Older women are most likely to work in 'administrative and secretarial', 'personal service', and 'professional' occupations; combined 52% do so. In contrast, 55% of older men are employed as 'managers and senior officials', 'professionals' and in 'skilled trades'. What this demonstrates is that gender segregation also persists over the life course. However, whilst the trend in the nature of men's employment is more or less stable, women in the younger age group (25–49) are better represented among managers, professionals and associate professionals. It is also worth noting that the gender pay gap widens with age with women between the ages of 50 and 59 earning 73% of the average hourly wage of men of the same age. It is possible that women never recover the earnings potential they lose earlier in their working lives during the

Table 2.6 Workers by Occupation, Age and Gender

	16–24			25–49			50–59/64		
	All (%)	Men (%)	Women (%)	All (%)	Men (%)	Women (%)	All (%)	Men (%)	Women (%)
Managers and senior officials	3.6	3.8	3.4	17.5	21.3	13.3	16.7	20.6	11.0
Professional	4.4	5.1	3.7	14.4	15.2	13.5	15.0	15.1	14.8
Associate professional and technical	10.6	10.3	10.9	16.3	14.3	18.4	11.9	11.4	12.5
Administrative and secretarial	12.1	7.2	17.3	11.4	4.2	19.5	12.1	4.5	23.3
Skilled trades	11.5	21.4	1.2	10.6	18.4	1.8	12.5	19.4	2.3
Personal service occupations	9.6	3.4	16.1	7.9	2.0	14.6	7.1	2.5	13.9
Sales and customer service	21.6	16.3	27.0	5.5	3.0	8.4	4.9	2.6	8.4
Elementary occupations	22.0	25.4	18.4	9.1	9.6	8.6	10.1	9.5	11.0
Process, plant and machine operators	4.6	7.3	1.9	7.3	11.9	1.9	9.7	14.5	2.7

Source: National Statistics web site: www.statistics.gov.uk.
Crown Copyright material is reproduced with the permission of the Controller of HMSO.

child-rearing years when they often work in low-level part-time employment. On the other hand, men's average gross hourly wages decline more significantly than women's between 50 and 65 (DWP, 2007).

2.5.1 Education and training

It might be tempting to explain any age gaps in employment as a function of education and training gaps. It remains the case that older workers are typically less well qualified than younger ones, partly due to the expansion of further and higher education over time. Relatively few adults acquire new qualifications beyond the age of around 25. Around 14% of older workers have no formal qualifications, compared with just 6% of those aged 25–49; around 20% of older workers have degrees compared with 27% of the 25–49 age group (DWP, 2007). Education gaps between younger and older age groups are narrowing, but what is more worrying is that there is also evidence that older people generally receive less employer training than younger people (Dixon, 2003). In the 1990s, there was evidence that employers held negative attitudes towards older people, including the view that they are less trainable, less interested in developing their careers and suitable only for low-skill, low-responsibility jobs (Taylor and Walker, 1994). Thus, older people's lesser level of formal (academic or vocational) qualifications was further compounded by employers' reluctance to train them to adjust to the skill demands of a restructured labour market. Taylor and Walker's (1994: 577) study found that 13% of employers did not train management past the age of 50, while 17% did not train other staff past the age of 50. This was despite the fact that (male) employees in this age group still had another 15 years before SPA. It is important to note that this employer reluctance to invest in older people in terms of recruitment and training at this time was set against a context of labour and skills shortages in some sectors and occupations. Employers' preferred response to this problem might be to recruit young, female or migrant labour rather than older people. This interpretation was borne out by the findings of Taylor and Walker's early 1990s (*ibid*) study, which found that the employment of greater numbers of older people was not a priority for most employers. Nevertheless, there are now signs that employers are adopting age-friendly HR practices, especially around recruitment and retention (DWP, 2007). Some organisations in the service sector, such as 'do-it-yourself' stores and supermarkets, do now actively recruit older people, although mostly into low-paying part-time employment. Employers also now report being willing to invest in training older workers, but many claim that older workers themselves do not request training. What impact the recession (at the time of writing) will have on older workers remains to be seen; only time will tell whether the more recent age-friendly HR practices will survive (DWP, 2007).

2.5.2 Older women's employment

We have seen earlier that women's career trajectories are different from men's largely because women's labour market participation is so intensely bound up with their childcare role. It is interesting that fewer women in their 50s than in their 40s are in paid work when we consider that most women do not have dependent children when they reach their 50s. Women in their 50s are, in theory at least, released from earlier responsibilities constraining their labour market participation. But, instead of rising, the proportion of women in employment declines somewhat in the 15 years before reaching SPA from 74% of the 25–49 group to 70% of the 50–64 group. Further, part-time working increases from 39% of the 25–49 age group to 43% of the 50–64 group (DWP, 2007). Part of the explanation lies in the fact that older women often assume new domestic responsibilities including caring for grandchildren, elderly relatives or adult children, reducing their propensity to be in employment. Ginn and Arber (1995) argued that other factors contributing to older married women's reduced employment included low financial and intrinsic rewards, an unemployed husband or a high-earning husband. They based their arguments on a reading of the data showing that older women without educational qualifications in manual occupations had lower rates of employment, were likely to be low paid and reap fewer intrinsic rewards from work. They found that older women with husbands in receipt of some state benefits were unlikely to be in work, largely because of means testing and the taking into account of a couple's combined income, which created a disincentive for women to work. Conversely, older women with high-earning husbands were also less likely to be in work, possibly because financial necessity is reduced (Ginn and Arber, 1995). Many of these factors remain relevant some 15 years later. The data still support the idea that personal, financial and family circumstances shape older women's labour market participation. But these circumstances are likely to intersect with negative employment experiences and employer attitudes, to reduce the likelihood of older women continuing to work.

2.5.3 Ageism

This brings us to ageism. Ageism is an issue that is increasingly receiving the attention of policy-makers, partly because of the changing age structure of the British workforce, but also because of the introduction in 2006 of legislation outlawing age discrimination (see Chapter 6). Employer attitudes, rooted in negative stereotypes of older people, are thought to be one of the main barriers to the continued employment of older workers. Ageism has a gendered dimension in that youth is frequently an implicit, if not explicit, requirement for many of the jobs dominated by women – for example, the jobs of secretary, receptionist or flight attendant all seemingly 'require' youth (look at television adverts, etc.). Young workers between the ages of 16 and 21 may also encounter employment discrimination of course, but the causes usually relate more to lack of qualifications and work experience, rather than to age per se. In the 1990s, evidence was found that some employers considered people too old to recruit after the age of 50 (Taylor and Walker, 1994). To what extent attitudes have now changed is unclear, but employers are less likely to be open about discriminatory attitudes now that the anti-age discrimination regulations are in place. In the years leading up to the introduction of legislation in 2006 to tackle age discrimination (see Chapter 6), employers certainly gradually began to place less overt emphasis on age as a job requirement. As early as 1998, only around 10% of job adverts used numerical age limits compared with 30% in 1993 (EOR, 1998). Initially, this reduction in overt discrimination occurred against a background of government campaigns against ageism and subsequent voluntary measures among some employers and parts of the job advertising and recruitment industries. For example, by 1998 the Chartered Institute of Personnel and Development (CIPD) no longer accepted job advertisements containing age limits. Nevertheless, thinly veiled messages about the desired age groups continued to litter recruitment advertisements, arguably deterring older people from applying for jobs for which they possessed the necessary experience, skills and qualifications. As stated above, employers are generally more age friendly now than previously, but this does not mean that age discrimination has disappeared.

Key learning points

- Negative attitudes towards older workers among employers seem to have diminished, but by no means disappeared. Employers now report a greater willingness to recruit and train older people. Nevertheless, many older people have difficulty in finding employment and continuing to participate in the labour market until SPA.
- There is no specific labour market for older workers. However, it is notable that part-time work increases for men as they get older and men's average earnings decrease significantly with age.
- Older women's labour market participation is shaped by a combination of family and financial circumstances and negative employment experiences.

Activity 2.4

Britain needs the wisdom of older workers more than ever

It may seem odd, but this recession has produced a cheerful rhetoric, as well as gloomy headlines. It comes from ministers and it goes like this: 'Here is a perfect time for Britain to gear up for the future, reshaping herself as a greener, fairer and more efficient country for the good years to come. Let's buckle down, let's not lose heart.' This will sound hollow to lots of people. One group in particular, though, has good reason to blow angry raspberries. Bad times distort society and produce their own varieties of unfairness; and this time it seems to be older workers, or would-be workers, who are in special trouble. As companies shed jobs, they are handing out P45s to mature employees first. In the last quarter, the number of people aged over 50 who were unemployed for up to 6 months jumped by nearly 30%, compared to just 5% among 25- to 49-year-olds. Unemployed men and women over 50 have only a one in five chances of being in work 2 years later, and their chances of getting another job fall by a quarter for each year they are out of work.

A new documentary for Channel 4's Dispatches, to be broadcast next week, provides chilling evidence of what this means. It details the weasel words being used by recruitment agencies and employers to reject older job applicants – 'too experienced', 'over-qualified' and even unlikely to fit in 'culturally'. Alternatively they simply ask for 'dynamic' staff, and we all know what that means. In one undercover sequence, the programme takes 56-year-old chartered accountant, Martin Lloyd-Penny, and his daughter Tanne, 25, who is still to qualify as an accountant, and follows their job-hunting. Martin has 30 years experience; Tanne is by contrast a complete beginner. Yet, week after week, he finds it impossible even to get replies to his applications while she is eagerly pursued for positions, and even cold-called by eager employers. His humiliation and bemusement are awful to watch. Now you could, I suppose, say that in tough times, favouring younger workers is not only necessary, but right. Companies are like any other human organisation: they need fresh blood and youth to move forward. Aren't they right to focus on the young, and the future, when forced to make hard choices? How would we feel if things were the other way about, and it was the younger workers, fresh from college or in their early years at work, who were being sacked and discriminated against? Before looking at that more closely, let's add another salient fact into the picture – the introduction of the so-called 'default retirement age' in 2006, which allows employers to sack people aged 65 or more immediately because of their age. The government had been thinking of setting this at 70, not 65, but according to Ros Altman, a government adviser at the time, ministers 'bottled it, in the face of intensive lobbying from big business'.

Employers are now saying quite openly that they will enforce retirement ages more vigorously. Meanwhile, if you do batter your head against this form of discrimination, don't think you will get much help from employment law: though complaints to tribunals about age discrimination have risen by 60%, just 3% of them are successful.

So what about the 'fresh blood' argument? Well yes, of course, companies must recruit younger people. They shouldn't discriminate against any group, as such. But the madness is that our whole society is ageing, that we are all living longer, and the younger people being employed cannot possibly sustain an ever-larger group of jobless pensioners. This is, or should be, a familiar fact. As a society ages, people need to work for longer, or it needs to import very large numbers of young migrant workers. Otherwise the sums don't add up. People in their 50s expect a reasonably healthy 20 years or so after the age of 60. They are well fed, often pretty fit, and represent a massive investment in education and training. The waste in consigning such people to the economic scrapheap is obvious. Their taxes are needed, as is their experience. After decades of juggling tasks, bringing up children and working, older workers are also notably reliable and hardworking. Companies like B&Q, which employ more of them, report that it's a great success. There is a wider point still. Older people, so long as they are fit and eager, provide wisdom. Wherever employment law in this sense doesn't apply, in self-employment or in specialised areas, we readily acknowledge it. Would it have been a good idea to forcibly retire John Updike or John Mortimer at 65? How about Ken Clarke? As an oldie, is he less effective than George Osborne? In the arts, in intellectual pursuits, it is assumed that so long as you keep your marbles you have a chance of getting better, or at least of working in ways that are just as useful. Anyone who started work in a newspaper office in the 1970s knows how much raw recruits learned from the experienced old salts. Yet now we have plenty of outfits that have forgotten what happened only a few years ago. Would the hideous mistakes of the banking world have happened had there been more people in charge who were in their 60s, and fewer brash young men in top jobs in their 30s?

The other side of this is that, if we work longer, we can't expect to hog the best jobs. Careers and salaries, like markets, must go down as well as up. But in companies, as in life, the generational transmission of experience is a key way we learn. Far from equipping the country better for the future, by ditching more experienced workers, we are piling up problems for the public finances - where there are plenty of problems already - and weakening corporate culture when it needs to be stronger. Add to that the human misery. According to a YouGov poll for the same Dispatches programme, 67% of those who retired at 65 said that they felt forced to do so when they were not ready. These days, with falling markets and zero interest rates, they must cope not only with idleness but collapsing pensions - oh yes, and the ageism which even doctors report is rampant in the National Health Service (NHS) as well. This has all the elements of a catastrophic policy failure. What's needed, as Age Concern says, is to scrap the retirement age and to allow people to keep working so long as they are fit and keen. And as Help the Aged is urging, the new Equality bill - which outlaws certain forms of age discrimination - needs a fast track on to the statute book. Let's take ministers at their word and point out that a Britain which emerged from recession stripped of experience would be not stronger at all, but much weaker.

(*Source: The Guardian*, 2 February 2009)

Questions

1. Discuss why employers might have been so against a 'default retirement age' of 70.
2. Examine the social and economic arguments *for* employing older workers. Is there a 'business case' to be made?
3. What difference has legislation outlawing age discrimination made?

2.6 LESBIANS AND GAY MEN AND EMPLOYMENT IN THE UK – TRENDS AND PATTERNS

Stonewall, the widely known campaign organisation, has stated that there are 1.7 million gay people in the UK workforce (Stonewall, 2009). The issues for lesbians and gay men in employment are somewhat different than those for the other groups we have so far considered. First, it is not possible to set out the employment locations and concentrations (if any) of lesbians and gay men, because the main data sources do not ask questions about sexual orientation. However, this is set to change with the ONS now developing and piloting questions on this equality and diversity strand. Second, there is unlikely to be a specific labour market for lesbian and gay people, although some employers might be more 'gay friendly' than others. Third, sexual orientation can be concealed far more easily than can gender, race, disability or age. Some lesbians and gay men may choose to conceal their sexual orientation in order to avoid discrimination and harassment. With regard to the tangible employment disadvantages of being lesbian or gay, for example, overt discrimination in recruitment, promotion and in access to employee benefits, the law now prohibits discrimination on grounds of sexual orientation (see Chapter 6). It is too early to determine whether and how the existence of legislation will reduce or prevent discrimination or disadvantage.

2.6.1 Discrimination in recruitment and promotion

Historically, women and men who were either openly lesbian or gay commonly experienced overt discrimination by employers based on their sexual orientation. This is confirmed by survey evidence gathered in the 1990s, which revealed that between 10 and 14% of lesbians and gay men believed that they had either been refused a job or denied promotion because of their sexuality (Palmer, 1993; Snape et al., 1995). Another third suspected discrimination (Palmer, 1993). Heterosexual people also believed that employers treated gay men and lesbians less favourably (Snape et al., 1995). High-earners reportedly found it more difficult to be open about their sexuality at work (Palmer, 1993) and survey respondents believed that it was considered unacceptable to be openly lesbian or gay in certain professional fields such as teaching, the health service and the military (Snape et al., 1995). Not surprisingly then, there was evidence of widespread concealment of sexuality among lesbians and gay men. In one survey, over half of the lesbian and gay respondents reported that none of their work colleagues knew about their sexuality and only two-fifths said that all their colleagues knew, whilst some people confided in a few trusted colleagues (Snape et al., 1995). How far have things changed? Based on its recent research, Stonewall reports that around one-third of gay workers still feel unable to be open about their sexual orientation (Stonewall, 2009).

2.6.2 Access to employee benefits

Although now illegal, one significant way in which lesbians and gay men have been historically disadvantaged in employment is in unequal access to employee benefits such as special leave arrangements, health insurance, pensions, staff discounts and so on. Until fairly recently these benefits were usually extended to spouses or to opposite-sex partners, but not to same-sex partners. In the case of special leave, this meant, for example, that time-off to care for a sick partner or compassionate leave following the death of a partner might only apply to employees with opposite-sex partners. Employees with same-sex partners would either be denied special leave or would have to use annual leave. This of course effectively resulted in the lower remuneration of lesbians and gay men.

Similarly, the remunerative loss to lesbians and gay men of not having access to certain other employee benefits was often considerable. For example, dependants' benefits from pension schemes usually specified that the widow's or widower's pension could only be paid to a married partner (EOR, 1997) effectively excluding same-sex couples. Even in organisations where benefits were available to same-sex partners, it was of course necessary to disclose sexual orientation in order to claim them. To do this, lesbians and gay men obviously needed to be confident that this would not have adverse effects on their employment security and prospects.

The latest available research from Stonewall suggests that attitudes towards lesbian and gay people in the workplace are changing. In its latest survey (Stonewall 2009), Stonewall found that two-thirds of individual respondents believed that gay people should be able to be open at work about their sexual orientation and 75% of lesbian and gay workers agreed that their workplace culture was inclusive. However, one of the remaining challenges that Stonewall identified was for organisations to promote the availability of benefits such as parental leave to lesbian and gay employees in order to encourage take-up – at present only 38% of organisations did so and consequently take-up is usually low. Another remaining challenge is to open up higher-level jobs to lesbian and gay workers – only 38% of the organisations identified as in the top 100 of a sexual orientation workplace equality index, had openly lesbian and gay people in their top three staff levels.

Key learning points

- There is evidence to suggest that lesbians and gay men have historically experienced discrimination and disadvantage in employment. Those who are open about their sexual orientation still risk discrimination at the point of recruitment and in promotion.
- To avoid discrimination many lesbians and gay men actively seek to conceal their sexuality from employers and colleagues.

Activity 2.5

Banks and police among most gay-friendly employers

The police service, banks and management consultants top the league table of gay-friendly employers in Britain, outperforming the public sector, the media and education, according to the latest workplace equality index. High street and investment banks fared particularly well, with Lloyds TSB rising from sixth in the 2008 table to take the number one slot this year, and Goldman Sachs winning 13th place. Three police services featured in the top 10 including Hampshire constabulary in second place and Kent police at fourth, while 17 forces were listed in the top 100. The metropolitan police came in at number 35. Professional services companies also performed impressively with KPMG, Ernst and Young and PricewaterhouseCoopers all making the top 25.

Now in its fifth year, the index from campaigning group Stonewall tracks the impact of workplace culture on gay, lesbian and bisexual employees. It has quickly become a key barometer of diversity practices. The 2009 index, which also included a survey of more than 7000 gay and lesbian employees, had a record 371 entries across 23 sectors. This is more than double the number of submissions in the 2005 launch year. Some sectors, such as law and housing, have improved markedly year on year.

Organisations that apply to be included on the index are examined on the success of their diversity policies and the extent to which they encourage job applications from lesbian and gay workers. Stonewall also surveys gay employees on whether their workplace experiences match up to the claims made by employers. As well as shining a spotlight on the top performing organisations, the index also notes those sectors such as media, retail, construction and the National Health Service (NHS) that consistently fail to make the grade, shown by their absence or low rankings.

'There are sectors such as the police which perform exceptionally well in the index but then there are sectors such as construction and media which don't,' David Shields, director of Stonewall's Workplace Programmes said. 'But it can take a few years from when an organisation decides to improve in this area to begin to see some results. We are always working with organisations in [under-represented] sectors such as the NHS, retail and the media to help them improve.' The country's single largest employer, the NHS, was notable for its absence in the upper reaches of the index. Only one NHS trust, Tower Hamlets, was among the best, ranked at 58. The public sector's performance was shored up by local authorities with 49 entries submitted, the largest tranche from a single sector. Fourteen councils made the top 100 with three reaching the top 10, including Brighton and Hove which took third place. Three of the 20 fire services that entered also made the top 100, while the Home Office made the top 20. The voluntary sector did not feature strongly, although last year's overall winner, the crime charity Nacro, remained in the top 10. The media industry, which might have been expected to perform better, has consistently failed to make an impression on the index. Only five media companies entered this year and just one, Time Warner, made it into the top 100, in 90th place.

According to Shields, it can be difficult to pinpoint why some sectors far outstrip others. The strides made by so many police forces may be part of 'a broader effort to effect cultural change' he suggested, adding that complacency may have something to do with why media companies barely feature. 'I think for banks, for example, there is a real emphasis on the bottom line and they are recognising that fair employment practices directly impact on performance. I wonder if with the education or media sectors they believe they are already good and don't feel the need to measure it.'

Fiona Cannon, head of equality and diversity at Lloyds TSB, said good diversity policies 'simply make good business sense'. 'I think the financial services sector is good at recognising this. At Lloyds we have worked hard and it's wonderful that it's paying off.'

Gavin Wills, managing director for corporate services and real estate at Goldman Sachs, said the Stonewall index had provided considerable impetus for many organisations within the investment banking sector. 'The index has been a phenomenal success for Stonewall over the years. You start getting employers who you never would have dreamed were supportive of lesbian, gay and bisexual professionals competing to get on to it.'

Chief executive of Stonewall, Ben Summerskill, said the bar was set even higher for the 2009 index than in previous years, with additional proof of long-term effectiveness required from entrants. 'To make the top 100 this year, employers had to demonstrate that equality and diversity were not optional extras but core values. Ninety-seven percent of the top 100 had an organisation-wide equality and diversity strategy which links LGB equality into wider organisational aims.'

(*Source: The Guardian*, 7 January 2009)

Questions

1. Discuss whether there is a business case for policy-making on sexual orientation issues.
2. Why do you think that banks and the police service might be the most gay-friendly employers?
3. Discuss the value of a workplace equality index.

2.7 WORKFORCE DIVERSITY IN THE BROADER EUROPEAN CONTEXT

This section presents a sketch of the macro-level labour market trends and patterns of diverse social groups across the 27 countries of the European Union (EU). The overall picture is one of diversity, discrimination and disadvantage across a number of equality and diversity strands. Although collection and analysis of data in the Member States are overall improving, there remain inconsistencies. For example, there are more concrete data on some equality and diversity strands (gender for example) compared with others (disability for example). There is also more detailed information available for the EU-15 countries than for the newer Member States of Central and Eastern Europe. This reflects the different amounts of research carried out and different accounting and monitoring procedures in the different countries. This obviously limits the comparisons that can be made between countries.

2.7.1 Women's employment – European trends and patterns

There is considerable similarity between the patterns of women's labour market participation in the UK and across Europe, with rising rates of female employment being the long-term trend in most countries. The average EU female participation rate stands at 57% rising from less than 50% in the early 1990s. However, the proportion of women in employment varies between countries from just over 73% in Denmark and just under 71% in Sweden to just over 46% in Italy and only 35% in Malta. Further, the employment rate of both men and women is lower in the newer EU Member States in Central and Eastern Europe than before the transition when everyone able to do so was expected to work. In many of the countries, however, the rate has risen over recent years. In contrast, the employment of men has tended to change relatively little in most of these countries (Eurostat, 2008).

Women's increased employment participation has not necessarily led to increased equality for women within the labour market. Women across the EU tend to be found in the lowest paid, lowest status and most vulnerable jobs. In many countries, with the exception of the Central and Eastern European countries, in line with the situation in the UK, the expansion of women's employment has mainly been in part-time jobs. Overall, 36% of employed women in Europe work part-time (compared with just 6% of men). However, there are huge variations between Member States. The Netherlands has the highest female part-time working rate at 73%. In contrast, in Greece, Portugal, Finland and all the new Member States (except Malta), the proportion of women working part-time is only around 20%. In these countries women tend to work either full-time or not at all. In many Central and Eastern European countries part-time working for women is at an extremely low 10%. A growth in temporary and fixed-term working is also a common trend across the EU, with an almost equal take-up by both men and women (Eurostat, 2008). This indicates that the move to flexible and short-term contracts is a wider feature of labour market trends and not specifically related to gender. However, the higher numbers of women in part-time work in some Member States is an important policy issue because part-time jobs are typically lower level and lower paid.

Women throughout Europe still face horizontal and vertical segregation, with women continuing to work predominantly within feminised sectors and occupations. Around 61% of women in employment in the EU-27 work in just six sectors of activity. All of these are in the service industry – healthcare and social work (in which 17% of all women in work were employed), retailing (12.5%), education (11.5%), public administration (7%), business activities (7%) and hotels and restaurants (5%). In comparison, for men, the degree of concentration is much less than for women. The six most important sectors, three of which are also the most important for women, employ 42% of men in work in the EU-27. They are construction (employing 13% of all men as against just 1.5% of women); public administration (7%, much the same as for women); retailing (6%, half the proportion of women); business activities (6%, slightly less than for women); agriculture (5% as against 4% of women) and land transport (4%, four times the share for women). These six sectors accounted for 33% of women in employment. Concentration is highest in the Netherlands and Sweden (71% of all women employed working in the top six sectors), in Norway, the figure was even higher at 73%, followed by the UK, Belgium and Romania (68–69%). Concentration is lowest in the Czech Republic and Estonia (52–53% of women being employed in the top six sectors). Thus, women's employment is more concentrated than men's. Further, gender segregation has increased in the 2000s. The average picture of gender segregation for the EU-15 Member States is largely replicated at the individual country level (Eurostat, 2008). Therefore, the increasing number of women within the European labour market has had little if any effect on gender segregation.

When it comes to occupations we also see gender segregation, with more pronounced concentration of women in a relatively small range of jobs. More than one-third of employed women in the EU work in just six of the 130 standard occupational categories, whereas the proportion of men in the top six male jobs is one-quarter (Eurostat, 2008). Broadly speaking, women's jobs involve caring, nurturing and service activities; the top six female jobs are shop salespersons and demonstrators; domestic and related helpers; personal care; office clerks; administrative and associate professionals; and housekeeping and restaurant services. In contrast, men monopolise management and manual and technical jobs. Whilst women have increased their representation in management and certain professional occupations (e.g. law, medicine, accountancy), vertical segregation is still pronounced across all European countries. There are only two EU Member States – Bulgaria and Slovenia – in which women are presidents or chairpersons of more than 10% of the largest 50 enterprises and none in which the figure is over 20%. Moreover, there are only two other countries, Latvia and Poland, in which women are the heads of over 5% of the largest 50 enterprises, and in 13 of the remaining 23 EU Member States, all the heads of the 50 enterprises concerned are men (Eurostat, 2008). This includes the so-called egalitarian countries of Scandinavia with the highest female participation rates. Indeed Plantenga's (1995) research indicated that the highest level of gender segregation by sex is found in Denmark, a somewhat surprising finding, given Denmark's generally positive record on equality issues as will be discussed in Chapter 10.

Why does gender segregation matter? One consequence is the considerable pay gap between men's and women's pay that continues to exist in all European countries despite women's increased participation in employment (Eurostat, 2008). Since 1995 the average earnings of women have risen relative to those of men in most Member States. However, the rise has been small and on average the gender pay gap is now 15%. There are only three countries – Belgium, Malta and Slovenia – where the gender pay gap is less than 9%. In six countries – Germany, Estonia, Cyprus, Slovakia, Finland and the UK – the gap is 20% or more (Eurostat, 2008).

There is also variation by occupation, with the pay gap wider in male-dominated skilled manual jobs and lower in jobs where women either dominate or are well represented, such as clerks and salespersons. Average female rates of pay in management jobs are only around 70% of the male rates of pay. Slovenia is the only country where women managers' pay is only slightly below men's. In Italy women managers earn just 65% of male managers' pay. At the top end of the pay hierarchy, the top 10% female wage earners achieved 35% less pay than the top 10% of male earners, and this was especially marked in France, Italy and the UK (EC, 2001). It is also interesting to note that paradoxically the gender pay gap appears to increase the more education is gained, with female university graduates earning on average 31% less than their male counterparts. Only in Denmark, Romania and Slovenia women graduates' earnings are over 80% of men's. Nearly two decades ago Pillinger (1992: 1) identified two trends in the labour markets of Europe, the feminisation of the labour market and the *feminisation of poverty* – all the signs are that the latter remains a key challenge within the EU.

2.7.2 Black and minority ethnic employment – European trends and patterns

On a European scale, identifying employment trends and patterns among different ethnic groups is a more complex task than we find when considering the UK alone. Across the EU there are a variety of ways in which the BME population is defined and the collection of data by ethnicity is in some countries prohibited by law and in others either non-existent or patchy. Yet Europe is historically, and continues to be, a continent of migration; in the present period, especially following the enlargement of the EU, there is a renewed policy emphasis on the economic impact of migration. In this section we focus on non-EU born minorities. There are around 27 million non-EU born people (so-called 'third-country nationals') resident in the EU (or 5.6% of the population). The highest shares are found in Estonia and Latvia (14–18%); Austria (9.1%); Cyprus (8.6%); and the Netherlands (8.4%). The main movement into the EU is from neighbouring countries, Africa and South America (EC, 2008). It is useful to make a distinction between non-nationals moving from country to country, predominantly for work – migrant workers – and non-nationals who intend on residing permanently in the country of migration – immigrant workers. However, even this twofold categorisation does not necessarily capture all BME workers, because the extent of monitoring and ways of recording ethnic origin vary from country to country. In fact most Member States do not record ethnic or national origin in their official statistics, although two-thirds do provide statistics comparing 'citizens of countries outside the EU' and 'citizens of Member States'. This means that the available data are limited for examining discrimination and disadvantage on the basis of race and ethnicity (EC, 2007a). As Wrench et al. (2003) argue the concepts of migrants and minorities can assume very different meanings in different national contexts and this is often a controversial area.

Wrench et al. (2003) provide a useful summary of the historical background to migration of labour within the EU-15 prior to enlargement. First, there is the group of countries with a long history of colonial immigration (France, Netherlands, UK), which have more extensive and open citizenship rights. Second, are countries with the category 'active guest worker' (Austria, Belgium, Denmark, Germany, Luxembourg, Sweden), where migrant workers were specifically encouraged to fill vacant jobs in the 1960s and 1970s. Finally, there is the group of 'new immigration' countries (Greece, Spain, Italy, Portugal, Finland, Ireland), where substantial immigration has occurred relatively recently, since the 1980s. Across the EU-15, BME groups have lower economic activity rates and face dramatically higher rates of unemployment than the majority population (Wrench et al., 2003). These disadvantages are particularly pronounced for certain groups, for example those dominating recent refugee flows, such as Afghanis, Iraqis, Iranian, Somalis, who face an unemployment rate of up to 50%, as do Roma and Travellers (Wrench et al., 2003: 6). More recent data covering the EU-27 suggest that in many Member States the group with the highest unemployment rate is the Roma. In Belgium, the highest unemployment rates amongst all groups are those for Turkish and Moroccan nationals (45% for males and 56% for females) compared to 10% for Belgian nationals (EC, 2007a).

When it comes to sectors and jobs, non-EU (or third country) nationals tend to be the most disadvantaged in the labour markets of the EU-15, concentrated in so-called '3-D Jobs' – dirty, dangerous and demanding (Wrench et al., 2003: 6). These BME workers are the most vulnerable and least protected groups of workers in the EU. Third-country migrants tend to be concentrated in certain sectors, particularly manufacturing (which has faced dramatic decline over more than two decades), plus construction, personal services, and sectors open to seasonal fluctuations, such as tourism and agriculture (Wrench et al., 2003: 37). They are also over-represented in blue-collar and low-skilled jobs. As in the UK, the heterogeneity of the BME employment experience is also identified across the EU-15. Wrench et al. (2003: 37) document the 'ethnic hierarchy' which exists for different BME groups within different Member States. For example in Greece – Albanians and Roma are in low-skilled agriculture and construction; Poles and Romanians are in skilled manual labour; Filapina are domestic workers; Pakistanis, Indians and Bangladeshis are in unskilled factory work; and Africans are small traders and street vendors.

More recently, the European Commission reminds us that statistics of higher unemployment rates for migrants and minorities do not in themselves represent evidence of discrimination. However, the Commission's report on racism and xenophobia in the EU-27 goes on to state that when unequal circumstances remain for equally-qualified people, even when other variables are controlled, then discrimination stands out as a more likely cause. The examples of Austria, France and Sweden are provided. In Austria there is evidence that the concentration of third-country nationals in insecure work cannot exclusively be explained by lower levels of education, and it was also found that almost 50% of higher qualified people with a background outside the EU are employed in jobs below their qualification levels. In France, a 2005 study of the immigrant population in Ile-de-France – where nearly 40% of this population lives – concluded that whatever the age or education level, the active immigrant population is more affected by unemployment and work insecurity than the population as a whole. In Sweden there is still a major difference in the rate of employment between natives and foreign-born that cannot be explained by differences in human capital, such as educational level. Irrespective of age, level of education, civil status or the time spent in the country, the gap remains, particularly for people from Asia and Africa (EC, 2008).

Herzing (1995) illustrated how gender and ethnicity interconnect, with comparative research in the Netherlands, Belgium, Germany and the UK indicating that BME women have a particularly unfavourable position in terms of pay and status compared to men and women of the 'majority' culture (see also Wrench et al., 2003). Herzing was also able to identify which ethnic groups were worse off than others. For example, particularly low participation and high unemployment rates were found among Moroccan, Turkish, Pakistani and Bengali women, while higher rates were found among Surinamese, Antillean and West Indian women. However, similar education levels among the latter still did not lead to parity of pay and status with the white population. As in the UK, explanations for this disparity were largely focused around discrimination by employers and within wider society, as well as state policy on citizenship and caring responsibilities (discussed further in Chapter 3 and in a specific EU context in Chapter 10).

Chapter 10 elaborates on how immigration policies and procedures for gaining citizenship and denizenship, which define eligibility for social and legal protection, have been found to formally and informally discriminate against BME workers. In some countries, third-country nationals are directly excluded from certain jobs, especially those in the public sector. In addition, the presence of illegal workers is seen as an expanding problem, particularly in the countries of Southern Europe. Estimates of numbers indicate around 350,000 in Greece alone (8% of the registered workforce); while in Spain illegal workers are estimated to account for as much as 60% of workers from non-EU countries. This is significant when considering employment disadvantage, as illegal workers have no rights to employment protection. For example, in Portugal, around half of BME workers have no employment contract, legal protection or welfare rights. Illegal migrants work mostly in low-skilled sectors, such as in construction, agriculture, catering or cleaning and housekeeping services. Often they are hired for the so-called 3-D jobs rejected by the domestic workforce (EC, 2008).

2.7.3 Workers with disabilities – European employment trends and patterns

The difficulties, identified earlier within the UK context, in identifying employment trends and patterns among disabled workers are increased when a view across Europe is taken. Comparison is complicated by the fact that Member States have their own ways of defining the disabled population legally and for the purposes of data collection and different methods of assessing disability for welfare benefits. For example, some of the definitions used blur the boundary between old age and disability by operating early retirement provisions where some sort of limitation to work has to be shown. This makes comparisons of things such as rates of disability and rates of disabled unemployment between countries difficult. Definitions also vary on the extent to which they draw on a medical model of disability – focusing on the individual's impairment – or on a social model – focusing on the environment in which disabled people live (Wynne and McAnaney, 2008).

In total, disabled people comprise approximately 16% of the EU's working-age population. There are large variations between Member States in the number of people of working age reporting a disability, from just below 7% in Italy to around 32% in Finland. Similarly, there are variations in the number of people with disabilities in work, from just below 4% in Italy to 22.5% in Finland (Wynne and McAnaney, 2008). In comparison with the total workforce, the number of people with disabilities who are *in employment* is very small. The labour market share of people with disabilities is less than 1% in seven countries (Portugal, Spain, Finland, Belgium, Slovenia, Latvia and Luxembourg). The highest share (6%) is in Poland followed by the UK and Ireland (5% and 4% respectively) (EC, 2007b).

However, one-third of the 16% of men and women aged 16–64 years in the EU who report having a long-standing health problem or disability indicate that they are not restricted in the kind or amount of work they can do or in their mobility to and from work. Those who are restricted in work or mobility are much less likely to be in employment than those who are not. Further, educational attainment levels have a major effect on the relative employment rates. Among disabled people with higher education qualifications in the EU, 48% of those who are considerably restricted were in employment compared with 85% of those not restricted. Among people with only basic schooling, only 20% of those who are considerably restricted were in employment compared with 6% of those not restricted (Giaccone and Bucalossi, 2008). As discussed earlier, employment rates are somewhat deceptive, as the figures do not take into account those who are inactive, but capable and willing to work and who favour the alternative of long-term social security benefits because they are so discouraged by the discriminatory environment they meet (Hyde, 1996). Nevertheless, most people with disabilities participate in the open labour market, rather than in sheltered employment designated specifically for disabled people (EC, 2007b).

Despite there clearly being an ongoing challenge in terms of integrating disabled people into the labour markets of the European Union, there are positive signs of recent change. In most countries the employment of disabled people has increased since 2000. Unemployment of disabled people declined in the Czech Republic, Germany, France, Austria, Poland, Slovakia, Finland and the UK. However, it rose in seven countries (EC, 2007b). Further, in a European-wide survey of attitudes towards discrimination and equal opportunities, 41% of respondents felt that disability was the fourth most likely factor to put job candidates at a disadvantage. Forty-five percent of respondents felt that disability discrimination was widespread; however, around 67% of respondents felt that it was less widespread than 5 years ago. Nevertheless, 31% of disabled respondents reported having experienced disability discrimination in the last year (Eurobarometer, 2008).

2.7.4 Older workers – European employment trends and patterns

In the context of the Europe before enlargement, Hugman (1994: 1) identified three major trends: (i) an increase in the proportion of people aged over 65 years; (ii) an increase in the absolute numbers of older people; and (iii) an overall increase in life expectancy. The ageing of the population has major consequences both for the workforce and for social protection and welfare/pension benefits. It has therefore become an increasingly important policy issue within the EU.

For the great majority of people in the EU, the retirement age is from 60 upwards. However, a significant proportion of women and men are not in employment after age 55. In the EU-27 the proportion of people aged 55–64 still in employment is 42.5%. There are just eight Member States where this proportion exceeds 50% – the three Nordic countries, Estonia, Ireland, Cyprus, Portugal and the UK. A much smaller proportion of women than men in this age group remain in employment – 34%, compared with 52%. There are large gender variations between countries. The employment rate for women ranges from over 70% in Denmark, Estonia and Sweden and over 60% in Lithuania, Finland and the UK to only around 30% or just over in Belgium, Greece, Italy and Slovenia and 23% in Poland and Slovakia. The reasons for relatively low employment rates of older workers in many countries are in part a tendency to take early retirement and in part a function of lack of job opportunities. Few women and men in most Member States remain in employment after the official retirement age – on average only 5% of women aged 65–69 and 11% of men. However, there are significant country-by-country variations. For example, in Latvia 15% of women in this age group were in employment; in Portugal 22% and in Romania 25%. A significant proportion of men in these countries also remained employed between 65 and 69. In these countries older workers are usually employed in agriculture. The rate of employment of those aged over 55 is related to education level. Older workers with higher education have an above average employment rate of 70% in the EU as a whole. The preretirement years also see an increase in part-time working for both women and men. It is also the case that there is a clear link between disability and age – nearly half of workers classified as disabled within the EU are within the 50–64 age group (EC, 2008).

Social beliefs and attitudes are bound to impact on the employment participation of older workers. Evidence shows that perceptions of unfair discrimination against older workers are commonplace across the EU-27 countries. For example, the Eurobarometer (2008) survey finds that 42% of people in Europe believe that age discrimination is widespread, although 51% believe that it is now less widespread than 5 years ago. Respondents in Hungary and the Czech Republic are most likely to believe that age discrimination is widespread. Overall 57% feel that people over 50 are considered to be no longer capable of working; 69% saw being over 50 as a disadvantage in society today; 49% believe that the over 50s are disadvantaged in getting jobs; 78% believe that a person over 50 is less likely than someone under 50 with equivalent skills/qualifications to get a job, training or promotion at work. Six percent of respondents reported having personally experienced age discrimination in the last year.

2.7.5 Lesbian and gay workers – European employment trends and patterns

As noted above in the section on lesbian and gay workers in the UK, it is not possible to determine with any degree of accuracy whether or not lesbian and gay workers are under- or over-represented in certain sectors and occupations. However, what we can say (to be discussed more extensively in Chapter 10) is that wider social attitudes and prejudices, combined with the legacy of (until recently) legal discrimination, mean that gay and lesbian workers have faced and are likely to continue to face significant discrimination and disadvantage within the European labour market. Studies indicate widespread perceptions of employment discrimination. For example, the Euro-barometer (2008) survey found that discrimination on the basis of sexual orientation is regarded as the second most widespread form of discrimination in the EU (after discrimination on the basis of ethnic origin). Sexual orientation discrimination is seen as being particularly widespread in many of the Mediterranean countries. However, in virtually all EU countries this form of discrimination is seen as less widespread in 2008 when compared with the 2003 survey. Six percent of people indicated that they had witnessed discrimination on the basis of sexuality.

Key learning points

- Overall women's employment in Europe has increased over time. The European labour market is highly gender segregated both horizontally and vertically. Women are more highly concentrated in a small range of occupations when compared with men.
- Data on BME employment are hard to capture across the EU because of the variety of classifications and monitoring systems. Illegal workers are in a particularly vulnerable position in the EU, most of whom are from non-European BME backgrounds, and who are predominantly concentrated in the worst-paid and lowest-status jobs, with little or no employment protection.
- While differences in definition can skew the statistics in cross-EU comparisons, disabled people are more likely to be unemployed or inactive in the labour market, and to hold lower-paid and lower-status jobs than people without disabilities.
- Demographic statistics identify the accelerating trend towards an ageing population in all EU countries. This is of concern because the labour market participation of older workers is disproportionately low and there are fears that if older workers are not gaining employment, or retirement ages are not raised, then there will be a significant decline in the working-age population.
- Gay and lesbian workers continue to face discrimination despite recent legislation. Evidence suggests that discrimination on the basis of sexual orientation remains widespread.

2.8 CONCLUSION

By examining macro-level data in the UK and broader European contexts, this chapter has shown that the labour market differentiates between different groups of employees on the basis of demographic and identity characteristics. The result for employees is unequal outcomes and opportunities and from an employer perspective, the under-utilisation of certain segments of the workforce. Claims frequently made by employers to treat everyone the same or as individuals are likely to prove naïve or unfounded. The data presented here reveal distinctive employment trends and patterns and significant disadvantage for certain social groups. Thus, labour market opportunities are mediated and constrained by gender, race, age, disability and sexual orientation, albeit in qualitatively different ways. By examining labour market trends and patterns along the lines of social group membership, a complex picture emerges, which is ever changing, partly in response to wider social and economic changes.

REVIEW AND DISCUSSION QUESTIONS

1. Why should UK and European policy-makers prioritise gender segregation of the labour market?

2. Explore the changing trends and patterns in BME employment in the UK and the wider Europe. How much progress has been made by BME groups?

3. Based on the evidence, is it justified to say that discrimination and disadvantage remain widespread in the labour markets of the UK and Europe?

FURTHER READING

For reliable labour market information and data, visit the following web sites for downloadable fact sheets and reports:

Department for Business, Enterprise and Regulatory Reform http://www.berr.gov.uk/

Department for Work and Pensions http://www.dwp.gov.uk/

Equality and Human Rights Commission http://www.equalityhumanrights.com/en/Pages/default.aspx

European Commission http://epp.eurostat.ec.europa.eu/

European Foundation for the Improvement of Living and Working Conditions http://www.eurofound.europa.eu/

Government Equalities Office http://www.equalities.gov.uk/

REFERENCES

Anthias, F., Yuval-Davis, N., 1992. Racialised Boundaries. Routledge, London.

Aston, J., et al., 2004. Interim Update of Key Indicators of Women's Position in Britain. Women and Equality unit/Department of Trade and Industry, London.

Barnes, C., 1992. Disability and employment. Personnel Review 21 (6), 55-73.

Blackburn, R., Browne, J., Brooks, B., Jarman, L., 2002. Explaining Gender Segregation. British Journal of Sociology 53 (4), 513-536.

Blackwell, L., 2001. Occupational sex segregation and part-time work in modern Britain. Gender, Work and Organisation 8 (2), 146-163.

Brah, A., 1994. South Asian young Muslim women and the labour market. In: Afshar, H., Maynard, M., (Eds.), The Dynamics of 'Race' and Gender. Taylor & Francis, London.

Brown, C., 1992. Same difference: the persistence of racial disadvantage in the British employment market. In: Braham, P., Rattansi, A., Skellington, R. (Eds.), Racism and Antiracism: Inequalities, Opportunities and Policies. Sage, London.

Clark, K., Drinkwater, S., 2007. Dynamics and Diversity: Ethnic Minorities in the UK Labour Market. Policy Press, Bristol.

CRE, 2006. Employment and Ethnicity. Factfile 1. Commission for Racial Equality, London.

Dale, A., Shaheen, N., Fieldhouse, E., Kalra, V., 2002. The labour market prospects for Pakistani and Bangladeshi women. Work, Employment and Society 16 (1), 5-25.

Dixon, S., 2003. Implications of population ageing for the labour market. Labour Market Trends, February 2003, 67-76.

DWP, 2003. Factors affecting the labour market participation of older workers. Research Report 200: Department for Work and Pensions.

DWP, 2007. Older Workers: Statistical Information Booklet. Department for Work and Pensions, London.

EC, 2001. Gender Equality Magazine, 11, European Commission.

EC, 2007a. Report on Racism and Xenophobia in the Member States of the European Union. European Commission, Brussels.

EC, 2007b. Study of Compilation of Disability Statistical Data from the Administrative Registers of the Member States. European Commission, Brussels.

EC, 2008. Employment in Europe 2008. Directorate-General for Employment, Social Affairs and Equal Opportunities. European Commission, Brussels.

EOC, 2006. Facts About Women and Men in Great Britain 2003. Equal Opportunities Commission, Manchester.

EOR, 1997. Equality for lesbians and gay men in the workplace. Equal Opportunities Review 74, 20-28.

EOR, 1998. Tackling age bias: code or law? Equal Opportunities Review 80, 30-31.

EOR, 2001. Trends in female employment. Equal Opportunities Review 96, 29.

Eurobarometer, 2008. Discrimination in the European Union: Perceptions, Experiences and Attitudes. European Commission, Brussels.

Eurostat, 2008. The life of women and men in Europe - A statistical portrait, European Commission.

Fagan, C., Burchell, B., 2002. Gender, Jobs and Working Conditions in the European Union. European Foundation for the Improvement of Living and Working Conditions, Dublin.

Giaccone, M., Bucalossi, G., 2008. Annual Review of Working Conditions in the EU, 2007-2008. European Foundation for the Improvement of Living and Working Conditions, Dublin.

Ginn, J., Arber, S., 1995. Exploring mid-life women's employment. Sociology 29 (1), 73-95.

Goldstone, C., Meager, N., 2002. Barriers to Employment for Disabled People. Department of Work and Pensions, Leeds.

Hakim, C., 1993. The myth of rising female employment. Work, Employment and Society 7 (1), 97-120.

Heath, A., Cheung, S., 2006. Ethnic Penalties in the Labour Market: Employers and Discrimination. Department for Work and Pensions, London.

Herzing, A., 1995. The labour market position of women from ethnic minorities: A comparison of four European countries. In: Doorne-Huiskes, A.V., Van Hopf, J., Roelofs, R. (Eds.), Women and the European Labour Market, Ch. 1. Open University, The Netherlands.

Holdsworth, C., Dale, A., 1997. Ethnic differences in women's employment. Work, Employment and Society 11 (3), 435-457.

Hugman, R., 1994. Ageing and the Case of Older People in Europe. Macmillan, London.

Hyde, M., 1996. Fifty years of failure: employment services for disabled people in the UK. Work, Employment and Society 10 (4), 683-700.

Joshi, H., Layard, R., Owen, S., 1985. Why are more women working in Britain ? In: Leaker, D., (Ed.), 2008. The Gender Pay Gap in the UK Economic and Labour Market Review 2(4), 19-24.

Leaker, D., 2008. The gender pay gap in the UK. Economic and Labour Market Review 2 (4), 19-24.

McNair, S., Flynn, M., 2007. Employer Responses to an Ageing Workforce: A Qualitative Study. Department for Work and Pensions, London.

Millward, N., Woodland, S., 1995. Gender segregation and male/female wage differences. Economics of Equal Opportunities. Humphries, J., Rubery, J. Manchester, Equal Opportunities Commission.

Modood, T., Berthoud, R., Lakey, J., Nazroo, J., Smith, P., Virdee, S., Beishon, S., 1997. Ethnic Minorities in Britain: Diversity and Disadvantage. Policy Studies Institute, London.

Palmer, A., 1993. Less Equal than Others. Stonewall.

Pillinger, J., 1992. Feminising the Market: Women's Pay and Employment in the European Community. Macmillan, London.

Plantenga, J., 1995. Labour market participation of women in the EU. In: Doorne-Huiskes, A.V., Van Hopf, J., Roelofs, R. (Eds.), Women and the European Labour Market, Ch. 1. Open University, The Netherlands.

Platt, L., 2006. Pay Gaps: The Position of Ethnic Minority Women And Men. Equal Opportunities Commission, Manchester.

Smith, A., Twomey, B., 2002. Labour market experiences of people with disabilities. Labour Market Trends, August 2002, 415-427.

Smith, S., 1992. Disabled in the Labour Market. Employment Policy Institute, London.

Snape, D., Thomson, K., Chetwynd, M., 1995. Discrimination Against Gay Men and Lesbians. SCPR, London.

Stonewall, 2009. Stonewall Top 100 Employers 2009: The Workplace Equality Index. Stonewall, London.

Taylor, P., Walker, A., 1994. The ageing workforce: employers' attitudes towards older people. Work, Employment and Society 8 (4), 569-591.

TUC, 2008. Ten Years After. Trades Union Congress, London.

Walby, S., Armstrong, J., 2008. Review of Equality Statistics. Equality and Human Rights Commission Manchester.

Walling, A., 2007. Understanding statistics on full-time/part-time employment. Economic and Labour Market Review 1 (2), 26-44.

Wrench, J., Jandl, M., Kraler, A., and Stepien, A., 2003. Migrants, Minorities and Employment: Exclusion, Discrimination and Anti-discrimination in the 15 Member States of the EU. European Monitoring Centre on Racism and Xenaphobia (EUMC), October, Brussels.

Wynne, R., McAnaney, D., 2008. Employment Guidance Services for People with Disabilities. European Foundation for the Improvement of Living and Working Conditions, Dublin.

Theorizing employment segregation

3

Aim

To provide the conceptual and theoretical underpinning necessary to develop a critical analysis of the employment trends and patterns outlined in Chapter 2.

Objectives

- To present the main theoretical explanations for employment segregation.
- To provide a critical analysis of these theoretical explanations, highlighting strengths and weaknesses.

3.1 INTRODUCTION

Chapter 2 outlined the segregated and segmented nature of the European labour market. We also showed that employment segregation produces and reinforces inequalities, disadvantage and discrimination. This chapter aims to present a brief outline of the various theoretical explanations for the group-based differential employment trends and patterns described in Chapter 2. It draws on classical theories as well as more recent ones. It explores both demand and supply side arguments, and critically appraises their ability to offer a complete explanation for labour market segmentation and segregation. For utility, a distinction is made between neoclassical and human capital theories, labour market segmentation theories and social identity theories. It should be recognized that these overlap and interconnect, but the distinction provides a useful classificatory tool for the purpose of analysis.

3.1.1 Employment segregation

The five social groups that are the focus of this book experience, to one degree or another, employment segregation. Employment segregation operates at different levels – industrial, sectoral and occupational. At the occupational level it involves both vertical and horizontal segregation where women, black and minority ethnic (BME), disabled and older workers are more likely to hold lower status, lower paid jobs with less chance of promotion, training and career opportunities. Given the invisibility of sexual orientation, it is more difficult to determine whether or not the labour market is segmented by sexual orientation, but it is certain that gay and lesbian workers experience disadvantage in the labour market (as shown in Chapter 2).

Why does employment segregation matter? From an economic perspective, it is argued that employment segregation causes labour market rigidity and inefficiency; it is wasteful of human resources and a source of inflexibility within a context of globalization, where the importance of flexibility is stressed (Anker, 1997). More importantly for our discussion, employment segregation is clearly detrimental to marginalized groups of workers, having a negative effect on employment opportunities, occupational attainment and pay. In particular, gender segregation is pronounced in all industrialized countries and it is generally agreed that it is by far the most important explanation of the gender pay gap and women's disadvantage in the labour market (Anker, 1997).

3.2 EXPLAINING EMPLOYMENT SEGREGATION – THE NEOCLASSICAL APPROACH

Within an economic paradigm, the neoclassical approach places an emphasis on the rational and efficient functioning of the labour market (for a summary see Beardwell and Holden, 2004). According to neoclassical economic theory, irrational prejudice and discrimination against certain groups of workers distort the rational and efficient functioning of the market and therefore should not exist. However, there is plenty of evidence that discrimination and disadvantage *do* exist, so how does neoclassical theory explain this? First, from a supply side perspective, the focus is on choices and preferences of workers, which market forces then have to accommodate. From a demand side perspective, employers try to maximize profits and minimize costs, which may involve discriminating against particular individuals or groups of individuals. These arguments are now discussed in further detail.

3.2.1 Supply side arguments

From the labour supply point of view, a neoclassical approach to explaining employment segregation is based around rational choice of individuals with regard to their occupation. This in turn is linked to differences in workers' human capital – that is, the skills, qualifications and training that workers bring to the labour market, and the human capital that is acquired after joining the labour market (work experience). Therefore, a person's rational choice of industry, sector or occupation is dependent on what is attainable, which in turn depends on the level of human capital that person has (Blackburn et al., 2002). Neoclassical theorists see human capital as the outcome of deliberate investment by an individual (perhaps incurring some present costs) for the sake of future benefits (Becker, 1964).

Chapter 2 highlighted the fact that there is not a level playing field prior to entering the labour market as there is also segregation and unevenness within the education system. For instance, females tend to choose to study subjects within the arts and humanities, whilst men lean towards the sciences, including subjects like engineering. Also, some BME groups have lower rates of higher education than others (EOC, 2006).

Prior education and qualifications inevitably open up some career paths and close off others. Thus, certain groups (e.g. women or BME workers) are said to come to the labour market with less human capital, which then shapes the opportunities available to them. In addition, Chapter 2 indicated that while the 'traditional' family structure has declined, women are still almost exclusively responsible for housework and childcare. Family responsibilities mean that many women gain less paid work experience than men owing either to their early and permanent withdrawal from employment or career breaks to care for young children. According to human capital theory, in anticipation of future family responsibilities, women rationally choose occupations with relatively high starting pay, relatively low returns to experience, and relatively low penalties for temporary withdrawal from the labour force (Anker, 1997; England, 1982). This also makes occupations that offer flexible terms and conditions more attractive to women.

To expand on this, the disproportionate representation of women in lower skilled occupations and part-time work is seen as due to women's own choices. Women accept the differentials (including lower pay) as a trade-off for the other responsibilities they have (Anker, 1997: 4). Thus, it is argued that women engage in less training because they expect to work less and they choose occupations where interruptions (career breaks) are not costly. In addition, women's careers continue to be severely affected by the uneven gender division of household and parental responsibilities. Women's employment is still typically characterized by one or more career breaks, and this is found to have a particularly detrimental effect on women's job prospects in the medium to long term (Hardill and Watson, 2004). Even for presently childless women, it is likely that the prospect of future child-rearing responsibilities influences them to some extent when making decisions about human capital investment (Blackburn et al., 2002). Two main factors that are thought to positively influence career progression are a full-time uninterrupted working life and demonstrating the ability to appear as a long-term prospect, particularly showing career commitment by working long hours (Liff and Ward, 2001). Thus, women are often disadvantaged, when the model of career is based on that of a male full-time employee.

There is some empirical support for a human capital explanation of gender segregation, although Hakim's (1991, 1998, 2000) influential assertions to this effect have been the subject of controversy (Crompton and Harris, 1998a, Blackburn et al., 2002). Hakim used her research to attempt to counter explanations that positioned women as 'victims' of social structures and attitudes. Her main argument was that while women are disproportionately in the lowest status and lowest paid jobs, they are also disproportionately satisfied with their jobs. Hakim explained this by arguing that the majority of women aim for a 'homemaker' career and work is seen as of peripheral importance. Hakim identified three groups of women workers – the first two are polarized between the 'work-centred' (a small minority who work full-time and have strong work commitment), and the 'home-centred' (a larger minority of part-time women workers who have lower levels of work commitment than men). Hakim labelled the third and largest group as 'adaptive' women who actively seek to combine work and family, or women with no clear career strategy. In some ways, 'adaptive' women present a contradiction of human capital theory as they do not always make 'rational' economic use of their qualifications (Blackburn et al., 2002). However, Hakim (2000) also talks about 'marriage markets' arguing that some women invest in higher education in order to find a 'suitable' partner. Hakim (2000) also challenges human capital explanations for seeing preferences as stable and static, recognizing that women may have considerable choice and changing preferences over their life cycles. However, 'adaptive' women's work still does not dominate their life preferences, and they are not found to be ambitious for career success, often 'preferring' (for a variety of reasons) to work part-time in female occupations. Thus, they contribute to the maintenance of gender segregation. The overall argument is that gender segregation ultimately derives from women's work orientations and life priorities. Hakim goes so far as to state: '...*most women have actively colluded in their own imprisonment in unpaid work in the home and low-paid, low status jobs in the workforce' (1991: 110).*

To summarize the supply side perspective, a person's occupation is seen as the outcome of individual agency (active preferences and choices) and rational human capital investment decisions. Further, this perspective would argue that women, BME, disabled and even perhaps older workers are over-represented in lower paid jobs and certain occupations because of their different (often perceived as inferior) types and levels of human capital when compared to white, male, non-disabled, younger workers.

3.2.2 Demand side arguments

Many of the factors influencing individual preferences for particular occupations also influence employer's preferences for particular types of workers. It is argued that jobs requiring a relatively high level of education, and those where experience and on-the-job training are relatively important, are more likely to be offered to men than women (Anker, 1997). One reason is that women are considered to be higher cost workers because they are assumed to demand higher indirect labour costs, including statutory costs such as maternity leave. Women are also perceived to have higher rates of absenteeism and lateness, and higher turnover rates (largely due to caring responsibilities).

While discrimination (the application of various criteria to choose between people) is part of an employer's expected role in recruitment and selection processes, Noon and Blyton (2002: 168) distinguish between 'fair' and 'unfair' discrimination. 'Unfair' discrimination is based on unjustifiable, unfair criteria, usually based around stereotypes. Stereotyping is particularly apparent in a discussion of why many employers see older workers as having less human capital. The education system is seen as playing an important part in the relationship between age and employment (Branine and Glover, 1997: 239). The British education system requires that subject choices are made at an early age and these choices inevitably have a bearing on future career opportunities and decisions. Although it is theoretically possible to return to education later in order to open up new career paths, mature graduates and people who gain qualifications later in life are generally disadvantaged when they seek employment, training and promotion. There is also a perceived belief, mirroring the perceived higher indirect costs women carry, that older workers cost companies more due to higher healthcare costs. In addition, older workers are stereotyped as lacking energy, flexibility and ability and willingness to learn, all of which can make organisations less willing to employ them (Branine and Glover, 1997: 240). More than two decades ago, Pringle (1989: 170) pointed to the overtly discriminatory attitudes of managers responsible for recruitment on the basis of age *and* gender. She argued that managers make decisions based on stereotyping which casts women over the age of 40 years as being increasingly domesticated and uninterested in business issues. Thus, the role of stereotyping in constraining women's opportunities becomes exacerbated as women get older. Furthermore, Oswick and Rosenthal's (2001: 168) research indicates that stereotypes can work to the disadvantage of both older and younger workers, with some jobs classified as older or younger jobs. For example, employers are likely to discriminate in favour of older workers where a job requires stability, loyalty and maturity, but in favour of younger workers where the job is physically demanding, whether or not such skills/attributes are real.

The case of age stereotypes is just one example – stereotypes, often negative, are also attached to gender, disability, race/ethnicity and sexuality. It is clear that negative stereotyping leads not only to disadvantage in recruitment but also in job progression. Kamenou and Fearfull (2003) find that gender and ethnicity clearly interact in the formation of stereotypes. Their research considered issues around self-presentation, particularly whether an employee is seen as 'Westernized'. This had an effect on how someone was accepted in a predominantly white organisational context and consequently had an impact on career opportunities. For example, wearing traditional Muslim dress is found to lead to perceptions of the woman as passive, fundamentalist, less professional, less business-oriented and less committed to work. Pakistani Muslim women in Kamenou and Fearfull's study felt that they were not perceived as 'career women' regardless of their performance. While lower levels of human capital, combined with household responsibilities are seen as a key to some BME women's disadvantaged position in the labour market, for some BME women *supposed* 'language' difficulties and 'lack of skills' are seen as *doubly disadvantaging* them (Phizacklea, 1994: 179). However, it should be recognized that female workers from minority ethnic groups cannot just be seen as 'doubly discriminated' as their experience is likely to be qualitatively different, and not just an issue of amount of discrimination (Maynard, 1994: 13).

According to an influential model of employer behaviour developed by Becker (1971), employers are prejudiced against certain groups of workers. Because of this prejudice, employers are said to sustain a cost when they hire someone from the group discriminated against. Therefore, according to this theory, employers act rationally when they hire fewer people from that group since they wish to avoid this 'cost'. This can be termed 'statistical discrimination', where employers discriminate against individuals on the basis of perceived group characteristics (Anker, 1997). Such stereotypes are bound up with perceptions of what is acceptable in an employee and generally lead to a preference for a white man or woman over a person of minority ethnic origin or for a younger worker over an older one, a non-disabled person rather than a disabled person and so on. Thus, a vicious circle exists where employment segregation is perpetuated and jobs become stereotyped through a combination of institutional discrimination and limited expectations of job seekers themselves.

3.3 EXPLAINING EMPLOYMENT SEGREGATION – LABOUR SEGMENTATION THEORIES

This section focuses on theories arguing that access to occupations and progression within them are determined by the structure of the labour market. These theories grew out of analysis of the economic and labour market conditions in the post-war era up to the late 1970s. The theory was that within existing structural conditions, employer choices ensured that disadvantaged groups only rarely gained the opportunity to improve their circumstances. Capital accumulation is seen as predicated on the exploitation of resources, including women and BME labour. Labour markets are seen as segmented with different groups of workers compartmentalized and isolated and receiving different rewards and opportunities for otherwise comparable attributes (Watts and Rich, 1993: 160).

Perhaps the best known of these is dual labour market theory (Doeringer and Piore, 1971). Here, a primary sector is distinguished from the secondary sector. Jobs in the primary sector are relatively good in terms of pay, security and opportunities for advancement and working conditions. In contrast, secondary sector jobs tend to be relatively poorly paid with few chances for promotion, poor working conditions and little job security. As Anker (1997) pointed out, the concept of dual markets could be adapted to explain employment segregation, where the primary sector is said to hold mainly 'male', 'white' jobs, and the secondary sector, 'female', 'older worker' and 'BME' jobs. Within this theory, men would be favoured by primary sector employers on account of their more continuous work experience and the fact that primary sector jobs tend to accord a relatively high value to firm-specific experience and low labour turnover. It has been argued that the dual labour market derives from clear control strategies by employers. The argument was that in the face of a highly organized and highly skilled workforce, employers consciously exploited race, ethnic and gender antagonisms in order to undercut trade union strength (when trade union membership was high).

With regard to race and ethnicity, it is argued that in the 1950s and 1960s the British government and employers had a clear strategy to segment the market by deliberately employing people from BME groups to fill jobs at the lower end of the labour market, within the 'secondary' sector (Cockburn, 1991; Anthias and Yuval-Davis, 1992). Chapter 2 emphasized that a historical analysis is required to understand how the labour market came to be segregated by race. 'Mass' migration of labour is linked to demand during the post-war period of economic development. The economic boom from 1945 to the late 1960s, which saw a growing number of white women entered the British labour market, also led to the recruitment of workers from Britain's former colonies. Immigrant workers provided a so-called 'reserve army of labour' – a pool of workers drawn upon in a time of labour shortages. The degree to which these 'reserve armies' were integrated into the labour market varies from country to country and between different ethnic groups. However, generally speaking they were assigned to an inferior position in Britain.

The significance of the segregation of workers is that once entrenched within the secondary labour market, it is difficult both for individuals and groups to move out because they do not acquire the human capital necessary to do so. This is not to say that social mobility is not possible. Indeed there are clear illustrations of groups moving out of a disadvantaged position – for example certain BME groups (see Pilkington, 2001). However, dual labour market theorists argue that individuals and groups can become trapped by stigmatization and thus labour market segregation is perpetuated into the next generation. In essence, the segregation process becomes self-reinforcing (Watts and Rich, 1993).

Key learning points

- Neoclassical explanations for employment segregation stress differences in workers' human capital. The supply side argument considers differences in education and training and the uneven division of household responsibilities. The demand side argument stresses the rational preferences of employers for low-cost employees based on stereotypes of certain groups, leading in turn to statistical discrimination.
- Labour market segmentation theories posit that segmentation leads to a vicious circle of segregation for 'minority' workers.

3.4 WEAKNESSES IN NEOCLASSICAL AND LABOUR MARKET SEGMENTATION THEORIES

Neoclassical and labour market segmentation theories certainly make a contribution to understanding employment segregation. The neoclassical approach highlights the important role played by individual preferences and choices and differences in the human capital accumulated by diverse social groups. Labour market segmentation theories are useful for understanding how, historically, industries, sectors and occupations become segregated. However, there are also strong criticisms particularly if these approaches are taken as the only explanations of employment segregation. The first major criticism is that the changing trends and patterns in the labour market participation of diverse social groups do not always provide support for these theories. The second is that explanatory gaps remain. These criticisms are now explored in more detail.

3.4.1 The changing evidence base

The most obvious issue to turn to in order to highlight the weaknesses of neoclassical and labour segmentation theories is gender. Chapter 2 pointed to the fact that women's labour market activity has increased exponentially over the last few decades. In addition, there is evidence of the breakdown of traditional family and household structures. The type of household that was the most common in post-war Britain was the traditional male breadwinner type. By the mid-1980s, only 7% of couple families with a child under six were of the 'dual breadwinner' type, where both parents are in full-time employment. But, by the end of the twentieth century, this figure had trebled. Marked increase has also taken place in households where there is a child under the age of six and where the man works full-time and the woman part-time. This all indicates major gendered social change (Glover and Kirton, 2006). Further, women are gaining greater labour market experience, which, according to neoclassical theory, means that they have increased human capital, which should lead to changes in the types of occupation women are able to access. However, the picture is uneven. Certainly in the 2000s we can see signs of women's progress. It is argued that white, highly qualified (often child-free) women who are willing and able to meet the expectations of the male norm of full-time, continuous employment and of privileging work over home and family appear to be 'winning' in the labour market. These women have now increased their share of relatively highly paid managerial and professional work enabling them to buy substitute childcare and household labour (Glover and Kirton, 2006: 17). But, less highly qualified women still remain stuck in feminized sectors and occupations, where pay is relatively poor. Thus, some commentators argue that there is increased polarization among women – the highly qualified are doing quite well and the more poorly qualified less well. However, even for highly qualified women the picture is not wholly positive. Purcell's (2002) research on male and female graduates shows that even when women's qualifications are in applied subjects that are particularly relevant for the labour market, such as languages, engineering and business studies, substantial numbers of them are employed in routine, non-graduate-level jobs. This uneven picture challenges the value of neoclassical theories.

Another criticism arises from the (dual labour market theory) assumption that primary sector jobs necessarily require more continuity of experience than those in the secondary sector. Anker (1997: 320) compares the male job of a delivery truck driver with that of the female job of a secretary. He argues that a secretary requires considerably more knowledge and skills. From a human capital perspective, the predominance of women in the secondary labour market is explained by the fact that women who plan to spend time out of the labour market will choose jobs with low penalties for intermittent employment. However, more than 25 years ago England (1982) established that female-dominated occupations (often in the secondary labour market) did not consistently show lower penalties for intermittent employment when compared with male-dominated jobs. In other words, the supply side theory of gender segregation cannot explain women's predominance within a relatively narrow range of female occupations at each skill level (Watts and Rich, 1993).

In addition, the assumption (for example in Hakim's work drawing on rational choice theory) that women have lesser work commitment and that is why they have such a strong tendency to work part-time, leads to a second assumption that part-time work is necessarily less demanding than full-time. Research has found both assumptions to be flawed arguing that part-time work can be just as, if not more demanding than full-time work. Therefore there is an argument to be made that work or career commitment should not be measured primarily in terms of work hours (Scheibl, 1996).

With regard to demand side explanations, it is disputed whether there are in practice higher direct and indirect labour costs associated with female workers. It is true to say though that labour laws and regulations can increase the comparative cost of employing female workers if they decide to have children for maternity leave costs. However, on other points of higher cost, there does not seem to be a gender difference, for example survey evidence indicates that there are similar turnover and absenteeism rates for women and men (Anker, 1997). This leads us to challenge the extent to which employers make recruitment and selection decisions based on unfounded negative stereotypes and outdated assumptions or on 'real' differences in skills, experience, costs, etc. This point can be illustrated by reference to BME workers. There is little evidence to suggest that people from BME groups today have lower career aspirations or even lower qualifications and skills, but there remain 'ethnic penalties' in the labour market even when education and qualifications are controlled (Heath and Cheung, 2006). Formal education does not seem to act as the buffer against unemployment and under-employment for workers from BME groups to quite the same extent as it does for white workers. Similarly, there is little concrete evidence for popular stereotypes of older workers. A review of studies of age and job performance finds older workers to be as productive as their younger counter-parts, despite the fact that they are often perceived as having less energy, being less able and less willing to learn (Lackzo and Philopson, 1991). In conclusion, the available evidence does not lend total support to neoclassical and labour market segmentation theories.

3.4.2 Theoretical gaps

Neoclassical and labour market segmentation theories provide only incomplete expla-nations. Human capital theory highlights how some groups are less well-qualified than others for certain occupations. Rational choice theory states that a person's occupation is an outcome of individual preferences and choices. Labour market segmentation theories indicate that labour markets are segmented and that this leads to the repro-duction of disadvantage for marginalized social groups.

However, questions remain. Why do certain social groups on average come to the labour market either with lower levels of education or with qualifications in subjects seen as 'less relevant'? Why are housework, childcare and eldercare almost always the responsibility of women? Why does employment segregation persist despite a large overlap in the abilities of advantaged and disadvantaged groups? Blackburn et al. provide a useful summary of the critiques of human capital theory, and highlight in particular their circular nature: '...*we are told that women's qualifications are worth less, and therefore are paid less. How do we know they are worth less? Because women are paid less.'* (2002: 518–519). What human capital theory cannot explain is the persistent undervaluing of women's occupations (Anker, 1997) which will be discussed later in this chapter.

Crompton and Harris (1998a,b) dispute Hakim's (1991, 1998) notion that variations in women's preferences and orientations to work are the major determinant explaining their employment patterns. Like the women in Crompton and Harris' (1998) research, the women in Scheibl's (1996) study had reluctantly accepted a household career path, despite their earlier intentions to have a career in the labour market. Therefore, we need to recognize that choices are made in the knowledge of available opportunities and constraints. More important for Crompton, Harris and Scheibl, but neglected by Hakim, are the processes of choice making: *'Preferences may shape choices, but they do not... determine them'* (Crompton and Harris, 1998b: 131). One question we must ask is how and why are people's occupational choices constrained and facilitated, and how does social group membership influence these opportunities and constraints? Finally, the disadvantages faced by disabled workers and gay and lesbian workers are not dealt with specifically as part of, and cannot be explained by, human capital theory. This silence is significant in highlighting the inability of economic theories to provide a full explanation for employment segregation.

Key learning points

- There are clear weaknesses if human capital and labour market segmentation theories are used as the only explanations for employment segregation. There is a lack of evidence for the negative characteristics ascribed to certain groups of workers and the approaches do not explain why such attitudes have come about in the first place and continue to be perpetuated in changed economic and social contexts.
- Neoclassical and labour market segmentation theories are almost exclusively focused on gender and race segmentation and do not adequately explain the employment disadvantage met by disabled and gay and lesbian workers.

3.5 EXPLAINING EMPLOYMENT SEGREGATION – SOCIAL IDENTITY THEORIES

Social identity has become a major preoccupation of the social sciences with many disciplines and perspectives grappling with what identity means and why it matters (Jenkins, 2004). The literature is vast and complex. In this section we limit our discussion to drawing out the main implications for theorizing inequalities, discrimination and disadvantage in employment.

3.5.1 Identity formation processes

In his book *Social Identity* (1996), Richard Jenkins relates an incident where he meets his neighbour's daughter and her daughter Helena for the first time:

> *'I cannot... forget that Mrs. Oswald's daughter is female. Otherwise she would be Mrs. Oswald's son, and she could not possibly be Helena's mother. And the relevance of gender depends upon the point of view: whether "I" am male or female... nor is ethnicity disregardable: "my" ethnic point of view matters depending on context. When I first encountered the woman who I now know to be Helena's mother, that she was Afro-Caribbean may have been the first significant thing that I noticed about her. And is Mrs. Oswald Afro-Caribbean? And what might tell me if she were not? Similarly, the fact that her daughter owns a red Mazda tells me something about her class, which in itself may call up knowledge about her profession...' (1996: 116).*

This passage illustrates a process of categorization or identification that occurs continually in our interactions with other people. Concepts of social identity are necessary to query and confirm who we are and who others are, and are an integral part of society (Jenkins, 1996: 6). Elaborating on this in the second edition of his book, Jenkins (2004) argues that:

> *'We try to work out who strangers are even when merely observing them. We work at presenting ourselves so that others will work out who we are along the lines that*

we wish them to. We wonder whether so-and-so is doing that *because of "their identity". ...We talk about whether people are born gay or become gay because of their upbringing... About the differences between the English and the Scots. ...We talk about identity all the time (although we may not always use the word itself).'*

Thus, Jenkins establishes identity as a two-way process – discussed further below. Identity is something others attach to us, but we also attempt to create our own identities so that others will understand who we are. Inevitably, these processes of deciding 'who's who and what's what' (social identification) (Jenkins, 2004) influence the employment relationship just as much as other social relations. For our discussion, the main concern is that social identity matters for employment experiences and outcomes. Some groups are negatively affected by the social identities that others perceive them to possess and even though they may attempt to project a positive self-identity, this can be undermined by the negative stereotypes others might attach to them. In comparison to the neoclassical explanations, social identity perspectives highlight that whatever group of workers we are looking at, it must be acknowledged that preferences and choices are shaped by the opportunity structures that exist in society. Choices are enabled and constrained within the limits set by rules, norms and expectations within any given social context. People need personal, material and social resources if they are to challenge these social constraints.

3.5.1.1 *Ascribed and achieved identities*

A distinction can be made between different types of identities (Jenkins, 2004). *Ascribed* identities are socially constructed on the basis of contingencies of birth and include our gender, race/ethnicity, socio-economic background, etc. These identities are rooted in very early experience and according to Jenkins (2004: 148) are 'massively implicated in the embodied point of view of selfhood'. *Achieved* identities are acquired or assumed through the life course and are an outcome of at least some degree of self-direction. In competitive organisational recruitment, *ascribed* identities are most likely to influence the notion of '*acceptability*' (whether or not a person will 'fit in' to the social networks and relationships of the organisation – the 'right kind of person'). For example, a woman might be deemed 'wrong' for a job on a construction site, based on the gender identity ascribed to her and the employer's understanding of 'what a woman is'. This is in contrast to the notion of '*suitability*', which is usually based on achieved or assumed characteristics (for example skills, education, interests). As Jenkins (2004: 154) asserts, it is from the point of view of acceptability criteria that stereotypes become important. Being 'suitable' for a job does not guarantee a person's recruitment to it because meeting all the objective criteria does not guarantee that 'your face fits' (discussed in greater detail in Chapter 4). This was clearly demonstrated by Collinson et al. (1990) in a seminal study that provided stark examples of discriminatory practices in the insurance industry. Their research highlighted that organisations might be formally open to all, but effectively closed to many groups who are excluded on the basis of acceptability criteria. In their case study organisations, routine recruitment procedures seemed to legitimate racist and sexist practices, with interviewers making decisions based on stereotypes, but justifying them on grounds of what was acceptable to the organisation.

Cockburn (1991: 175) has pointed out that in most cases an *acceptable* worker is a trouble free one and so, for example, employers might refuse to appoint a black applicant in order to avoid racist reactions from existing workers which they would then need to deal with. Disabled workers are similarly seen as an extra cost which the employer wants to avoid paying. Cockburn (1991) found that disabled people seldom got shortlisted for jobs and some managers had overtly discriminatory attitudes towards disabled workers. The existence of informal methods of recruitment, or a strong internal labour market can also encourage the perpetuation of a workforce that may not include disabled workers. In the 1999 BBC documentary, *Disabled Century,* in answer to the question from the floor 'what defines disability', a woman on the panel commented that she did not consider herself disabled; she stated that it was non-disabled people who defined her in that way. For her, the way in which she lived her life was simply different. It seems that such an attitude could apply to many disadvantaged groups and illustrates the explanatory power that social identity perspectives have in understanding the ways in which the labour market becomes segmented.

Turning to women, they are seen primarily as workers with domestic ties (impacting on their work commitment), regardless of their individual circumstances. This ascribed gender identity casts women as troublesome workers, whilst their lower earning capacity and their subordination to men in the workplace also diminish their standing within the household (Cockburn, 1991: 76). The self-reinforcing nature of employment inequality is demonstrated by the fact that because women *do* predominantly take responsibility for childcare, they are often seen as meeting their stereotype in practice. Women in Cockburn's (1991: 86) study found that the difficulty of combining a demanding paid job and family responsibilities meant that they were prevented from taking promotion opportunities. Women were often required to state that they would not put their family first if they wanted to get ahead in their careers. This debate rages on today, but it is of course inequitable because a man would not usually be asked to make the same decision (regardless of the fact that men have families too). Thus, while women may meet the stereotype in practice, this is certainly not a free or rational choice. It is important to avoid biological determinism – the idea that just because women can have children they are automatically the ones who must be the lifelong primary carers in the family or the ones to do the household chores. The fact that this is often the case is the consequence of societal norms and attitudes, rather than biology. As Armstrong and Armstrong point out: *'That women have babies, albeit under a variety of conditions, does not necessarily mean that they will rear the children or clean the toilets'* *(1985: 32).*

3.5.2 Feminist and gender theories

Despite having become a major theme of academic writing, Jenkins informs us that an interest in social identity is not new. It has been a preoccupation in philosophical writings for many hundreds of years. Its origins as a 'modern' project can arguably be traced back to the women's movement of the 1960s (Jenkins, 1996: 13; see also

Giddens, 1991). Feminist and gender theories are primarily concerned with explaining women's inequality; however, as this chapter will demonstrate, the arguments also have some purchase for explanation of the employment disadvantage experienced by other groups.

Feminist theories emerged out of a critique of Marxist theories as failing to take account of the gendered nature of the labour market (See Hartmann, 1979; Beechey, 1987; Walby, 1990). Marxist theories focusing on the oppression of the working class by capitalists failed to distinguish individuals by gender, when evidence seemed to point to the obvious distinction made by employers between the two sexes and as we have pointed out earlier, between different ethnic groups. While Marxist thinkers such as Lenin and Engels stated that women would be emancipated from the oppression of family life by their entry into the productive labour force, the overall experience of women in the twentieth century demonstrated that women's oppression as a sex continued (Cockburn, 1991: 22). To explain this, feminist analysis has challenged and developed Marxist theory in new directions.

3.5.3 Patriarchy

The concept of patriarchy lies at the heart of classic feminist theories. Walby defines patriarchy as '*a system of social structures and practices in which men dominate, oppress and exploit women*' (1990: 20). The theory of patriarchy holds that patriarchal relations both at home and in the workplace give rise to gender inequalities in the labour market. It should be noted that patriarchy is seen to predate capitalism – there is no suggestion that as a social system, patriarchy was created by the forces of capitalism, but nevertheless capitalism is seen as benefiting from patriarchy. What patriarchal theorists refer to as 'the domestic mode of production' (women's role in the household) was seen as the 'super-exploitation' of women (Cockburn, 1991: 23). This is because while women's work in the home can be seen as a form of production (because all the tasks of household labour could be purchased in the market), this labour goes uncompensated by pay and thus women are positioned as the exploited labourers of men in the home. The argument continues that women subsidize the employer by looking after male workers (husbands and sons who need to be clothed and fed). Additionally, women continue to suffer the effects of their unpaid household labour when entering the paid workplace. Women's wages have come to be seen as a secondary income to the male breadwinner wage contributing to the forces that created the gender pay gap. This overarching system of patriarchal relations structures the way in which women and men are treated as workers.

There are several different strands within feminist theories that draw on the concept of patriarchy. Marxist feminists emphasize the need to consider the structures of patriarchy, as well as those of capitalism, in order to understand gender inequality in the labour market (Walby, 1986; Hartmann, 1979; Cockburn, 1983). Patriarchal structures and attitudes within society distinguish between the female as the 'homemaker' and the male as the 'breadwinner', thus enforcing a view of childcare and housework (household labour) as the chief responsibility of women. As Cockburn (1991: 100; see also Dex and Joshi, 1999) highlights, the gender division of roles intensifies with parenthood, with evidence still indicating that men with young families work the longest hours, while women with young children work the least. This directly relates to the provision of state childcare facilities in Britain which as explained in Chapter 2 is relatively poor compared to many other European countries. Patriarchal theorists argue that the 'public' (e.g. the labour market) and 'private' (the home) spheres are thus separated, with notions of womanhood being linked with childbearing, childrearing and domestic life (Mills, 1989). There is an asymmetrical relationship in this gendered division, where the public sphere is accorded greater cultural worth than the private sphere thus disadvantaging women (Mills, 1989; Gardiner, 1998).

There has been considerable critique of the concept of patriarchy, which space does not allow full discussion of here (see Bradley and Healy, 2008; Gottfried, 1998; Pollert, 1996). To summarize, critics have argued that as a 'grand theory' patriarchy is flawed – it is more of a description than an explanation; it denies the role of individual agency (i.e. women are seen as victims); it does not reflect the fluid nature of gender relations (e.g. what role fathers are expected to play is changing), and that as a universal theory it does not explain the differential experiences of diverse women (e.g. why it is that some women are doing fairly well in the labour market and others less well). Regardless of the controversy surrounding the continued usefulness of the concept of patriarchy, however, it did enable feminist theorizing to emerge, helping us to see and understand how men's concerns and interests have come to dominate and define public and political agendas (Cockburn, 1991). More recently authors tend to talk about 'gender' rather than 'patriarchy' – for example, gender relations, gender regimes, gendered attitudes, etc. Gender is a more elastic concept than patriarchy, but still holds the male and female and the masculine and feminine as central to our understanding of social relations.

3.5.4 Changing gendered attitudes

One of the problems with the concept of patriarchy is that it cannot easily accommodate the changing gendered attitudes that are indicative of changing gender relations. As we have seen in Chapter 2, women's employment participation has increased dramatically. Alongside this, there is also evidence of changing social attitudes towards women in paid work. Evidence from UK attitude surveys in the early 1990s indicated that compared to the 1960s there had been a significant fall in the number of women who felt mothers with children under five years old should stay at home. However, there was also evidence of the upholding of traditional attitudes with a large proportion of women agreeing that a husband's job was to earn money and a wife's to care for the home and family (supporting the traditional 'homemaker/ breadwinner' distinction) (Newell, 1993). For women there is evidence that paid work is still perceived as something that has to be accommodated alongside household demands, particularly childcare responsibilities. Despite some glimmers of progress, the continued segregation of unpaid household work is clear. Warren (2003), using the 1995 British Households Panel Survey, found scant evidence of substantial moves towards equity between the sexes regarding household work. Indeed, while there were some class differences, overall, three-quarters of dual waged couples had a male breadwinner arrangement (Warren, 2003: 743). Moreover, almost all couples could be classified as having a female carer arrangement, where the percentage of household tasks undertaken by women across all classes was above 70%. For women to break out of these unequal gendered arrangements, a radical transformation of the relationship between the household and the public sphere of work is needed, for which the existing attitudinal evidence does not bode well. In addition, the available evidence indicates that even if the provision and opportunity were there for men to take an increased household role, there would be a general reluctance to do so. Only a minority of men would welcome the idea of a greater share of parental work and the extension of family-friendly provisions such as those that exist in Sweden (discussed in Chapter 10). Gender role stereotyping within society is therefore deeply embedded and is continually perpetuated by the attitudes and actions of individual women and men.

Much of the stereotyping occurs prior to entry to the labour market. Psychological literature suggests that boys and girls are raised in ways that tend to foster consistency with traditional sex roles (Jenkins, 1996: 58). Corcoran and Courant's (1995) study from the 1990s provided a summary of this literature as well as empirical evidence that families treated boys and girls differently, so that the two sexes developed gendered characteristics and attitudes that advantage boys once they enter the labour market. It is believed that more still needs to be done to break down gender stereotypes as early on as possible and certainly while children are still in school in order to support greater equality between women and men (EC, 2008). Human capital differences can arise from early socialization in the family and schools and can provide a background against which women and men develop gendered preferences and exercise gendered 'choices'. This provides an alternative explanation for why boys and girls choose different subjects at school and why girls might value (feminine) characteristics and skills that are less profitable in the labour market. It also leads men to devalue feminine characteristics and skills and ultimately produces motivation for future gender-based discrimination (England and McCreary, 1986).

Gendered constructions of skill are also evident. This links back to the earlier discussion about whether or not employers' stereotypes of women's skills are based on 'real' skill differences or whether the assessment of skills conceals value judgements. The skills required by jobs seen as 'women's jobs' mirror the stereotypes of women and their supposed natural abilities. Anker (1997) draws up a list of 'feminine' characteristics often required for 'women's jobs'; for example, a caring nature, greater manual dexterity, greater honesty, attractive physical appearance, disinclination to supervise, lesser physical strength, lesser ability in mathematics and science, greater willingness to take orders, greater interest in working at home and greater tolerance of repetitive work. These stereotyped skills would seem to have a great influence on the general characteristics which typify 'female' occupations. Neoclassical economic theorists would explain this as due to women's preferences and biological differences. However, feminist theory suggests an alternative, that gender stereotyping is the outcome of organisational power relations and social, economic and ideological forces shaping the gender-segregated nature of labour market practices (Collinson et al., 1990; Blackburn et al., 2002). Gardiner (1998) summarized the ways in which the skills utilized in what is considered to be 'women's work' are persistently devalued.

She argued that improving women's economic position within households and the labour market would require a revaluing and reconceptualization of the labour processes involved in household work. It is not at all evident that we have yet reached this point.

From a social identity perspective, the view that the occupational position of women derives from rational choice, is: '...*a construction of reality that shifts the blame for women's difficulties to themselves rather than recognising the socially instituted and internalized stereotypes that underpin those choices.*' (Newell, 1993: 287)

In addition, the complexity of the choices women make is emphasized, pointing out that part-time work and home working are not freely chosen, but are chosen from the limited range of options available to most women (Scheibl, 1996; Cockburn, 1991: 82). Women typically occupy two roles which are to some extent incompatible, particularly in a labour market where promotion and earning potential are based around issues of longevity of employment, ability to work long hours and uninterrupted careers.

Overall, the division of household responsibility between the sexes and the patriarchal ordering of society are important in explaining why women usually accumulate less human capital compared with men. It also accounts for the statistical discrimination faced by women from employers once in the labour market. Finally, it explains why women are perceived as having less need for labour market skills and why they so often acquire less human capital once in the labour market through work experience as many of them withdraw from the labour market early or temporarily. Social identity explanations emphasize the importance of socially embedded gendered attitudes. As Anker highlights,

> '...*the fact that these societal norms and perceptions bear little relation to the daily lives of many women, men and families does not detract from their influence on people's behaviour and their contribution to gender-based discrimination against women*'.

(Anker, 1997: 326)

These socially embedded attitudes thus affect employers' and workers' labour market behaviour. Patriarchal theory also lays the responsibility for the exclusion of disadvantaged groups and their segregation into the secondary labour market on the active behaviour of men as a group. Cockburn (1983) subjected craft trade unions to an extensive feminist critique, identifying how the exclusionary practices of male-dominated trade unionists reproduced and protected segmented work patterns. This involved the influence of men (and white, heterosexual, non-disabled men) over recruitment and training and in defining the skill content of jobs. Similarly, Walby (1986) looked at the role of trade unions historically in the reproduction of job segregation in engineering, cotton textiles and clerical work. For example, in cotton textiles, from the nineteenth century, women were actively excluded from union membership and male trade unionists actively resisted the entry of women into the highly skilled spinning jobs. Other studies have pointed to the sexualization of roles and masculine cultures within trade unions which have marginalized and oppressed women who take an active role in modern trade unions (Kirton and Healy, 1999).

Key learning points

- A distinction can be made between ascribed and achieved social identities. Ascribed identities affect whether an individual is seen as 'acceptable' for a job, with stereotypes negatively influencing recruitment and selection processes.
- Feminist and gender theories explore the way in which disadvantage in the labour market is caused by, and is a reflection of, societal structures and attitudes. While the focus has primarily been women's inequality, the arguments made have pertinence for the explanation of the disadvantaged position of other groups within the labour market.
- Feminist theory holds that the patriarchal or gendered structure of society leads to the construction of a distinction between the public and private spheres where women are primarily characterized as workers with domestic ties. Feminist/gender theories see this as an important aspect of women's disadvantage in the labour market.
- Attitudes towards the gendered distinction between breadwinner/homemaker, public/household roles are deeply embedded and there is clear evidence that much sex stereotyping occurs prior to entry to the labour market. There is also little evidence of widespread change in these attitudes, even in more egalitarian societies.
- The division of responsibility between the sexes and patriarchal ordering of society is important in explaining why women accumulate less human capital compared to men. It also accounts for the statistical discrimination experienced by women.
- The active behaviour of employers, employees and trade unions encourages the employment segregation of different social groups.

Activity 3.1

Read the following article and discuss answers to the questions below:

Twisted sisterhood

Women have the feminist movement to thank for fairer working policies and attitudes. So why don't they want to be associated with it? Natalie Hanman investigates our fear of the f-word. The statistics are stark. Just one British woman in four calls herself a feminist. While most men and women in the workplace support feminist ideals, such as equal pay, flexible working and an end to sex discrimination, the f-word itself seems to have fallen out of fashion. For many women, the problem with feminism – and what makes it pretty impossible to adopt – is its image. From bra-burners to ball-breakers, the stereotypical face of feminism isn't pretty.

But how can workers claim to support the positive impact feminism has had on their lives and yet be afraid of identifying with the f-word? How can anyone expect to challenge ongoing gender inequality – from the pay gap to the poor representation of women in positions of power – without supporting the feminist movement? Tamara (not her real name), a 26-year-old public relations consultant, says the term has too much cultural baggage and that using it would make it harder for her to move up the career ladder. 'Even in the friendliest of workplaces, there is a reticence to discuss politics, as it's seen as a bit of a taboo, divisive subject, along with religion and sexuality,' she says. This is a long way from Betty Friedan's 1963 declaration in The Feminine Mystique that 'the personal is political'. Today's office workers seem to think being apolitical is a better route into the boardroom. Tamara, along with many other women I spoke to, did not even want to use their real names in case their employers caught them discussing the forbidden f-word. But surely there's a hint of hypocrisy in reaping the benefits of feminism without joining the movement? Feminism has, after all, achieved a lot and it needed the support of many to do so. Thirty years ago, a woman could be legally sacked for being pregnant, denied a job just because she was a woman or paid less than a man doing the same job. Thanks to women who were proud to call themselves feminists, new gender equality laws were introduced in the 1970s, including the Equal Pay Act, the Sex Discrimination Act and the Employment Protection Act, which made maternity leave a statutory right. Instead of embracing such historic victories, office workers, such as Charlotte Rigby, a 29-year-old solicitor, says being a feminist 'would scare our male colleagues', while Stella (not her real name), 22, who works in the media, says that in her workplace the term means 'man-hater'. She adds: 'I don't think it is perceived as very fashionable to be feminist and most of the women in my office seem to be more concerned with being fashionable than happy.'

Even the older generation, who have witnessed the positive changes feminism has brought to the workplace, tend to agree. Gail, a surveyor in her 50s, thinks the word has 'unpleasant, unattractive connotations'. None of her colleagues, men and women, aged from their late 30s to 60s, would call themselves a feminist. 'I think we should all have equal pay and rights and I will fight to obtain this, but I do not consider this feminism,' Gail argues. 'There are other ways of obtaining what you want without resorting to a head-on feminist approach [and] alienating blokes who then feel threatened.'

So, are women really against feminism or more subtly afraid of being associated with the word? Even some of those at the forefront of the fight for women's rights have their doubts. Thirty years ago, Belinda Price, now 65, won one of the first cases to be brought under the Sex Discrimination Act, but she would not call herself a feminist. 'I think that what people do is more important than the labels you put on them,' she says. 'Feminism isn't a big issue, so far as I'm concerned. It was in the past and I'm sure it needed to be then, but I'm not sure it's a label which needs to be bandied around now.' Others, however, are not ready to ditch the f-word just yet. Stella is a feminist. To her it means, 'not letting my gender hold me back in life'. But every day at work she sees that there is still much more that feminism can do.

'One year into my working life, I am completely stunned at how sexist the workplace is. I was brought up under the impression that work would be one area where things would be more equal, but that couldn't be further from the truth. This goes for the sort of jobs that men and women are deemed suitable for and the attitudes a lot of men seem to have towards their female colleagues. I don't know how the female bosses can put up with it.' Helen Tennison, 34, a theatre director, agrees. 'As an attractive woman, flirting rather than facts is what gets your point across quickly,' she says. 'Being a feminist gives me some kind of solace when deciding whether it is worth the indignity of resorting to an eyelid flutter in order to get my voice heard.' And there are valid reasons to keep fighting for feminism. Even though there are now equal numbers of women and men in employment, with women free to pursue careers of their choice, there is still not equality at work.

The Fawcett Society, a gender equality campaign organisation, reports that last year, the hourly pay gap between women and men stood at 18.4%, compared with 29% in 1975. For part-time work, the gap has hardly changed over the past 30 years – it was 42% in 1975 and 40% in 2005. The gap is even bigger for black and minority ethnic women. Furthermore, women still experience sticky floors and glass ceilings: in 2003, just 3.7% of Financial Times and London Stock Exchange (FTSE) 100 executive directors were women. While the right to request flexible working has been snapped up by many employees, issues such as paternity and maternity leave, work-life balance and women's pensions still need to be tackled.

Edward Lewin, 26, who works in government relations, is positive about feminism's future. 'It's probably a bit simple to say, "Yes, I'm a feminist" – that really doesn't tell you much… It's the role of society, rather than feminism, to ensure there's a greater representation of women in the workplace. It's for everyone to ensure that happens, not just the group of women it affects.' Clare Ettinghausen, 32, chief executive of the Hansard Society and a feminist, argues that feminism is finding its feet in a wider fight for social justice. 'I've seen a dramatic change not only in terms of the rights of women, but also race and disability,' she says. 'Do teenagers identify with feminism less because it has become more mainstream?' So, although many people shy away from the terminology, most seem to agree that gender equality is a worthwhile aim. Katherine Rake, director of the Fawcett Society, recently wrote an impassioned plea in this newspaper to see off the feminist-bashers. She argues that the challenge now is to harness the movement's third wave by uniting around core concerns and building a campaign that people are proud to join. 'Fawcett is determined to create a feminism fit for the twenty-first century that is inspiring and empowering and inclusive of all women and men,' she told me. 'It is not standing alone that we will reclaim the f-word, but together.'

(*Source: The Guardian,* 21 August 2006)

Questions

1. Discuss the contribution that feminism has made to advancing women's equality in employment.
2. How relevant is feminism as a theory and a movement in the twenty-first century?

3.5.5 Connecting race and gender – intersectionality

The black feminist critique of feminism was central to developing thought about the intricate links between gender, race, ethnicity and class (Anthias and Yuval-Davis, 1993). Black feminists pointed to the ethnocentric nature of Western feminism, arguing that its priorities did not take into account the experiences of black or developing world women. The critique highlighted how feminism assumed a unity on the basis of white experiences, rendering BME women invisible and denied a voice. It was argued that there is an inherent racism in analyses and practices which assume the white experience to be the norm.

Nevertheless, many BME feminist authors argued that gender and ethnic divisions can be linked (Anthias and Yuval-Davis, 1993: 111). Both divisions involve practices of exclusion and structuring of disadvantage in favour of a dominant group and both race and gender divisions involve differential access to resources and power. While gender relates to the social construction, representation and organisation of sexual difference and biological reproduction, gender cannot be reduced to biology. The practices around gender originate in social relations, which include race. We cannot understand racism except in its intersection with ethnicity, nationalism, class, gender and state. The conditions of the reproduction of ethnic groups are centrally linked to other primary social divisions of class and gender. While the particular discourses of sexism and racism can be separated, the experiences of the groups affected intersect. Thus, Brah (1994: 151) talks of the 'racialized gendering of labour markets'.

Citizenship is one such gendered and racialized concept affecting labour market position (discussed on a European scale in Chapter 10). Differences in immigration and nationality laws often cast women as men's dependants, and ethnocentrism and racism function to exclude certain groups of people from full citizenship (Anthias and Yuval-Davis, 1993: 127; Allen, 1994). This has an impact on the social stereotypes of different groups and the jobs they will be seen as suitable for. Brah pointed to the discriminatory impact that immigration legislation has had on the status of minority ethnic workers:

> '*Whilst the Asian male was defined as a prospective worker posing a threat to the employment prospects of white men, Asian women were defined in immigration law as "dependants". The social imagery of Asian women as hapless dependants who would most likely be married off at the earliest opportunity has played an important role in shaping the views that teachers or careers officers might hold of young Muslim women's education and employment prospects*'.
>
> **(Brah, 1994: 157)**

Brah (1994) also provided a summary of the extensive literature on direct and indirect employment discrimination against BME workers. Here, social agency as highlighted in feminist/gender theories of employment segregation is emphasized. Discriminatory practices are socially constructed and involve a racialized discourse that stereotypes and stigmatizes BME workers, in the same way that patriarchal discourses stigmatize women. Thus, racialized discourses have relevance for the perceived suitability of a social group for certain types of jobs and positions (Brah, 1994: 157). The actions of male employers, employees and trade unions are also implicated in creating employment disadvantage for BME workers, just as for women (Cockburn, 1991: 180).

Gender stereotyping interacts with ethnic boundaries; indeed cultural restrictions can contribute to the establishment of what is seen as acceptable work for women. For example, the concept of 'purdah'; 'a series of norms and practices which limit women's participation in public life' can have an influence (Brah, 1994: 158). This cultural constraint is often invoked for Muslim women, but different versions of 'purdah' have been found among other minority ethnic groups such as Hindus and Sikhs. Sharma (1983) suggests that 'purdah' can be applied in a wider context, applicable in all societies. The intersection of gender and race is clear here, where woman in all societies face ideologies and practices that influence the ways in which they can participate in the 'public' sphere. Wider patriarchal ideologies and practices can be seen as forms of 'purdah'.

These ideas first put forward by BME feminist authors about the intersections between gender, ethnicity and class have now been taken up by many researchers writing about gender and work. Bradley and Healy (2008) in their research on BME women and work, for example, state that they do not seek to prioritise gender, ethnicity/race or class. They claim that an intersectional approach seeks to understand the connections between various dimensions of social difference. This approach reflects the United Nations' definition of intersectionality:

> *Intersectionality is an integrated approach that addresses forms of multiple discrimination on the basis of racism, racial discrimination, xenophobia and related intolerance as they intersect with gender, age, sexual orientation, disability, migrant, socio-economic or other status. Intersectional discrimination is a form of racism and racial discrimination which is not the sum of race PLUS another form of discrimination to be dealt with separately but is a distinct and particular experience of discrimination unified in one person or group.*
>
> **(UN, 2001)**

Key learning points

- While black feminism has criticized Western feminism for its assumption that the white experience is the norm, gender and race divisions do intersect. Both involve differential access to resources and power and both involve policies of exclusion. Thus, gender and race can be said to intersect.
- There is extensive literature on direct and indirect employment discrimination against BME workers. This reflects conclusions drawn from feminist/gender theories about the interaction between attitudes, childhood socialization, levels of human capital, and individual experiences of employment practices, as explanations for employment segmentation.
- Intersectionality is a concept that now underpins much of the research on gender and work.

3.5.6 The sexuality of the workplace

It is also important to recognize the sexualized character of the workplace. There is now well-established literature in this area. Hearn and Parkin (1987: 83) commented on the way that the role stereotyping of 'women's jobs' often includes the harnessing of sexuality in certain jobs and subtle pressures for women to behave in a sexual manner at work. For example, women in many female jobs such as receptionists, secretaries, salespersons and flight attendants often find themselves expected to 'sell their sexuality' as part of their job in a way that men in male jobs typically are not. Thus, the sexual aspects of the female role in the private sphere are carried over to the public sphere of work and can override a view of a woman as a capable, committed worker (Gutek, 1989). Not burdened with the stereotype of domestication, the situation for men is different where men are seen as the natural inhabitants of organisations.

This has relevance for the discussion of the experiences of gay and lesbian workers in organisations. It is argued that the workplace is heterosexualized (see discussion in Chapter 4). Pringle (1989: 164) highlighted that the normality of sexuality in daily life is heterosexual, involving both the domination of male heterosexuality and the subordination of other forms of sexuality. It is only from 2003 that lesbian and gay workers have been protected by law from discrimination in employment (see Chapter 6). Around 20 years ago, Pringle (1989) noted how striking it was that they found few lesbian and gay employees in their study. She argued that this reflected a latent homophobia within organisations that led to lesbian and gay employees being driven underground. Hall (1989) summarized the possible choices that lesbian and gay workers had within organisational settings, making the point that while there is an argument that a person's sexuality is a private affair and need not be publicly disclosed, many lesbian and gay workers felt that non-disclosure led to 'living a lie' and feelings of betrayal. On the other hand, many lesbian and gay workers also felt that being open about their sexuality led to the loss of promotion opportunities. Thus, like the stereotyping of women and BME employees, sexualized discourses can also have material consequences. Again drawing on feminist/gender perspectives, wider embedded social attitudes are seen to have significant consequences for lesbian and gay employees within the labour market. As stated in Chapter 2, there is now evidence of less widespread homophobia, but that does not mean that organisations are free of bias and prejudice against lesbian and gay workers or that heterosexualized discourses and practices no longer infuse organisations (see Chapter 4).

Key learning points

- The heterosexualized nature of the workplace has consequences in terms of the perpetuation of the gendered stereotyping of work, where women are frequently called upon to harness their sexuality in their work in ways that men are not.
- The heterosexuality of organisation also has consequences for the lesbian and gay workers who are disadvantaged by the supposed threat they pose to the patriarchal authority structures, leading to discrimination and loss of opportunities.

3.5.7 The question of diversity within social groups

Finally, it is important to recognize the enormous diversity within different social groups. The discussion throughout this book emphasizes that women, lesbian and gay, older, BME and disabled workers are not mutually exclusive categories. Thus, no social group is entirely homogenous. This is where the weaknesses (and dangers) of theories may lie. It is important, for example, that theorizing takes account of the fact that women differ in their material and social resources in their individual career aspirations. The ethnocentric nature of Western feminism has also been discussed. Black feminist theories reject an assumption that there is a unity of women's interests and reject the idea that women's interests can be identified on the basis of white experience (Anthias and Yuval-Davis, 1993). Social identities are complex and multi-faceted, where other social divisions intersect with gender.

As Collinson et al. (1990: 192–212) summarize, stereotyping and discriminatory practices can be seen as relating to wider social identity categorization. Different groups within the workplace are constructed as threats and opportunities in different contexts and circumstances. Thus, there is no common experience of disadvantage or no single united disadvantaged group. The white male is not the common 'enemy' of all other groups of worker. Women do not always stand up for other women who are being discriminated against (Collinson et al., 1990) because of their need to maintain their own identities and statuses within the heterosexualized organisation. Oswick and Rosenthal (2001) argued that there is no single discriminating group when it comes to age discrimination – older people sometimes discriminate against other older people. BME men can be sexist in ways that are damaging to all women, including BME women. White women can be racist and not form alliances with BME women. Heterosexual people from many groups can be homophobic, non-disabled people from all groups can ignore the plight of disabled workers. Cockburn (1991: 188) pointed to misogyny with elements of male gay culture. Yet, groups can face a common condition uniting them across certain boundaries; for example, experiences of racism can unite BME women with BME men on racial grounds (Anthias and Yuval-Davis, 1993: 106).

Key learning points

- It is important to recognize that social groups are not homogenous and shared disadvantage does not necessarily lead to the formation of alliances across social groups.

3.6 CONCLUSION

This chapter has summarized the main theories that help us to explain employment segregation. It was concluded that neoclassical and labour segmentation theories offer only a partial explanation. A particular weakness is the emphasis placed on the notion of free or rational 'choice' by labour market actors. Social identity theories offer a fuller explanation, linking employment segregation and disadvantage to embedded norms and attitudes that have developed as a consequence of wider social identity categorization. Feminist theorizing focuses on the ways in which patriarchal or gendered structures disadvantage women in the labour market, and have been further developed to explain the employment experiences of other social groups. Social group stereotypes are found to be particularly influential in recruitment and selection, where decisions made on the basis of acceptability criteria can lead to discrimination and disadvantage for 'minority' workers.

The discussion in the next chapter moves from the theoretical and macro-level analysis of this chapter, to the level of the organisation when identity issues are dealt with in terms of organisational cultures and practices.

Activity 3.2

Race rows start ripple of anxiety

Black police officers all over Britain have reacted with shock and anger to the latest twist of the race row in the Metropolitan Police. After last week's decision to suspend the country's most senior Asian officer – assistant commissioner Tarique Ghaffur, who is taking the force to an employment tribunal over claims of discrimination – the Metropolitan Black Police Association (MBPA) said it had fielded phone calls from officers in virtually every force in the country.

'Black officers... are phenomenally nervous, and there is a lot of anger,' said Alfred John, chairman of the MBPA. 'We have been taking continuous calls from other areas, asking what is going on in the Met.'

Ghaffur, No. 3 in the Met's hierarchy, was suspended last week after the commissioner, Sir Ian Blair, said that his 'personal conduct' and 'media campaign' were affecting the operational effectiveness of the Metropolitan Police. One black officer expressed the view that the Met is out to 'get' Ghaffur, who earns £180,000 a year and is a CBE. The fear was heightened recently when a tribunal rejected the discrimination claims of another officer, Commander Shabir Hussain.

Yasmin Rehman, director of partnerships and diversity for territorial policing, and the Met's most senior Muslim woman, is also reported to be planning to lodge a claim. Met figures show a total of 23 internal allegations of racial discrimination currently under investigation. A further 19 cases involve some element of racial discrimination. 'We have cases going on that are a lot more serious than Tarique Ghaffur's', said John. 'People are concerned about what will happen if they use the complaints procedures. If we can't gain the confidence of the people who work for us, how on earth can we expect to gain the confidence of the people of London?'

In a statement after Ghaffur's suspension, the MBPA chairman said: 'The message this sends to black and minority ethnic officers and staff is clear – exercise your right to challenge unfairness and discrimination at your peril. You will not be listened to, and you and your supporters are likely to be victimised.' Hussain said that he intends to stay in his post as head of transport and aviation security at Scotland Yard and still believes he will see improvements in police procedures, despite the employment tribunal ruling against him. He is due to meet the Met's director of human resources, Martin Tiplady, soon to discuss the outcome of his case. Even so, black senior officers are saying privately he has no future in the police. Several of the most senior black officers in the Met have been involved in legal action against the commissioner. Ghaffur has gone to an employment tribunal claiming that he has been 'sidelined' for promotion. He said he had hired private security guards after receiving threats. At a press conference he claimed that he had been unfairly removed from his role heading security for the 2012 Olympics, and alleged he had been discriminated against, subjected to racist comments and threatened with the sack unless he dropped his complaints. A tribunal is to hear his case next year. Outside the Metropolitan Police, race-equality campaigners in the legal profession see links with disputes in other professions.

'Without going into the details, I see a clear connection with the Hussain and Ghaffur cases,' said barrister Sailesh Mehta, spokesman for the Society of Asian Lawyers. 'They are symptomatic of the response within the professions when people from the ethnic minorities start to seek promotion.' 'A lot of officers, like lawyers, entered the professions at a time when it was difficult to do so, and now they are hitting the glass ceiling. It is a disaster if the Metropolitan Police are using the Shabir Hussain case simply to say "I told you so", and pretend there isn't a problem. The fact an officer of his rank felt he had to go to a tribunal should make them take notice of the situation.' Hussain claimed that he had repeatedly been overlooked for promotion and that a 'golden circle' of favoured candidates was groomed for promotion and received preferential treatment. The tribunal ruled: 'On the evidence provided we are not satisfied, and we do not find that there was such a "golden circle".' Hussain had also claimed official guidelines on awarding promotion, followed by other forces, were ignored in the Metropolitan Police. 'I am disappointed by the outcome of the case, but it did highlight what I felt were shortcomings of the promotion process in the Met,' he said. 'The tribunal said they wanted the Met, the police authority, and me to come together and try to work out a way forward after the judgement, and that's now happening. I don't know enough about other cases to comment on them,' he said. In particular, despite what the press has suggested about our cases being linked, my case has nothing to do with Ghaffur's. My action was about me – all I was looking for was old-fashioned fairness.'

For his part, Blair said Ghaffur's suspension had nothing to do with discrimination. 'I have reflected whether operational effectiveness, leadership and confidence in the Metropolitan Police Service and the security and safety concerns of Londoners are being affected,' he said, 'It is also clear this is having a negative impact on the London 2012 Olympic security programme and risks undermining confidence in it. Certainly, it is the case that the interests of Londoners are not being well served by this current situation.' Blair said he was still anxious to resolve Ghaffur's complaints through mediation.

(*Source: The Sunday Times,* 14 September 2008)

Questions

1. Think about the social identity issues involved in this example. Discuss how ascribed identities impact on the employment opportunities available to BME police officers.

2. Would you say the Metropolitan Police seems to be making decisions on the basis of acceptability criteria?
3. How could explanations of vertical employment segregation be applied in the situation described above?

REVIEW AND DISCUSSION QUESTIONS

1. Identify and summarize the main arguments of each of the theories discussed in this chapter - neoclassical, labour market segmentation and social identity.

2. What contribution does each theory make to explaining employment segregation and what are the weaknesses of each theory?

3. Discuss how the arguments within feminist/gender theories can help to explain the employment segregation and disadvantage experienced by groups of workers other than women.

FURTHER READING

Afshar, H., Maynard, M., 1994.

  Extends discussion of feminist theory, highlighting the links between gender, class, race and ethnicity.

Anker, R., 1997.

  Summary of theories of gender segregation, outlining the strengths and weaknesses of human capital, institutional and feminist/gender theories.

Bradley, H., Healy, G., 2008.

  Theoretical contribution on intersectionality and empirical study of BME women and work.

Collinson, D., Knights, D., Collinson, M., 1990.

  Seminal study of the processes of employment segregation, containing theoretical and empirical contributions.

Jenkins, R., 2004.

  Theoretical text examining conceptualizations of social identity and processes of social identity construction.

REFERENCES

Allen, S., 1994. Some questions of identity. In: Afshar, H., Maynard, M. (Eds.), The Dynamics of Race and Gender: Some Feminist Interventions. Taylor and Francis, London.

Anker, R., 1997. Theories of occupational segregation be sex: an overview. International Labour Review, Autumn 136 (7), 315-340.

Anthias, F., Yuval-Davis, N., 1993. Racialized Boundaries: Race, Nation, Gender, Colour and Class and the Anti-Racist Struggle. Routledge, London.

Armstrong, P., Armstrong, H., 1985. Beyond sexless class and classless sex: towards feminist Marxism. In: Armstrong, P., Connelly, A., Miles, A. (Eds.), Feminist Marxism and Marxist Feminism, Garamond Press, Toronto.

Beardwell, I., Holden, L., 2004. Human Resource Management: A Contemporary Perspective. Financial Times Management, London.

Becker, G., 1964. Human Capital: a Theoretical and Empirical Analysis. Columbia University Press, New York.

Becker, G., 1971. The Economics of Discrimination. Chicago University Press, Chicago.

Becker, G., 1974. A theory of marriage. In: Schultz, T.W. (Ed.), Economics of the Family: Marriage, Children and Human Capital. University of Chicago Press, Chicago, pp. 299-344.

Beechey, V., 1980. Unequal Work. Verso, London.

Blackburn, R.M., Browne, J., Brooks, B., Jarman, J., 2002. Explaining gender segregation. British Journal of Sociology 53 (4), 513-536.

Bradley, H., Healy, G., 2008. Ethnicity and Gender at Work: Inequalities, Careers and Employment Relations. Palgrave Macmillan, Basingstoke.

Brah, A., 1994. 'Race' and 'Culture' in the gendering of labour markets: South Asian young Muslim women and the labour market. In: Afshar, H., Maynard, M. (Eds.), The Dynamics of Race and Gender: Some Feminist Interventions. Taylor and Francis, London.

Branine, M., Glover, I., 1997. Ageism in work and employment: thinking about connections. Personnel Review 26 (4), 233-244.

Cockburn, C. 1983. Brothers: Male Dominance and Technological Change. Pluto Press, London.

Cockburn, C., 1991. In the Way of Women: Men's Resistance to Sex Equality in Organisations. Macmillan, Basingstoke.

Collinson, D., Knights, D., Collinson, M., 1990. Managing to Discriminate. Routledge, London.

Corcoran, M., Courant, P., 1995. Sex role socialization and occupational segregation: an exploratory investigation. In: Humphries, J., E. Elgar, (Eds.), Gender and Economics, Cheltenham.

Crompton, R., Harris, F., 1998a. A reply to Hakim. British Journal of Sociology 49 (1), 144-149.

Crompton, R., Harris, F., 1998b. Explaining women's employment patterns: orientations to work revisited. British Journal of Sociology 49 (1), 118-136.

Dex, S., Joshi, H., 1999. Careers and motherhood: policies for compatibility. Cambridge Journal of Economics 23 (5), 641-659.

Doeringer, P., Piore, M., 1971. Internal Labour Markets and Manpower Analysis. DC Heath and Co. Lexington, MA.

EC, 2008. Equality Between Women and Men - 2008. European Commission, Brussels.

England, P., 1982. The failure of human capital theory to explain occupational sex segregation. In: Humphries, J., Elgar, E., (Eds.), Gender and Economics, Cheltenham. 1995.

England, P., McCreary, L., 1986. Gender inequality in paid employment. In: Humphries, J., Elgar, E. (Eds.), Gender and Economics, Cheltenham.

EOC, 2006. Facts about Women and Men. Equal Opportunities Commission, Manchester.

Gardiner, J., 1998. Beyond human capital: households in the macroeconomy. New Political Economy 3 (2), 209-221.

Giddens, A., 1991. Modernity and Self-Identity: Self and Society in the Late Modern Age. Polity Press Cambridge.

Glover, J., Kirton, G., 2006. Women, Employment and Organisations. Routledge, London.

Gottfried, H., 1998. Beyond Patriarchy? Theorising Gender and Class. Sociology 32 (3), 451–468.

Gutek, B., 1989. Sexuality in the workplace: key issues in social research and organisational practice. In: Hearn, J., Sheppard, D., Tancred-Sheriff, P., Burrell, G. (Eds.), The Sexuality of Organisation. Sage. London.

Hall, M., 1989. Private experiences in the public domain:lesbians in organisations. In: Hearn, J., Sheppard, D., Tancred-Sheriff, P., Burrell, G. (Eds.), The Sexuality of Organisation. Sage, London.

Hakim, C., 1991. Grateful slaves and self made women: fact and fantasy in women's work orientations. European Sociological Review 7 (2), 101–118.

Hakim, C., 1998. Developing a sociology for the twenty-first century: preference theory. British Journal of Sociology 49 (1), 137–143.

Hakim, C., 2000. Work-Lifestyle Choices in the Twenty-First Century: Preference Theory. Oxford University Press, Oxford.

Hardill, I., Watson, R., 2004. Career priorities within dual career households: an analysis of the impact of child rearing upon gender participation rates and earnings. Industrial Relations Journal 35 (1), 19–37.

Hartmann, H., 1979. Capitalism, patriarchy and job segregation by sex. In: Eisenstein, Z. (Ed.), Capitalist Patriarchy and the Case for Socialist Feminism. Monthly Review Press, New York.

Hearn, J., Parkin, W., 1987. 'Sex' and 'work': the power and paraox of organisation sexuality. Wheatsheaf, Brighton.

Heath, A., Cheung. S.Y. Ethnic penalties in the labour market: Employers and discrimination. Department for Work and Pensions Research Report No 341.

Jenkins, R., 1996. (2004 second ed.). Social Identity. Routledge, London.

Kamenou, N. Fearfull, A. Organisational well-being or organisations being, well, discriminatory? A critical analysis of ethnic minorities' struggles to fit in with organisational requirements. In: Paper Presented at the 21st Standing Conference on Organisational Symbolism, Cambridge, July 9–12.

Kirton, G., Healy, G., 1999. Transforming union women: the role of women trade union officials in union renewal. Industrial Relations Journal 30 (1), 31–46.

Lackzo, F., Philopson, C., 1991. Changing Work and Retirement. Open University Press, Buckingham.

Liff, S., Ward, K., 2001. Distorted views through the glass ceiling: the construction of women's understandings of promotion and senior management positions. Gender, Work and Organisation 8 (1), 19–36.

Maynard, M., 1994. 'Race', gender and the concept of 'Difference' in feminist thought. In: Afshar, H., Maynard, M. (Eds.), The Dynamics of Race and Gender: Some Feminist Interventions. Taylor and Francis, London.

Mills, A., 1989. Gender, sexuality and organisation theory. In: Hearn, J., Sheppard, D., Tancred-Sheriff, P., Burrell, G. (Eds.), The Sexuality of Organisation. Sage, London.

Newell, S., 1993. The superwoman syndrome: gender differences in attitudes towards equal opportunities at work and towards domestic responsibilities at home. Work, Employment and Society 7 (2), 275–289.

Noon, M., Blyton, P., 2002. The Realities of Work, second ed. Macmillan, London.

Oswick, C., Rosenthal, P., 2001. Towards a relevant theory of age discrimination in employment. In: Noon, M., Ogbonna, E. (Eds.), Equality, Diversity and Disadvantage in Employment. Palgrave, Basingstoke.

Pilkington, A., 2001. Beyond racial dualism: racial disadvantage and ethnic diversity in the labour market. In: Noon, M., Ogbonna, E. (Eds.), Equality, Diversity and Disadvantage in Employment. Palgrave, Basingstoke.

Phizacklea, A., 1994. A single or segregated market? Gendered and racialized divisions. In: Afshar, H., Maynard, M. (Eds.), The Dynamics of Race and Gender: Some Feminist Interventions. Taylor and Francis, London.

Pollert, A., 1996. Gender and Class Revisited; or the Poverty of Patriarchy. Sociology 30 (4), 639–659.

Pringle, R., 1989. Bureaucracy, rationality and sexuality: the case of secretaries. In: Hearn, J., Sheppard, D., Tancred-Sheriff, P., Burrell, G. (Eds.), The Sexuality of Organisation. Sage, London.

Purcell, K., 2002. Qualifications and Careers: Equal Opportunities and Earnings among Graduates. Equal Opportunities Commission, Manchester.

Scheibl, F., 1996. Part Time Workers: Grateful Slaves or Rational Time Maximising Individuals? An Examination of Fact and Fiction in Recent Explanations of Women's' Preferences for Part Time Working. Employment Studies Unit Paper 4, University of Hertfordshire.

Sharma, U., 1983. Women, Work and Property in North West India. Tavistock Publications, London.

UN, 2001. Background briefing on intersectionality. In: Working Group on Women and Human Rights, 45th Session of the UN CSW. Available from: http://www.cwgl.rutgers.edu/csw01/background.htm.

Walby, S., 1986. Patriarchy at Work. Polity Press, Oxford.

Walby, S., 1990. Theorizing Patriarchy. Blackwell, Oxford.

Warren, T., 2003. Class and gender-based working time? Time poverty and the division of domestic labour. Sociology 37 (4), 733–752.

Watts, M., Rich, J., 1993. Occupational sex segregation in Britain 1979-1989: the persistence of sexual stereotyping. Cambridge Journal of Economics 17, 159-177.

CHAPTER

Diversity in work organisations

4

Aim

To examine diversity, equality and discrimination issues in work organisations.

Objectives

- To outline the development of approaches to organisational analysis.
- To discuss the concept of cultural hegemony and how it contributes to the reproduction of inequalities.
- To explore organisational life from the perspectives of diverse social groups.

4.1 INTRODUCTION

Chapter 2 outlined employment trends among diverse social groups highlighting systemic inequalities and disadvantages across the dimensions of race, gender, disability, age and sexual orientation. Chapter 3 explored a range of theoretical explanations for employment segregation. In this chapter the focus shifts to diversity in work organisations. Here, we explore how organisations contribute to reproducing and reinforcing external patterns of inequality and disadvantage. This chapter begins by examining developments in approaches to organisational analysis, in particular the emergence of gendered organisational analysis and diversity perspectives. The discussion is then organized around the five social groups this book focuses on. Before proceeding, it is important to note that we do not intend to give the impression that organisational life has only negative consequences for the groups we focus on. On the contrary, work and organisations can offer opportunities for socializing, personal growth and development, and of course financial security.

4.2 A 'NEW' APPROACH TO ORGANISATIONAL ANALYSIS

What is organisational analysis? Organisational analysis is concerned with 'the process and dynamics that create and maintain given organisational realities and, from a radical perspective, the impact of those realities upon the construction of social relationships' (Mills and Tancred, 1992: 49). Organisational analysis is important for helping us to understand working life at the meso and micro levels – what goes on inside organisations from the perspectives of organisational members. From the late 1980s onwards, a number of organisational theorists writing from a feminist or pro-feminist perspective began to criticize the organisation studies literature for its neglect of gender and diversity. Cianni and Romberger (1997: 116), for example, argued that organisational analysis usually occurred through a white, male lens. This dominant lens led to the acceptance (particularly in the management literature) of white, non-disabled, heterosexual men's experiences and interpretations of organ-isational life as universally applicable (Alvesson and Billing, 1997). The neglect of gender and diversity came about partly because organisation studies often focused on senior levels of the hierarchy, where white, non-disabled men predominated. It was thus easy not to see gender and diversity issues (Acker and Van Houton, 1992). White, non-disabled males also dominated the research process itself, with most showing little interest in gender and diversity (Alvesson and Billing, 1997; Hearn and Parkin, 1992, Tancred-Sheriff and Campbell, 1992). The relatively recent attention to gender in organisational analysis has exposed the ubiquity of gendered relations, male power and masculine bias within organisations (Burrell and Hearn, 1989; Hearn and Parkin, 1992). The vast 'women in management' literature is an example of this. Authors are now arguing for gendered organisational analysis to be extended to include a multiplicity of intersecting dimensions of diversity, for example, race, disability, age and sexual orientation.

This approach is exemplified by the work of Joan Acker, who has extended her critique of traditional organisational analysis and its lack of attention to gender to highlight the neglect of other intersecting diversity strands. Acker (2006: 443) proposes the concept of inequality regimes as an analytic approach to under-standing the creation of inequalities in organisations. Inequality regimes, she argues, are embedded in all organisations, and are defined as: 'interrelated practices, processes, actions and meanings that result in and maintain class, gender and racial inequalities'. Acker (*ibid*: 443) defines inequality in organisations as 'systematic disparities between participants in power and control over goals, resources, and outcomes; workplace decisions such as how to organize work; opportunities for promotion and interesting work; security in employment and benefits; pay and other monetary rewards; respect and pleasures in work and work relations.' Acker (*ibid*: 444–455) identifies six components of inequality regimes: (i) the bases of inequality (e.g. class, gender, race); (ii) shape and degree of inequality (e.g. employment segregation); (iii) organizing processes that produce inequality (e.g. recruitment and selection practices); (iv) the visibility of inequalities (degree of awareness of inequalities in the organisation); (v) the legitimacy of inequalities (the degree to which different types of inequality are accepted or challenged); and (vi) control and compliance (e.g. how the power of managers is maintained and how the organisation ensures employees work towards its goals). As well as being a useful analytical approach, Acker's concept of inequality regimes might also serve a more practical purpose. Acker (*ibid*: 460) argues that 'looking at organisations as inequality regimes may give some clues about why change projects designed to increase equality are so often less than successful.' This is something we take a more detailed look at in Chapter 8.

Key learning points

- Historically, organisational analysis has tended to ignore the salience of gender and diversity. An approach that sees gender as integral to organisational analysis emerged in the late 1980s and this has been extended to include other diversity strands.

4.3 UNDERSTANDING ORGANISATIONAL CULTURE

Organisational culture is traditionally defined in terms of shared symbols, language, practices and deeply embedded beliefs and values (Newman, 1995). Newman is among the many writers who argue that each of these manifestations of organisational culture is gendered, because, she argues, organisations are important sites in which gendered meanings, identities, practices and power relations are sustained (1995:11). From a diversity perspective, we would add that organisations are sites for the creation, reproduction and enactment of *multiple* (diverse) meanings and intersecting identities. This perspective questions the traditionalist assumption of 'shared beliefs and values'.

However, there can hardly be any doubt that some groups in organisations are more powerful than others. It is senior people who are in a position to manipulate the cultural signals and messages, which the organisation projects both internally and externally. This is how the espoused values of the dominant group come to be seen as the reality of the organisational culture. Therefore, an understanding of power, its locations and its exercise is essential in order to understand how dominant cultures are produced and reproduced (Newman, 1995).

Newman (1995: 22) criticizes orthodox management models of organisational culture on the grounds that six spurious assumptions underpin them. First, the idea that cultures are 'closed societies' is an assumption which leads to neglect of the impact of the external environment, including for example discrimination and social disadvantages in wider society. Second, the belief that 'cultures are integrated wholes' is a unitary concept, ignoring the diversity of interests and values in the organisation. Third, the assumption that 'cultures are consensual' downplays the existence of conflict and resistance within organisations. Fourth, the belief that 'culture is objective reality' with a distinct set of uncontested and incontestable characteristics ignores subjective and diverse experiences of organisational cultures. Fifth, the assumption that 'culture is static' fails to recognize that culture is adaptable and responsive to changing circumstances. Sixth, the belief that 'culture can be changed through new symbols' wrongly suggests that management interventions can create new *shared* values.

The critical literature argues that it is necessary to reconceptualize organisational culture if the embedded nature of inequalities is to be understood. For example, Mills (1992: 98) identified three crucial factors, which studies of organisational culture need to reflect: (i) the relationship between societal values and organisational behaviour, (ii) the importance of powerful actors in the development of value systems and (iii) the significance of organisation as a subjective experience. From this perspective the study of organisational cultures is concerned with the qualitative and symbolic aspects of organisational life, which require interpretation rather than straightforward discovery (Mills, 1992). The critical approach therefore provides an avenue for exploring organisational life from the perspectives of diverse social groups and for investigating how social inequalities are reproduced within organisations.

Key learning points

- The orthodox notion of 'shared values' existing in organisations is exposed as flawed when organisations are interpreted from a gender or diversity perspective.
- The study of organisational culture is concerned with exploring the qualitative and symbolic aspects of organisational life.

4.3.1 The hegemony of organisational culture

The concept of hegemony refers to the predominant influences that one group has over another. The power of hegemony occurs through coercion by a dominant group and (often unwitting) consent by subordinate groups. There are a number of seminal studies from the 1990s that attempted to reveal the hegemony of organisational culture. In their case study research within the insurance industry Collinson et al. (1990) showed how women were excluded from sales jobs through both the conscious and unconscious practices and assumptions of male managers and how they were channelled into more 'gender appropriate' clerical work. Cockburn (1991) described processes such as these as *masculine hegemony* – 'sway exerted over women and men alike, not by legal coercion or economic compulsion but by cultural means, by force of ideas' (1991: 168). Widely held (hegemonic) beliefs about masculinity and femininity are central to understanding how jobs become sex-typed and how gender structures in organisations are produced and reproduced. Most types of work and occupations are associated with masculine or feminine characteristics – for a detailed discussion of masculinities and femininities see Alvesson and Billing (1997) or Collinson and Collinson (1997). Alvesson and Billing (1997) argued that work and occupations are also infused with gender symbolism. They suggested that occupations with a strong masculine symbolism included fire fighter (despite the name change from 'fireman') and army officer. Examples they gave of occupations with a strong feminine symbolism include secretary and nurse (1997: 90). Cockburn's (1991) and Collinson et al.'s (1990) work drew similar conclusions, with the jobs of trade union official and insurance sales person permeated with masculine meaning and the jobs of retail sales assistant and clerical support worker with feminine meaning. This powerful gender symbolism means that individual women or men who transcend the traditional occupational boundaries (e.g. women fire fighters, male nurses) often find themselves in a vulnerable and isolated position. This contributes to explaining why both sexes more typically keep to 'gender appropriate' jobs. Of course there are also financial disadvantages associated with work constructed as feminine, because it is generally lower paid with fewer opportunities for advancement. In contrast, management, leadership and high-powered jobs are traditionally constructed as masculine (Collinson and Hearn, 1994). This means that women tend to lose out in hegemonic processes.

The negative stereotyping of other social groups is also reflected in organisational cultures. For example, Cockburn applied her ideas on hegemonic culture to the issue of ethnicity, arguing that a 'national hegemony' is created by 'a white ruling group' (1991: 185). According to this account, black and minority ethnic (BME) workers must integrate and become acceptable to their white 'hosts'. Similarly, lesbians and gay men must conceal their sexual orientation in order to be acceptable within a hegemonic heterosexualized culture. The prevalent discourse in organisations is one where 'deviants' from the norm are regarded as 'other' and are excluded if not literally then symbolically (Gherardi, 1996). Gherardi suggested that there are various types of organisational cultures whose gender relations are characterized by a 'guest-host' dynamic, in which women are constructed as the guests and men as the hosts (1996: 199). Again, this argument can be applied to other social groups, who may also be constructed as 'guests' or 'other' for failing to conform to the expected norm and thereby challenging the hegemonic culture.

Alvesson and Billing talked about the 'pressure for homogeneity and culturally competent behaviour' (1997: 107) (see also Sheridan and O'Sullivan, 2003). This involves individuals, consciously or unconsciously, conforming and adapting to the norms of the hegemonic culture. People do this by adopting the expected language, behaviour, style, appearance and so on. People constructed as 'other', most likely including women, BME workers, lesbians and gay men and disabled workers, are required to make the most adaptations in order to conform. The demand for 'cultural competence' within the hegemonic culture serves the self-perpetuating function of both reinforcing and reproducing the dominant monoculture.

Key learning points

- Organisational culture is generally masculine-biased and women and other 'minority' groups are often constructed and treated as 'other' (different from the dominant norm) or as 'guests' (who must live by the existing norms and rules).
- Within organisations there are pressures for conformity, assimilation and homogeneity, which marginalize or exclude those who are 'other' – different from the dominant norm.

4.4 ORGANISATIONAL CULTURE: UNPACKING DIVERSITY ISSUES

4.4.1 Women in organisations

In this section we illustrate how organisational cultures are gendered and we explore some of the ways in which women are disadvantaged by male-gendered organisational culture. We examine some of the gendered actions, events, objects and language through which organisational culture manifests (Alvesson and Billing, 1997).

4.4.1.1 *The gender hierarchy*

The gender hierarchy – male dominance and female subordination (Itzin, 1995b) – is manifest in a number of organisational 'rules' (written or unwritten, formal or informal) and practices. For example, the gender hierarchy is often reflected in meetings, where the authority of senior male managers is underscored by their domination of meetings (Alvesson and Billing, 1997). Hierarchical gender relations may also be visible at meetings through formal seating arrangements – for example, the top table being reserved for the most senior members of the group – in most settings predominantly white, males. The gender hierarchy might also be revealed by the formal servicing of meetings – the minutes being taken by the female secretary and refreshments served by the female catering staff. These are examples of the way in which gender segregation can produce a gendered hierarchical order that is so 'normal' as to go unnoticed.

In a now classic study, Pringle (1989) argued that nowhere is the gender hierarchy more evident than in the boss–secretary relationship. Pringle argued that gender and sexuality are central to all workplace power relations, but that the boss–secretary relationship provides the most vivid illustration of this. It is, she said, the 'paradigm case' of gender relations in organisations (1989: 158). The male boss–female secretary relationship is also heterosexualized. Secretaries are often described as 'office wives' – the private secretary typically has a close personal relationship with her boss, reflected in the personal services she provides to him, organizing his personal as well as work life. The informal rules of the boss–secretary relationship also demand her loyalty to him and she derives *her* status and power from that of her boss.

One of the most powerful symbols of gendered organisational culture and of the gender hierarchy is probably the way workers are required or expected to dress. Based on her research conducted around 20 years ago, Cockburn (1991) argued that in most organisations women were still made to feel uncomfortable wearing trousers, even if they were not explicitly forbidden to do so. Uniforms were used in certain jobs deliberately to sexualize or eroticize women, for example some waitress or flight attendant uniforms. Reflecting changes in women's status in wider society and in the workplace, in many occupations and organisations, dress is now less gender differentiated than it once was. For example, female and male police officers have very similar uniforms; flight attendants' uniforms have become less sexualized. However, in others there may remain unwritten 'rules' and norms surrounding dress expectations for women and men. In her study of a retail company, Cockburn (*ibid*) described how women retail and office workers were 'required' to adopt a feminine, though not sexual appearance. She contrasted this with the appearance of male workers, '*The men move together, a solid mass of grey, conversing in deep tones. The women by contrast tap-tap along, chatting and laughing, colourful as a bunch of flowers. Gender differentiation is total*' (1991: 151). Cockburn argued that gendered dress differentiation was deeply symbolic of male authority, with men's appearance and behaviour appearing more earnest. Similar observations could still be made today by looking around many office buildings.

So why does dress matter? While at one level it is a matter of personal choice, it can also be argued that internalized notions of femininity and masculinity are expressed through dress. From this perspective, dress is gender differentiated by the powerful social norms guiding women and men, leaving individuals little choice over how to dress, particularly if they wish to succeed in their careers (Cockburn, 1991). Dress has been one of the issues explored by researchers interested in women's experiences in management roles. One argument is that because it is men who are viewed as analytical, logical and assertive, women who do not adopt masculine modes of appearance and behaviour will generally be perceived as lacking the abilities necessary for management (Gutek, 1989: 60). Sheridan and O'Sullivan (2003: 302) demonstrate this in their analysis of the film *Working Girl* in which 'a brassy blonde' secretary surreptitiously appropriates the identity, and with it the 'corporate wardrobe' of her female boss in her bid to 'pass as a legitimate participant in the corporate world'. Dress can be viewed as one dimension of a 'symbolic order of gender' (Gherardi, 1996: 190), a means of constructing and underscoring gender difference and at the same time, women's subordination. As suggested above, dress at work is also significant in that it has the potential to purvey sexual attractiveness. There are many examples of jobs dominated by women, which often implicitly require sexual attractiveness – receptionist, secretary, flight attendant and some sales assistant jobs. By contrast, there are very few jobs, unconnected with the sex industry, which require the same of men. Therefore, dress carries a potent symbolism for women. In her research Gutek found that when at work women wanted to be recognized for their accomplishments, rather than their sexual attractiveness (1989:65). Gutek went on to argue that when sexual attractiveness is perceived to be the key qualification for a job, then that work will be devalued and trivialized. This means that many women managers and professionals may seek to establish, through dress, difference between themselves and lower status women (Sheppard, 1989). As in the case of the secretary in the film *Working Girl*, this involves selectively borrowing masculine modes of appearance – the muted colours, the tailored suit, short or medium length hair. But at the same time, it is believed to be important for women to retain a degree of gender appropriateness, in order to avoid being seen as too masculine (Cianni and Romberger, 1997). Dress is often regarded as especially problematic for women managers, who walk a tightrope between appearing to be overly masculine and overly feminine, both of which could be detrimental to the exercise of managerial authority (Gutek, 1989; Sheppard, 1989). Thus, women managers are required to *manage* their femininity at the workplace (Gutek, 1989), whereas, as Cockburn (1991) suggested, manual and lower skill women workers have more freedom and flexibility in the way that they dress.

4.4.1.2 *Gendered organisational practices*

Earlier in this chapter we argued that most organisational cultures are permeated with masculine values and characteristics, what does this mean for everyday organisational practices? One example relates to patterns and hours of work. The so-called 'long hours culture' – the requirement to demonstrate commitment to the organisation by working beyond contractual hours – is widely held to be a masculine model of work (Collinson and Hearn, 1994). Working long hours does not necessarily improve individual performance, but it is seen as symbolic of full commitment to the organisation and the pressure to do so is entrenched (Hicks-Clarke and Iles, 2003). The 'long hours culture' is particularly problematic for women because it is typically women who assume responsibility for the family, bringing time pressures to bear on women to a far greater degree than on men. Gendered family ideologies therefore influence the way women manage their careers, the jobs and professions they choose and the decisions they make to balance paid and unpaid (family/household) work (Evetts, 2000). Another example is the assumption that people committed to their careers will have a continuous, unbroken record of full-time employment. To the extent that in reality this is more of a male than a female career pattern, we can argue that the concept of 'career' itself is a masculine construct. The popular concept of the 'career woman' is synonymous with either a woman who has chosen not to have children, or a woman who has sacrificed the primacy of her mothering role to her paid work. This leads to part-time work being seen as the option for noncareer-oriented women. In turn, progression opportunities are usually fairly limited in most part-time jobs. The same family constraints do not apply to men, because it is generally assumed that men's main life activity will be paid work even if they are fathers, i.e. the concept of 'career man' does not exist.

Gendered time constraints also come to bear on the issue of accessing business and career networks, as social activities often take place outside normal working hours. In this way, the dynamics of organisational social life can be said to be gendered. This has especially adverse consequences for women managers and professionals and is partly responsible for the construction of the so-called 'glass ceiling' – the invisible barrier to women's advancement. Obvious examples include the 'pub' or 'golf club' cultures, where business relationships are often cemented outside of normal working hours. These activities do not formally exclude women, but because of gendered social divisions, women typically feel less comfortable in these traditionally male social settings (Cianni and Romberger, 1997) and have less time to take part in any case. Cianni and Romberger (1997) suggest that social networks provide access to vital information and afford opportunities to form strategic alliances, both of which are essential for women managers and professionals.

Women are also informally excluded from male-dominated social networks by the behaviour and practices of male colleagues. Sexual humour is one practice that both senior and lower level men can use to exclude and control women. Collinson and Collinson's research on the shop floor uncovered the everyday utilization of sexual humour, which constructed an image of men as *assertive, independent, powerful and sexually insatiable* (1989:95). In contrast, women were constructed as passive and dependent. In her research in a retail company, Cockburn recounted events at a team meeting of the computer division. In introducing the meeting, a senior manager produced a life-sized photograph of a bare-breasted model and proceeded with an 'ice-breaker' of sexist jokes and sexual innuendo (1991:153). Cockburn argued that this example of 'male clubbing' in senior ranks produces a culture which, *'includes women but marginalizes and controls them'* (1991:153, original emphasis). In this way the sexualization of the workplace and objectification of women through humour trivialize and undermine women as organisational beings. It also creates a sense of in-group organisational identity for men, where women are the outsiders (Cianni and Romberger, 1997). Women can of course join in with sexualized banter, but they risk being perceived negatively as unfeminine, lesbian or feminist (Cockburn, 1991). Collinson and Collinson also found that men who did not participate in sexual banter 'had questions raised about their masculinity' (1989:96). There are therefore powerful cultural forces encouraging men to participate. Sexual humour can also be more serious as it can easily spill over and become sexual harassment. It is now widely accepted that sexual harassment undermines the dignity of women at work. It has been described as *'one of the most demeaning experiences an employee can suffer'* (Rubenstein 1989: 229). Sexual harassment is unwanted and unwelcome behaviour that arguably reflects *'broader patterns of sexual expression which are culturally acceptable in the wider society'* (Collinson and Collinson, 1992: 11–12). Sexual harassment can occur at work social events, but it also takes place in the normal work environment. From a feminist perspective, sexual harassment can be interpreted as a gendered power struggle (Cockburn, 1991). Two categories of women are thought to be particularly vulnerable to sexual harassment – women who transcend either vertical or horizontal gendered job boundaries (DiTomaso, 1989). Women who climb the organisational ladder and assume positions of authority, especially if they manage men, are vulnerable to sexual harassment. Equally vulnerable are women who enter traditional male (dominated) occupations, where their presence challenges masculine culture. Either way, women are competing with men for jobs and are therefore challenging traditional gender-role stereotyping. Sexual harassment becomes a controlling behaviour, reminding women that they remain vulnerable to men's power even if they are hierarchically superior (Cockburn, 1991; Collinson and Collinson, 1997).

Key learning points

- Organisational cultures are infused with gendered meanings, which are often unarticulated and therefore invisible. The gendered hierarchy, unwritten gendered codes, rules, customs and habits are examples, which guide gendered behaviour and underpin expectations of women and men.
- Sexual harassment and the use of sexual humour can be used to control and subordinate women.

Activity 4:1

Dresdner sued for $1.4 bn in sex discrimination case

Six female employees of the investment bank Dresdner Kleinwort Wasserstein filed a $1.4 bn (£793 m) sexual discrimination lawsuit yesterday, claiming unfair and abusive treatment. The suit, believed to be the biggest of its kind, is the latest in a growing number of legal challenges exposing the dark side of the clubby world of the City and Wall Street. According to the suit women are denied top jobs at Dresdner's London and New York offices, are paid less and are made to work in a hostile environment. In lurid detail, it claims that male colleagues would boast of strip club visits, bring prostitutes to the office and repeatedly subject female workers to coarse remarks. Women were hired as 'eye candy' and one was referred to as the 'Pamela Anderson of trading', the suit said.

The firm is part of Germany's Dresdner Bank, the banking arm of Allianz Holding. The suit was filed in a US district court in Manhattan. 'Although we live in 2006, the "glass ceiling" is alive and well at this German investment bank, where women are treated as second-class citizens,' it read. Several Wall Street banks have been forced to make payouts to female employees. Morgan Stanley agreed to pay $54 m to settle discrimination charges filed against it in July 2004 on behalf of a former bond trader and 340 other women. Perhaps wanting to avoid a costly repeat of that episode, Morgan Stanley fired four male employees last week after they accompanied a client to a strip club in New York. Last April UBS, Europe's biggest bank, agreed to pay $29 m to Laura Zubulake, who had worked on its Asian equities sales desk in the US, one of the biggest discrimination awards to an individual on record. At the time, she encouraged other women on Wall Street suffering abusive behaviour to speak out, no matter how tough it was to do so. Four women filed a case against Smith Barney, a part of Citigroup, last year alleging they were denied promotions and were paid less than male colleagues.

The suit against Dresdner contains a slew of statistics to back its claim of discrimination. It notes, for instance, that only about 1% of women in the capital markets division are managing directors while 15% of men hold that position. It says that the lack of women in senior positions contributes to a 'pervasive discriminatory culture' and includes a litany of anecdotal evidence. One plaintiff, Jyoti Ruta, works in the firm's capital markets division in New York. She alleges she was put under pressure by a supervisor and colleague to leave a dinner celebrating the closure of a large deal, so the male clients and bank employees could visit a strip club. Another plaintiff, Katherine Smith, a director in equity sales trading in London, says she was subjected to vulgar remarks from her boss, who simply laughed when she objected. During a working lunch to welcome a new person to the firm, her boss allegedly referred to her as the 'Pamela Anderson of trading', a reference to the former Baywatch actor.

A vice-president of corporate communications in New York, Maria Rubashkina, says she was aware of a male managing director who routinely brought prostitutes to the office during lunch hour. Kathleen Treglia, a vice-president of fixed income in New York, says salesmen on her desk openly commented that they hired females in junior positions because they wanted 'eye candy', and they were unabashed in recounting visits to strip clubs. The suit alleges the bank looked the other way when senior executives had relationships with junior members of staff.

The other two plaintiffs are Joanne Hart, a director of investor relations in New York and Traci Holt, a vice-president in the structured finance group in New York. In a statement, Dresdner said it intends to defend itself against the suit. The company, it added, 'fully complies with all applicable employment-related laws and is confident that any claims to the contrary are without merit'. A report by the American securities industry association said last year that more than 70% of all investment bankers, traders and brokers in management positions in the US were white men. Few women have reached the very top on Wall Street or in the City. One exception is London Stock Exchange boss Clara Furse. Sallie Krawcheck, chief financial officer at Citigroup, is arguably the most powerful woman in American finance.

In Britain, sex discrimination cases against banks have met with less success. The most high-profile failure was that of Stephanie Villalba, a former Merrill Lynch executive, whose £7.5 m claim was thrown out in December 2004. Julie Bower, dismissed as an analyst by Schroder Securities in London, is among those who have won payouts. A note from her boss said she 'had cancer, been a pain, now pregnant'. She received £1.4 m. In 2000, Kay Swinburne launched a claim against

Deutsche Bank in the UK after being called a 'bit of skirt' and being denied promotion. She reportedly settled for £1 m.

(*Source: The Guardian*, 10 January 2006)

Questions

1. Should women speak out or keep quiet about the kinds of treatment described in the article? What are the advantages and disadvantages?
2. How would you describe a workplace where it is considered acceptable to bring prostitutes into the office and to visit strip clubs?
3. How does what you have read in this chapter help you to explain the culture of the City of London and Wall Street?

4.4.2 Black and minority ethnic workers in organisations

Many of the issues discussed above in relation to women and the gendering of organisational cultures have racialized dimensions. For example, we have explored in some detail the issue of dress and appearance. As we have seen, dress is an important way of underscoring difference between women and men, which can have the effect of indirectly reinforcing the gendered hierarchy. Dress is also often a visible feature of ethnic difference, laden with symbolism. Over a decade ago, Modood (1997: 326) found that 'indigenous' people often resented the wearing of 'traditional clothes' by minority ethnic people. Around the same time, there were also a number of employment tribunal cases concerning the right of BME employees to wear traditional clothes and hairstyles at work. Modood's detailed examination of clothes and appearance among BME groups found, for example, that only 1% of men and 12% of women sometimes wore Asian clothes at work. He also identified a generational decline in the use of traditional Asian clothes at work (especially among Hindus and Sikhs), but people of Caribbean background were using dress or hair as a means of consciously marking a cultural dimension to their ethnicity (Modood, 1997: 328). To what extent are these attitudes and practices still prevalent? Some research suggests that BME people still believe that certain embodiments of ethnicity can lead to discrimination in the organisational context. In the present era, Muslim women in particular perceive prejudice against Muslim-style clothing as a significant problem (Botcherby 2006; Kirton, 2009; Tyrer and Ahmad, 2006).

Research has argued that racial stereotypes often inform recruitment decisions and the allocation of types of work (Cockburn, 1991; Jenkins, 1985). In contrast to sex stereotyping, which can result in a *preference* for women in certain occupations (for example, women are generally preferred in secretarial work and many caring roles), race stereotyping rarely results in a preference for BME people (Cockburn, 1991). Race stereotypes are almost always negative. However, different BME groups are stereotyped differently and stereotyping is not simply a crude response to skin colour. For example, positive race stereotypes underpin the idea that certain ethnic groups have a strong work ethic or are suited to particular types of jobs (Kirton, 2009). Jenkins argued that racial stereotyping informs managers' conceptions of 'acceptability' for the job. Even if a job applicant has the relevant skills and qualifications, a judgement has to be made about whether she/he will fit in, i.e. be acceptable to the organisation. Thus, the non-specific and subjective criteria of acceptability shape the final decision (1985: 149). Jenkins divided the criteria of acceptability into three categories, primary, secondary and tertiary, according to their significance to managers. For Jenkins, primary criteria included appearance, manner and attitude and maturity; secondary criteria included gut feeling, speech style, age and the ability to 'fit in'; and tertiary criteria were English language competence and employer references (1985: 149). Many of these criteria are not only highly subjective, but also racialized, and often irrelevant to the job. Different ethnic groups may be ascribed cultural traits, which are praised or condemned (Modood, 1997: 149) and which impact on perceptions of their ability to 'fit in'.

Several studies on race and organisational culture can be found in the US literature. DiTomaso (1989) found that BME women's experiences of discrimination and harassment in organisations were qualitatively different from that of white women. White and Hispanic females were most likely to see their *gender* as the cause of discrimination, whilst most black women felt they had experienced *race* discrimination. Both black women and black men believed they had experienced worse treatment at the hands of their supervisors than their white or Hispanic counterparts (1989: 84). This echoes Cianni and Romberger's (1997) later study, which found all ethnic groups believing there to exist racial and ethnic barriers to success within large organisations. These barriers included language skills, accents, stereotyping, differences in cultural values and experiences. Further, the use of racist jokes and humour served to reinforce and reproduce stereotyped beliefs about BME groups at the same time as leading to negative organisational experiences. Women and BME employees referred to the 'automatic camaraderie' among white men, which conferred inclusion in important and powerful informal networks (*ibid* 1997: 120). The overwhelming majority (96%) of white participants in the study reported having supervisors of the same race, whilst almost all black participants had supervisors of a different race. This raises the question of mentoring, career sponsorship and more generally the importance of racialized social relations in the workplace, and the role they play in reproducing inequality or in constructing the so-called 'concrete ceiling' – the almost impenetrable barrier to BME workers' advancement. A more recent study found that Hispanic women often believed themselves to be tokens in white dominated organisations, where they felt they had to prove and reprove themselves continually (Hite, 2007). Although these studies are situated in the US context, they demonstrate the value of researching diverse experiences of organisational cultures in order to gain a more complete, textured picture. Further, these studies underscore the way in which subjective experiences of organisations are mediated by both gender and race.

Key learning points

- Organisational cultures are 'racialized' and this contributes to the social construction of race inequalities.
- Negative racial stereotypes are frequently used to guide decision-making in employment.

Activity 4.2

Barack Obama is an inspirational mentor for black Britons

When I joined the banking sector in the City more than 15 years ago, I really was in the minority as a man of colour. These days, it is a different place. The bank that I work in, and all the other banks, has recognized the power of diversity and the importance of including a wealth of different talents in their staff.

Barack Obama's election highlights, on the world stage, just how far we have come. It has been an enormous transformation from ignorance to awareness, from discrimination to inclusion. For a man of colour to have got to the highest position in America is a tremendous achievement. We've had many generations of black people, across the world, that have been frustrated and unable to rise to the top. Now, we are the legacy of our ancestors who strove so hard to create change and to move things forward – their battles allow us to achieve our dreams. Mr Obama is living proof that the ability to rise has never been better. His election will have practical impact in Britain, changing mentalities and raising hope about the opportunities for change and illustrating how we might better ourselves. What better role model and mentor for young, black Britons than an inspirational president? He has achieved his dreams: what is to stop us achieving ours? It is momentous, particularly for the next generation of young people, in the sense that they will never think: 'Not in my lifetime.' It is normal for them: it will be a daily occurrence to see a black president. It raises a level of consciousness and a level of awareness that are unprecedented.

The US is slightly ahead of Britain in many aspects – for generations, black people have achieved power at local and state levels. But we're catching up and we're not that far behind. Mr Obama's inauguration is the encouragement, and the impetus, that we need.

Frank Makan is a senior manager at a leading American investment bank and co-chairman of the City's Multicultural Professional Network.

(*Source: The Times*, 18 January 2009)

Questions

1. In the light of what you have read in this chapter, how important do you think it is to have 'minority' role models in top positions?
2. What impact would you expect the election of the first black president of the US to have on the culture of organisations in the industrialized world?

4.4.3 Lesbians and gay men in organisations

Most organisational studies of sexual harassment and sexuality focus on heterosexuality (Burrell and Hearn, 1989: 21). This has led to a research gap and lack of theorizing on the collective organisational experiences of lesbians and gay men (Oerton, 1996a). However, it is widely recognized in the literature that '*all the assumptions in everyday relationship and discourse are heterosexual*' (Cockburn, 1991: 186). Cockburn also argued that men negotiate male solidarity around a heterosexual principle (*ibid*: 193). Consequently, within organisations lesbians and gay men are constructed as 'other' and in opposition to heterosexual masculine identity and discourse. Organisations are often hostile toward lesbians and gay men, many of whom conceal their sexual orientation to avoid discrimination and harassment (Oerton, 1996b). A paradoxical situation exists where homosexuality in organisations is ubiquitous, yet often invisible, because of widespread non-disclosure of sexual identity (Hall, 1989).

It is argued that the informal 'rules of behaviour' within organisations favour heterosexuality because heterosexuality is a symbol of gendered power relations both within the organisation and wider society (Mills, 1989). In these 'rules' homosexuality is subordinate because it poses a threat to the maintenance of the gender hierarchy which depends on (implicit and symbolic) sexualized relations between women and men (Oerton, 1996b). Further, in terms of power and gender relations it is argued that men cannot easily 'control' lesbians because their sense of sexual attractiveness or femininity is not dependent on male approval. Therefore patriarchal gender relations do not impact on lesbian women in the same way as on heterosexual women (Cockburn, 1991). Thus, a type of heterosexual hegemony can be said to dominate the culture and discourse of organisations (Mills, 1998; Oerton, 1996a). Oerton (1996a) characterizes male-dominated hierarchies as *oppressively* heterosexist and homosocial. This is reflected in workplace social relations, where, for example, sexual banter and joking are often of a heterosexual nature, marginalizing both lesbians and gay men. Despite the fact that heterosexual men often eroticize lesbianism, lesbians are less likely to engage in sexual banter with men (Oerton, 1996a). Lesbians' rejection or lack of interest in male sexual advances violates gendered expectations and often meets with retaliation or harassment (Hall, 1989). Gay men are also excluded from participating in heterosexual masculine humour and are more likely to be on the receiving end. Jokes about gay men are often used to reinforce notions of heterosexual masculinity and may be used by heterosexual men to avoid any implication that they might be gay.

Organisational *social life* is also heterosexualized. For example, despite the now widespread usage of the more neutral term 'partner' (to replace wife/husband, boyfriend/girlfriend), couples are still generally assumed to consist of a man and a woman. This heterosexual assumption leads some lesbians and gay men to keep secret their partners to avoid disclosure of their own sexual identity. Non-disclosure is a strategy used by some lesbians and gay men to avoid potential discrimination and harassment. But feeling unable to participate in the social life of the organisation forces separation between work and leisure, which can lead to exclusion from important business networks or simply from some of the more pleasurable aspects of work (Hall, 1989).

Cockburn (1991) suggested that equality for lesbians and gay men is the most contested and conflictual of equality projects, because of the lack of consensus over the moral worthiness of the gay rights project. Cockburn (1991) cited the AIDS panic of the 1980s as one of the primary reasons for the growth of animosity against gay men. Being gay is often 'pathologized' in popular discourse and associated with alcohol and drug abuse, obsession with sex and molestation (Cockburn, 1991). Further, it is still popularly assumed that people have a choice over whether or not to be lesbian/gay, whereas there is no choice with regard to gender, ethnicity, age or disability (Cockburn, 1991: 192).

The implication is that if a lesbian or gay identity is a 'lifestyle choice', then people must accept any negativity surrounding it.

Although homosexuality stands in opposition to heterosexuality, lesbians and gay men are not a unitary category and in many ways gender divides the group. For example, gay men undoubtedly challenge the norms and 'rules' of gendered behaviour and the heterosexual principle, but they might also sometimes hold misogynistic views about women, including lesbians (Cockburn, 1991). Gay men are not always united with lesbian women in opposing the norms and values generated by heterosexual men. This is because, according to Cockburn (1991), gay men want to retain their superior position in the male-gendered hierarchy. Further, lesbianism may worry heterosexual women just as much as men and therefore lesbians may experience a female-dominated environment as equally hostile as a male dominated one (Cockburn, 1991). However, lesbians and gay men do share many common experiences of organisations, for example the fears surrounding disclosure of sexual orientation, or the consequences of being 'outed' by anyone who discovers their sexuality. 'Coming out' is regarded as the essential ingredient of lesbian and gay equality. The process is less problematic in organisations with supportive lesbian and gay networks and policies (Creed, 2006).

Key learning points

- The dominant discourse in organisations is heterosexual, which constructs heterosexuality as the norm and lesbians and gay men as 'deviant' or 'other'.

Activity 4.3

Outed in the city

- As Lord Browne discovered this week, the professional lives of gay and lesbian workers in the Square Mile can be a web of secrets and innuendo.

The globe-trotting, multimillionaire businessman who dines with politicians and this week ended up in court is adamant: 'If I could be born again for business purposes I would be straight,' he says. Being gay has made his professional life tough. Being openly gay has made it even tougher. But this is not Lord Browne, who on Tuesday resigned as chief executive of BP because his reluctance to be outed ended with a lie in court and a judgement against him. This is Ivan Massow at the end of a successful week in which the entrepreneur who made his fortune providing insurance for gay clients was praised by a judge as a 'trailblazer' for gay rights and allowed to take a case against the Zurich group to trial.

For ambitious people working relentless hours behind computers and on trading floors across the City, the end of Browne's career at BP – topped off with a wreath of spiteful tabloid headlines from 'Silly old fuel' to 'Fetish

Petroleum' – would appear a compelling reason to keep their sexuality secret. Even Massow agrees. 'I would recommend it fully–stay in,' he says.

None of the FTSE 100 companies in Britain is run by an openly gay person. A list of 101 powerful gay and lesbian professionals in Britain published last year was topped by actor Sir Ian McKellen but, excluding advertising executives and media bosses such as Dawn Airey and Charles Allen, it featured only three people in senior roles in big business and the City. Many believe there is a 'pink plateau' preventing them winning directorships or breaking into boardrooms. 'At the moment some of the banks are keen to have young gay men working for them because they are easier to relocate and they wear nice shirts and ties. But they don't seem to get any higher,' says Massow, who has a feel for City opinion from running Jake, a networking Website used by 30,000 gay professionals. Rabid homophobic abuse, getting dragged to lapdancing clubs, water cooler chat and work dinners entirely based on heterosexual family life and the hypocrisy of colleagues who sleep with men but go home to their wives – the professional lives of some gay and lesbian City workers feature long hours of disingenuousness and discrimination.

Ben, 26, works for an investment bank in London. Like many people interviewed for this piece he is open about his sexuality at work but preferred not to out himself in a newspaper. He switched to a back office role after a stint on an 'aggressive, macho' trading floor. 'You're supposed to accept casual homophobic comments, but people wouldn't accept casual racism,' he says. He knows plenty of bankers who keep their sexuality under wraps. 'Everyone who is gay and high up in banking is closeted and they tell me I'm mad to be out.' With few role models, even successful gay businesspeople are wary of speaking out. Sir Michael Bishop, 64, the chairman of airline BMI, this week celebrated a threefold rise in pre-tax profits, but would not talk about how he had beaten homophobia in his career. 'He keeps his private life just that,' says a spokesperson for BMI.

Many in the City seem to operate a version of the 'don't ask, don't tell' policy that prohibits gays and lesbians in the US armed forces from disclosing their sexual orientation. The fact that so many remain in the closet at work implies that they experience or perceive a disadvantage with being openly gay in their professional lives. Lesbian employees in the City are three times more likely than gay men to keep their sexuality secret, according to a recent survey.

As a board member of the firm KPMG, Ashley Steel is probably the most senior lesbian in the City and champions her company's excellence on diversity issues. She believes people suffer professionally when they don't come out, but then she fully understands why so many stay in the closet. 'I just know that in most of the City and business generally, many gay and lesbian people cannot feel what I feel and they continue to have to work in a very difficult environment. There are tens of thousands of people out there now who are everyday feeling uncomfortable in certain situations,' she says. She came out several years ago. 'It was tricky, but it was the best thing I have done in my whole life.'

Employees are far more productive if they are as open as they want to be at work, she argues. Before she came out at work, she and her partner had been the victims of homophobic abuse and vandalism. Soiled men's underpants were even stuffed up her car exhaust pipe. 'I used to have to come into the office as if nothing had happened. A straight couple could have had a sympathetic ear at work,' she says. 'I believe it costs businesses when employees cannot be themselves. I'm a more confident and better business adviser as a result of being able to be myself. There is undoubtedly a cost when people are not operating in a optimal way because they can't be out in the workplace.'

Openly gay people in the City tend to be robust individuals who swipe aside gloomy talk of discrimination and a macho environment they supposedly cannot master. 'People say the City is a difficult environment for gay people. Why? Because it has this competitive, go-getting atmosphere. Are these just characteristics of straight white men? No,' says a senior gay banker. With its onus on individual achievement and entrepreneurship, the City's successful gay businesspeople often frame issues of sexuality as something they as individuals are responsible for managing at work. Ben, the investment banker, feels some of his gay friends have mismanaged their careers by choosing the closet – where they are now stuck, he says, because they have told so many 'lies' they cannot come out without damaging their credibility.

Lee Marshall, an openly gay senior manager at Ernst & Young (EY), feels his decision not to come out for several years was not because of the risk to his career but due to personal anxieties. While there is much 'marketing fluff on diversity', Marshall feels the partnership structure of EY genuinely supports gay staff. 'I never felt pressured or held back. It was self-imposed by my own insecurities.' He believes that similar insecurities prevent others being open about their sexuality at work.

Many gay people, however, do feel disadvantaged in relation to the social networking that is so crucial to climbing the career ladder in big business, particularly in firms with a partnership structure. Family and football are the only two things partners talk about, says one senior banker. While client entertainment such as lapdancing is often officially forbidden, it still goes on informally and can be excruciating for gay employees who aren't out (as well as women and many straight men). When he has been dragged along with colleagues sizing up girls in foreign strip joints, a gay City executive who writes an anonymous blog under the pseudonym GB says he wriggles out of awkward situations by saying: 'I'm just a voyeur.'

Marshall believes dinners and social events are an important part of his work. 'It is almost frowned upon if you go to those events single,' he says. His boyfriend is now a regular fixture at staff functions and in the past couple of years he has felt comfortable enough to bring him to the Christmas party. 'The partner I work with knows my boyfriend well. We've dined together and been to each other's houses. When he started, he knew I was gay and came up to me and said "so, do you have a boyfriend?" It was nice – an attempt to find something in common we could talk about because he talks about his wife.'

In recent years, big businesses have rushed to reform their unreconstructed ways, in part to comply with the extension of anti-discrimination laws to include gay and lesbian employees in 2003. In a survey of more than 20,000 City candidates by headhunters Joslin Rowe, 5.9% of respondents anonymously identified themselves as gay or lesbian in 2004, rising to 6.3% last year. Many big firms have sought the advice of Stonewall – IBM was top of the campaign group's latest

Corporate Equality Index with companies Lloyds TSB, Goldman Sachs and KPMG also in the top 10. Deutsche Bank has a Global Rainbow Group; Barclays supports a similar internal gay network called Spectrum. Stonewall says most members of internal gay networks in the companies it works with are back office staff. 'There are very few coming from the trading floor or senior staff,' says a spokesperson.

Barclays says it gets good feedback on gay and diversity issues from its staff surveys. Its workers include gay couples who have children and bring them to employee family days, for instance. But a spokesman for the bank admits it is difficult to monitor the effectiveness of its diversity policies. 'When it comes to women and ethnic minorities you can officially count them, but for gay people it requires them to come out or be recorded as gay in an employee opinion survey. You can put the best policies in place, but when it comes to auditing the impact of those policies, it requires people to volunteer to be counted.'

Casual homophobia is not really the issue, according to Steel. The most important thing is for it to be obvious to employees that they will suffer no handicap for being open about their sexuality. She believes that there is a real lack of leadership in the City and, whether gay or not, company bosses must speak out. 'What bothers me is a working environment where people do not know what reaction they would get if they did come out. The only way companies can counter that is for chairmen or CEOs to be saying, "It's okay to be out" and openly sponsoring gay and lesbian people in their office.'

Lord Browne's experience may not at first encourage people to speak out, but Ben Summerskill, the chief executive of Stonewall, reports an increase this week in the number of companies contacting the group for help on diversity issues. He agrees with Steel that it is a question of leading by example. 'People at CEO level have to say this is important and take what is sometimes perceived as very harsh action against those who are making the workplace extremely uncomfortable for other talented staff.'

(*Source: The Guardian*, 5 May 2007)

Questions

1. Based on what you have read in this chapter, what would your advice be to someone lesbian or gay – stay in 'the closet' or 'come out' at work?
2. Discuss the concept of the 'pink plateau'. How, why and by whom is it constructed?
3. Is it up to individuals to manage their sexuality at work or is this something that organisations should be addressing?

4.4.4 Disability in organisations

Most non-disabled people have very little personal contact with disabled people. It is possible, therefore, for non-disabled people to journey through childhood and adulthood with very little contact with disability. This narrows the perspectives of non-disabled people on disability (Reynolds et al., 2001). Non-disabled people's lack of contact with disability is thought to be a powerful obstacle to employment equality for disabled people. Personal contact between disabled and non-disabled people is 'an important ingredient in bringing about positive attitude change' (French, 1996: 159). French is mostly concerned with the relationship between health professionals and disabled people, but much of what she says has relevance for the social relations between non-disabled and disabled people within work organisations. For example, she argues that *equal status* contact between disabled and non-disabled people is especially important because it is the opportunity for disabled people to present themselves as capable and as multifaceted (1996: 160). It is against this background that it is necessary to set a discussion about organisational culture because individual attitudes towards disability are formed in the wider social environment. Ignorance of disability contributes to the pervasiveness of the many myths and negative stereotypes surrounding disabled workers. In contrast, familiarity with disability outside the workplace tends to engender more positive attitudes (Woodhams and Danieli, 2003).

There are two main approaches to understanding disability and its effects on individuals. Within the 'medical model', it is the physical disability and/or its psychological consequences, which prevent disabled individuals from participating in the labour market (Barnes, 1992). Within this model, disabled people are often represented as victims of some kind of personal tragedy, often attracting sympathy, but not equal status or worth. Opposing this approach, is the 'social model' which holds that disabled people are among the most excluded in society because of the *attitudes* of others rather than because of their disability *per se*. Disabled people experience work organisations as hostile, with a substantial proportion believing that attitudinal barriers render it almost impossible to find employment (Reynolds et al., 2001). Most social research on disability now reflects the social model. In this vein, Hyde argued that '*discriminating employers are the main factor underlying disadvantage*' (1996:683). Thus, what is needed is the removal of the environmental and social barriers which prevent disabled people from participating fully in society. According to the social model, disadvantage does not arise inevitably because of physical impairment as in the medical model (Hyde, 1996). It is work organisations which need to change rather than disabled people needing to be 'cured'. There are an infinite variety of causes of both mental and physical disability and the extent to which impairment is experienced as disabling depends on the context and the demands and constraints of that context (Honey et al., 1993). Thus, it is not inevitable that disabled people will experience work organisations negatively, although many do.

Employment is an important social activity, which gives access to opportunity, status and self-worth. Disabled people are influenced by the same expectations and aspirations towards work as the non-disabled population (Smith, 1996). However, most employed disabled people are concentrated in low-paid, low-skilled and low-status jobs and there are relatively few disabled role models in senior positions (Thornton and Lunt, 1995). Negative employment experiences are thought to lead many disabled people to expect to fail at work, creating a 'discouraged worker' syndrome, which results in some disabled people opting not to work and to rely instead on state financial benefits (Hyde, 1996; Smith, 1996).

Many myths, stereotypes and negative attitudes help to create negative experiences of work organisations among disabled people. It is argued that the disabilities most 'disliked' by the general population include alcoholism, mental illness, mental impairment and hunchback (French, 1996). According to the various pieces of research French reports on, physical disabilities, especially invisible ones are disliked the least. Any disability perceived to be self-inflicted (for example, disability arising from drug abuse or even AIDS) carries its own particular stigma and does not attract the sympathy reserved for 'victims' of other disabilities (French, 1996). When evaluating a disabled person's suitability for employment, non-disabled people tend to focus on *disability* rather than *ability* even though disability is not the deterministic indicator of ability it is widely held to be (Woodhams and Danieli, 2003). Disabled people are generally regarded as 'hard to employ' (Reynolds et al., 2001). The main misconceptions are that disabled people represent a health and safety risk (both to themselves, other employees and customers), that they will have higher sickness absence rates, that they will be less productive, perform less well and be generally more expensive to employ (Honey et al., 1993; Roberts, 1996). It is also often claimed that disabled people will not fit in with other employees, who may feel unease or embarrassment at their presence (Honey et al., 1993). Thus, we can see how Jenkins' (1985) ideas (discussed earlier in relation to race and ethnicity) on the importance of 'suitability' and 'acceptability' criteria have salience for disability. Many of the perceived difficulties in employing disabled people expose stereotypical beliefs about disability – a focus on wheelchair users is commonplace for example. Alternatively, disability is equated with illness and it is widely believed that disabled people will have higher sickness absence rates and will have to be 'carried' by their colleagues (Reynolds et al., 2001). What these stereotypes fail to acknowledge is the multiplicity of disability. Disability is often hidden and employees may prefer not to reveal it, for fear of encountering discrimination and negative attitudes and behaviour (Reynolds et al., 2001). Disability also varies considerably in type and severity and it can be temporary as well as permanent or recurring. The consequence of negative stereotyping is the expectation that the performance of disabled people is predictable and therefore that disability can be used as a criterion to frame valid and reliable selection decisions. Many disabled people perceive that a major barrier to career progression is the lack of support from line managers (Reynolds et al., 2001).

How are negative attitudes towards disability explained? It is argued that disability is deeply feared by non-disabled people (Cockburn, 1991; Roberts, 1996). This is partly because illness and injury can unexpectedly cause disability to anyone at any time. Indeed, the majority of disabled people nowadays have become disabled in adulthood (Reynolds et al., 2001). The presence of a disabled person serves as an uncomfortable reminder of everyone's vulnerability to disability. Holding stereotypical beliefs about disability helps non-disabled people to psychologically distance themselves, whilst reserving some pity or sympathy for some disabilities,– hence the tendency to distinguish between those who 'deserve' their disability (i.e. it is perceived to be self-inflicted, by, for example, alcohol or drug abuse) and those who do not. People 'who do not deserve their disability' are the most patent reminder that disability is not entirely within our personal control and whilst they attract greater sympathy, non-disabled people prefer not to be around them.

Although disabled people's experiences of organisational life vary according to the type and severity of disability, organisations are often hostile to disability. Habits, social norms and group pressure also influence organisational culture (French, 1996). A discrimination complicit culture can develop through, for example, the use of humour. Disability is often the butt of jokes which ridicule difference, as Cockburn (1991) demonstrated in her case studies.

Key learning points

- Non-disabled people's lack of contact with disability serves to reinforce the widespread fear and ignorance and to perpetuate the many myths and stereotypes surrounding disabled people and their 'fitness' for employment.
- Many disabled people have negative experiences of work organisations because of the attitudes of others rather than because of the physical barriers they encounter.

Activity 4.4

Living with a label

- Despite long standing legislation against disability discrimination, serious prejudice and misunderstanding still exist. With one in five adults classed as disabled, a government rethink is needed.

The Disability Discrimination Act (DDA), which made it on to the statute book in 1995, was a key victory for campaigners. It began a process of securing legal protection from discrimination and raised hopes of transforming society's attitudes towards disabled people. So why does a national survey published 11 years later conclude that the public is confused about what constitutes a disability and that serious prejudice persists?

The latest British Social Attitudes Survey, published today, concludes that disability is still largely perceived in the narrow and outdated sense of visible physical disability, such as wheelchair use, even though the DDA has a much broader definition that incorporates conditions such as long-term debilitating illness. It also reveals worrying levels of prejudice against some groups defined as disabled under the act – in particular, people with mental illness.

According to the study, 52% of those surveyed did not think of someone with schizophrenia as being disabled and only 44% regarded an older person with a hearing aid as having a disability, yet 31% regarded a person with a broken leg who needed to use crutches as disabled. 'The general public tends not to draw the definition as wide as the DDA does,' the report's authors conclude. 'Mental health conditions are often not seen as disabilities. Nor are long-standing illnesses, such as cancer or HIV/AIDS, included by most people.'

But if the public appears confused about what a disability is – under the DDA definition, one in five adults, around 10 m, in the UK is disabled – some of the study's findings on perception of prejudice will concern campaigners. According to the survey, 75% of people believe disabled people experience 'a little' prejudice, but only 25% think they face 'a lot'. For many charities and campaign groups, this is far from the reality of everyday life for disabled people.

Face ignorance

In addition, the survey concludes that some groups appear to face ignorance and even fear of their disability. More than 70% of people interviewed said they would 'not feel comfortable' living next door to someone with schizophrenia, and half would not want someone with depression as a neighbour. There is much confusion when it comes to who is most likely to encounter prejudice. Those groups least likely to be seen by the wider public as disabled are, in fact, perceived as the most discriminated against. For example, 46% of the population believes that people with schizophrenia experience a lot of prejudice, yet other groups, such as deaf people, are viewed as facing very little. Some 42% of people believe that deaf people experience 'hardly any or no' prejudice and that only 13% face a lot. A spokesman for the Royal National Institute for Deaf people (RNID) says that, for deaf people, the figures are worrying and 'in no way reflect the true extent' of the difficulties faced.

The muddled perceptions exposed by the report, about both the nature of disability and the reality of prejudice, highlight that there is still some way to go to change attitudes to disability. 'Most people say they would not be very comfortable living next door to someone with a mental health condition and the prejudice is more pronounced when they were asked how they would feel if a close relative married someone with a long-term health condition like Multiple Sclerosis (MS) or severe arthritis,' says Bert Massie, chairman of the Disability Rights Commission (DRC). 'These findings catalogue a degree of social repulsion to disabled people that is unparalleled with any other group. If these attitudes are allowed to fester unchecked, we will only be encouraging a segregated society. Despite 12 years of disability discrimination legislation, the report reveals that disabled people are still struggling to rid themselves of the tag "second class citizens". We clearly have a long way to go before disabled and non-disabled people work together, learn together, and share the same communities. As countless other examples show, it is only in this way that prejudice is broken down.'

The study's authors argue that their findings could have profound implications for how greater awareness of disability and changes in attitudes are to be achieved in the long term. The DDA - which has been introduced in stages since 1995 and covers a range of protection against discrimination, including that experienced in employment and education - is regarded by many as a huge step forward in the campaign for disabled rights. So too was the setting up seven years ago of the DRC, with a remit to eradicate discrimination and pursue equal opportunities. They are examples of how the effort behind campaigning has been focused, understandably, on cementing legal rights.

But what needs to be done now? And will the findings in today's report really help shape what happens? The consensus from charities and campaigners is that the research has highlighted how essential it is not to become complacent. In many ways, it backs up surveys conducted in recent years by the DRC and advocacy groups such as Leonard Cheshire, which found that disabled people continue to experience substantial prejudice in their everyday lives, not just in areas that are legislated for such as the workplace. A spokesman for Leonard Cheshire says the study may be an indication that while the DDA has helped raise awareness of discrimination, people nevertheless 'still don't seem to fully understand what a disability is'. It is a long-term issue, he says, and one that will require ongoing effort by campaigners. 'You don't just change attitudes the moment a new act is passed.'

Brian Lamb, director of communications at the RNID, agrees. 'I think there needs to be a huge long-term awareness campaign,' he says. 'We're not really going to get change without changes in work, but people need to meet disabled people in social life and other areas.'

Policy initiatives

Many campaigners are also demanding that the government learns a lesson from the survey and puts more resources and cash into campaigns designed to change attitudes, such as anti-stigma campaigns on behalf of people with mental illness. A spokesman for the mental health charity, Mind, says charities cannot do it on their own and that the government should take heed of policy initiatives elsewhere. 'In New Zealand, they have been successful at raising awareness, thanks to high profile TV campaigns,' he says. 'But it takes money. The sector is very keen to do it, but you can't do it for nothing.'

Despite the pessimistic picture painted by the report, it does include several positive points. For example, it finds that where someone knows or is related to a disabled person, they have a greater understanding of the issues and are much less likely to hold negative attitudes. The report concludes that this is a clear argument in favour of policy continuing to focus on the inclusion of disabled people in wider society.

Lamb agrees. 'It's getting better. We now have whole generations of children growing up with disabled children in their classroom. This is a very positive thing.' In February, the DRC will launch its new Disability Agenda, in which it will lay out guidance on the direction that future public policy should take. It has been put together in advance of the body being absorbed in the autumn by the new Commission for Equality and Human Rights and will recommend policies promoting further integration of disabled people into mainstream society. It will aim to 'tackle the most deep-rooted and persistent disadvantage experienced by disabled people', a spokesman says.

But even if the agenda does succeed in injecting a fresh focus into disability policy, campaigners say that government needs to play its part, and that a key lesson to be taken from today's survey is that legislation is merely the beginning.

(*Source*: *The Guardian*, 24 January 2007)

Questions

1. Discuss the survey findings summarized in the article and the implications for disability equality within organisations.
2. The article stresses the role that the government should take, but what kinds of action might organisations take to improve understanding of disability?

4.4.5 Older workers in organisations

Unlike other diversity strands, age is something we are all certain to be affected by as we move in and out of disadvantaged age groups over the life course. Perhaps because of this, age discrimination has an air of legitimacy that other forms of discrimination do not have (Oswick and Rosenthal, 2001). Certainly, age has received less attention than other forms of discrimination within the diversity and equality literature. The issue of age is undoubtedly complex as it intersects in different ways with other diversity strands, so that the effects of age on organisational experiences cannot be fully understood without reference to other overlapping social groups. For example, the incidence of disability and health problems rises with age, so it might sometimes be difficult to disentangle age from disability discrimination. In Chapter 2 we examined trends and patterns in older people's labour market participation. The age of 50 appears to be a turning point in the life cycle in terms of employment experiences when many people feel they meet age discrimination (McKay, 1998). This section considers the issue of ageist attitudes embedded in organisational cultures.

Many managers have found themselves the victims of 'downsizing' and restructuring and having been displaced from senior and well-paid positions, find themselves competing for jobs with younger candidates and encountering ageist attitudes. There is evidence, discussed in Chapter 2, that older workers find it harder to find a job than younger, suggesting that recruiters favour younger workers. Employer ageism is sometimes reflected in recruitment advertisements, which can carry coded messages about the desired age range, even though the use of numerical age limits in job advertisements has been illegal in the UK since the introduction of anti-age discrimination regulations in 2006 (see Chapter 6). For example, adverts might use words or phrases to suggest that the ideal candidate is a younger person – 'first jobber', 'young, fast-moving entrepreneurial company'. These coded messages imply that a younger person would fit in better and are likely to deter older workers from applying. Jobs can become age-typed, with some jobs being seen as more appropriate for younger workers and others for older workers (Perry and Parlamis, 2006). Interestingly, an *employer's* age is not found to have any significant effect on ageist attitudes. In other words, older managers are just as likely to discriminate against older employees as younger ones (Oswick and Rosenthal, 2001). Therefore the social identity of discriminators and discriminated is not as clearly differentiated as with other forms of discrimination.

The question is whether chronological age really does tell us anything about a person's skills and abilities. There are more myths and stereotypes underpinning the negative attitudes towards older employees than hard facts and a physically fit older person could outperform a younger less fit one in many types of job (Brotherton, 2003). Myths include the belief that older people are less productive, inflexible, resistant to change and less easy to train. These views are apparently widespread among line managers. Set against this, studies have found some positive attributes consistently related to greater age – positive stereotyping. These include being conscientious, modest, careful in interaction, sympathetic and helpful, all characteristics that ought to make older workers highly valued (Brotherton, 2003).

There are signs that some employers are becoming more positive towards older workers, especially with regard to their perceived loyalty and reliability. However, with negative attitudes outweighing positive, the jobs for which older employees are deemed particularly suitable are typically lower skill, lower status and lower paid, for example, in the do-it-yourself stores and other parts of the service industry. In view of present demographic trends, it could be argued that these positive signs are simply examples of employer responses to labour shortages, rather than indicative of deep-seated cultural change. Whether more positive attitudes towards older workers will survive the recession the UK is experiencing at the time of writing, remains to be seen.

Age has particular salience for women. Gendered ageism is a significant, deep-rooted cultural phenomenon. In general women are perceived as being 'older' at a chronologically younger age than men (Itzin and Phillipson, 1995). Youth is a gendered requirement of some types of female-typed jobs, especially those where feminine beauty and female sexual attractiveness are requirements. In some instances female youth and beauty are 'sold' as part of the service. The female flight attendant is a good example of this. Up until the early 1970s, it was standard practice in the airline industry to dismiss women when they reached a certain age (usually 32) (Mills, 1998). Equality laws brought an end to this directly discriminatory practice, but the job of flight attendant remains associated with images of femininity, youth and attractiveness.

On the other hand, some employers might prefer younger women who are in the first phase of their working lives (before having children). For example, talking about secretarial work Pringle (1989) argued that male bosses often avoided women with young children because of the perceived difficulties in getting them to work long hours and also because they perceived mothers as less committed to their work. Women managers often meet a 'glass ceiling of age' (Itzin and Phillipson, 1995). The career break often takes women out of employment during the years, which for men are considered to be the 'golden decade' – between 30 and 40. When they return, women managers frequently find themselves competing with younger men and the double bind of gender and age stereotyping kicks in. What this discussion reveals is that gendered ageism is firmly linked to male perceptions of women. What women should be like, look like or be doing at any given age are all defined by men because they predominate in organisational decision-making (Itzin and Phillipson, 1995). However, gendered attitudes towards age are also internalized by women, whose own behaviour and actions may reinforce male perceptions (Itzin and Phillipson, 1995).

Key learning points

- Employer ageism impacts on older workers in multiple ways. Age intersects with other diversity strands.
- Myths, stereotypes and value judgements underpin the negative attitudes towards older workers.
- Gendered ageism is a significant and deep-rooted cultural phenomenon, which is manifest in certain workplace relationships, in workplace social relations and in the requirements of some jobs.

Activity 4.4

City lawyers feel chill of recession

Britain's top law firms expanded dramatically during the financial boom but, just as they rose with the City, they are now declining with it. One lawyer said: 'Two American firms have gone under. I don't think that's going to happen in the UK, but we're expecting a lot of jobs to be lost.' Partners, especially those with equity in the business, should be particularly worried. They were once guaranteed jobs for life and earnings of more than £1 m a year. Now more than 15% of the 12,000 partners in the City's top firms could go.

Michael (not his real name) has been a partner in a second-tier law firm for more than 20 years. 'My firm isn't restructuring yet, but obviously we're hearing about the top firms – the so called "magic circle" – shedding dozens of partners in a bid to maintain profitability,' he said. 'I'm worried about my performance – if I don't deliver a certain profit, I earn less. But I'm not worried about my job yet because my firm is more collegiate and less cutthroat.'

It has been a miserable time for City law firms. Clifford Chance, Addleshaw Goddard, SJ Berwin and Baker & McKenzie have announced a series of redundancies that brings the total number of law jobs lost during the credit crunch to more than 2000. Some partners will not lose their jobs but will be stripped of equity. Last week there was a leak that Linklaters, the world's second-largest law firm, could cut 70 of its 540 partners, and 10% of more junior lawyers, as it focuses on fewer, more profitable, clients. Law firms are in uncharted waters. In recent years many have undergone a change from a collegiate model to a corporate one. Some insiders claim that respect for 'old-fashioned law' with a premium on technical excellence has now been replaced by the need for senior staff to generate business and manage client relationships. 'I hustle,' said Michael. 'I go on trips. I contact potential clients. I take new products to sell. Big firms have institutional clients, who get handed on from generation to generation. If you have been sitting at your desk, waiting for your client to ring up and tell you what to do, life is now going to be tough. Who will want you?'

Catrin Griffiths, editor of *The Lawyer*, described the climate as a 'perfect storm' and went on to predict that nearly all law firms would make redundancies, with women in junior positions possibly bearing the brunt of the job losses. 'There are now more women than men entering the profession,' she said. 'It has been hugely popular for graduates because, until recently, it has been seen as more secure than the City.'

According to Griffiths, the recession and dearth of work from some areas, such as private equity and property, have combined with a drive for greater professionalism and corporate management. 'Top law firms have already been looking at outsourcing work, sometimes sending it to India. They have been looking at using agency lawyers. Now they are looking at which areas they are going to get work from in the next 3 years, and making adjustments accordingly.'

While mid-sized and regional firms across Britain struggled in the last quarter of 2008, larger firms continued to see profits from international work in the Middle East, the Far East and Russia, paid for in Euros and Dollars, which have appreciated greatly against sterling. Senior partners were often shuffled off overseas rather than face redundancies at home. But that source of work has begun drying up too as the recession goes global, and those partners have been brought home to face a bleak future. 'Even Dubai is quiet,' one lawyer reported glumly.

Legal work on complicated financial products may have vanished, but some firms will be able to benefit from a surge in work on restructuring, insolvency and litigation. The bigger deals could lead to fees of more than £30 m and are likely to be fought over by many firms. Linklaters has more than 100 lawyers working on the Lehman Brothers administration. Slaughter and May, one of the City's most traditional and successful practices, bagged the role of legal adviser to the Treasury and has worked on the nationalisation of Northern Rock.

Griffiths said: 'It's about retooling. There are new areas. As a partner it is no longer enough to be a good lawyer. You have to be all-singing and all-dancing – technically excellent but also a mentor and an income generator. 'Another aspect to consider is that law firms are structured on the basis that people will rise through the ranks and then leave. When there is a recession fewer people leave because there are fewer opportunities. At the moment law firms have hangers-on. Some will have to go.'

With many of those hangers-on at the senior end of the profession, employment lawyer James Davies from Lewis Silkin solicitors warns that firms should be careful of age discrimination. 'If you are a partner and you are 55, you probably know that you will not be getting another job. You have nothing to lose by claiming age discrimination against your former employer and asking for up to £4 m,' he said. 'It is easier to get rid of partners than salaried staff, but because the process is also less transparent, firms should ensure that they can justify their decision-making.'

(*Source*: *The Sunday Times*, 1 February 2009)

Questions

1. Identify the changes in the culture of law firms and discuss why the new culture might impact negatively on older workers.
2. Why might law firms target older partners for redundancy?
3. To what extent and how might age stereotypes inform notions of the ideal legal worker?

4.5 CONCLUSION

This chapter has demonstrated that organisational cultures are not neutral. In order to understand organisations fully an interpretative approach is required, focusing on the qualitative and symbolic aspects of work organisations. This chapter has focused on the organisational experiences of diverse social groups. It is necessary to explore these experiences in order to understand the deeply embedded nature of inequalities and disadvantage at the meso level. Two important concluding points arise from the 'unpacking' of diversity issues within work organisations. Firstly, there is a dearth of role models in senior positions in many organisations for some social groups. This can create barriers to accessing important work-related social networks and in receiving career sponsorship. Secondly, myths, stereotypes and the use of harassment and humour, underpinned by deep-seated cultural norms and values, contribute to reinforcing and reproducing the inequalities and disadvantage experienced by the five social groups we focus on.

REVIEW AND DISCUSSION QUESTIONS

1. Based on what you have read in this chapter, discuss the value of Acker's (2006) concept of inequality regimes.

2. Why are some forms of discrimination seen as more legitimate than others?

3. Discuss what is meant by 'glass' and 'concrete' ceilings. How are these barriers constructed and manifested within organisations?

FURTHER READING

Acker, J., 2006.

An article addressing how to theorize intersectionality and how to identify barriers to creating equality in work organisations.

Ely, R., Foldy, E., Scully, M., 2003.

An edited collection of articles with gender at the centre, but also considering intersecting diversity strands.

REFERENCES

Acker, J., 2006. Inequality regimes: gender, class and race in organisations. Gender and Society 204, 441–464.

Acker, J., Van Houton, D., 1992. Differential recruitment and control: the sex structuring of organisations. In: Mills, A., Tancred, P. (Eds.), Gendering Organisational Analysis. Sage, London.

Alvesson, M., Billing, Y., 1997. Understanding Gender and Organisations. Sage, London.

Barnes, C., 1992. Disability and employment. Personnel Review 216, 55–73.

Botcherby, S., 2006. Pakistani, Bangladeshi and Black Caribbean women and employment survey: aspirations, experiences and choices. Moving on up? Ethnic minority women and work. Manchester, Equal Opportunities Commission.

Brotherton, C., 2003. Is diversity inevitable? Age and ageism in the future of employment. In: M. Davidson, M., Fielden, S. (Eds.), Individual Diversity and Psychology in Organisations. John Wiley, Chichester.

Burrell, G., Hearn, J., 1989. The sexuality of organisation. In: Hearn, J., Sheppard, D., Tancred-Sheriff, P., Burrell, G. (Eds.), The Sexuality of Organisation. Sage, London.

Cianni, M., Romberger, B., 1997. Life in the corporation: a multi-method study of the experiences of male and female Asian, Black, Hispanic and White employees. Gender, Work and Organisation 4 (2), 116-127.

Cockburn, C., 1991. In the Way of Women. Macmillan, Basingstoke.

Collinson, D., Collinson, M., 1989. Sexuality in the workplace: the domination of men's sexuality. In: Hearn, J., Sheppard, D., Tancred-Sheriff, P., Burrell, G. (Eds.), The Sexuality of Organisation. Sage, London.

Collinson, D., Collinson, M., 1992. Mismanaging sexual harassment. Women in Management Review 7 (7), 11-16.

Collinson, M., Collinson, D., 1997. It's only Dick: the sexual harassment of women managers in insurance sales. Work, Employment and Society 10 (1), 11-32.

Collinson, D., Hearn, J., 1994. Naming men as men: implications for work, organisation and management. Gender, Work and Organisation 1 (1), 3-22.

Collinson, D., Knights, D., Collinson, M., 1990. Managing to Discriminate. Routledge, London.

Creed, D., 2006. Seven conversations about the same thing: homophobia and heterosexism in the workplace. In: Konrad, A., Prasad, P., Pringle, J. (Eds.), Handbook of Workplace Diversity. Sage, London, pp. 371-400.

DiTomaso, 1989. Sexuality in the workplace: discrimination and harassment. In: Hearn, J., Sheppard, D., Tancred-Sheriff, P., Burrell, G. (Eds.), The Sexuality of Organisation. Sage, London.

Evetts, J., 2000. Analysing change in women's careers: culture, structure and action dimensions. Gender, Work and Organisation 7 (1), 57-67.

French, S., 1996. The attitudes of health professionals towards disabled people. In: Hales, G. (Ed.), Beyond Disability, Towards an Enabling Society. Sage, London.

French, S., 1996. Simulation exercises in disability awareness training: a critique'. In: Hales, G. (Ed.), Beyond Disability: Towards an Enabling Society. Sage, London.

Gherardi, S., 1996. Gendered organisational cultures: narratives of women travellers in a male world. Gender, Work and Organisation 34, 187-201.

Gutek, B., 1989. Sexuality in the workplace: key issues in social research and organisational practice. In: Hearn, J., Sheppard, D., Tancred-Sheriff, P., Burrell, G. (Eds.), The Sexuality of Organisation. Sage, London.

Hall, M., 1989. Private experiences in the public domain: lesbians in organisations. In: Hearn, J., Sheppard, D., Tancred-Sheriff, P., Burrell, G. (Eds.), The Sexuality of Organisation. Sage, London.

Hearn, J., Parkin, W., 1992. Gender and organisations: a selective review and a critique of a neglected area. In: Mills, A., Tancred, P. (Eds.), Gendering Organisational Analysis. Sage, London.

Hicks-Clarke, D., Iles, P., 2003. Gender diversity and organisational performance. In: Davidson, M., Fielden, S. (Eds.), Individual Diversity and Psychology in Organisations. John Wiley, Chichester.

Hite, L., 2007. Hispanic women managers and professionals: reflections on life and work. Gender, Work and Organisation 14, 120-136.

Honey, S., Meager, N., Williams, M., 1993. Employers' Attitudes Towards People with Disabilities. Institute of Manpower Studies, Brighton.

Hyde, M., 1996. Fifty years of failure: employment services for disabled people in the UK. Work, Employment and Society 10 (4), 701-715.

Itzin, C., Phillipson, C., 1995. Gendered ageism: a double jeopardy for women in organisations. In: Itzin, C., Newman, J. (Eds.), Gender, Culture and Organisational Change. Routledge, London.

Jenkins, R., 1985. Black workers in the labour market: the price of recession. In: Braham, P., Rattansi, A., Skellington, R. (Eds.), Racism and Antiracism. Sage, London.

Kirton, G., 2009. Career plans and aspirations of recent black and minority ethnic business graduates. Work, Employment and Society 23 (1), 12-29.

McKay, S., 1998. Older workers in the labour market. Labour Market Trends, July, 365-369.

Mills, A., 1989. Gender, sexuality and organisation theory. In: Hearn, J., Sheppard, D., Tancred-Sheriff, P., Burrell, G. (Eds.), The Sexuality of Organisation. Sage, London.

Mills, A., 1992. Organisation, gender, and culture. In: Mills, A., Tancred, P. (Eds.), Gendering Organisational Analysis. Sage, London.

Mills, A., 1998. Cockpits, hangars, boys and galleys: corporate masculinities and the development of British airways. Gender, Work and Organisation 5 (3), 172-188.

Mills, A., Tancred, P., 1992. Gendering Organisational Analysis. Sage, London.

Modood, T., 1997. In: Modood, T., Berthoud, R., Lakey, J., Nazroo, L., Smith, P., Virdee, S., Beishon, S. (Eds.), Ethnic Minorities in Britain: Diversity and Disadvantage. PSI, London.

Newman, J., 1995. Gender and cultural change. In: Itzin, C., Newman, J. (Eds.), Gender, Culture and Organisational Change. Routledge, London.

Oerton, S., 1996a. Sexualizing the organisation, lesbianizing the women: gender, sexuality and 'Flat' organisations. Gender: Work and Organisation 31, 26-37.

Oerton, S., 1996b. Beyond Hierarchy: Gender, Sexuality and the Social Economy. Taylor and Francis London.

Oswick, C., Rosenthal, P., 2001. Towards a relevant theory of age discrimination in employment. In: Noon, M., Ogbonna, E. (Eds.), Equality, Diversity and Disadvantage in Employment. Palgrave, Basingstoke.

Perry, E., Parlamis, J., 2006. Age and ageism in organisations: a review and consideration of national culture. In: Konrad, A., Prasad, P., Pringle, J. (Eds.), Handbook of Workplace Diversity. Sage, London, pp. 345-370.

Pringle, R., 1989. Bureaucracy, rationality and sexuality: the case of secretaries. In: Hearn, J., Sheppard, D., Tancred-Sheriff, P., Burrell, G. (Eds.), The Sexuality of Organisation. Sage, London.

Reynolds, G., Nicholls, P., Alferoff, C., 2001. Disabled people, retraining and employment: a qualitative exploration of exclusion. In: Noon, M., Ogbonna, E. (Eds.), Equality, Diversity and Disadvantage in Employment. Palgrave, Basingstoke.

Roberts, K., 1996. Managing disability-based diversity. In: Kossek, E., Lobel, S. (Eds.), Managing Diversity: Human Resource Strategies for Transforming the Workplace. Blackwell, Oxford.

Rubenstein, M., 1989. Preventing sexual harassment at work. Industrial Relations Journal 20 (2), 226-236.

Sheppard, D., 1989. Organisations, power and sexuality: the image and self-image of women managers. In: Hearn, J., Sheppard, D., Tancred-Sheriff, Burrell, G. (Eds.), The Sexuality of Organisation. Sage, London.

Sheridan, A., O'Sullivan, J., 2003. What you see is what you get: popular culture, gender and workplace diversity. In: Davidson, M., Fielden, S. (Eds.), Individual Diversity and Psychology in Organisations. John Wiley, Chichester.

Smith, B., 1996. Working choices. In: Hales, G. (Ed.), Beyond Disability: Towards an Enabling Society. Sage, London.

Tancred-Sheriff, P., Campbell, E., 1992. Room for women: a case study in the sociology of organisations. In: Mills, A., Tancred, P. (Eds.), Gendering Organisational Analysis. Sage, London.

Thornton, P., Lunt, N., 1995. Employment for Disabled People: Social Obligation or Individual Responsibility? Social Policy Research Unit, York.

Tyrer, D., Ahmad, F., 2006. Muslim women and higher education: identities, experiences and prospects. Liverpool John Moores University, Liverpool.

Woodhams, C., Danieli, A., 2003. Analysing the operation of diversity on the basis of disability. In: Davidson, M., Fielden, S. (Eds.), Individual Diversity and Psychology in Organisations. John Wiley, Chichester.

Theorizing policy approaches to equality and diversity

5

Aim

To provide a summary of the conceptual and theoretical underpinning of equality and diversity policies.

Objectives

- To present the main theoretical approaches to equality and diversity.
- To identify the chronological shift from equality to diversity.
- To provide an analysis of similarities and differences between 'equal opportunities' and 'diversity management'.

5.1 INTRODUCTION

This chapter aims to present a summary of the concepts and theories underpinning equality and diversity policies. As Webb (1997) pointed out, over the 1990s there were changes in the meanings attached to equality. Early policies were founded on a 'sameness' model and in the UK policies were firmly connected to the legislation enacted in the 1970s. 'Equal opportunities' (EO) became the most common label for organisational policies, even though, as we discuss later, it became a 'catch-all' for a range of distinctly different types of equality policy. The chapter offers a summary of the critiques of traditional equality concepts that set the scene for the emergence of the diversity concept. Diversity management (DM), as a policy approach, was founded on a 'difference' model and emerged in the mid to late 1990s in the UK. As Kaler (2001: 51) has pointed out, there are difficulties in determining the precise relationship of DM to the older concept of EO – whether diversity should be considered as a new and different concept or one that builds on the older concept. Does diversity pursue different ends by different means or do EO and DM overlap to the extent that diversity can be seen as pursuing the same ends by different means? Finally, the chapter considers the present state of theorizing on equality and diversity, together with future prospects. We believe that it is important to understand how traditional concepts of equality live on in contemporary DM policy and practice, even if the label and rhetoric have changed.

Thus, the chronological account presented below should be read as outlining dominant thinking on equality and diversity in the different periods, but in reality we will show that the theoretical approaches are interconnected.

Equality is undoubtedly a difficult area to theorize because of the wide variety of meanings attached to the concept. Is the concern with the principles of equality, the type of equality, the implementation of equality policies or the effectiveness of past and present equality initiatives? Salient questions include: what types of equality are organisational policies intended to achieve – for example, equality of treatment, equality of opportunity or equality of outcome? What types of discrimination are policies intended to overcome and in what ways? Does equality mean treating people the same, or differently? Should we be thinking of employees as neutral individuals who contribute the same abilities, and who should receive the same access to opportunities and rewards and be assessed in the same way, regardless of social group characteristics? Should we play down the differences between people or should we value the very existence of those differences? Should we look at differences between individuals, or does it still make sense to talk about group differences among women, black and minority ethnic (BME) workers, older workers, lesbian and gay workers or disabled workers? Do members of these groups face similar problems to each other and might they benefit from similar solutions? Or is everyone a unique individual with no special connection to others? For the purposes of our discussion, questions such as these are significant because they point to the lack of conceptual clarity that often surrounds organisational policies. But, it is important for organisational policies to be specific about what they are aiming to accomplish, otherwise there can be no means of evaluating what has been achieved.

5.2 THE EQUALITY AGENDA 1970s–1980s: LIBERAL AND RADICAL APPROACHES

A good starting point is to look in some detail at Jewson and Mason's (1986) influential article on the theory and practice of equality policies. They identify, compare and contrast liberal and radical approaches to equality policy-making.

5.2.1 The liberal approach

The liberal approach to equality essentially derives from political ideals of classic liberalism and liberal democracy (Jewson and Mason, 1986). It is based around a belief in the rights of the individual to universally applicable standards of justice and citizenship (Webb, 1997). Therefore, *'equality of opportunity exists when all individuals are enabled freely and equally to compete for social rewards'* (Jewson and Mason, 1986: 307). The model is predicated on a philosophy of 'sameness' – the idea that people should have access to and be assessed within the workplace as individuals, *regardless* of social group. The focus is on the individual, where people are required to deny or attempt to minimize differences and compete for jobs solely on the basis of individual merit (Liff and Wajcman, 1996; Kaler, 2001). Job selection on the basis of individual merit is seen as fair. Conceptions of merit typically include factors such as experience, educational qualifications, commitment and so on (Kaler, 2001: 53).

Policies based on the notion of the neutral individual are seen as the most efficient means of achieving a fair distribution of rewards and resources in the workplace. This standpoint has grounding in the philosophy of free market competition and thus can be linked to neoclassical theories of employment segregation (Chapter 3). Within neoclassical theory, unfair discrimination is not an inherent or intrinsic feature of capitalist labour markets, but is a distortion of an otherwise rational market. Notions of the free market are central to the liberal approach to equality and therefore, equality policy within the liberal approach is focused on what Jewson and Mason (1986) call 'positive action'. Positive action involves implementing measures to remove obstacles to the operation of the free labour market and to meritocratic competition. This should not be confused with 'affirmative action' which derives from the US and reflects a more radical approach (see Table 5.1). Affirmative action is more akin to what in the UK is called 'positive discrimination' (discussed later). Positive action might include initiatives such as advertising campaigns reassuring candidates that all applications will be judged solely on their merits, crèche facilities in the workplace (allowing parents – mostly mothers – to balance work and family), etc. It can also include equality training to teach recruiters how to use non-biased procedures and methods in recruitment and selection.

The liberal approach to equality influenced the campaign for anti-discrimination legislation in Britain in the 1970s, leading to the Sex Discrimination Act (1975), Race Relations Act (1976) and Equal Pay Act (1970). At this time, the emphasis was on encouraging employers to develop formal procedures for ensuring fair and meritocratic methods of selection for jobs, training and promotion. It was believed that this would lead to the development of a 'metaphorical level playing field' (Webb, 1997). Thus, the liberal approach to equality rests on bureaucratization and formalization of procedures so as to ensure that processes are formally fair within organisations – an approach also known as procedural justice.

5.2.2 The radical approach

In contrast to the liberal approach, the radical approach emphasizes the need for direct intervention in order to work towards not only equality of opportunity, but also equality of outcome. This means that the objective is not only to achieve fair procedures (as in the liberal approach), but also to achieve fair distribution of rewards. What is meant by fair distribution of rewards? If, for example, women or BME workers are under-represented in middle and senior management, this would be seen as unfair distribution of rewards, which should be tackled by the equality policy (by introducing, for example, targets or even quotas for under-represented groups). To emphasize, the focus of the radical approach is not on individuals, but on groups, recognizing that while discrimination affects individuals, it is at the group level that systemic discrimination can be identified. The idea that all people are equal regardless of social group membership should be reflected in the even distribution of rewards in the workplace. The absence of fair distribution is read as evidence of unfair discrimination. The ideal of the radical approach is a situation where every workforce is representative of all the social groups available to it (Kaler, 2001: 53). This stands in contrast to the liberal approach where the principle of selection on merit alone does not require even group representativeness. The question posed by the radical approach is – what is merit? The radical approach

Table 5.1 Comparison of Equality and Diversity Approaches

Approach	Principle	Strategy	Method	Type of Equality
Liberal	Fair equal opportunity	Level playing field	Policy statement, equality proof recruitment and selection procedures	Equality of opportunity
	Positive action	Assistance to disadvantaged social groups	Monitoring, pre-entry training, in-service training, special courses, elevate equality within management	Equality of opportunity
	Strong positive action	Give positive preference to certain groups	Family friendly policies, improve access for disabled, make harassment a disciplinary offence	Moving towards equality of outcome
Radical	Positive discrimination (or more radical forms of positive action)	Proportional equal representation	Preferential selection, quotas	Equality of outcome
Diversity	Maximize individual potential	Use employee diversity to add value	Vision statement, organisation audit, business-related objectives, communication and accountability, change culture	Equality means profit aligned with organisational objectives

Source: Based on Miller, 1996: 205, 206.

does not see ability or talent as neutral, but claims that notions of ability and talent contain and conceal a series of value judgements and stereotypes. Negative value judgements and stereotypes are attached to 'minorities' by dominant groups, so that minorities are less likely to be seen as appointable on merit. Discrimination is not, therefore, simply a distortion of the free labour market but is a socially constructed feature of the market process. Whilst the aim of the radical approach is to achieve equality of outcome for all on the same terms, it contains elements of a 'difference' perspective. The radical approach recognizes the existence of differential treatment based on social group membership and the way that some groups are socially constructed as possessing fewer talents and abilities than others.

The policies associated with the radical approach include 'positive discrimination', where employment practices are explicitly geared towards obtaining a fair distribution of disadvantaged groups in the workplace (Jewson and Mason, 1986). For example, where BME people were under-represented, they would be given preferential treatment in recruitment and selection until a fair distribution had been achieved. Whilst the liberal approach emphasizes the need to formalize procedures, the radical approach emphasizes the need to politicize the processes of decision making. Theoretically, policies could involve the imposition of quotas. However, radical measures are largely outlawed in Britain (see Chapter 6), although there are *elements* of the radical approach within the legislation and within organisational equality policies and practices (Liff and Wacjman, 1996; Miller, 1996).

5.2.2.1 *Linking liberal and radical approaches*

In practice, there are elements of a 'difference' or radical approach within the largely 'sameness' or liberal approach of the British equality legislation. For example, the concept of indirect discrimination is where a condition is applied equally to all, but a larger proportion of people from one social group find it more difficult to comply with it than people from another social group (see more detailed discussion in Chapter 6). Liff and Wajcman (1996) argued that the legal definition of indirect discrimination was used to remove the age restrictions for promotion to the more senior Civil Service grades. The age restriction was established as disadvantaging (indirectly discriminating against) women who had been out of employment due to family responsibilities and when they returned found they were too old for promotion. Age criteria – specifically requiring 'maturity' – could also be seen as indirectly discriminatory on grounds of ethnicity, as the BME population is comparatively youthful.

Work-life-balance policies designed to enable women to combine work and family responsibilities could be seen theoretically as an example of either the liberal or radical approaches. On the one hand, work-life-balance policies 'level the playing field' in the way that the liberal approach requires; on the other hand, such policies could be read as an example of the direct intervention to influence equality outcomes that the radical approach requires.

Thus, it seems that some elements of contemporary policy and legislation would seem to breach the liberal view that all people should receive the same treatment, regardless of social group membership. However, whilst social group-based differences *should* be irrelevant in terms of the meritocratic free labour market, it is quite clearly recognized by the law that sometimes policy measures might be needed to ensure that everyone can truly participate on the same terms. Thus, while legislation and organisational policies largely reflect the liberal approach, elements of the radical approach and acknowledgement of 'difference' have emerged. In Liff and Wajcman's (1996: 82) words, '*organisations which are proactive on equality issues have stretched and re-interpreted the equal treatment model in a number of ways*'.

This mix of radical and liberal approaches within equality policies is symptomatic of the ambiguous nature of traditional conceptualizations of equality. In their study, Jewson and Mason (1986) found that individuals and groups frequently invoked various aspects of both conceptions, depending on the circumstances and their needs. This was often due to confusion and misunderstandings surrounding the policy and practice of equality. In addition, Jewson and Mason also found more conscious and deliberate attempts to mislead and mystify opponents and outsiders. Similarly, Cockburn (1989) found that people interpreted workplace equality policies differently, depending on what they expected and desired from them. Cockburn identified various interest groups – the shareholder who has a strong personal commitment to equality; the executive team who sees a business case for equality; the lawyers who want equality initiatives in order to avoid legal claims of discrimination; the personnel managers who see equality as part of wider management trends; and line managers who are only concerned with equality if it does not conflict with maintaining work discipline and cost budgeting (Greene and Kirton, 2009). In essence, equality policies are part of the wider, complex and multi-faceted nature of workplace relations within the social structures and systems of wider society.

Key learning points

- There is a variety of meanings and approaches attached to the concept of equality. Key approaches identified include liberal and radical.
- Equality approaches can be based on 'sameness' or on 'difference'.
- Free market theory underpins the liberal approach based on 'sameness'. It is predicated on the premise that people should have access to opportunities at the workplace as individuals, regardless of social group membership. Policies within this approach emphasize the formalization of procedures and 'positive action' measures to ensure that the 'rules of the game' are fair.
- The radical approach attempts to ensure equality of outcome as well as equality of opportunity. It recognizes that discrimination is a socially constructed part of the market process. Policies emphasize direct intervention in order to work towards achieving a fair distribution of rewards in the workplace.
- Equality legislation in Britain mainly reflects the liberal 'sameness' approach, although elements of a radical 'difference' approach are evident. The legislation establishes the concept of indirect discrimination.

5.2.3 A critique of liberal and radical equality approaches

There can be no doubt that the dominant liberal approach to equality has achieved a degree of success in tackling inequalities, discrimination and disadvantage. With regard to gender inequality, for example, Webb (1997) pointed to the rising number of women in the workforce, the increasing number of women in the professions and the growth in the numbers of women achieving some degree of economic independence. Chapter 2 identified the main changes in the UK labour market with regard to different social groups, some of which have been positive from an equality perspective. However, there are also criticisms of the liberal approach and it has its weaknesses, focused as it is on procedural justice and equality of opportunity rather than equality of outcome.

One longstanding criticism is that equality legislation and policies might appear strong, but are in fact weak in practice. Collinson et al. (1990) and Cockburn (1991) provided multiple examples of where legislation was being ignored in everyday organisational practices and where discrimination continued unabated. Explanations for this gap between the rhetoric and reality of equality policies include the lack of political will underlying the legislation (as evidenced by the limited resources of the equality bodies such as the former Equal Opportunities Commission and the former Commission for Racial Equality); the institutional weakness of personnel or human resources managers in organisations (the people largely responsible for implementing equality policy); and the lack of support from senior management for equality initiatives (Webb, 1997).

Another criticism concerns the belief at the heart of the liberal approach that fair procedures lead to fair outcomes (Jewson and Mason, 1986). Many researchers and writers have argued that procedural formalization is by no means a guarantee of fairness in practice (Richards, 2001; Webb, 1997; Liff, 1996; Cockburn, 1991). Webb (1997) highlighted the ways that procedures could be evaded, especially with many managers having substantial managerial discretion over how they make decisions and how they implement equality initiatives. Also, in most organisations, monitoring of the ongoing processes of equality policies is patchy at best (Dickens, 1994; Richards, 2001). A reliance on procedures and increased bureaucratization also seems at odds with the trends towards deregulation and flexibility, and such an approach has come to be seen as unfair and restrictive within the laissez-faire economy (Rees, 1998). Moreover, Jewson and Mason's (1986) research showed that many aspects of work life are very difficult to bureaucratize. They pointed to the numerous informal norms and codes of behaviour that exist no matter how formalized an organisation is.

In particular, many writers (Webb, 1997; Cockburn, 1991) have focused on the fact that the liberal approach to equality assumes that acceptability and suitability criteria for jobs could be separated. An equality policy might require that procedures are followed to ensure that candidates are chosen on the basis of their suitability and merit for the job, but in reality, the labour supply is gendered, racialized, aged and sexualized from the start, making the holy grail of rational, unbiased decision making impossible to achieve. For example, prevalent stereotypes attached to groups of workers mean that some 'types' of people might be judged more acceptable than others. As Webb pointed out with regard to gender, *'aspects of masculinity and femininity become established as indicators of suitability'* (1997: 161). A belief that a woman would not be 'acceptable' as a top manager due to her supposed inability to put in long hours at work means that this gender stereotype becomes a measure of suitability for her appointment, regardless of her skills and qualifications (Chapter 3).

As discussed, British equality legislation generally focuses on procedures, not outcomes, and therefore it can be characterised as an attempt to treat the symptoms of disadvantage and discrimination rather than the causes (Rees, 1998). The focus on individuals within the dominant 'sameness' model is also a weakness, suggesting that people should be treated as neutral individuals without recognizing the impact of culturally reproduced and socially constructed group membership. Jewson and Mason (1986) similarly pointed out that the liberal approach ignores or cannot accommodate the structural sources of social capacities and skills. The traditional liberal approach leaves the prejudices and stereotypes unchallenged and so is seen as ineffective in leading to change, but instead is accused of reproducing the inequalities of the broader context (Rees, 1998). The position of women in the workforce serves as an example. Rees (1998) emphasized the importance of the fact that within the traditional, liberal equality approach, there is little acknowledgement of the way that household arrangements impact on participation in the workplace. Thus, she argues *'granting equal access to men and women will only benefit certain women: those whose cultural capital, experiences, family circumstances and share of domestic responsibilities are similar to those of* [white] *men as a group'* (Rees, 1998: 29). All in all, equality of access is an illusion while the white, male, full-time worker, with few domestic responsibilities, is seen as the norm and as the standard by which skills and abilities are measured.

The radical approach also has its critics. While on the one hand it recognizes the fact that formal procedures do not necessarily lead to fair outcomes, its attempt to intervene to change the status quo carries its own dangers. Cockburn (1989, 1991) identified how initiatives aiming to enhance the position of workers from disadvantaged social groups are often seen negatively as meaning 'special treatment'. The women and BME workers in Cockburn's research disliked the idea of what they saw as favouritism because they feared a backlash by dominant groups. Rees (1998) discussed the furore over the Labour Party's 1996 all-women shortlists for nominated candidates in certain parliamentary seats. This was a radical interventionist measure designed to redress the gender imbalance in Members of Parliament. The policy met opposition from both men and women because it was felt by some to be unfair or to be 'reverse discrimination'.

Perhaps more significantly, however, initiatives to improve the position of particular groups are not always felt to lead to any overall change in the nature of the organisation (Cockburn, 1989). As Cockburn argued, both liberal and radical approaches seek '*to give disadvantaged groups a boost up the ladder, while leaving the structure of that ladder and the disadvantage it entails just as before*' (1989: 217). While the rhetoric of equality policies is changed, the reality is more static.

The lack of transformation could mean that the radical approach will continue to be seen as unfair and as unnecessary or as unwanted 'special treatment' (Liff, 1996). Being critical of both liberal and radical approaches to equality for their lack of success in achieving organisational transformation, Cockburn developed the concept of 'short' and 'long' equality agendas (1991, 1989). The 'short' agenda is similar to the traditional liberal approach emphasizing the need to treat the symptoms of discrimination and disadvantage, or to develop special policies to protect or enhance the position of disadvantaged social groups. The 'long' agenda seeks to change the unequal systems and structures of organisations, alter the nature and distribution of power and thus transform the organisation. The long agenda requires organisational actors to be fully committed to a transformative aim of equality policies (Richards, 2001: 19).

Liberal and radical approaches have both been criticized for being too simplistic, underestimating the complexity of organisations. The reality is that employee interests are heterogeneous, meaning that it is difficult to conceive of an equality policy that would meet the needs of all and be felt fair by all. For example, there are different interests among women, between the young and old, and between those with children and without. Different ethnic groups have different interests relating to cultural background and religious affiliation. The liberal, 'sameness' approach has been criticized for failing to advance the position of disadvantaged groups and for failing to change unequal systems, structures and hierarchies. Workers are expected to assimilate and to dilute or deny their differences in order to meet the expectation of the norm, usually that of a white, non-disabled, heterosexual, man, aged 25–40 years. Meanwhile the radical approach is deemed to rest on the implementation of change strategies that are themselves felt unfair. A possible move away from traditional approaches is seen in concepts of diversity or 'difference'.

Key learning points

- Liberal and radical approaches to equality have been criticized for failing to deliver equality of outcome. Critics highlight continuing inequalities, discrimination and disadvantage and the fact that suitability criteria continue to be judged against the dominant white, male norm.
- Policies associated with the radical approach can be criticized as involving 'special treatment'.
- Equality policies based on the concept of 'sameness' are criticized for benefiting only a minority of workers from disadvantaged groups who can most easily meet the dominant norm. This is

because a 'sameness' approach does not transform organisational culture, but perpetuates unfair structures and systems within organisations and wider society.

- Both liberal and radical approaches to equality tend to follow a 'short agenda' rather than a 'long agenda'. The latter would seek to change unequal systems and structures and transform organisational cultures.

Activity 5.1

Police consider quotas to boost force diversity

Senior police officers are discussing whether to introduce quotas for black and Asian recruits in a last-ditch attempt to make forces more representative, it was revealed today. The Association of Chief Police Officers (ACPO) is to consider whether it should press for a change in the law to allow "affirmative action" to recruit minorities. However, the Commission for Racial Equality (CRE) dismissed the idea as a "smokescreen" and said more attention should be paid to why more people of ethnic minorities are not applying to become officers. Home Office figures last month revealed that the proportion of ethnic minority police in England and Wales reached 3.7% in 2005/06 – below a 4% target forces were supposed to reach 2 years earlier.

Ministers have set a final 7% target for 2009. An Acpo spokeswoman said "At a conservative estimate, it would take 23 years to reach that target with current legislation. Chief constables are going to start a debate on whether we need to change the law to enable us to reach those employment targets." In all, there were 5236 black and Asian officers in the 43 police forces in England and Wales at the end of March last year, excluding the National Crime Squad and the National Criminal Intelligence Service, which have since been disbanded. The Acpo spokeswoman said a report being presented to the association's council meeting this morning by the Cheshire chief constable, Peter Fahy, would float the idea of introducing quotas and allowing forces to use affirmative action to meet them. It would also seek to boost the number of women in the police, who are currently "grossly under-represented", the Acpo spokeswoman said.

Affirmative action describes the process of prioritizing minorities once they have passed initial selection procedures. It differs from "positive discrimination" which means hiring minorities, regardless of whether they are qualified for a job. Acpo will not make a decision today on whether to lobby for a change in the law. But chief constables are thought to be keen to begin a wider debate on the move, in consultation with bodies such as the CRE. A spokeswoman for the CRE said it would not support the move. "The CRE doesn't support positive discrimination and affirmative action," she said. "These forms of 'reverse discrimination' could actually increase community tensions, rather than ease them." In many areas forces are struggling to recruit people from diverse backgrounds because of people's negative perceptions and experiences. This is the real problem that needs to be addressed." She added "The police ought to stop hiding behind the smokescreen of 'affirmative action' and start looking at the real reasons why ethnic minorities are not applying to become police officers."

(*Source*: www.guardian.co.uk, 19 April 2007)

Questions

1. Consider whether introducing quotas would be considered a liberal or radical equality approach. Explain your categorization.
2. Why would there be controversy around such an initiative and how does this fit into the critique of equality approaches?
3. Why might such an initiative be deemed necessary in order to combat organisational inequalities? You might refer back to the discussion in Chapter 3 on employment segregation.

5.3 THE EQUALITY AGENDA 1990s: DIVERSITY APPROACHES

It is self-evident that organisational policies are influenced by wider economic, political and ideological trends. Thus, a shift in thought about equality also accompanied the late 1980s and 1990s trend towards deregulation, flexibility, new managerialism and human resource management (Webb, 1997; also see Chapter 10). There was also a shift in feminist consciousness led by an increasing backlash to feminism and feminists (Cockburn, 1989, 1991; Webb, 1997). At the same time there was a growing belief in the need to downplay the innate 'sameness' of gendered groups and to move away from the idea that women's interests would best be served by challenging men (as a group). Further, as discussed in Chapter 3, the black feminist critique of western feminism focused on the way that it denied the differences among women. These developments in feminist thinking helped to engender a shift in thought towards a 'difference' approach to conceptualizing inequalities, discrimination and disadvantage.

There are a variety of ways in which 'difference' or diversity approaches have been understood. The management and organisation literature finds diversity variously presented as (i) an evolutionary step from equality (Chartered Institute of Personnel Development: Kandola and Fullerton, 1994, 1998); (ii) a sophistication of the equality approach (Rubin in Overell, 1996); (iii) a repackaging of equality (Ford, 1996); (iv) more negatively as a sanitized, politically unthreatening and market-oriented notion (Webb, 1997); (v) a 'comfort zone', allowing employers to avoid actively fighting discrimination (Ouseley in Overell, 1996). Kandola and Fullerton (1994) provided a summary of the development of the diversity concept in the US, locating it to 1987 when an influential report – *Workforce 2000* – by Johnston and Packer highlighted the implications of the increasing diversity of the American workforce. *Workforce 2000* predicted that by 2000, white male employees would comprise a minority of new entrants to the workforce. This prompted widespread discussion in the media, business and academic forums of the greater need for organisations to recognize the importance of managing a diverse or multi-cultural workforce. Kandola and Fullerton began their discussion of the diversity approach with the statement: '*managing diversity* [diversity management] *means different things to different people*' (1998: 6). Reflecting this there are many different definitions, but Kandola and Fullerton's captures the main principles and aims of diversity approaches:

> '*The basic concept of managing diversity [diversity management] accepts that the workforce consists of a diverse population of people. The diversity consists of visible and non-visible differences which will include factors such as sex, age, background, race, disability and work style. It is founded on the premise that harnessing these differences will create a productive environment in which everybody feels valued, where their talents are being fully utilised and in which organisational goals are met*'

> **Kandola and Fullerton, 1998: 8**

Compared with the state of the field when the first edition of our book was published in 2000, there are now a number of detailed expositions of diversity approaches. The contemporary literature discusses the ways in which diversity differs from traditional 'equality' approaches and evaluations of its strengths and weaknesses are offered (for example, Cornelius, 2002; Kirton, 2008; Noon and Ogbonna, 2001; Lorbiecki and Jack, 2000; Liff, 1999, 1997). Most writers agree on the essential dimensions of the diversity approach.

First, at the heart of diversity approaches lies the premise that difference should be positively recognized, nurtured and rewarded rather than denied or diluted (Liff, 1996). There is a move away from the idea that everyone should assimilate in order to meet an organisational norm. The employer is expected to be committed to creating a workplace that facilitates the inclusion of all, enabling everyone to contribute in their own way to the organisation (Webb, 1997). Thus, rather than difference being viewed negatively, there should be recognition of the inherent strengths of employee diversity based on cultural background, gender or age, or differential experience. It is expected that work organisations will gain from employee diversity. The focus moves away from a rights-based agenda focused on discrimination and disadvantage. In this way the equality agenda is rendered less controversial and less sensitive to backlash from dominant or 'advantaged' groups and individuals (Sinclair, 2000).

Second, difference is viewed as being *individually* based. Diversity approaches would thus have an individualistic policy focus (Liff and Wajcman, 1996), moving away from standardized procedures to eliminate discrimination and positive action to redress historical disadvantage of particular social groups. Therefore, diversity approaches involve a broader range of people than the social groups usually covered in 'EO' policies, moving beyond the equality strands (race/ethnicity, gender, age, sexual orientation, religion and disability) towards individual differences. Of particular note is the inclusion of individual 'non-visible' differences and personal characteristics such as 'work style' (Kandola and Fullerton, 1998).

Third, a diversity approach aims to meet organisational goals. In this sense it is a business-driven approach, rather than one underpinned by broader notions of social justice (i.e. as in equality approaches) (Kaler, 2001). Indeed Noon and Ogbonna (2001) argue that this is the key analytical differentiation between 'EO' and 'DM'. While 'EO' policies may utilize business rationales to achieve moral/social justice ends, diversity policies can be seen to have an exclusive focus on business case (Kaler, 2001: 59). The diversity approach appeals to critics of traditional equality approaches, who have argued that the moral cause of 'equality' has little purchase in the competitive world of business. Thus, employee diversity is valued as a direct contribution to the success of an organisation.

Finally, the diversity approach is presented as not only concerned with numerical representation of different 'types' of employees, but as an attempt to change the culture of organisations. This element of diversity meets one of the major criticisms of the dominant liberal equality approach seen as too focused on procedures to stimulate culture change. It has become widely accepted that organisational cultures need to change significantly so that employee differences are viewed as positive. Rees (1998) saw diversity approaches as facilitating more 'mainstreaming' of equality (i.e. equality issues being included in every part of strategy and policy, rather than simply having dedicated equality policies). Mainstreaming requires a shift in organisational culture in the same way as demanded by diversity approaches. Rees (1998) saw the mainstreaming project as seeking to *transform organisations and create a culture of diversity in which people of a much broader range of characteristics and background may confidently flourish* (Rees, 1998: 27). The objective of culture transformation also has echoes of Cockburn's (1991, 1989) 'long agenda', where the aim is to bring about greater equality by changing cultures, systems and structures.

There are different conceptualizations of diversity that impact on equality and diversity policy and practice. Kandola and Fullerton's approach (1994, 1998), which they call 'Managing the Mosaic', highlights the business case for employee diversity, particularly due to demographic shifts in the labour market. This moves away from the traditional, rights-based agenda of 'EO'. Gagnon and Cornelius (2002) outline a 'capabilities' approach to diversity, where diversity policies revolve around identifying the choices that people have, facilitating those choices, and providing the organisational environment in which individuals can make the fullest use of their individual set of capabilities. For them, embracing diversity involves ensuring that individuals feel that their treatment is fair, requiring changes in organisation cultures, structures and communications to allow people at all levels to have a voice in the development of policies.

Liff's (1997) typology of DM approaches, despite being over a decade old, retains its usefulness as an analytical framework. This differentiates between four sets of underlying policy principles and aims that recognize to different degrees the legacy and imprint of traditional EO-type approaches that most organisations are still likely to be working with today. The framework also fits well with debates about sameness and difference approaches to equality discussed earlier. The two caveats are first that in practice, organisations' policy aims might be multi-dimensional and complex and therefore, might not fit neatly into any of the approaches that Liff identifies; second that the diversity debate and policy and practice have moved on in the decade since Liff wrote her paper (Greene and Kirton, 2009).

The first approach Liff (1997) identifies is *dissolving differences*. Here, differences between people are not seen as based on social group membership (such as gender or race), but are individual based. It follows that initiatives would seek to respond to individual rather than group needs, for example individual career management policies. If someone has training needs, this should be addressed regardless of whether they are a man or a woman, or black or white. The point is for people to see themselves as individuals, rather than identify with similar others based on social group characteristics. Further, monitoring the workforce by characteristics such as gender, race and ethnicity would be seen to offer little of value or might even be counter-productive to a dissolving differences approach. Essentially, this approach ignores or downplays the wider social causes of inequality, including unequal access to training and education and does not see inequality as patterned by social group membership. This approach has echoes of EO insofar as the underlying aim is to treat people the same, regardless of social group characteristics. The second approach is *valuing differences*. Here, Liff (1997) refers to social group-based rather than individual differences, with policy recognition of the way in which gender or race, for example, can contribute to patterns of under-representation and inequality. Positive action initiatives would be included – such as, for example, provision of training for employees from under-represented groups to help them succeed in the organisation and to help overcome past group disadvantage. There would also be some adaptation of organisational policies in order to recognize different holidays and diets, for example. The third approach is *accommodating differences*, where there is a commitment to creating policies that open up opportunities (such as flexible working patterns) to under-represented groups. This approach might be found where the most compelling business case for diversity relates to the changing demographic composition of the labour market, for example, a need to recruit more women. This approach is very similar to the liberal equality approach and whilst it goes some way to recognizing both individual and socially based differences, it does not question the fundamental social or organisational structures of inequality. The final approach is *utilizing differences* where social group-based differences are recognized and provide the basis for different treatment. This approach is not concerned with social justice, rather employee differences will be put to use for the benefit of the organisation. This might be described as a 'special contribution' perspective which argues that different people (women, BME people, etc.) might be able to contribute to organisations in different ways with their different values, experiences, ways of thinking etc. (Billing and Sundin, 2006). Liff suggests that policy initiatives designed to tap gender-based differences might include different career tracks for 'career' and 'family' women.

In many respects, as suggested by Liff's typology, there is some similarity between equality and diversity approaches, and a glance at a practitioner guide for DM such as Kandola and Fullerton (1994) demonstrates that many of the measures involved within a diversity approach would not be alien to a traditional equality approach (see also Liff, 1999; Kirton, 2002; Gagnon and Cornelius, 2002). However, DM is often presented as significantly different from 'EO', the implications of which form part of the discussion in the next section.

Key learning points

- Diversity is a 'difference' approach that seeks to recognize, value and utilize differences between individuals rather than dilute or deny differences.
- Four main characteristics differentiate diversity from equality approaches: (i) differences are viewed positively; (ii) differences attached to group membership are downplayed; (iii) the

business case rather than the social justice case is predominant; and (iv) there must be a trans-formation in organisational cultures.

5.3.1 A critique of diversity approaches

One of the most significant criticisms of the diversity approach is that just like equality approaches, it seems to promise more than it can deliver. Indeed Kandola and Fullerton (1998), for all their positive proclamation of the diversity approach, recognized that the long list of 'benefits' are debatable and concluded that much more research was needed to establish whether their model was successful (1998: 52). Even more than a decade later, there is still no solid evidence that diversity policies are any more successful than traditional 'equal opportunity' ones (Greene and Kirton, 2009). There are, however, suggestions that diversity policies can deliver organisational benefits if initiatives are formulated in ways that are sensitive to the existing culture and practices and if some of the potential dilemmas and challenges are dealt with (Cornelius et al., 2000; Sinclair, 2000; Maxwell et al., 2001).

5.3.1.1 *What is distinctive about a diversity approach?*

Part of the problem lies in the difficulties in differentiating DM from EO in practice. Whilst many organisations now claim to have adopted a diversity approach, there is a lack of evidence of the success of such an approach and it is not always clear that the 'new approach' is anything more than just a name change (Greene and Kirton, 2009). Webb (1997) found that while her case study firm proclaimed a diversity approach, the policies actually introduced offered no challenge to the structure and culture of the organisation in the way that DM is meant to do. In fact, as opposed to the rhetoric of difference, the policies in reality tended to reflect a 'sameness' approach. Similar points were made by Liff (1999) in her research at British Telecom (BT), where she found that the bulk of policies could be categorized as a 'valuing diversity' approach (fitting closely with the traditional liberal equality approach). Dean (2009) and Greene and Kirton (2009) found only limited evidence of inclusion of a broader range of employee differences (a key element of the diversity approach) in both private and public sector diversity policies. The evidence begs the question – is diversity in practice no more than a name change? Also, if this is the case, what benefits does the name change bring both for organisations and for employees? Or does, as some commentators argue, diversity represent a distinctively different approach in practice (Kandola and Fullerton, 1998: 11)? If so, what are these differences and what are the consequences in equality terms? Critical authors argue that there are a number of serious problems with the diversity approach that are often glossed over in the management and practitioner literature.

5.3.1.2 *Problems with the business case*

The crucial area of debate has been whether the business and social justice cases are competing rationales (Noon and Ogbonna, 2001). This of course is linked to the question of whether diversity is a new *approach* or simply a new *label*. It might be argued that the business case has traditionally been an important element of equality approaches. Some commentators go further and talk about the social justice and business cases coinciding. The argument here is that social justice aims can lead to organisational benefits – for example, the marketing potential and enhancement of reputation that come with being (perceived as) an ethical business, or the benefits from being seen as an 'employer of choice' (Gagnon and Cornelius, 2002; Liff and Dickens, 2000; Dickens, 2000; Dickens, 1999). There are obvious pragmatic issues here and arguably social justice arguments will probably be most persuasive when they are combined with the business case (Dickens, 2000: 144).

However, some authors highlight the dangers of the business case (Noon and Ogbonna, 2001; Kaler, 2001; Greene and Kirton, 2009; Kirton, 2008; Lorbiecki and Jack, 2000; Dickens, 1997; Webb, 1997). The problem is whether the social justice aim of achieving fair representation can be met solely by the business case (Kaler, 2001: 59). Dickens (1997) emphasized the dangers for equality policies of the business case, stating that it is always contingent on factors such as the profitability of the firm or nature of the product market. What happens in times of economic downturn? What happens if a return on investment cannot be proven? What happens if the nature of the firm and its markets simply mean that employee diversity does not add value? More fundamentally, where is the moral imperative underpinning ethical business practice and corporate social responsibility? As Kaler comments, '*Under certain pressing conditions, there will always be much to lose from being ethical and much to gain from being unethical*' (2001: 60 from Chryssides and Kaler, 1993). There are too many cases when it could be argued that it will not pay to pursue diversity. If organisations are only going to introduce diversity policies if they have a business end, surely we can think of many instances when the customer, supplier or employer preference may be for a homogenous work-force (Kaler, 2001: 62). Finally, is it morally right for diversity to be promoted simply on business case terms or, as discussed below, could this be seen as the exploitation of difference?

5.3.1.3 *The exploitation of difference?*

Jones (2004) sees diversity as a 'discourse of exploitation' rather than the new paradigm for equality policy-making. It has been argued that emphasising employee differences might be used to reassert inferiority and justify exclusion (Webb, 1997). Webb used a quote from Cockburn (1991) stating that there is little room for difference *not* to be constructed as something inferior, '…*the dominant group know you are different and continue to treat you as different, but if you yourself specify your difference, your claim to equality will be null*' (1991: 219). Thus, a diversity approach may give ammunition to those who believe that being 'different' to the dominant norm disqual-ifies 'outsiders' from full inclusion and allows differences to be used in a way which is detrimental to equality (Liff, 1996). Individuals from 'minority' groups are thus vulnerable to becoming 'ghettoized' and exploited for the purposes of organisational gains – the 'utilizing diversity' approach.

The 'utilizing diversity' approach might also serve to reinforce stereotyping, which, as discussed in Chapter 3, can contribute to the perpetuation of disadvantage (see also Kaler, 2001: 63). As Liff (1996) stated, people may talk about the value of women's skills, such as 'caring attitudes', but in reality such 'feminine' skills continue to be undervalued in terms of pay and status. Thus, discourses of difference can often be used to support the 'normalcy' of employment segregation and pay gaps. An opposing argument is that employers should be able to articulate that people from different cultures, backgrounds and genders have different inherent aptitudes and skills, for example, the idea that *'women do well in social services and education'* or that *'Asians, having an aptitude for math, excel at engineering'* or, *'that blacks [sic] have some advantage in achieving success in basketball'* (Chen, 1992: 33). However, the counter-claim is that these alleged differences are no more than a reflection of dominant stereotypes with little basis in reality. This reliance on stereotypes and myths of difference tends to go unrecognized by 'utilizing and valuing diversity' approaches. According to this critique, the diversity approach does little to transform attitudes and cultures to make organisations more inclusive.

5.3.1.4 *Neglecting the realities of unfair discrimination and disadvantage*

As discussed above, the diversity approach emphasizes employee differences and their value to organisations. Celebratory rhetoric and metaphors are often used in diversity statements, making the policies sound far more positive than EO policies with their emphasis on discrimination. However, Kirton (2008) argues that the rhetoric of diversity could be used to conceal organisational 'non-action' on discrimination and inequalities and to convey the impression that 'there's no problem here'. If everyone is different and has different needs, aspirations etc. why does it matter if there are different outcomes? Kirton (2008) goes on to argue that when this kind of neoliberal thinking underpins policy and practice, unequal outcomes can easily be presented as simply different. Thus, the diversity approach can be used to deny the existence of injustice, inequalities and discrimination and to deny the need to challenge these things.

Another factor that could potentially lead to policy neglect of disadvantage is the fact that despite the difference rhetoric within the diversity approach, a 'difference' approach is not necessarily taken in practice. Paradoxically, it could even be argued that a 'sameness' approach is implicit in Liff's (1996) 'dissolving differences' diversity approach, with its requirement that everyone is treated the same, regardless of group characteristics. As we argued in reference to the liberal equality approach, 'same treatment' does not necessarily lead to equal outcomes. Elements of a 'sameness' approach, which could lead to the neglect of disadvantage, can also be identified within the model of DM espoused by Kandola and Fullerton (1998). Their model positions all differences on the same or similar terms; none are seen as more salient than others in leading to disadvantage in the workplace. For example, individual personality characteristics such as 'workstyle' are seen as being as significant as, and independent of, gender or ethnicity. We argue that while we need to recognize the transient nature of some forms of disadvantage (for example disability – Woodhams and Danieli 2000, or age – Oswick and Rosenthal 2001), and the fact that individuals within a social group do not all share the same forms of disadvantage all the time, certain identities affect life chances more than others. We argue, for example, that race and gender are particularly salient in the structuring of opportunities and of disadvantage. Whilst we acknowledge that categorizing individuals in reference to their social group characteristics may be constraining in some respects, social group membership needs to be recognized as a fundamental contributing factor to patterns of inequality and disadvantage.

Even Kandola and Fullerton (1998: 103) acknowledge that some of the work conducted in the name of diversity could enhance rather than reduce the effects of stereotypes, potentially reinforcing inequalities. As a necessary requirement of diversity policies therefore, Ford (1996) suggested that there is a need to ensure that all human resources processes in organisations are intrinsically fair and based on individual ability. However, the question to ask is, against what criteria is something judged fair and who develops the criteria for evaluating individual ability? Further, who decides what the norms or benchmarks are against which someone is judged to be the same or different? Liff and Wacjman (1996) took up this point, arguing that these questions signal a weakness in the dichotomy which opposes 'sameness' and 'difference' when, in fact, the terms are only relative to each other. In reality, what tends to happen in organisations is that fairness and ability, 'sameness' and 'difference' continue to be judged by those most powerful (typically white males) against the same dominant norm (white males).

Another problem that limits the capacity of the diversity approach to tackle discrimination is that it is largely introspective, focusing more on the movement of people within organisations rather than the barriers existing in the wider labour market (Miller, 1996). It could be argued that the diversity approach implicitly presupposes that equality already exists within the organisation so that employee differences can be celebrated. As Thomas (1990) pointed out, you cannot 'manage diversity' unless you have a diverse workforce to begin with. There are without doubt more factors involved in the perpetuation of inequalities and disadvantage than direct discrimination at the entry point to organisations. Wider workplace culture, attitudes and values have an impact and these are very difficult to manage. The fact that line managers do not always 'buy into' the diversity approach remains a significant barrier (Greene and Kirton, 2009). Kandola and Fullerton commented that diversity policy is not about *removing our prejudices. It is about recognising they exist and then questioning them before we act*' (1998: 13). This statement seems to imply that it is enough to recognize that prejudices exist. While it would be a difficult, if not impossible, task for an organisation to remove prejudices from all employees, it is necessary for organisations to attempt to prevent prejudices from influencing decision-making on staffing matters.

Finally, in de-emphasizing systemic inequalities and disadvantage, the diversity approach seems to miss the opportunity for bottom-up, employee-led challenge and action. If we think of people as members of social groups, people are not equally powerful in society. Highlighting the interests and differences of *individuals* may only serve to maintain the power of the dominant groups because the power structures remain taken-for-granted within an individualistic lens (Liff, 1996). An emphasis on individual differences weakens the ties that people can forge through recognition of common experiences, based for example, on being a woman or being disabled. These common experiences can foster the necessary collectivist orientation to encourage groups to push for action. However, where people perceive themselves simply as individuals, they are also likely to feel alone and isolated in their struggles (Cockburn, 1989). As Kandola and Fullerton (1998: 109) acknowledge, there may be dangers in ignoring what is *similar* to emphasize difference. For example, the diversity approach could be disempowering for individuals as dissolving collective identity can lead to dissolving collective strength. In Dickens' (1997) ideal model of equality practice, the role of trade unions, with their emphasis on collective action, is seen as a vital piece of the 'jigsaw' making up the campaign for equality in the workplace (see also Greene and Kirton, 2002).

5.3.1.5 *Can an individualized business case be made?*

Completing the circle of our discussion brings us back to the question of whether a diversity approach can advance the equality agenda. Reflecting many elements of the above discussion, a key question is, whether a business case can be made for valuing *individual* differences? The problem is that, in practice this appears to be very difficult. We have already established that in practice, many diversity policies look very similar to traditional equality policies with social groups still appearing significant, despite the rhetoric of individual difference. It is clear that in practice, organisations do not see a complete separation between equality and diversity approaches (Liff, 1999; Kirton, 2002: 7; Cornelius, 2002a; Greene and Kirton, 2002). Much of this overlap appears to occur because developing policy on the basis of individual differences is problematic in practice. Liff provided a good illustration of this with reference to policies at BT, where she highlighted the difficulties of having a policy that aimed to simultaneously *ignore* and *respond* to differences. There was little understanding within the organisation of the basis for deciding when it is appropriate to recognize differences and when to ignore them (1999: 73). Woodhams and Danieli (2000) clearly illustrate the difficulty of the business case for diversity in relation to disabled employees. Disability is perhaps the most obvious example of the deficiencies of the diversity approach. Paradoxically, disability is also the most obvious example of where individual differences are most salient because impairment is necessarily individual. Yet, in the case of disability, it would be hard to justify diversity policies in purely business case terms because the degree of individuality inevitably leads to increased costs in identifying and implementing policy measures. Therefore, the conclusion we must draw is that a diversity policy has to have at least a degree of focus on groups. Woodhams and Danieli's analysis is important in touching on the inherent contradiction within the rhetoric of diversity. This is that the business case for recognizing diversity is prioritized; however, if this is conceptualized solely as concerned with individual differences, identified and dealt with on an individual basis, then it becomes very difficult to make a viable business case.

5.4 HOW CAN EQUALITY AND DIVERSITY BE THEORIZED IN THE 2000s?

Based on the critiques above, we can see that neither an equality approach nor a diversity approach provides us with a perfect solution. The debate on sameness versus difference in relation to women is illustrative here:

> '...the 'sameness' alternative is insufficiently critical of the status quo. The 'difference' option <u>is</u> critical...but seems to conjecture that women can exist in some sort of separate world. Seeing women as <u>the same as men</u> prevents us from challenging the model, against which women are being compared; seeing women as different prevents us from changing it'
>
> **Bacchi, 1990: 262, quoted in Webb, 1997**

While the point above relates specifically to the case of gender, it can be utilized to highlight the weaknesses of the sameness and difference approaches more generally.

Working from within a sameness approach, equality policies often aim to make workers from disadvantaged groups fit the dominant norm, while a focus on 'differences' only seems to further reproduce the disadvantage faced by those groups. People may want to be treated neither the same nor differently at all times with respect to all aspects of their work lives (Liff and Wajcman, 1996). This returns to a point made earlier about the inseparability of 'sameness' and 'difference'. People possess what Liff and Wajcman call '*mobile subjectivities*' where people have both multiple differences and similarities. So for example, people may want to be treated the same for recruitment purposes, regardless of their ethnicity or gender, but may want their rights recognized to have flexible work arrangements to look after a dependent or to have special arrangements for religious worship, without suffering a long-term career detriment. People are the same and different simultaneously. The problem is that this debate does not provide any solution as to how policy could be constructed without falling foul of the criticisms noted in this chapter. It is difficult to identify how to develop policy that would take account of both sameness and difference and it is difficult to identify what policy measures would be appropriate in all the different circumstances.

One of the main issues is that neither the equality nor the diversity approach in practice is transformative enough. Rees (1998) stated that in practice, there can be short and long diversity agendas, just as with equality. Within the 'mainstreaming' approach that Rees advocated, there is a need for organisational cultures to be 'transformed', building upon the politics of difference. But this is clearly no easy task, especially when organisations face external pressures such as competition in the market or periods of recession. Thus, Rees concluded that in reality, many organisations simply 'tinker' with or 'tailor' existing initiatives and procedures which do not challenge the inherent inequalities within the structures, systems and cultures.

With regard to how to achieve greater gender equality, Liff and Wajcman (1996) suggested that what was needed was the construction of a new norm of work based on women's needs and interests, so that women can be assessed in their own right and not as 'not men' or 'other'. It is not easy to define exactly what are 'women's interests'; indeed, the diversity of interests within social groups is a recurring theme in this book. However, it would certainly be helpful if the norm of work was not full-time, uninterrupted service, as this disproportionately disadvantages many women, especially those who work part-time or who have domestic responsibilities. The experience of Sweden is cited as demonstrating where an equality strategy sees typically female patterns of work as the norm. For example, the extensive parental leave provisions, available to both men and women in Sweden, challenge the male breadwinner stereotype that militates against men taking more domestic responsibility. Gardiner (1998) proposed that skills developed in domestic work should be revalued as important to the labour market, and that breaks from paid work could still seen as periods of valuable skills development.

There are, however, obvious problems with moving to a new norm. The first is clearly that it would require considerable transformation in attitudes and power structures, and it is therefore a utopian conception. Having the *opportunity* to assume more domestic responsibility does not necessarily mean that men will *actually* take it. Therefore, for a new norm to establish itself, at least some of the challenge to the status quo has to come from the dominant group (in this case men); otherwise, 'differences' are likely to remain identified with inferiority (Webb, 1997). Secondly, and perhaps more importantly, as Liff and Wajcman (1996) acknowledged, a fundamental criticism of the 'female norm' approach is that gender is privileged over other social divisions such as ethnicity, disability, sexuality or class. Any new norm would have to ensure that there was enough space for workers from other social groups too. However, as is highlighted throughout this book, the issue is not that other identities should be treated as equally significant as gender, but that a new norm has to recognize intersectionality.

5.4.1 An integration of approaches

The pragmatic solution would be to have a mixture of equality and diversity, sameness and difference approaches. However, Liff's (1999) comments above about the difficulties of achieving this need to be borne in mind here. There are dangers if the diversity approach is seen as something totally new that does not require the maintenance of the basic safeguards and protections contained within the liberal equality approach. If diversity is presented as an alternative to equality, then this threatens to sever the link between organisational strategies and the realities of labour market disadvantage (Miller, 1996). We would agree with Kaler (2001) and Liff (1999) that the safer option, with more prospects for greater equality, is to ensure that the traditional equality paradigm underpins the newer diversity approach. Recognizing individual differences within groups and people's different and changing needs over time becomes a 'bonus' if basic equality work is being done.

Key learning points

- There is still limited evidence as to the success of diversity policies. In addition, there are examples of where the 'difference' approach can be used to reassert the inferiority and justify the exclusion of disadvantaged groups.
- There is still a lack of clarity about how to achieve equality in the workplace. Suggestions include recognizing that people are both similar and different simultaneously. Therefore, 'sameness' and 'difference' should not be placed in opposition. This leads to the need to maintain traditional equality approaches alongside more recent diversity approaches.
- There are a variety of different conceptualizations of diversity, including 'mainstreaming', which seek to transform organisational cultures. Short and long diversity agendas can also be identified.

Activity 5.2

Police halt jobs diversity scheme after discrimination claims

A pioneering campaign by Avon and Somerset police to increase the number of women and ethnic minority officers in its ranks has been withdrawn following advice that it may discriminate against white men. The scheme, launched last summer, was intended to "redress under-representation" of the area's "diverse communities" but resulted in complaints to the Commission for Racial Equality and the Equal Opportunities Commission. Applications from 186 white males were rejected before the interview stage in favour of those from women and from non-white backgrounds.

"Positive action" - helping applicants prepare for recruitment procedures or advertising in ethnic minority publications - is permitted but positive discrimination is illegal. The chief constable, Colin Port, yesterday defended the "innovative" approach: "Last summer we tried to do something different. Through use of positive action and using the model of the Disability Discrimination Act we intended to recruit officers that more accurately reflect the diverse communities we serve. We considered this represented an untried and untested area. It was not and has never been our intention to discriminate against anyone who applies for a position with the Avon and Somerset constabulary.... We will think again about how we can continue to recruit from under-represented groups...until that balance has been redressed." The force added: "In order to redress the situation we have... offered to reconsider all of the applicants excluded."

Around 3.9% of Avon and Somerset's population of around 1.5 million is from a non-white background. Peter Fahy, chairman of the race and diversity committee of the Association of Chief Police Officers, said police forces were being damned for failing to recruit enough ethnic minority and women officers, and damned when they tried new ways of diversifying their workforce.

(*Source*: *The Guardian*, 8 March 2006)

Questions

1. Drawing on the chapter's discussion, consider why this scheme attracted such controversy.
2. Given that the scheme was legal, was the police department right to back down in the face of complaints?
3. Does the scheme fit within either an equality or diversity approach?

5.5 CONCLUSION

This chapter has summarised the key conceptualizations of equality and diversity approaches and highlighted their strengths and weaknesses. What has emerged from the discussion is the lack of clarity about how to achieve equality – whether through 'sameness' or 'difference'. There is no clear and undisputed conceptualization of equality or diversity and no clear guidance as to the future direction of the equality project. It is of course always much easier to find weaknesses and criticisms than it is to construct new ways of doing things. Many of these problems will be discussed further in the following four chapters dealing with the translation of theoretical approaches into policy and practice within the law, trade unions, organisations and management thinking. The theoretical perspectives presented here will provide a useful background which can be used to help make sense of, and assess the success of, the various policy initiatives presented.

Activity 5.3

Understanding equality approaches

Undertake an internet search of the equality and diversity statements made on web sites by major work organisations in the UK and elsewhere. Try to include organisations from different sectors (e.g. retail, banking, local government) and of different sizes (large multi-national as well as medium-sized organisations). List the types of policies organisations have.

Questions

1. Do the policy *statements* seem to reflect the equality or diversity approach? Offer explanations for how you would categorize the statements.
2. Do the policy *initiatives* described seem to fit into either the equality or diversity approach?
3. Discuss the fit between the various policies and initiatives and the rationale organisations give for them.
4. Critically evaluate the potential that the diversity statements and the policies have for leading to 'transformation' in organisations.

REVIEW AND DISCUSSION QUESTIONS

1. What are the differences and similarities among the liberal, radical and diversity approaches? What types of equality do they address?

2. What are the strengths and weaknesses of each of the approaches?

3. How does such an analysis help us to conceptualize the direction that equality policies will or should take in the 21st century?

4. *'Managing diversity'* [diversity management] *is not anything new. It is simply another renaming exercise to enhance the image of existing 'equal opportunities' initiatives* (Hollinshead et al., 1999: 451). Discuss this statement.

FURTHER READING

Cockburn, C., 1989 and Jewson, N., Mason, D., 1986.

These two articles are widely cited as they provide critical analyses of traditional equality approaches and a starting point for theorizing in the contemporary period.

Konrad, A., Prasad, P., and Pringle, J., 2006.

A comprehensive volume of diversity research containing several theoretical contributions.

Liff, S., Wajcman, J., 1996.

An insightful analysis of the 'sameness' and 'difference' approaches to equality, identifying key strengths and weaknesses and providing a multi-dimensional model of diversity.

Noon, M., Ogbonna, E., 2001.

A useful collection of papers, which discuss the theoretical and policy debates around equality and diversity, and which present empirical research examining the experiences of different social groups.

REFERENCES

Bacchi, C., 1990. Same Difference: Feminism and Sexual Difference. Allen and Unwin, Sydney.

Billing, Y., Sundin, E., 2006. From managing equality to managing diversity: a critical scandinavian perspective on gender and workplace diversity. In: Konrad, A., Prasad, P., Pringle, J. (Eds.), Handbook of Workplace Diversity. Sage, London, pp. 95-120.

Chen, C., 1992. The diversity paradox: personnel management and cultural diversity. Personnel Journal 71 (1), 32-35.

Chryssides, G.D., Kaler, J., 1993. An Introduction to Business Ethics. Chapman & Hall, London.

Cockburn, C., 1989. Equality: the long and short agenda. Industrial Relations Journal 20 (3), 213-225.

Cockburn, C., 1991. In the Way of Women: Men's Resistance to Sex Equality in Organisations. Macmillan, Basingstoke.

Collinson, D., Knights, D., Collinson, M., 1990. Managing to Discriminate. Routledge, London.

Cornelius, N. (Ed.), 2002. Building Workplace Equality: Ethics, Diversity and Inclusion. Thomson, London.

Cornelius, N., 2002a. Introduction and overview. In: Cornelius, N. (Ed.), Building Workplace Equality: Ethics, Diversity and Inclusion. Thomson, London, pp. 1-5.

Dean, D., 2009. Diversity management in the private sector. In: Greene, A.M., Kirton, G. (Eds.), Diversity Management in the UK - Organisational and Stakeholder Experiences. Routledge, London, pp. 90-114.

Dickens, L., 1994. Wasted resources? Equality in employment. In: Sisson, K. (Ed.), Personnel Management. Blackwell, Oxford.

Dickens, L., 1997. Gender, race and employment equality in Britain: inadequate strategies and the role of industrial relations actors. Industrial Relations Journal 28 (4), 282-289.

Dickens, L., 1999. Beyond the Business Case: a Three-Progned Approach to Equality Action. Human Resource Management Journal 9 (1), 9-19.

Dickens, L., 2000. Still wasting resources? Equality in employment? In: Bach, S., Sisson, K. (Eds.), Personnel Management: a Comprehensive Guide to Theory and Practice, third ed. Blackwell, Oxford.

Ford, V., 1996. Partnership is the secret of progress: equality policy and diversity programs. People Management 2 (3), 34-36.

Gagnon, S., Cornelius, N., 2002. From equality to managing diversity to capabilities: a new theory of workplace diversity. In: Cornelius, N. (Ed.), Building Workplace Equality: Ethics, Diversity and Inclusion. Thomson, London, pp. 13-58.

Gardiner, J., 1998. Beyond human capital: households in the macroeconomy. New Political Economy, 3 (2), 209-221.

Greene, A.M., Kirton, G., 2002. Trade Unions and Managing Diversity. Presented at the 18th EGOS (European Group of Organisation Studies) Colloquium, July, Barcelona.

Greene, A.M., Kirton, G., 2009. Diversity Management in the UK, Organisational and Stakeholder Experiences. Routledge, London.

Hollinshead, G., Nicholls, P., Tailby, S., 1999. Employee Relations, Financial Times. Pitman Publishing, London.

Jewson, N., Mason, D., 1986. The theory and practice of equality policies: liberal and radical approaches. The Sociological Review 34 (2), 307-334.

Jones, D., 2004. Screwing diversity out of the workers? Reading diversity. Journal of Organisational Change Management 17 (3), 281–291.

Kaler, J., 2001. Diversity, equality and morality. In: Noon, M., Ogbonna, E. (Eds.), Equality, Diversity and Disadvantage in Employment. Palgrave, Basingstoke.

Kandola, R., Fullerton, J., 1991. Equality can damage your health. Equal Opportunities Review p.38.

Kandola, R., Fullerton, J., 1994. Managing the Mosaic: Diversity in Action. Institute of Personnel and Development (IPD), London.

Kandola, R., Fullerton, J., 1998. Managing the Mosaic: Diversity in Action. Institute of Personnel and Development (IPD), London.

Kirton, G., 2002. What is diversity? In: Johnstone, S. (Ed.), Managing Diversity in the Workplace. IRS, London, pp. 1–22.

Kirton, G., 2008. Managing multi-culturally in organisations in a diverse society. In: Clegg, S., Cooper, C. (Eds.), Handbook of Macro-Organisational Behaviour. Sage, London.

Konrad, A., Prasad, P., Pringle, J., 2006. Handbook of Workplace Diversity. Sage, London.

Liff, S., 1996. Two routes to managing diversity: individual differences or social group characteristics. Employee Relations 19 (1), 11-26.

Liff, S., Wajcman, J., 1996. 'Sameness' and 'difference' revisited: which way forward for equal opportunity initiatives? Journal of Management Studies 33 (1), 79-95.

Liff, S., 1997. Two routes to managing diversity: individual differences or social group characteristics. Employee Relations 19 (1), 11-26.

Liff, S., 1999. Diversity and equality: room for a constructive compromise? Human Resource Management Journal 9 (1), 65-75.

Liff, S., Dickens, L., 2000. Ethics and equality: reconciling false dilemmas. In: Winstanley, E., Woodall, J. (Eds.), Ethical Issues in Contemporary Human Resource Management. Macmillan, Basingstoke, pp. 85-101.

Lorbiecki, A., Jack, G., 2000. Critical Turns in the Evolution of Diversity Management. British Journal of Management 11 (Special issue), S17-S31.

Maxwell, G., Blair, S., McDougall, M., 2001. Edging towards managing diversity in practice. Employee Relations 23 (5), 468-482.

Miller, D., 1996. Equality Management: Towards a Materialist Approach. Gender, Work and Organisation 3 (4), 202-214.

Noon, M., Ogbonna, E., 2001. Equality, Diversity and Disadvantage in Employment. Palgrave, Basingstoke.

Oswick, C., Rosenthal, P., 2001. Towards a relevant theory of age discrimination in employment. In: Noon, M., Ogbonna, E. (Eds.), Equality, Diversity and Disadvantage in Employment. Palgrave, Basingstoke.

Overell, S., 1996. Ouseley in assault on diversity. People Management 2 (9), 7-9.

Rees, T., 1998. Mainstreaming Equality in the European Union: Education, Training and Labour Market Policies. Routledge, London.

Richards, W., 2001. Evaluating equality initiatives: the case for a 'transformative' agenda. In: Noon, M., Ogbonna, E. (Eds.), Equality, Diversity and Disadvantage in Employment. Palgrave, Basingstoke.

Sinclair, A., 2000. Women within diversity: risks and possibilities. Women in Management Review 15 (5/6), 237-245.

Thomas, R., 1990. From affirmative action to affirming diversity. Harvard Business Review March 68 (2), 107-117.

Webb, J., 1997. The politics of equal opportunity. Gender, Work and Organisation 4 (3), 159-167.

Woodhams, C., Danieli, A., 2000. Disability and diversity – a difference too far? Personnel Review 29, 402-416.

PART 2

Policy
and Practice

Equality, diversity and the law

6

Linda Johnson and Sue Johnstone

Aim

To present an overview of the legislative framework on discrimination in the UK; to critically examine the current and future nature and content of that legislation; and to critically analyse how the law impacts on diversity management in the workplace.

Objectives

- To examine the framework of discrimination law as a driving force for diversity.
- To look at different approaches to discrimination and equality legislation and examine how far the British system supports the promotion of workplace equality and diversity policies.
- To explain the role and impact of the European Union (EU) in the development of legislation in the UK and to discuss contemporary issues arising from recent developments.

6.1 INTRODUCTION

There are moral, business and legal reasons for employing a diverse workforce. This chapter explores the legal imperative in adopting an equality and diversity policy. But how far does the UK legal framework support, or encourage, the management of diversity? There is no doubt that breach of the discrimination legislation can be costly for employers. However, the traditional legal approach has been to compensate individuals who have been discriminated against rather than to create an ethos of valuing and encouraging workforce diversity. Developments since 2000 have demonstrated a shift in emphasis, by placing a positive duty on public sector employers to promote equality. Positive duties were introduced by the Race Relations (Amendment) Act (RR[A]A) 2000 in relation to race, and extended to disability by the Disability Discrimination Act (DDA) 2005 (from December 2006) and to gender by the Equality Act 2006 (from April 2007).

At the time of writing, there are proposals to extend these duties to all the other strands of discrimination covered by legislation (see Equality Bill below). Whether or not they become law will depend on how quickly the Bill receives Royal Assent, or the outcome of a general election. The law here is presented as at 1 June 2009.

6.2 LEGAL SYSTEM

This chapter provides a brief overview of the English legal system and EU law. Students who need more detailed understanding are referred to further reading at the end of this chapter.

The sources of English employment law are common law (decisions made by judges), legislation (also referred to as Acts of Parliament or Statute law) and European Law. (English law refers to the law of England and Wales although these laws can be [and often are] extended to Scotland and Northern Ireland. Although there are differences in the common law, all the discrimination legislation discussed in this chapter applies in Scotland. There is a separate statutory framework in Northern Ireland.) There are also Statutory Codes of Practice (for example the Code of Practice on Equal Pay 2003), which do not have the full force of law, but can be used as evidence in a court or tribunal.

Bodies involved in the enforcement of employment law include the Advisory Conciliation and Arbitration Service (ACAS) and the Central Arbitration Committee (CAC). Most importantly in relation to equality, there is the Equality and Human Rights Commission (EHRC), established by the Equality Act 2006 and operational from October 2007. The EHRC replaced three existing commissions – the legacy commissions (Equal Opportunities Commission (EOC), Commission for Racial Equality (CRE) and Disability Rights Commission (DRC)) – and took on additional responsibilities in relation to the newer discrimination strands (sexual orientation, religion or belief, age and transgender) as well as human rights.

The broad remit of the EHRC and its extensive enforcement powers have increased expectations. O'Cinneide (2007) comments '... its troubled birth, the pressure of expectation, the ever-increasing complexity of enforcing anti-discrimination legislation and the tensions that lurk within its broad remit present substantial challenges for the new Commission. It will have to be flexible, creative, strategic and tough-minded where required if it is to win credibility and ensure respect for anti-discrimination and human rights values.' It is still early days for the EHRC but it has not been without its critics. The strength of the previous equality commissions lay in their ability to mount strategic litigation campaigns, and all eyes have been on the new commission's litigation strategy. A major part of the EHRC's legal strategy is to use its power to intervene in legal proceedings, and so far, it has used its powers to intervene in cases to great effect (EOR, 2009a).

Employment Tribunals deal with claims arising under employment law. Tribunal cases do not create legally binding judgments and legal aid is not available, although the EHRC may provide help and advice through its helpline. Some lawyers will do pro bono work in employment tribunals, or assistance may also be provided by a trade union where appropriate. There has also been a growth of 'no win, no fee' lawyers, particularly in relation to equal pay claims, whereby lawyers will represent claimants and be paid a proportion of the compensation awarded if the case is successful.

Appeals from employment tribunals are heard in the Employment Appeal Tribunal (EAT), which hears appeals on points of law, but not questions of fact.

The employment tribunal system was set up to process disputes with the minimum amount of legalism, but employment rights have become increasingly complex – none more so than in the area of discrimination – as legislation has grown, largely influenced by EU law. This requires statutory interpretation by the courts and tribunals, and has resulted in tensions between the aims of the tribunal system and the need for assistance from experienced legal representatives in order for cases to succeed.

6.3 PUBLIC POLICY

Issues of public policy play a significant role in the development of employment law. Legislation is informed by the economic and political climate of the day and by the views of society and is therefore quite fluid and, at times, responsive to the organisational actors and pressure groups involved.

At common law, under contracts of employment, the employment relationship is generally weighted in favour of the employer, and UK governments, particularly over the past 40 years, have sought, in various ways, to protect employees from unfair employment practices. However, strategies vary with some governments adopting an interventionist approach while others, such as the Conservative Governments from 1979 to 1997, adopting a strategy of minimum intervention, in line with free-market economic policy.

In relation to discrimination law, much of the driving force for change has come from the EU (see below). However, the Labour Government elected in 1997 has also pursued an agenda of 'family-friendly' policies, resulting in maternity rights that are amongst the best in the European Community, and recognition of the need for flexible working to ensure work–life balance.

6.4 APPROACHES TO DISCRIMINATION LAW – EQUALITY OR DIVERSITY?

The extent to which government will legislate to protect vulnerable members of society from discriminatory treatment is often informed by what governments believe the electorate will tolerate, as illustrated by the history of the UK race relations legislation discussed below (Bindman and Lester, 1972).

6.4.1 Different approaches

States vary in their legislative approaches towards preventing discrimination. The complaints based approach, which concentrates on redressing discrimination against individuals rather than seeking to eradicate social disadvantage, has historically been predominant in most European countries. This anti-discrimination law approach uses the law to redress injustice and inequality and to protect members of particular vulnerable groups in society. However, there has been a move towards legislation which recognizes the need to *promote* equality; for example, by the positive duties upon public bodies to eliminate discrimination and promote equality. This is a relatively new direction for equality law in Great Britain, whereas in Northern Ireland the concept of promoting equality has long been part of discrimination law.

The White Papers leading to the sex discrimination and race relations legislation in Britain in the 1960s and 1970s, detailed below, acknowledged that there was 'active prejudice' operating against disadvantaged groups in society and that discrimination was institutionalized (Ellis, 1997: 15). The White Paper on the Race Relations Act 1976 (RRA), a piece of legislation modeled on the Sex Discrimination Act 1975 (SDA), aimed to 'reduce discrimination' thereby breaking the 'familiar cycle of cumulative disadvantage'. However, that legislation did not really seek to *promote* equality. It has been argued that the White Paper on sex discrimination did not attempt to deal with the social problems facing women (Bamforth, 1996: 49) and the RRA has been criticized for failing to tackle institutionalized discrimination (MacPherson Report, 1999).

It has been suggested that '*anti*' or '*non-discrimination*' approaches are negative while an '*equality*' approach is more wide-ranging and positive (Lustgarten, 1992: 455). It is arguable that anti-discrimination legislation supports an 'equal opportunities' (EO) approach to equality, where an organisation adopts a well-meaning policy, which in theory addresses issues of equality. In reality it often becomes an add-on policy stating the laudable aim of creating equality of opportunity for all but which ignores the fact that in order to achieve equality, the differences between groups and individuals within those groups have to be accommodated.

Weaknesses of the traditional equality approach are discussed in Chapter 5. The EO approach seeks to ensure that individuals will be treated 'equally'. However, the 'diversity' argument is that it is not always appropriate to treat people the same way; for example, why are there still relatively few women in senior management, particularly at Board level? The opportunity to progress to these positions may be the same for women and men, but women may be hampered by career breaks, childcare responsibilities or lack of role models. It is only by addressing these barriers that women will have the opportunity to break through the 'glass ceiling'. A further limitation of the current legislative approach is that it fails to take account of 'multiple discrimination'. A black woman may be treated less favourably than a white woman, but also than a black man. The law currently allows her only to bring two separate claims – for sex discrimination and race discrimination – but neither will be successful, if it is only her sex plus her minority ethnic status that has led to the discrimination (EOR, 2008a).

The effectiveness of any legal measures adopted may be hampered by the individual nature of the system. If a system relies on the courage and resilience of individuals to pursue a claim it is likely to result in some injustice. The US system of class actions permits individuals who have been affected by identical discrimination to be given the same remedy as the person who was successful in a particular case. In Britain each person affected has to bring an individual claim. It has been argued that the US system is more forward-looking and results in a 'cost maximizing' deterrent for American employers as they will have to deal with huge compensation payouts (Lustgarten and Edwards, 1992; MacEwen, 1995; Lacey, 1992). It also has the benefit of applying to a whole disadvantaged group rather than to one individual who receives compensation but leaves the employer free to continue to discriminate against other people in the workforce who are subjected to the same disadvantage. There have been calls for class, or representative, actions to be allowed in UK discrimination law, but the government's Discrimination Law Review (2007) came out against such a move, stating that representative actions 'are often seen as a major factor in developing an undesirable litigation culture.'

6.4.2 Groups protected by law

Debates continue as to who should be covered by anti-discrimination or equality law. Until 1995, the law in Great Britain was narrowly confined to gender and race. Disability discrimination became unlawful in 1995, and transsexual people were protected from discrimination in employment from 1999. Sexual orientation and religion or belief have been grounds for discrimination claims since December 2003, and age discrimination since October 2006. Rubenstein (EOR, 2007a) asks 'What is the next frontier for discrimination law?' and highlights 'three candidates' for future legislation: genetic information, personal appearance and social class. Problems associated with obesity in the workplace have also been highlighted by other commentators (Chamberlain, 2005). Indeed, personal appearance has become the 'next frontier' in parts of US; for example, Washington DC. The Equality Bill presently before Parliament raises 'socio-economic' issues. These will be considered later in 'Future Developments'.

Key learning points

- Public policy considerations play a significant role in the development of employment law. Legislation is influenced by the economic and political climate of the day and by the views of society.
- The role of governments in upholding the rule of law varies as do approaches to anti-discrimination or equality law.
- Anti-discrimination law attempts to use the law to redress injustice and inequality and to protect vulnerable members of particular groups in society. An 'equality' approach is more wide-ranging and positive and includes affirmative action and the use of quotas. Either system may be hampered by its individual nature.
- The anti-discrimination legislation supports an 'EO' culture, but a more proactive approach to the law is needed to encourage a diversity strategy.
- Valuing diversity is not a concept recognized by law and the UK legal framework does not on the whole address societal issues that have led to disadvantage.

6.5 THE ROLE AND IMPACT OF EU LAW ON THE UK

6.5.1 Brief background

The EU law-making process and machinery are somewhat complex and the original European Commission (EC) Treaty has been amended and revised since its inception. For example, the Single European Act 1986, the Treaty on European Union 1993, and the Treaty of Amsterdam 1997, which introduced the competence to legislate on discrimination and the Treaty of Nice 2000, which 'solemnly proclaimed' the Charter of Fundamental Rights, were later adopted in the Lisbon Treaty 2007. The Lisbon Treaty attempted to raise the status of the Charter but has been somewhat controversial and is not yet ratified by all member states with some negotiating opt-outs. The UK has a written guarantee that the charter cannot be used by the European Court of Human Rights to alter British labour law, or other laws that deal with social rights. How effective this opt-out will be is debatable but has not yet been tested.

The EU derives its competence from the Treaties and secondary legislation requires a specific legal Treaty base to ensure its validity. Directives are the most common form of secondary legislation used in the social policy and employment field of EU law; for example, the Equal Treatment Directive 1976, which has since been revised (Equal Treatment Directive 2002/73).

6.5.2 Impact on sex discrimination

Equality of treatment between men and women has had a fairly high profile in the EU. Article 141 EC on equal pay for equal work in the EC Treaty provided the base for the Directive on Equal Pay 1975 and former Article 308 EC was used to enact the Equal Treatment Directive 1976, which introduced the principle of equal treatment relating to access to employment, vocational training, promotion and working conditions and was revised and expanded in 2006. Subsequent European Court of Justice (ECJ) judgments have assisted in elevating the principle of equal treatment as one of the fundamental rights protected by Community law (Nielsen and Szyszczak, 1997: 151). EU law has had a major impact on sex equality law. By 1979 it was apparent that the sex equality legislation needed some assistance to challenge the deep-rooted discriminatory practices. EU law in cases such as *Defrenne* (1971, 1976 and 1978) led the way for further challenges in the ECJ.

Criticism has been levelled at the ECJ for its 'market ideology' approach (Nielsen and Szyszczak, 1997: 209). The court has been seen to take a narrow approach restricted to its economic base, and therefore supporting business, rather than looking at wider social or human rights and although the ECJ recognized the general principle of equality in some early cases, it has had, it was argued, '... *a suffocating effect on the development of the principle of equality*' (Barnard, 1995: 71). Hepple (1997: 142) argues that the Court '... *has not been prepared to treat a breach of the fundamental right to equality as a free-standing basis for legal action by individuals*' and Ellis (1997: 174) has observed that '... *a number of the Court's decisions have failed to tackle the issue with the robustness of former decisions*' and that the Court in recent years, '*seems to have lost sight of the objectives of the legislation and to be operating as a drag on the system*' (Ellis, 1998: 379). For example, although the ECJ was prepared to recognize the rights of transsexual people in 1996 (in *P and S v Cornwall CC* 1996), it subsequently ruled that discrimination on grounds of sexual orientation did not amount to sex discrimination in *Grant v South West Trains* 1998.

However, there has been a shift in emphasis in EU legislation towards greater social policy intervention, resulting in the Employment Framework Directive (Directive 2000/78/EC establishing a general framework for equal treatment in employment and occupation) and the Race Discrimination Directive (Directive 2000/43/EC implementing the principle of equal treatment between persons irrespective of racial or ethnic origin), and this has resulted in the ECJ playing an important role in progressing the new legislation.

6.5.3 Impact on other forms of discrimination

The influence of the EU in areas of equality such as sexual orientation, religion, disability, age and race was less marked until a non-discrimination clause (Article 13) was introduced into the EC Treaty by the Treaty of Amsterdam in 1997. The Race and

Employment Framework Directives have their basis in Article 13, and for the first time the EU directly legislated on discrimination in those areas.

The extension of EU law has had an impact in the UK, but probably not as much as in some other EU states, as the UK already had well-established race and disability laws. However, it did require legislation to prohibit discrimination on grounds of sexual orientation and religion or belief, which came into effect in 2003. Because of an opt-out allowing the UK to delay implementation, age discrimination provisions came into effect later, in October 2006.

The 'new' role of the ECJ in upholding the new rights has been witnessed in recent decisions relating to age discrimination. For example in *Mangold v Helm* (2005), a German law that excluded workers over the age of 52 was ruled to be contrary to the principle of equality on grounds of age, even though the time limit for implementing the directive had not passed. It was described as a *'remarkable decision'* (Barnard, 2006). However, in a later case – the *Heyday* challenge – the ECJ did not condemn outright UK legislation that allows age discrimination; the court did not state that the default retirement age in the UK law was incompatible with the Employment Equality Framework Directive, but stated that such a policy needed to be justified, applying the test laid down in EU law.

The UK government chose to implement most of EU law by way of Regulations, which are introduced by Statutory Instrument relying on delegated power. This meant that the government had power to introduce only those rights set out in the Directives – they could not go beyond that. The Employment Framework Directive is limited in its application, applying only to discrimination in employment (not the provision of goods or services), and the Race Directive contains a definition of 'race' that is narrower than that in existing UK law. This has led to inconsistent and piecemeal legislation where different rights apply to different groups even within the same piece of legislation, which is not conducive to establishing a holistic approach to diversity within organisations. One aim of the Equality Bill is to harmonize the UK legislation and remove inconsistencies (see below).

EU law in this area does not stand still. For example, research commissioned by the EC recently on multiple discrimination was presented in December 2007 (European Commission, 2007) and is still being debated. It has led to a bill, passed in April 2009 by the European Parliament, to extend EU anti-discrimination legislation to areas beyond employment and to introduce specific provisions to deal with multiple discrimination. The draft law is expected to be debated by member states towards the end of 2009 (EOR, 2008b).

Key learning points

- If the UK legislation and EU law clash, EU law takes precedence.
- EU law has historically had a significant impact on British sex discrimination legislation but has now extended its reach to race, disability, sexual orientation, religion or belief and age.
- The ECJ has had a major impact on sex equality law developments but has been criticized for allowing economic rights to take precedence over social rights. However, there has been a shift towards support for social policy, as signalled by the introduction of Article 13, and the ECJ is likely to play an important role in progressing the new discrimination legislation. Already important case law is emerging from the court.

6.6 DISCRIMINATION LEGISLATION IN BRITAIN

Under the common law, an employer is free to enter into an employment contract with whosoever they choose, on whatever terms are agreed. However, discrimination legislation overrides the common law and the terms of the employment contract and provides rights for specified groups of people who are refused employment or who are in other ways disadvantaged by an employer's discriminatory exercise of that right to freedom of contract.

As indicated above, historically the legislative approach has been one of reacting to discrimination rather than promoting equality and the legislation has adopted a complaints based culture requiring individuals to pursue complaints of discrimination rather than imposing any duty on employers to prevent discrimination or promote equality.

There is a raft of legislative provisions, providing a complex framework of individual rights. The main statutes are shown in Table 6.1.

As highlighted in this chapter, the many separate pieces of legislation have resulted in unnecessary complexity and inconsistency in British discrimination law. There have long been calls for a single equality act (Bob Hepple QC (Hon); Lord Lester of Herne Hill QC; Professor Evelyn Ellis; Dinah Rose, barrister; and Rabinder Singh, barrister – Runnymede Trust 1997; Hepple, Coussey, Choudhury 2000; Fredman 2002). The argument for a single overarching framework is now overwhelming and the introduction of the EHRC, which deals with all strands of discrimination, has provided further support for the arguments for an overhaul of the legislation.

At the same time as calling for single equality legislation, the argument has been put forward for a proactive approach to equality, similar to that now applying to the public sector, which would mean requiring all employers to *promote* equality. It has been argued that legislation should focus on prevention not litigation (Spencer and Fredman, 2003; McColgan, 2003). At the time of writing, a single Equality Bill is proceeding through Parliament and, if it becomes statute, will improve the current inconsistencies.

Table 6.1 Main Equality Statutes
Sex Discrimination Act 1975
Race Relations Act 1976
Disability Discrimination Act 1995
Sex Discrimination (Gender Reassignment) Regulations 1999
Race Relations (Amendment) Act 2000
Sex Discrimination Act 1975 (Amendment) Regulations 2003
Race Relations Act 1976 (Amendment) Regulations 2003
Disability Discrimination Act 1995 (Amendment) Regulations 2003
Employment Equality (Religion Or Belief) Regulations 2003
Employment Equality (Sexual Orientation) Regulations 2003
Employment Equality (Age) Regulations 2006

However, the Bill has been criticized for not going 'far enough'. Rubenstein (EOR, 2009b), for example, argues that the 'positive action' provisions in the Bill appear to be unworkable, and the proposed changes to the powers of tribunals regarding making recommendations (see below), are 'toothless'. There have also been calls to use the opportunity of single equality legislation to address conflicting equality rights (Malik, 2009), but these have not been met.

6.6.1 Scope of the legislation

Within UK legislation individuals can claim discrimination on grounds of gender, married or civil partnership status, race, disability, gender reassignment, sexual orientation, religion or belief and age. Outside of this legislative framework, there is no law to prevent an employer from discriminating against someone on any ground they choose; because of, say, their political beliefs, or because they have red hair. The legislation does not require employers to treat employees well, just equally. If an employer treats all employees badly, regardless of sex or race for example, a claim of discrimination will fail, as in the case of *Zafar v Glasgow City Council* 1998 IRLR 36, where the House of Lords found that an employer had treated the employee, Mr Zafar, who is black, as unfavourably as other employees and therefore there was no discrimination.

This section considers in more detail the grounds upon which discrimination is prohibited. The legislation provides very specific definitions of the grounds upon which a claim can be made, and claimants can fall at the first hurdle and lose their case on what appears a very technical legalistic detail. Thus, it becomes about who can win a legal argument, rather than providing support for an inclusive, holistic approach which is associated with diversity.

6.6.2 Sex discrimination

The SDA covers discrimination against women (or men, s.2) and married persons (s.3) in all aspects of employment (recruitment, terms and conditions, access to training and promotion, dismissal or any other detriment – s.6) and against transsexual people, in relation only to recruitment, promotion and training (s.2A).

Discrimination in relation to remuneration is covered by the Equal Pay Act 1970 (as amended) which came into force in December 1975. It is beyond the scope of this chapter to consider equal pay legislation in detail but it is worth noting that it is one of the most controversial areas of discrimination law. It has been the fastest-growing area in terms of the number of claims submitted each year, with equal pay claims outnumbering for the first time unfair dismissal claims, in the most recent Annual Report from the Tribunal Service (2008). Despite the large number of claims, fuelled by public sector disputes that involve many thousands of claimants (EOR, 2008c), many problems remain with this legislation and although some concerns are addressed by the Equality Bill, nothing short of a complete overhaul will help overcome the issues.

6.6.3 Race discrimination

The RRA applies to discrimination on 'racial grounds', defined in s.3 of the Act as grounds of 'colour, race, nationality or ethnic or national origins'. This definition has not been without its problems, particularly in relation to the meaning of 'ethnic origin'. The leading case is *Mandla v Dowell Lee* (1983), where the House of Lords decided that 'ethnic origin' was wider than 'racial origin' and that it could cover religious and cultural differences. The test is whether the group constitutes a separate and distinct community by virtue of characteristics, which are commonly associated with racial origin. Applying this test, it has been possible to include some religious groups within the definition, such as Sikhs, whereas others have been excluded. For example, in *J H Walker Ltd v Hussain* (1996) it was held that Muslims could not be treated as an ethnic group although the decision in *Khanum v IBC Vehicles* (1998) adopted a different approach. In *Dawkins v Department of the Environment* (1993) it was held that Rastafarians did not constitute a racial group, as they were not a distinct group within the African-Caribbean community.

6.6.4 Disability discrimination

One of the more controversial areas of the DDA is the definition of disability. Only applicants who can show that they have a disability *within the definition of the Act* can claim unlawful discrimination. What the Act fails to do is to take account of the 'social model' of disability, adopting instead a 'medical' model of disability, contrary to what most disability rights activists would have preferred. The social model focuses attention on how disabled people are treated. For example, if all buildings had entrance ramps, wheelchair users would not be disabled from gaining access to them.

Disability is defined in the DDA (s.1) as 'a physical or mental impairment, which has a substantial and long-term adverse effect on [the person's] ability to carry out normal day-to-day activities'. Many cases at employment tribunal have centred on whether or not the complainant does in fact have a disability within the meaning of the Act. Examples of conditions that have been held to amount to a disability include epilepsy, back injury, cerebral palsy, diabetes, migraines, dyslexia and chronic fatigue syndrome. Although there is no definitive list of what falls within the statute, certain conditions are excluded (such as drug addiction) and certain progressive conditions are expressly included, such as HIV or cancer, following amendments made by the DDA 2005. It made further amendments, making it easier for people with mental illness to show that they were disabled within the meaning of the Act, by removing the requirement that a condition had to be 'clinically well-recognized'. The 2003 Regulations, amending the 1995 version, which implemented the EU Directive, introduced the concept of 'disability-related' discrimination, which has given rise to problems of interpretation (see below).

A problem facing the tribunals when deciding if a claimant falls within the definition of disability is that they are not medically qualified, and it is not unusual for them to be faced with conflicting medical evidence from experts. The claimant's case can fail at this stage if the employer can produce a more compelling medical opinion. Another point where the disability provisions differ from other jurisdictions is that it applies only to those who are disabled and not to non-disabled people.

6.6.5 Discrimination on grounds of sexual orientation

The main legislation on sexual orientation is the Employment Equality (Sexual Orientation) Regulations 2003, which came into force on 1 December 2003. 'Sexual orientation' is defined in the Regulations to mean 'an orientation towards (a) persons of the same sex; (b) person of the opposite sex; or (c) persons of the same sex and of the opposite sex.' The definition applies to a person's 'orientation', but it is not clear how it will apply to a person's sexual behaviour or practices. It is still open to question whether or not the regulations will cover an employer who says, for example, that they are willing to employ gay men, so long as they do not look obviously gay as it may upset customers. However, the Regulations also include discrimination based on perceived sexual orientation. In other words, if it is wrongly assumed that someone is gay and they are treated less favourably as a result, the person discriminated against can bring a claim and there is no requirement for that person to disclose their sexuality at the hearing. Furthermore, recent case law has confirmed that harassment of an employee by suggesting that the employee is gay, when it is known that they are not, can amount to sexual orientation discrimination (*English v Thomas Sanderson Blinds Ltd* [2008] IRLR 342).

6.6.6 Discrimination on grounds of religion or belief

The main legislation on religion or belief is the Employment Equality (Religion or Belief) Regulations 2003, which came into force on 2 December 2003 and were amended by the Equality Act 2006. Religion is defined as 'any religion' and belief means 'any religious or, philosophical belief'. Thus, 'any religion' means the law will cover fringe religions and membership of cults. Also, 'religious belief' is likely to cover manifestations of a person's belief, i.e. the practice of their belief (unlike the sexual orientation provisions which do not specifically cover 'behaviour' relating to a person's sexual orientation).

The reference to 'philosophical belief' is not intended to cover political beliefs, and following the 2006 amendments, the definition now expressly includes 'lack of religion' or 'lack of belief'. It also refers to a lack of a 'particular' religion or belief, so would apply where a claimant is discriminated against because they do not share an employer's religion.

6.6.7 Age

The most recent strand of discrimination added to the legislation is that of age. The Employment Equality (Age) Regulations 2006 prohibit discrimination against people of any age, the comparison being between 'age groups'. It prohibits direct and indirect discrimination, as most other strands of discrimination, but with a crucial difference – both direct and indirect age discrimination are capable of objective justification. If an age barrier is a proportionate means of achieving a legitimate aim, it will be lawful. Indeed, the Government is hoping to prove that the exception to the law enshrined in the legislation – the default retirement age, whereby dismissal by reason of retirement at age 65 is lawful – is justifiable (Heyday, 2009).

6.6.8 Types of discrimination – direct, indirect, victimisation and harassment

The two main forms of discrimination are direct and indirect. These concepts are found in the legislation relating to all strands of discrimination, although the DDA is significantly different. There are some distinguishing features in relation to each of the strands and these are highlighted below where applicable.

6.6.8.1 *Direct discrimination*

Where a person from one group is treated less favourably than people not in that group (s.1[1][a], s.3[1][a] and s.2A SDA; s.1[1][a] RRA; Clause 3[1] RoB Regs; Clause 3[1] SO Regs; and Clause 3[1] Age Regs). This is the most blatant form of discrimination. For example, where an employer stated that it would not, 'take on a coloured girl when English girls are available', that was held to be direct discrimination (*Owen & Briggs v James* 1982). Similarly, where a woman is refused employment simply because she is female, she suffers direct discrimination.

Given the length of time discrimination legislation has been in place, such blatant discrimination is now rare, though not unknown, in the tribunals. However, the majority of cases reaching tribunal involve direct discrimination. It may be a case of a woman persistently being overlooked for promotion, where there is no explanation for such treatment other than her sex.

Another example of direct discrimination is where an employer uses gender-based criterion in their employment practice. The tribunals will apply a 'but for' test – 'but for' the sex of the complainant they would be treated differently. For example, in the House of Lords' decision in *James v Eastleigh Borough Council* (1990), where a Local Authority allowed free admission to a swimming pool for people of state pensionable age (60 for women and 65 for men), it was found to be discriminatory as Mrs James was admitted free whereas Mr James, who was the same age, had to pay. 'But for' his sex, Mr James would have been admitted free also. Although this example relates to the provision of services, the test is applied also to employment cases.

Discrimination on grounds of sexual orientation and religion or belief raises different issues from the sex and race provisions. Unlike sex and race, sexual orientation and religion are not visible. Thus, the Regulations will apply not only to *actual* sexual orientation or beliefs, but also to a person's *perception* of another's sexual orientation, or religion or belief.

The DDA has a different definition of direct discrimination. As well as less favourable treatment on grounds of disability, following amendments by the DDA (Amendment) Regulations 2003, disability discrimination has an additional form of direct discrimination – disability-related discrimination. This has been fraught with difficulties, which hopefully will be resolved if the Equality Bill becomes law. The problem revolves around the identification of a comparator for the purposes of deciding if there has been less favourable treatment for a reason related to disability. This has been considered by the ECJ in *London Borough of Lewisham v Malcolm* (2008) IRLR 700, where the House of Lords' interpretation undermines the concept of disability-related discrimination and renders it of negligible use in employment cases.

An area where the law has developed under this head, and where the ECJ has potentially created greater rights than the UK law apparently did, is 'associative discrimination'.

In *Coleman v Attridge Law* (2008) IRLR 722, the ECJ ruled that the Employment Framework Directive's prohibition of direct discrimination 'is not limited only to people who are themselves disabled. Where an employer treats an employee who is not himself disabled less favourably than another employee is, has been or would be treated in a comparable situation, and it is established that the less favourable treatment of that employee is based on the disability of his child, whose care is provided primarily by that employee, such treatment is contrary to the prohibition of direct discrimination laid down by Art. 2(2)(a).'

The employment tribunal has since decided in favour of the claimant, stating that UK law can be interpreted in such a way as to comply with the EU Directive. However, this has been appealed to the EAT. The impact of *Coleman* could be far reaching as discrimination by association could then be extended to other grounds such as caring for elderly relatives under age discrimination legislation.

Age discrimination raises its own issues. Unlike the other jurisdictions, direct age discrimination is capable of justification. If an employer can show that age discriminatory treatment (such as dismissing on grounds of retirement at, say, age 60) is a proportionate means of achieving a legitimate aim, then the discrimination will be lawful.

6.6.8.2 *Indirect discrimination*

This occurs where an apparently neutral employment practice has a disproportionately disadvantageous effect upon a particular group. Indirect discrimination covers employment practices that unintentionally have a discriminatory effect – although the legislation has been criticized for not eradicating institutionalized racism. There are two main definitions of indirect discrimination. However, the most recent and commonly used is where: a person (A) applies to another (B) a 'provision, criterion or practice' which puts people in the same group as B (for example, gay men) at a particular disadvantage (compared to others who do not fall within the same group as B, for example, heterosexual men), where B is put at that disadvantage and A cannot show that the provision, criterion or practice is 'a proportionate means of achieving a legitimate aim'. This definition follows the EU model, and is found in parts of the RRA (depending on which part of the definition of race is being used), the SDA in relation to employment and vocational training; and the newer Regulations applying to sexual orientation, religion or belief and age. The reason for the different definitions is due to the different ways in which the European Directives have been implemented into UK law.

Because of the different definitions, particularly within the RRA, different provisions apply in relation to the application of the various provisions. For example, the defence available differs under the different definitions. Clearly there are problems of inconsistency. Under the Equality Bill as currently drafted, the same definition of indirect discrimination would apply to all strands.

The DDA does not currently include indirect discrimination in its definition of discrimination, but this would change under the Equality Bill. The DDA places a duty on employers to make reasonable adjustments in relation to the arrangements they make for disabled people. Section 6 refers to '*arrangements*' or '*any physical feature of premises*' which place a disabled person at a '*substantial disadvantage*'. In that case, there is a duty on an employer to '*take such steps as it is reasonable, in all the circumstances of the case*' in order to prevent the arrangements or feature from having that effect. Unlike the other Acts, the DDA puts a positive obligation upon employers to take measures to prevent the discriminatory effect. The employer's duty is to do what is reasonable, with the tribunal deciding what is reasonable in all the circumstances.

Section 6(3) gives examples of steps, which an employer may have to take. These include making adjustments to premises, allocating some of the disabled person's duties to another person, transferring them to fill an existing vacancy, altering their working hours, acquiring or modifying equipment and modifying instructions or reference manuals. In determining whether a step is reasonable, s.6(4) requires a number of issues to be taken into account, including how effective the relevant step would be, the financial costs and the employer's financial and other resources. The EAT have taken a fairly wide view of the extent of this duty. In *London Borough of Hillingdon v Morgan 1999* the EAT made it clear that the Code of Practice had to be referred to when deciding what is reasonable. In that case, it was decided that the employer had failed to comply with the duty to make adjustments when they did not allow an employee who had become disabled to work from home temporarily in order to assist her transition back into full-time employment.

Tribunals will not accept an explanation from employers that they could not accommodate the person's disability – the employer must provide evidence of the steps that they had taken. Therefore employers are subject to an 'anticipatory duty' and this is a good example of how legislation can support the diversity argument. It requires employers to take account of the individual circumstances of employees or applicants. It remains fairly limited in its application though as employees may not wish to disclose their disability, so employers cannot reasonably be expected to take it into account. However, as soon as an employer knows, or should reasonably know, of a disability, it has a duty to make reasonable adjustments. Where an employer refuses to take reasonable steps the remedy in most cases remains compensation for the claimant, although, an order that the employer make the necessary arrangements may provide a more effective remedy.

The Equality Bill 2009 provides a new definition of indirect discrimination, applying it to disability discrimination for the first time. It attempts to address the House of Lords judgment in *London Borough of Lewisham v Malcom* (2008), discussed above. However, this is somewhat controversial, and there is concern that the DDA could be even more problematic than it is currently (Feinstein and Davies, 2009).

6.6.8.3 *Victimisation*

This applies to all strands of discrimination. It arises where an employee is treated less favourably because they have alleged discrimination, brought proceedings or given evidence relating to a discrimination claim. Examples include being subjected to disciplinary action, being denied promotion and being dismissed.

6.6.8.4 *Harassment*

This is a form of discrimination, which now has a free-standing definition. Until amendments to the law in 2003, employees claiming harassment had to rely upon the scope of direct discrimination to bring their claim within the SDA, RRA or DDA. There are numerous cases of sexual and racial harassment and, to a lesser extent, harassment on grounds of disability.

Harassment is defined as, 'unwanted conduct which has the purpose or effect of (a) violating that other person's dignity or (b) creating an intimidating, hostile, degrading, humiliating or offensive environment for him. Conduct shall be regarded as having the effect specified in paragraph (a) or (b) only if having regard to all the circumstances, including in particular the perception of that other person, it should reasonably be considered as having that effect'.

6.6.9 **Intention or motivation**

The intention and motive of a person who discriminates have been discussed in a number of cases, and it is clear that it is not relevant that an employer had no desire to discriminate or did so for the best of motives. The tribunal will look at the effect of the discriminatory act. A good example of this is the *James* case on direct discrimination referred to above. The council in that case argued that their concessionary rates were for the benefit of members of the community who were less well off. The House of Lords found that although the motive for the council's policy was to be applauded, the effect was discrimination and the motive was irrelevant.

The same principle also applies to indirect discrimination. This must be so, if the issue of institutional discrimination is to be tackled at all by the legislation. Employers may apply employment policies, which unwittingly have the effect of discriminating against a particular group. The law would be undermined if it was found that there was no discrimination in those cases simply because the employer had no intention to discriminate. This may seem harsh on employers but the repercussions for the employer may be mitigated in the tribunal's decision as to the amount of compensation to be paid by the employer to the complainant.

6.6.10 **Is the discrimination unlawful?**

If a person establishes that they have been discriminated against, either directly or indirectly, they must then go on to show that the discrimination is 'unlawful'. This means showing that the act of the employer falls within the situations specified in the legislation. Basically, it is unlawful to discriminate in all aspects of the employment relationship: from recruitment and selection to dismissal. Unlike most other employment statutes, the discrimination legislation applies not just to employees but also to job applicants. It is also unlawful to discriminate in the course of employment, for example, in promotion and training, and in relation to dismissal or by subjecting the applicant to 'any other detriment'. The only difference between the Acts is that the SDA does not apply to discrimination in pay – that is covered by the Equal Pay Act.

6.6.11 **When is discrimination lawful?**

There are exceptions to the rules. Again, there are differences in definitions following the implementation of the Race and Employment Framework Directives. In relation to sex, race, sexual orientation, religion or belief and age there are circumstances in which it is lawful to discriminate. The main definition is where there are 'genuine occupational requirements' (GORs) – it is lawful to discriminate where 'having regard to the nature of the employment or the context in which it is carried out' being of a particular group 'is a genuine and determining occupational requirement' and either a person cannot meet that requirement or, more controversially, the employer is not satisfied (where it is reasonable for them to do so) that the person meets it – in other words, it allows an employer to establish a defence on a reasonable perception about a person's ability to meet a requirement. This is open to challenge as regressive, as it is narrower than the old definition.

Another controversial area is the scope of this defence in relation to religion or belief and sexual orientation. The Religion or Belief Regulations contain a two-pronged defence. First, the general defence which applies to any organisation where religion or belief is a 'genuine and determining requirement'. Secondly, there is an exception which applies only to 'ethos based' organisations. In that case the GOR applies where being of a particular religion or belief is a genuine occupational requirement and, having regard to the ethos of an organisation which has an ethos based on religion or belief, a person does not meet the requirement, or the employer believes that they do not meet the requirement. In this case, the GOR is not a 'determining' factor as in the other definitions and so is broader than in the other circumstances. For example, it might permit an employer with a Roman Catholic ethos to reject an applicant who was divorced on the basis of a reasonable belief that they were not Catholic, even though the individual concerned might continue to define himself/herself as a Catholic.

The Sexual Orientation Regulations have similar provisions on GORs. Again, there are two sets of circumstances. First, there is the general GOR as set out above. Secondly, there is an additional exclusion 'for the purposes of an organized religion'. This applies where an organisation based on organized religion excludes individuals on the basis of sexual orientation, to comply with the doctrines of the religion or to avoid conflicting with the strongly held convictions of a significant number of the religion's followers. This was explained by the government in the House of Lords debate on the Regulations (Hansard, 17 June 2003), where it was stated 'When drafting reg. 7(3), we had in mind a very narrow range of employment: ministers of religion, plus a small number of posts outside the clergy, including those who exist to promote and represent religion...It is quite clear that reg. 7(3) does not apply to all jobs in a particular type of organisation. On the contrary, employers must be prepared to justify any requirement related to sexual orientation on a case-by-case basis. The rule only applies to employment which is for the purposes of "organized religion", not religious organisations. There is a clear distinction in meaning between the two. A religious organisation could be any organisation with an ethos based on religion or belief. However, employment for the purposes of an organized religion clearly means a job, such as a minister of religion, involving work for a church, synagogue or mosque.'

6.6.11.1 *Positive action and positive discrimination*

Positive action – encouraging people from particular groups to apply for jobs – is permitted where a particular group is under-represented in an organisation or at certain levels within the organisation. The provision is found in relation to all the strands of discrimination. It allows, for example, an employer to run management training programmes restricted to women employees in order to address the gender imbalance at senior levels. These are little used provisions. However, they do provide an organisation which seeks to promote diversity to lawfully take action in favour of under-represented groups. Although these provisions do not go so far as *promoting* diversity, they are certainly helpful where an organisation is seeking to address the barriers to employment or promotion for particular groups of employees.

There is generally support for the idea of positive action or duties, where obligations are placed upon employers to take a proactive stance to eliminate discrimination at the workplace. Positive or reverse discrimination, on the other hand, is a feature of the radical approach discussed in Chapter 5 and is more controversial. It involves giving preferential treatment to a member of a disadvantaged group in order to redress imbalance in representation of the group in the workplace.

The issues have been brought sharply into focus in the EU in recent years. Positive discrimination has been given limited acceptance within the EU, as demonstrated by the ECJ's decision in *Hellmut Marschall* 1998, where it was held that positive sex discrimination can be lawful if 'an objective assessment of each individual candidate, irrespective of sex of the candidate in question, is assured and that, accordingly, promotion of a male candidate is not excluded from the outset'. Furthermore, the EU Treaty amendment in Article 141 EC now allows some forms of positive discrimination (reflected in the subsequent Race and Employment Framework Directives), which has been endorsed by the ECJ in cases such as *Lommers* 2002 where the ECJ upheld a policy in a Dutch civil service department which offers subsidised childcare places only to female employees. The ECJ said that the scheme does not contravene EU law so long as it is also available on the same conditions to men who are single parents.

The government took advantage of these EU developments to introduce the Sex Discrimination (Election Candidates) Act 2002, which allows political parties to select women-only short lists. Although the government has amended race, disability and sex discrimination legislation to include positive duties as discussed above, any form of positive discrimination has historically been avoided. It is therefore unlawful in the UK, although a House of Lords ruling in *Archbold v Fife Council* (2004) pronounced that the duty to make reasonable adjustments may require an employer to treat a disabled person more favourably in order to counteract the disadvantage presented by the disability.

A bold move in the Equality Bill 2009 will allow a form of positive discrimination in a tie-break situation. Referred to as positive action measures, it would allow discrimination in favour of a candidate from an under-represented group where applicants are equally qualified.

6.6.11.2 *Proving discrimination*

Discrimination is notoriously difficult to prove. This was problematic for claimants when the burden of proving discrimination was placed upon them. However, changes to the burden of proof have strengthened the tribunal's ability to infer discrimination. Where a claimant has presented facts from which a tribunal could, in the absence of any other explanation, conclude that there has been discrimination, the burden of proof will shift to the employer, who will have to prove there has been no discrimination. Guidance in this area has been provided in cases including *Barton v Investec* (2003) and *Igen Ltd v Wong* (2005), with the latter setting out 13 points of guidance.

There is also a statutory questionnaire procedure, whereby complainants have a right to ask a number of questions of the employer/ex-employer, which can assist potential claimants to gather evidence. Employers are not obliged to answer the questionnaire but adverse inferences can be drawn if they fail to do so.

6.6.12 Remedies

The main remedy for unlawful discrimination, as may be expected with a complaints based system, is compensation for the individual who successfully claims discrimination. There are two other sanctions available to an employment tribunal: a declaration of the parties' rights in the matter and a recommendation that the employer takes action to reduce or obviate the discriminatory treatment of the claimant. Neither of these remedies is particularly effective in preventing discrimination, as a declaration simply provides vindication for the applicant, and tribunals do not have the power to enforce their recommendations. They only have the power to award additional compensation. As far as the individual is concerned monetary compensation is the best they can hope for. However, the amount of compensation that a successful claimant can expect to be paid is fairly low – the median award in 2008 was £9,845 (see Table 6.2). Compensation awards in discrimination cases differ from other areas, such as unfair dismissal, in that there is no statutory maximum in discrimination cases. So employers need to be aware that in some cases tribunals have awarded extremely high amounts; for example, in *Bower v Schroeder Securities Ltd* (2002) compensation of £1.4 million was awarded, and a recent race discrimination case saw an award of almost £3 million, although that amount is to be reassessed following a successful EAT appeal (*Chagger v Abbey National Building Society*). Although the amount of compensation in the vast majority of cases will not necessarily act as a deterrent to employers (and thus still cannot be seen as 'eradicating' discrimination), the high-profile cases where huge amounts have been awarded may well make some organisations reconsider their equality/diversity policies.

Discrimination compensation awards also differ from other areas in that it can include an amount for injury to feelings. Although the average and median awards under this head are not enormous, the assessment of the amount of hurt is necessarily subjective and the amounts awarded by tribunals are often inconsistent, despite

Table 6.2 Average and Median Compensation Awards in 2008		
	Average	**Median**
Age discrimination	£15,080	£4,503
Disability discrimination	£21,339	£8,000
Race discrimination	£18,200	£6,325
Religious discrimination	£8,248	£5,750
Sex discrimination	£13,312	£9,109
Sexual orientation discrimination	£33,724	£36,364
Combined jurisdiction	£37,655	£26,014
All discrimination awards	£17,099	£9,845

Source: EOR (2009b).

guidance from the Court of Appeal in the case of *Vento v Chief Constable of West Yorkshire Police* (2003).

6.6.12.1 *Vicarious liability*

Employers will be liable for discriminatory actions, and the resulting compensation, where the acts are carried out '*in the course of employment*' by fellow employees (see *Jones v Tower Boot Co Ltd [1997]*).

Activity 6.1

Table 6.2 shows figures relating to recent compensation awards. Examine the figures and identify where the highest awards are being made.

Questions

1. Discuss the possible influences on the amount of compensation being awarded.
2. Look at the average and median awards in Table 6.2 and consider what these show about the amount of award an individual could expect to get.
3. To what extent does the prospect of paying high levels of compensation influence employers' behaviour?
4. How do the levels of compensation shown support the legal argument for diversity?

6.7 PUBLIC SECTOR EQUALITY DUTIES

The introduction of public sector duties was a major change in direction, as organisations covered by these duties are required to eliminate unlawful discrimination and promote equality of opportunity. The EHRC is responsible for enforcement and can take legal action against public sector organisations that have not complied with the duties.

The duty introduced into the race discrimination legislation in 2000 and extended to disability in December 2006 and sex in April 2007 will be extended to the other strands via the Equality Bill 2009. All strands are required to comply with the general duty, and then specific duties are outlined for each strand. Codes of Practice accompany the law and recommend a number of key requirements including mainstreaming of the duty into such functions as business plans and budgets, for example, to enable the legislation. In effect, the duties require a change in culture which inevitably takes time to implement. Both the CRE and DRC, which had responsibility for enforcing the legislation prior to the establishment of the EHRC, published reports naming and shaming organisations failing to produce equality schemes or comply with their legal duty.

It is argued that surveys 'show that organisations can become too focused on process rather than outcomes' and that 'organisations can view the publishing of their equality scheme as the completion of the legal requirement, rather than the starting point' (EOR, 2007b). Research carried out in 2007 by Schneider Ross, diversity consultants, presents a more encouraging view. It is argued that the duty is resulting in a greater systematic approach to the equality agenda and that the existence of the race equality duty for a number of years has assisted the understanding of the duty. The research involved 113 organisations with 44% choosing to produce a single equality scheme across all strands or adopt a combined approach, largely for practical reasons such as avoiding duplication and reducing costs. An important factor in the success of schemes was deemed to be commitment at a senior level and that the role has to be 'strategic and influential' not merely focusing on operational matters.

6.7.1 **Impact of the law**

What does all this mean in practice for employers? As a legal driver for the promotion of equality and diversity there are a number of issues. First, employer liability – employers will incur the financial costs of discrimination by their employees. As we saw above, this can be substantial so it makes sense for employers to have policies in place that will avoid legal action against them. Secondly, if an employer does have to defend a claim in legal proceedings, the employment tribunal will be looking not just for the employer to have policies in place, but evidence that those policies are being properly implemented. In order to avoid complaints of unlawful discrimination and possible high levels of compensation awarded against them, employers need to adopt employment policies and practices which promote and support diversity within their workforce. Generally there is no formal requirement to review employment practice but employers clearly need to consider carefully the effect of their employment policies to ensure that they are not discriminatory.

The requirement now upon public sector organisations to promote race, disability and sex equality means that it is becoming more important for employers to adopt policies which are proactive rather than reactive. Although the public sector equality duties apply directly to specified public bodies, they have an impact on private sector organisations that provide public services. These too need to comply with the duty to promote equality and eliminate discrimination. Procurement policies are another area where the public sector requirements have an impact on the private sector. For example, Transport for London is using its multi-million pounds contracts to persuade contractors to adopt equality and diversity amongst their workforce by requiring contractors to demonstrate their commitment through equality and diversity schemes (EOR, 2009d).

Key learning points

- Legislation in Great Britain covers gender, married or civil partnership status, race, disability, gender reassignment, sexual orientation, religion or belief and age.
- The law recognizes direct (blatant) and indirect (more subtle and institutionalized) discrimination, as well as victimisation and harassment. The DDA goes further and requires employers to make reasonable adjustments to accommodate disability and remove disadvantages to a disabled person.

- Intention and motive are not relevant in cases of discrimination. The tribunal will look at the effect of the discriminatory act.
- Remedies are confined to redress for individuals with no real sanctions against employers. Class actions, such as apply in the US, appear to be effective but there is no precedent for this in Britain.
- The public sector is under a duty to promote equality and eliminate discrimination on grounds of race, disability and sex, with the prospect of this being extended to all strands of discrimination.

6.8 FUTURE DEVELOPMENTS

6.8.1 Equality bill

A major development is the introduction of the Equality Bill, which if it becomes statute means the first single Equality Act in UK law. Many commentators and lobby groups have welcomed the Bill, but it does have shortcomings, and many see it as a missed opportunity to sort out some of the pressing problems with current legislation. One key area is equal pay legislation.

Commentators have long argued for new strategies to break down the structures of discrimination in employment and promote equality (Hepple et al., 2000). Fredman (2002) called for the promotion of EO as a function of public authorities. McColgan (2003) argued that radical reform of the law was needed, in particular 'a more aggressive model of positive action to address entrenched inequalities'. The Government's Discrimination Law Review 2007 and the proposed Single Equality Act moves in this direction with its proposals for positive action measures and the extension of public sector duties. The main provisions of the Bill as on 1 June 2009 are set out in Table 6.3.

6.8.2 Constitutional rights

A number of recent commentators (Bamforth et al., 2008) have posed the question about 'constitutionalising' discrimination law, arguing that it could be seen as a 'constitutional commitment which happens in practice to have a particular impact on the employment relationship'. An exclusively constitutional approach which excluded the private employment relationship would of course be problematic but it is argued that the expansion of discrimination law beyond employment matters and the social injustice the law is seeking to address requires a different approach. Bamforth et al. also argue that constitutional aspects are raised by the potential clash of rights granted by different strands of discrimination law.

The expansion of discrimination law to cover a number of strands (defined as nine in the Equality Bill 2009) has led to 'equality conflicts' such as that witnessed in the case of *London Borough of Islington v Ladele* and others. Obviously it is difficult to eradicate equality conflicts. Whether they can be tackled at a general level by having a non-negotiable floor of human rights standards with equality law directly related to constitutional and human rights law by way of a purpose clause in the Single Equality Act (Malik, 2009) is debatable.

Table 6.3 Equality Bill 2009 – Main Provisions

- New definitions of direct and indirect discrimination

- 'Protected characteristics' – the new name for the discrimination strands and the means of bringing together all the jurisdictions into one piece of legislation

- General principles that apply to all the protected characteristics

- Specific rules that apply to particular characteristics; for example, disability discrimination is still capable of being justified

- Extends the definition to cover associative discrimination

- A free-standing, updated, definition of harassment that applied to all the protected characteristics

- Wider powers for tribunals to make recommendations

- Positive action measures in a tie-break situation in recruitment or promotion

- A single public sector equality duty taking the place of the three existing statutory duties and also covering religion or belief, sexual orientation and age. Public authorities will be required to have 'due regard to' the need to eliminate unlawful discrimination, advance equality of opportunity and foster good relations

- Regulations to impose duties on a public authority in connection with its public procurement functions.

- Provisions to allow for 'dual discrimination' claims

6.8.3 Promoting equality

The proposed extension of public sector duties to other strands has the potential to change the whole approach to discrimination legislation, to one of equality legislation. However, the government and EHRC have an important role to play in enforcing the duty and there seems to be little pressure so far on employers to comply. The legacy commissions had started to take action. The CRE warned in its final report, before its remit was transferred to the EHRC, that the EHRC will need the full support of government to use the range of powers at its disposal. The CRE (2007) report asserted that its work in this area was not well supported by government as when evidence of non-compliance was found there was an attempt to prevent the CRE from taking action, preferring instead to smooth things over rather than tackle the problems at hand. It pointed out that public authorities had been subject to the duties since 2000 yet a sizeable number had not complied, including 15 government departments. The DRC also named and shamed organisations failing to engage with the duty. Although the Schneider Ross (2007) research report paints a more encouraging picture as discussed above, the challenges of enforcing the duty across all strands will no doubt test the EHRC for years to come.

6.8.4 Positive discrimination

The concept of affirmative action originated in the US in the 1960s and includes positive steps to increase the representation of under-represented groups. Dupper (2006) identifies 'weak' affirmative action and 'strong' affirmative action. 'Weak' affirmative action is classified as positive action measures such as recruiting via targeted minority media and special training courses (such as that allowed in our system at present) whereas 'strong' affirmative action includes positive discrimination measures which give preferential treatment to applicants from under-represented groups. As indicated above, it is the latter which is controversial.

It has long been argued that only by favouring disadvantaged groups can true equality be achieved. Parekh (1992) argued that in Britain the policy is being increasingly used in practice. On the other hand, Pitt (1992) argued that the SDA and RRA have not had the desired effect of eliminating discrimination but reverse discrimination is a violation of the equality principle. She concluded though that perhaps public bodies should take the lead in positive action programmes and allow 'limited', closely monitored reverse/positive discrimination programmes. UK governments have traditionally shied away from radical positive discrimination measures, but the Equality Bill 2009 is set to test the legislators' nerve for this form of legislative intervention. When the Bill was introduced by Harriet Harman in Parliament, she was confronted with cries of 'outrageous' and 'disgusting' by Conservative backbenchers as there are fears that some groups will be 'more equal' than others. The proposals, allowing employers to choose a candidate from an under-represented group where the applicants are equally appointable, will have the potential to result in a more representative diverse workforce. There is a view that employers could be discouraged from 'taking the risk of using it' and that due to drafting problems in the Bill the provisions on positive action measures 'look unworkable' (EOR, 2009e).

In any event, it is argued that positive discrimination measures can be successful only in the short term. Recent experience in the US has demonstrated that where affirmative action programmes include positive or affirmative action, or discrimination, this can eventually lead to a backlash. Although the US Supreme Court ruled in 2003 that affirmative action is permitted, the court narrowed its application. The United Nations Human Rights Committee (UNHRC) and the International Labour Organisation (ILO) seem to view it as a temporary measure. The UNHRC states that 'such action may involve granting for a time to the part of the population concerned certain preferential treatment' and the ILO defines it as '...a coherent package of measures of a temporary character aimed specifically at correcting the position of members of a target group'. Arguably, positive discrimination, or the radical approach to equality, can be used only to kick-start a process to redress past inequalities and a long-term solution would be a diversity approach.

Key learning points

- New strategies are required to break down the structures of discrimination in employment. The law should take a more active involvement in promoting equality.
- Opinions are divided as to the merits or otherwise of positive discrimination in employment. Positive discrimination is outlawed in the UK but plans to allow positive discrimination in tie-break situations are included in the Equality Bill 2009.

Activity 6.2

XYZ is a public body employing 3000 staff. The following issues arise:

1. A is an Asian man who works in the customer service department. He has worked for the organisation for 7 years, and is very good at his job. His performance assessment has been outstanding. However, he has been turned down for promotion three times.

   The organisation employs 10% black and minority ethnic staff – a fair representation of the community in the area. However, further research would reveal that almost all the black and minority ethnic staff is on the lower grades and the majority of Asian staff are aged over 40.

2. B is a woman, and manager of a large department. While on maternity leave she made a request to work shorter hours on her return. Her request was turned down, and she has consequently decided not to return.

   Refusing such requests is in fact normal practice within the organisation, and research would show that only 25% of women return to their jobs after maternity leave, resulting in huge recruitment and training costs.

3. C is a gay man who works in the technical support service, in a job where there are skill shortages. He is competent at his job, but has asked for a transfer to another department. He has told his manager that he can no longer tolerate the taunts from colleagues about his sexuality. This has been happening for some time, but his manager, a devout catholic, has not taken his complaints seriously.

4. D is a disabled woman. She has a hearing impairment. She works as a clerk in the supply department and until recently her job has involved mainly paperwork. However, due to a restructuring and a change in the way the work is done, clerks in the department are now expected to spend much more time on the phone to suppliers. Due to her hearing impairment, D cannot use the phones. She has been told that as she cannot do that part of the job, she will be found alternative employment within the organisation. However, there are no vacancies at the moment and she has been told that if no suitable vacancies arise in the next month, her employment will be terminated.

5. E, a devout Muslim, was suspended recently from her post as a diversity trainer for wearing a niqab (a veil which covered her face). She has worked in the organisation for 2 months and her employer originally allowed her to wear the veil. However, following a number of workshop observations she was asked to remove it as it was claimed that verbal and non-verbal communication including facial expressions and eye contact was vital for the job.

   Other colleagues are permitted to wear religious symbols such as a crucifix and other Muslim women wear the headscarf but not the veil.

6. F recently applied to become an inspector in one of the organisation's laboratories but was not selected due to the fact that he was over the age of 55, the maximum permitted. The human resources department

informed F that due to health and safety issues they had to apply the age limit and that all inspectors were required to retire at 55 years of age.

Questions:

1. Discuss the possible legal consequences of the above situations.
2. Consider how each of the issues could be addressed.
3. How would a diversity approach have helped to improve the staffing situation?

6.9 CONCLUSION

Diversity management involves recognizing and accommodating diverse cultures and characteristics, not excluding them on arbitrary grounds. It is arguable that to truly value diversity there needs to be all encompassing legislation, which requires employers to justify all their employment practices on objective grounds. However, for any government this would be a far too interventionist approach and too great an imposition on business. The traditional UK reactive approach to discrimination legislation is changing. Although the law has difficulty in recognizing the concept of diversity, there are moves towards this approach as witnessed in the RR(A)A, subsequently extended to the DDA and SDA, which places a positive duty upon specified public sector employers and service providers to promote racial equality. In addition, changing public opinion and EC law have resulted in extending protection to groups not previously covered.

Even though the law has extended its reach, there will still be problems with implementation. As McColgan (2003) points out, 'the piecemeal approach serves only to make a bad situation worse'. It is pointed out that in 2000 there were 'no fewer than 30 Acts of Parliament, 38 Statutory Instruments, 11 Codes of Practice and 12 European Community Directives and Recommendations'. On top of that, there have been many additional provisions, again in a piecemeal way. Furthermore, the approach has not been consistent; for example, the different definitions of indirect discrimination. McColgan and other commentators have argued that a radical process of reform is needed. The proposed Equality Bill goes some way to introducing such reforms.

The use of the law as an instrument of social change is a controversial one. The law does not have mystical powers and is not a panacea, as demonstrated by the above review of the RR(A). The rule of law and legislation can, however, promote and encourage equality and diversity and provide some redress for victims of discrimination. Employment statistics continue to demonstrate the structural inequalities in the labour market and the existence of discrimination against disadvantaged groups. Employers should adopt employment policies and practices, which promote and support diversity within their workforce. Experience has shown that some employers are not willing to move voluntarily in this direction. The positive obligations incorporated into the race, disability and sex discrimination legislation are a step in the right direction and will no doubt be extended to other groups in the near future.

REVIEW AND DISCUSSION QUESTIONS

1. Provide examples of how public policy has influenced anti-discrimination law.

2. What remedies should be provided for individuals subjected to discrimination? Should discrimination be covered by criminal or civil law?

3. Explain the difference between direct and indirect discrimination, giving examples.

4. The law on discrimination has recently extended to groups previously unprotected by law. Has the law gone far enough, or too far?

5. The discrimination laws in the UK are criticized for being incoherent and inconsistent. Provide examples to support this criticism, and discuss whether or not a new approach is needed.

6. The law is moving towards a proactive approach to equality. How might this affect an organisation's view of equality and diversity?

FURTHER READING

Bamforth, N., Malik, M., O'Cinneide. 2008. Discrimination Law: Theory and Context: Text and Materials. Sweet and Maxwell.

Text attempts to provide an account of discrimination law from a constitutional point of view rather than just a branch of employment law.

Dine, J., Watt, B. 1996. Discrimination Law: Concepts, Limitations and Justifications Longman.

A collection of papers from a symposium entitled 'Justifying Discrimination' at Essex University.

Fredman, S. 2002. Discrimination Law. Oxford University Press.

Textbook examining the concepts of equality and discrimination and scope of discrimination law, including the issue of reverse discrimination.

Hepple, B., Szyzsczak E. 1992. Discrimination: the Limits of the Law. Mansell.

A collection of papers from the Hart Legal Workshop at the Institute of Advanced Legal Studies.

McColgan, A. 2000. Discrimination Law: Test, Cases and Materials. Hart Publishing.

Analytical text examining UK and EU law, including Northern Ireland's fair employment legislation.

Wiley, B. 2009. Employment Law in Context: an Introduction for HR Professionals. Pearsons.

Textbook on employment law, which examines the law alongside an examination of the social, economic and political context in which it develops.

REFERENCES

Annual Report from the Tribunal Service, 2008. http://www.employmenttribunals.gov.uk/Publications/publications.htm

Bamforth, N., 1996. Limits of anti-discrimination law. In: Dine, J., Watt, R.A. (Eds.), Discrimination Law: Concepts, Limitations and Justifications. Longman.

Bamforth, N., Malik, M., O'Cinneide, C., 2008. Discrimination Law: Theory and Context: Text and Materials. Sweet and Maxwell.

Barnard, C., 1995. A European litigation strategy: the case of the equal opportunities commission. In: Shaw, J., More, G., (Eds.), New Legal Dynamics of European Union. Clarendon.

Barnard, C., 2006. EC Employment Law. Oxford University Press.

Bindman, G., Lester, A., 1972. Race and Law. Penguin Books.

Chamberlain, J., 2005. Obesity in the workplace: overweight and over here. Employment Law Journal 62, 13-15.

Commission for Racial Equality, 2003. The Race Relations Act 1976 (Amendment) Regulations: Briefing by the CRE, June 2003. Commission for Racial Equality.

Commission for Racial Equality, 2007. CRE Monitoring and Enforcement Report, 2005/7. Commission for Racial Equality.

Dupper, O., 2006. Affirmative action in South Africa: (m)any lessons for Europe? Law and Politics in Africa, Asia and Latin America 59, 135-164.

Ellis, E., 1997. The Principle of Equality of Opportunity Irrespective of Sex: Some reflections on the present state of European Community law and its future development. In: Dashwood, A., O'Leary, S. (Eds.), The Principle of equal treatment in EC law. Sweet & Maxwell.

Ellis, E., 1998. Recent developments in European community sex equality law. Common Market Law Review 35, 379-408.

Equal Opportunities Review, 2003. Top QC Launches Attack on Labour's 'ham-fisted and narrow' Approach to Equality Laws, November, 123.

Equal Opportunities Review, 2007a. What is the Next Frontier for Discrimination Law? July, 166.

Equal Opportunities Review, 2007b. Positive Action: Possibilities and Limits, November, 170.

Equal Opportunities Review, 2008a. Multi-dimensional Discrimination: Justice for the Whole Person, February, 173.

Equal Opportunities Review, 2008b. Multiple Discrimination in the EU, February, 173.

Equal Opportunities Review, 2008c. Current Issues in Equal Pay in the Public Sector, March, 186.

Equal Opportunities Review, 2009a. EHRC Interventions, January, 184.

Equal Opportunities Review, 2009b. The EOR Guide to the Equality Bill: Part1 - General Principles, June, 189.

Equal Opportunities Review, 2009c. Transport for London: Contracting for Equality, February 2009.

Equal Opportunities Review, 2009d. Equality Bill Verdict: Could do Better, Rubenstein, M., June, 189.

European Commission, 2007. Tackling Multiple Discrimination - Practices, Policies and Laws, September 2007.

Feinstein, N., Davies, H., 2009. An uncertain prognosis. New Law Journal 8th May.

Freedman, S., Szyszczak, E., 1992. The Interaction of Race and Gender. In: Hepple, Szyszczak (Eds.), Discrimination: The Limits of the Law. Mansell.

Hepple, R., Lord Lester of Herne Hill QC, Ellis, E., Rose, D., Singh R., 1997. Improving Equality Law: the Options. The Runnymede Trust.

Hepple, B., 1997. The principle of equal treatment in article 119EC and the possibilities for reform. In: Dashwood, A., O'Leary, E. (Eds.).

Hepple, B., Coussey, M., Choudry, T., 2000. Equality: A New Framework Report of the Independent Review of the Enforcement of UK Anti-discrimination Law. Hart.

Lacey, N., 1992. From individual to group. In: Hepple, B., Szyzsczak, E. (Eds.), Discrimination: The Limits of the Law. Mansell.

Lustgarten, L., 1992. Racial inequality, public policy and the law: where are we going? In: Hepple, B., Szyszczak, E. (Eds.).

Lustgarten, L., Edwards, J., 1992. Racial inequality and the limits of law. In: Braham, P., Rattansi, A., Skellington, R. (Eds.), Racism and Antiracism. Open University Press.

MacEwen, M., 1995. Tackling Racism in Europe: an Examination of Anti-Discrimination Law in Practice, Berg.

Macpherson, W., 1999. Report from the Stephen Lawrence Inquiry. HMSO.

Malik, M., 2009. From Conflict to Cohesion: Competing Interests in Equality Law and policy. Equal Opportunities Review April.

McColgan, A. (Eds.), 2003. Achieving Equality at Work. Institute of Employment Rights.

Nielsen, R., Szyszczak, E., 1997. The Social Dimension of the European Union. Handelshojskolens Forlag.

O'Cinneide, C., 2007. The commission for equality and human rights: a new institution for new and uncertain times. Industrial Law Journal 36 (2), 141–162.

Parekh, B., 1992. A case for positive discrimination. In: Hepple, B., Szyzsczak, E. (Eds.), Discrimination: the Limits of the Law. Mansell.

Pitt, G., 1992. Can reverse discrimination be justified? In: Hepple, B., Szyzsczak, E. (Eds.), Discrimination: the Limits of the Law. Mansell.

Schneider-Ross, 2007. The Public Sector Equality Duties – Making an Impact, Schneider Ross diversity consultants, www.schneider-ross.com (Reported in EOR December 2007).

Spencer, S., Fredman, C., 2003. Age Equality Comes of Age: Delivering Change for Older People. Institute for Public Policy Research.

Trade unions and equality and diversity

7

Aim

To explore trade union approaches to equality and diversity.

Objectives

- To outline contemporary patterns of union membership and collective bargaining.
- To summarise union objectives, especially in relation to equality and diversity.
- To discuss trade union responses to diversity policies.
- To discuss diversity and equality in the internal context of trade union organisation and democracy.

7.1 INTRODUCTION

Chapter 6 showed the law to be a weak instrument in terms of actually promoting equality and diversity at work and eradicating discrimination, partly because of the lack of proactive measures required (in the private sector) and the prohibition of 'class action' within British law. We will also see in Chapter 8 that employers do not always voluntarily improve their policies and practices and consequently, 'bottom-up' pressure for equality from employees exerted through trade unions can be just as important as the 'top-down' commitment to diversity of senior management. Dickens et al. (1988: 65) highlighted this more than two decades ago, arguing that a 'review of discriminatory terms and practice is more likely to occur where there is some form of joint regulation [trade union or employee involvement] than where issues are unilaterally determined by employers'. More recent evidence indicates that unionized workforces generally experience less pronounced inequalities than non-unionized ones (Colling and Dickens, 2001) and that union involvement often results in more progressive equality and diversity policies (Greene and Kirton, 2009).

Broadly speaking, trade unions exist in order to protect employees, to further employee interests at the workplace and to work towards a fairer, more equal society. Their existence is underpinned by the assumption of inequalities of power between employers and employees, which means that employees need independent representation and need to act collectively in order to improve pay and conditions at work through negotiations with management. Unions have a longstanding interest in issues of equality and social justice although it is only fairly recently that they have begun to talk about promoting diversity.

This chapter discusses the role of trade unions in promoting an equality and diversity agenda in work organisations and in the wider political arena. It outlines the nature of contemporary trade unionism and trade union objectives. It pays particular attention to equality bargaining and to trade union responses to diversity management. It also considers how unions function, in particular, their internal equality and diversity contexts. We recognise that many students of equality and diversity modules on management and business studies courses will not have grounding in employment relations. Therefore, this chapter should be viewed as an introduction to the role of unions as a key industrial relations actor. It is the intention that its contents will be comprehensible to students with little prior knowledge of trade unions. Interested readers should consult the list of references for a more in-depth analysis of the issues raised here. The glossary will help to clarify any unfamiliar terminology.

7.2 HISTORICAL BACKGROUND

In order to understand contemporary trade unionism and in order to evaluate the potential for unions to promote equality and diversity, it is necessary to have some awareness of the history of British trade unionism. Early trade unions emerged in the first half of the nineteenth century and were formed largely by skilled male workers in order to protect their relatively privileged terms and conditions. By the end of the nineteenth century in the aftermath of the industrial revolution, unions of unskilled, male general workers had been formed, changing the character and objectives of the union movement. A concurrent development of the nineteenth century was the growth of separate women's trade unions. Women's unions emerged partly because women were often excluded from men's unions and partly because of the growing influence of the feminist movement, which believed that women needed to organize to fight for their own rights (Cunnison and Stageman, 1995). Trade union membership grew at a rapid rate before, during and after the First World War and by 1920 almost half the British workforce was trade union organized. In the 1920s, the separate women's unions merged with the male-dominated unions, which generally resulted in women losing influence over union objectives. Between 1920, and the late 1960s, union membership increased and declined in response to the economic and political climate. Women's union membership grew significantly during this period and they were an important source of members, although they were under-represented in union decision-making positions and bodies.

During the 1970s, union membership increased significantly, particularly among white-collar workers and among women. Between 1968 and 1978 women's membership had grown at more than three times the rate of men's (Cunnison and Stageman, 1995). Union membership was also becoming more racially diverse. During the post-war period, black migration to Britain gathered pace, reaching a peak in the 1960s. From these early days, black workers joined trade unions in greater proportions than white workers. In the mid-1970s, 61% of black male workers were union members compared to 47% of white males (Lee, 1987). However, union membership did not always seem to benefit black members as much as their white counterparts in terms of better pay and conditions. Union membership reached a peak in 1979 of around 13 million members, representing an overall union membership rate (density) of around 55%. To summarise, in little more than a century British trade unionism had risen from obscurity to occupy a prominent position in British social, economic and political life. However, the membership gains of the 1970s were totally nullified by the dramatic losses of the 1980s. The questions facing trade unions today are (i) whether they can reverse the massive membership decline of the 1980s or (ii) at least maintain the current membership rate in order to avoid returning to obscurity. Union stability and even growth are essential if unions are to play a significant role in promoting equality and diversity at work.

Key learning points

- Historically, trade unions were set up by and for white male workers. Union membership gradually became more diverse as greater numbers of women and black and minority ethnic (BME) people entered the British labour market.
- Union density has declined from its peak of 55% in 1979 to around 28% today, leaving the unions weaker and less influential.

7.3 CONTEMPORARY TRADE UNIONISM

Trade unions do not now wield the power and influence in the UK labour market that they once did. There has been a continuous downward trend in trade union membership since 1979 and whilst the majority of employees in the UK do not now belong to a trade union, a substantial 28% still do (Mercer and Notley, 2008). Although trade unions retain a significant presence overall, as will be discussed, the extent of union membership varies considerably between employment sectors, occupations and according to organisation size. This affects the degree of union influence at an organisational level. In certain employment contexts, the public sector for example, there is considerable potential for unions to exert pressure on employers to develop policies to combat discrimination and promote equality and diversity. Whilst in others, especially private sector employers, only a minority of organisations have a substantial trade union presence. Further, unions are widely criticised for having traditionally focused their bargaining efforts on improving basic terms and conditions of employment. This has rarely included the specific concerns of women or other diverse 'minority' groups; for example, issues such as childcare or religious leave have been neglected. This narrow perspective on union objectives has been widely criticised as being white-male biased and for failing to take account of the diversity of union membership (for example, Cockburn, 1991; Dickens, 1997; Rees, 1992). Loss of union membership and the decline in both union presence at the workplace and in collective bargaining coverage combine with white-male domination of union power structures to limit the unions' ability to promote equality and diversity at the workplace. The unions have, however, sought to tackle the problem of membership decline by active membership recruitment campaigns targeting diverse social groups. As discussed later, they also now actively seek to improve representation of diverse interests by a variety of methods designed to increase the representation of previously under-represented groups within union decision-making.

7.3.1 Union membership patterns

During the 20-year period after 1979, trade union membership declined by an enormous 40%, but membership has now stabilised and there was even a small growth in the early 2000s. Blyton and Turnball (1998) reviewed in detail the various explanations for the massive union decline of the 1980s and early 1990s. These can be briefly summarised as arising from a complex interaction of features of the political, economic, social, technological and legal contexts of the period.

There are currently around seven million trade union members constituting about 28% of all employees. The rate of union membership is far higher in the public sector (59% of employees) than in the private sector (16% of employees) (Mercer and Notley, 2008). Breaking this down further between industries, there is considerable variation ranging from a membership rate of 63% in education to just 13% in the industry category 'wholesale, retail and motor trade'. Union membership also varies according to workplace size, with a rate of 26% of employees in workplaces with fewer than 50 employees compared with a higher than average rate of 49% in workplaces with 50 or more employees (Mercer and Notley, 2008).

Within industries there are also significant occupational variations in union membership. For example, the rate is lowest in sales and customer service occupations at 11% and highest in professional occupations at 57% (Mercer and Notley, 2008). Other occupations with higher than average union membership are 'associate professional and technical workers' and 'process, plant and machine operatives'. In all occupations full-time employees are more highly unionized than part-time – 31% compared with 18% of part-timers. When men work part-time they are far less likely than female part-time workers to be union members. Thus, we can see how aggregate union membership data conceal significant variations across five dimensions – sector, industry, workplace size, occupation and hours of work.

Union members also display a range of diverse individual characteristics shown in Table 7.1. The characteristics of the 'typical' trade unionist have changed over time. In 1979 when trade union membership was at its peak, the 'typical' trade unionist was a male, full-time, manual worker in the production sector. Today, the 'typical' trade unionist is slightly more likely to be female than male and a non-manual rather than manual worker, more likely to work in the service than in the production sector, and be a highly qualified worker in the public sector. The one stable characteristic is that trade union members are mostly full-time workers. Individual and job-related characteristics have important implications for trade union recruitment strategies.

One of the interesting trends in union membership in the period of steep decline was the slower rate of decline in women's membership when compared with men's. As a result women now have a higher union membership rate than men. Approximately 26% of male employees are union members, compared with 30% of female (Mercer and Notley, 2008). This is interesting because it is a reversal of the traditional trend for men to have a far greater propensity to be union members. Whilst this trend might suggest that feminized employment makes fertile recruiting territory for unions, most of the

Table 7.1 UK Union Density by Various Characteristics

Sex	%	Highest Qualification	%	Industry	%
Men	26	Degree or equivalent	36	Agriculture, forestry, fishing	08
Women	30	Other higher education	41	Mining and quarrying	23
Age band		A-level or equivalent	26	Manufacturing	22
16–24	09	GCSE or equivalent	23	Energy and water	46
25–34	22	Other	22	Construction	16
35–49	34	No qualifications	20	Wholesale and retail trade	11
50 plus	35			Hotels and restaurants	05
		Full- or part-time work		Transport and communication	40
Ethnic group		Full-time	31	Financial intermediation	22
White	28	Part-time	18	Real estate and business services	10
Asian/Asian British	23			Public administration	57
Black/Black British	29	**Workplace size**		Education	55
Chinese/other ethnic group	17	Less than 50 employees	18	Health	43
		More than 50 employees	37	Other services	19

Source: Mercer and Notley (2007)

recent growth in women's employment has been in part-time work and in the service sector where unions are relatively weak. This means that unions would need to develop new strategies to reach greater numbers of presently non-unionized women workers. It is women's strong presence as workers in the public sector that largely accounts for their higher union membership rate.

Rates of union membership also vary according to a number of other individual characteristics, for example, ethnic origin. The data show that the rate of union membership is highest among 'black' workers at 29% and lowest among 'Chinese and other ethnic groups' at 17% (Mercer and Notley, 2008). White workers have a membership rate of 28% and the other minority groups analysed – Asian and mixed – have lower union membership at 23% and 22%, respectively. When it comes to women, black women have a significantly higher union membership rate than white women (35% compared with 30%). This is partly because black women are more likely than white to be in full-time employment and there is a strong association between full-time employment and trade union membership as stated earlier. Of particular concern to the trade unions is the age profile of membership. Employees aged 50 plus are most likely to be union members (35%), whilst among younger workers aged 25–34 only 22% are members. Some commentators have claimed that the evidence suggests that the greater likelihood of older employees belonging to a trade union reflects different attitudes to trade unions across age-based cohorts rather than changing attitudes to trade unions over the life course. This means that younger people will not necessarily join unions as they get older and therefore unions will need to strive to demonstrate their relevance to younger people, who may not share the views of their parents' generation. It is clear that unions need to recruit more women, young people and part-time workers if they are to reverse the trend of membership decline or even to maintain present membership rates.

What an analysis of contemporary union membership trends reveals is the uneven pattern of union coverage of sectors and industries and different membership rates according to individual and job-related characteristics. It goes without saying that unions are most able to advance an equality and diversity agenda in those areas where they have the strongest presence and the highest membership.

7.3.2 Collective bargaining coverage

Union recognition is where employers formally agree to negotiate terms and conditions of employment with trade unions, known as collective bargaining. Union recognition agreements set out the procedures and substance of collective bargaining, for example, when negotiations will take place and what will be covered. Union recognition is strongly associated with workplace size; the larger the workplace, the more likely there is to be a union recognition agreement. Overall, 36% of employees are covered by collective agreements. Again, this varies from 22% in the private sector to 73% in the public sector, and from industry to industry, with, for example, 48% of employees in transport and communication and 23% of employees in construction covered by collective bargaining. Overall then, only a (substantial) minority of employees is covered by collective bargaining but there are enormous sectoral and industrial variations. Nevertheless, there is some evidence of a 'strengthening platform' for collective bargaining in context of renewed political legitimacy granted to unions since the late 1990s (Colling and Dickens, 2001).

Key learning points

- Union density varies according to several job and industry-related characteristics. These include sector, industry, workplace size, occupation and hours of work. Union density is higher in the public than private sector.
- Certain individual characteristics are also important for patterns of trade union membership, particularly gender, ethnicity and age.
- The characteristics of the 'typical' trade union member have changed both in line with demographic changes and wider structural and economic changes impacting on the labour market.

7.4 TRADE UNION OBJECTIVES

As stated above, the trade union movement exists to defend and promote workers' rights. Achieving these objectives is a multi-faceted task, which involves campaigning and lobbying in the political arena and negotiation and advocacy at the workplace. With regard to political objectives, the Trades Union Congress (TUC) is the trade union movement's principal conduit for influencing the government and thereby influencing social and economic policies of concern to affiliated unions and by extension to trade union members. The TUC was established in 1868 and individual unions can affiliate to it. It currently has around 60 member unions, including most large unions, and represents the vast majority of trade unionists. During the post-war period and until 1979, the government generally consulted the TUC before introducing legislation or policy affecting the interests of the trade union movement. Following the election in 1979 of the Thatcher-led Conservative government, this dialogue was broken until the election of the Labour government in 1997. The 18-year period of Conservative government placed the TUC on the margins of British political life, unable to exert direct influence on the social, economic and legal policies of the period. In 1997 the Labour government re-opened the dialogue with unions, but famously promising them 'fairness not favours' (Blyton and Turnball, 1998: 127). In the light of the Labour government's commitment to retaining most of the employment legislation passed under the previous Conservative administration (much of which is hostile to trade union influence and power), the unions have concentrated their efforts on re-establishing their role as 'social partners' in the political process. Commentators are divided, but there is some evidence that a union role in the political process is valued by the present Labour government. For example, speaking in April 2008 at a conference in Glasgow – *The role of modern trade unions in the 21st century workplace* – the Rt. Hon. John Hutton MP commented:

> *We should celebrate the fact that the union movement has many strong links with the growth and success of this great city. Of course the unions continue to play an important part in helping to create the dynamic and vibrant city we see today. Because modern trade unions, I believe very strongly, have a crucial role to play in helping to sustain a successful and fair society – a society where every person has the chance to make the most of their talents and skills. And where there are no barriers to how far a person can rise.*
> **(http://www.berr.gov.uk/aboutus/ministerialteam/Speeches/page45773.html)**

Examples of the unions' political lobbying and campaigning work relating to equality and diversity can be found on both the TUC and individual unions' web sites. For instance, at the end of 2003 the TUC was invited to respond to the Treasury's 2004 spending review on childcare. The TUC highlighted gaps in childcare provision, recommended improvements which would make a difference to children and their families and gave an assessment of delivery of the government's childcare strategy so far. In 2003 the TUC organized a petition of trade union members calling for the government to introduce a new law to provide equal rights for disabled people and correct the weaknesses of the Disability Discrimination Act. More recently, in 2009, the TUC lobbied government to ensure that the present recession does not affect women disproportionately. The TUC argued for stronger maternity rights and better childcare provision as well as calling for the government to step up its efforts to tackle gender segregation and the gender pay gap. It joined forces with MP and government minister Vera Baird who spoke in the House of Commons on 'Safeguarding Women at Work during the Recession'. She said: 'these are turbulent economic times but I am confident that together, Government and the trade union movement can ensure that we come out of these difficulties stronger.'

The TUC consolidates its lobbying and campaigning work by publishing and disseminating research papers, discussion documents and policy statements. In addition, the latest available evidence shows that half of the unions have taken measures to make their campaigns and communications material available and accessible to people with visual and hearing impairments and to people whose first language is not English (TUC, 2007).

The trade union movement has managed to retain at least some influence in public life despite membership decline and a long period of political hostility, contrary to some popular representations of unions as a spent force. It is also clear that the unions now have equality and diversity issues firmly on their political campaigning agenda.

Turning to the workplace, unions' roles include (i) giving advice when members have a problem at work; (ii) representing members in discussion with employers; (iii) making sure that members' legal rights are enforced at work; (iv) helping members take cases to employment tribunals; (v) fighting discrimination; and (vi) helping to promote equality at work. There is evidence that union members highly value union support when they encounter problems at work – many people join unions precisely for this reason. The TUC and individual unions provide advice to union representatives on handling discrimination cases via web sites, publications and education programmes. However, discrimination is a sensitive issue and it is thought that some members, BME people for example, may lack confidence in their unions to handle discrimination cases effectively. To overcome these barriers to representing a diverse membership effectively, the TUC recommends that unions negotiate workplace procedures for dealing with cases of discrimination, that union representatives are trained in how to handle discrimination cases and that the assistance available is publicised. As important as it is for unions to represent individual members who experience discrimination, the greatest potential for unions to contribute to greater equality and diversity at workplace level lies in collective bargaining. The next section discusses equality bargaining.

Activity 7.1

Unions must not be made to feel like embarrassing relatives – nor Labour ministers like mill owners

In 1971 I was a 20-year-old postman on strike. That strike lasted 7 weeks and sparked my involvement with trade unions. But more than that, the experience of solidarity in the workplace moulded my political philosophy. Soon afterwards, unencumbered by any formal study of politics, I joined the Labour party, and ever since I have seen the link between party and unions as essential. A decade later, I was on the national executive of my union, watching Labour's self-destruction. That had a lasting effect. Eighteen years out of power changed our movement forever.

Before Margaret Thatcher, unions opposed every interference with free collective bargaining. We weren't just opposed to the European social model, we were opposed to Europe. We banked everything on legal immunity for trade unions and the concept that workers' rights came with their union cards. The notion that Labour was in the pocket of the unions, or vice versa, did damage to both. When Labour left office in 1979, it was in favour of secondary action but against the minimum wage. By 1997 the position had reversed, and 10 years later we can see the benefits for workers: a series of new rights – many of which I introduced – covering pay, holidays, grievance procedures, maternity leave, protection for short-term contractors and redress against all shades of discrimination. We have provided rights at work, but also the jobs in which these rights can be enjoyed.

Unions collectively enjoy new recognition rights, protection for strikers, a ban on blacklisting union activists and partnership over the minimum wage, pensions and skills. The healthy links with unions should be celebrated. Trade unionists have always presented a united front against racism. During the Troubles in Northern Ireland, theirs was the only non-sectarian voice consistently condemning the violence. Today they champion the rights of European Union (EU) migrant workers when the easier option would be to attack them. Unions play a big role in everything from pensions to skills to work–life balance and the impact of globalisation. Climate change and the environment are now so important that unions should have a role there as well. For example, the legal responsibilities of health and safety representatives could be extended to cover environmental protection as well.

The unions' link with Labour should be strengthened, not weakened. We need a constitutional and physical connection between constituency parties and local union branches. Any reform of the vote at conference should be accompanied by an increase in union representation on the party's national policy forum to one-third, and development of a mechanism to unite around positive policies for the future. A fresh impetus to the relationship works both ways – union leaders must do their bit too. The Tories are a real threat for the first time in years. They may seek to hug 'hoodies', but they remain the only mainstream centre-right party in Europe hostile to independent trade unionism. Cameron hasn't revealed many policies, yet he has pledged to withdraw from the EU social chapter, legislate against the Labour-union link and re-open the pensions settlement I brokered, and which protected the pensions of 3 million teachers, nurses and civil servants. Union leaders must recognise that there is no longer a soft option of Labour in power but disunited.

Unions should not be made to feel like embarrassing elderly relatives, and Labour ministers shouldn't be made to feel like recalcitrant mill owners. There is so much more we can do together in government, rather than separately in opposition.

(*Source:* Alan Johnson MP, *The Guardian*, 3rd May 2009)

Questions

1. What does the article reveal about the unions' changing political role?
2. What does the article reveal about the unions' stance on equality issues?
3. Do you agree that unions should work with the Labour Party in order to work towards a fairer and more equal society?

7.5 BARGAINING FOR EQUALITY AND DIVERSITY AT THE WORKPLACE

Although there is evidence that workplaces with recognised trade unions are more likely to have developed formal equality policies than non-unionized firms (Noon and Hoque, 2001), in practice trade unions have a 'mixed record' (Dickens et al., 1988: 65) in challenging discrimination and tackling inequalities. Until fairly recently, unions did not confront issues of membership diversity. For example, the unions' historical record of representing women is quite poor. Many unions originally sought to exclude women from certain trades, whilst others accepted women but only in segregated, lower-skill, lower paid jobs (Cockburn, 1991). The TUC supported the principle of equal pay for women since 1888, but did little to effect it until the 1970s (Walby, 1997). Similarly, there are instances from the past of where unions supported management's racist employment practices, which contributed to a generation of Asian and Caribbean workers being confined to low-paid, low-skill jobs (Phizacklea and Miles, 1987; Lee, 1987). Other groups, including disabled and lesbian and gay members, have remained invisible to the trade unions until relatively recently (Colgan, 1999). Overall, traditional liberal 'sameness' models of equality shaped the strategies and policies of trade unions until the late 1990s. This led critics to assert that the trade union agenda had not been as progressive as it might have been (Colling and Dickens, 2001).

Why were unions reluctant and slow to recognise diversity? Traditionally unions assumed that people working within the same industry, organisation or occupation shared the same interests and bargaining priorities, regardless of characteristics such as gender, race, etc. Unions feared that highlighting different interests might undermine solidarity over bargaining issues and thereby weaken their influence and power. However, unions now recognise that different groups prioritise different issues, for example, women are more likely than men to value the opportunity to take career breaks and job share, some BME groups are more likely than white employees to value alternative religious holidays, and so on.

It is quite clear that the contemporary policy position is for unions to support campaigning and bargaining for equality. The TUC has developed a model equality clause which its affiliates are strongly encouraged to adopt. The latest available evidence shows that 22 unions (40%) have done so. The clause states:

> 'The objects of the union shall include: (a) The promotion of equality for all including through: (i) collective bargaining, publicity material and campaigning, representation, union organisation and structures, education and training, organising and recruitment, the provision of all other services and benefits and all other activities; (ii) the union's own employment practices. (b) Active opposition to all forms of harassment, prejudice and unfair discrimination whether on the grounds of sex, race, ethnic or national origin, religion, colour, class, caring responsibilities, marital status, sexuality, disability, age, or other status or personal characteristic' (TUC, 2007).

7.5.1 **Equality reps**

Many unions have introduced workplace equality reps whose role is to raise the equality and diversity agenda among fellow workers and in their unions. Equality reps are also tasked with encouraging employers to make equality and diversity part of collective bargaining and to ensure that every worker receives fair treatment. In a recent evaluation, the TUC argued that union equality reps enormously enhance the work done by employers and unions to achieve workplace equality and diversity. However, the TUC also points out that currently, equality reps (unlike workplace reps, health and safety reps and learning reps) are not given paid time off to be trained or to carry out their duties. Due to the complexity of equality law, thorough training is essential for equality reps to be effective. Therefore, the TUC has called on the government to recognise equality reps in law and to accord them the same legal rights as the other union reps mentioned above (TUC, 2009).

7.5.2 **Conceptualising equality bargaining**

Equality bargaining can be defined as 'the collective negotiation of provisions that are of particular interest or benefit to diverse social groups and are likely to promote equality and diversity at work'. Influenced by Bercusson and Dickens' (1996) earlier work, we find it useful to analytically distinguish two main approaches to equality bargaining. The first approach consists of the '*equality and diversity dimension*' to the traditional union bargaining agenda. To illustrate what is meant by *dimension*, a specific instance is when unions negotiate on low pay. There can be no doubt that much of the disadvantage experienced by many employees relates to basic terms and conditions of employment such as pay, working hours and employment security. Low pay among women and BME workers, for example, is not necessarily a result of direct discrimination by employers (although it can be). Rather, low pay is often a feature of certain occupations and industries in which women and BME people 'just happen' to be concentrated. Therefore, it may appear to union negotiators that the general problem of low pay has no direct relevance to equality and diversity issues. Indeed, tackling low pay is a traditional or 'mainstream' union bargaining objective, because the eradication of low pay would benefit all low-paid workers. Yet an improvement in pay levels is often of disproportionate benefit to women and BME workers because they are over-represented in low-paid work. Therefore, when unions bargain around low pay it often has the effect of promoting gender and race equality whether or not this was the intention. This can be conceptualised as an 'equality and diversity dimension' to traditional collective bargaining. A formal equality and diversity policy need not provide the framework for this type of bargaining objective because equality and diversity benefits can be achieved without explicitly mentioning equality and diversity issues. However, conversely bargaining objectives, which do not *explicitly* promote equality and diversity, might discriminate indirectly or do little to address the concerns of disadvantaged groups. One example of this would be where a union negotiates to reduce the standard weekly working hours. Conceivably, men might value this more highly than women because women have a strong tendency to work part-time anyway. Therefore, benefits for disadvantaged social groups are by no means guaranteed unless equality and diversity issues are explicitly pursued.

So, if the traditional bargaining agenda does not necessarily address equality and diversity issues, where does this lead us? The second approach to equality and diversity bargaining is more explicit in its aim of promoting equality and diversity. Here we would expect to see an employer-led equality and diversity policy and/or a union-management negotiated equality and diversity agreement. There are five main areas that are typically covered:

- Pay and benefits discrimination

- Employment segregation

- Job access and security

- Work–life balance

- Harassment

7.5.2.1 *Pay and benefits discrimination*

Chapter 2 noted gender and race pay gaps, but there is evidence to suggest that unionization narrows the wage gap between male and female employees, full- and part-time, white and black, non-manual and manual, and healthy and those with health problems (Metcalf, 2000). Many of the employment tribunal claims for equal pay for work of equal value made by individual women came from unionized workplaces (Colling and Dickens, 1998). However, as can be seen from Activity 7.2, more recently the unions' approach to equal pay claims has met with some controversy.

Long before the regulations protecting workers against discrimination on the basis of sexuality were introduced, the unions also had some success in tackling the pay and benefits discrimination experienced by many lesbians and gay men. For example, British Telecom succumbed to union pressure to change its pension scheme enabling same-sex partners to receive death benefits, etc. In British Telecom and in the Civil Service, union negotiations ensured that all leave and relocation entitlements could be equally accessed by all staff, so that lesbians and gay men could no longer be denied bereavement leave on the death of a partner or carer's leave to nurse a sick partner, etc. (Labour Research, 1994).

7.5.2.2 *Employment segregation*

Employment segregation is produced and reinforced by discrimination and disadvantage in the labour market. Therefore, in order to promote equality and diversity, unions need to tackle employment segregation, which they can do by placing certain issues on the bargaining agenda. Firstly, it is critical to negotiate access to training that will enable under-represented groups either to climb the hierarchical ladder to more senior positions or to enter occupations where they are traditionally not well represented. Secondly, unions need to audit and monitor organisations' recruitment, selection and promotion policies, practices and outcomes to ensure that there are no barriers created either by the policies and procedures themselves or by managers' actions. Some of the unions representing highly qualified workers have mounted 'glass ceiling' campaigns to raise awareness of the barriers and what actions organisations might take. However, the reality is that there are few examples of actual bargaining on employment segregation.

7.5.2.3 *Job access and security for under-represented and marginalized groups*

This involves scrutinising organisational practices in the areas of recruitment and selection, redundancy, termination of contract and contractual status in order to identify any potentially discriminatory practices. Chapter 2 showed that women, BME workers, disabled people and older people are over-represented in insecure, non-standard forms of employment. Although it is true that some people, women for example, might 'choose' to work part-time, for many people, including women, insecure work is often involuntary. Negotiating greater access to better quality jobs with greater security undoubtedly promotes equality for disadvantaged groups. Job access and job security issues overlap with employment segregation, and training and recruitment and selection policies are particularly important areas for unions to negotiate around in order to promote equality and diversity.

7.5.2.4 *Work–life balance*

Work–life balance has become a prominent bargaining issue for many unions. Unions are increasingly bargaining around issues such as maternity and paternity leave and pay, childcare, working time and career breaks. There is potential here for unions to develop a progressive bargaining agenda seeking to ensure that maternity and paternity leave and childcare provisions allow and encourage both mothers and fathers to take an active parental role, rather than following the traditional assumption that looking after children is solely women's business. On its web site (http://www.tuc.org.uk/work_life/), the TUC states that achieving work–life balance requires management and unions to work together in partnership. According to the TUC, a genuine partnership has:

- A shared commitment to the success of the organisation
- A commitment by the employer to employment security
- A focus on the quality of working life
- Recognition of the legitimate roles of the employer and the trade union
- Openness on both sides and a willingness by the employer to share information and discuss the future plans for the organisation
- Added value – a shared understanding that the partnership is delivering measurable improvements for the employer, the union and employees

7.5.2.5 *Harassment*

Bullying and harassment is another issue that is high up on the bargaining agenda of many unions. Many unions hold their own equality and diversity awareness training to help members recognise and challenge harassment. Unions are also often instrumental in pushing for bullying and harassment training to be provided by work organisations. Many employers have harassment policies, but Cockburn (1991) argued that the real test of a harassment policy is whether or not cases of complaint are encouraged and whether action is taken against offenders. The TUC produces guidance on bullying and harassment for union negotiators, encouraging them to raise awareness at the workplace, to carry out surveys to find out the extent of the problem and to negotiate a policy.

Key learning points

- Trade unions seek to promote equality at work by supporting, representing and negotiating on behalf of employees in the workplace and by influencing politicians and government.
- There are two main approaches to equality and diversity bargaining: (i) negotiating measures *indirectly* tackling equality and diversity issues, (ii) negotiating initiatives with an *explicit* intention to promote equality and diversity.

Activity 7.2

Who's best at getting equal pay for women?

Unions face allegations of negligence, but claim they are still better than lawyers, says Jon Robins.

Thousands of women began legal proceedings against trade unions last week, claiming they have been negligent in handling equal pay claims. Newcastle law firm Stefan Cross has issued almost 3000 claims against Unison, GMB, Unite T&G and the Royal College of Nurses on behalf of cleaners, care workers and kitchen staff. 'The unions' failure to grasp the nettle of equal pay, be straight with their members and use the law on their behalf has been all too apparent,' says Stuart Hill of Action for Equality, a company owned by Stefan Cross.

Cath Mullins, 58, who has worked for Middlesbrough Council as a carer for 22 years, is one of the women arguing that her union has been negligent. She claims to have been advised that she had no equal pay claim by the GMB on the grounds that she was 'a white-collar worker' having moved into sheltered accommodation work. 'If I'm a white-collar worker, why do I wear plastic gloves and pinnies and clean commodes?' she says. Colleagues who did not make the move into sheltered accommodation work received up to £18,000 in back pay two years ago. 'If it's equal pay, surely everybody is entitled?' she adds.

This rash of legal action has come despite a judgment in favour of the GMB by the Employment Appeal Tribunal. In *GMB v Allen*, the court overturned last year's tribunal ruling in favour of female members of the GMB who had argued that their unions had not fought hard enough for them and that they had been sexually discriminated against in negotiations for its 'single status' pay deal introduced in January 2005, which was supposed to iron out pay differences between men and women. The women contended that the GMB had failed them by concentrating on the interests of men and not on winning them back pay. Brian Strutton, national secretary for public services with the GMB, says that unions received 'between 2000 and 3000' negligence claims earlier in the week. 'But we don't believe that we have been negligent, just as in *Allen* we didn't discriminate against women,' he says. He adds that 'the pleadings [statements of case] were appalling and we're trying to make sense of them'.

Unions had been hoping to see off 'no win, no fee' lawyers led by Stefan Cross, which has acted in 50,000 equal pay claims since 2003. They argue that lawyers are undermining collective negotiations with local authorities. By contrast, Hill accuses unions of 'conspiring to keep information hidden' from women members. He cites women such as Tracy, a 50-year-old site manager from Middlesbrough, who had been told by her union (Unison) that she did not have a claim. She has worked for the council for 15 years, as a cleaner at a leisure centre, then cleaning vacant council property and most recently as a school caretaker. 'I was told that because I moved over to being a caretaker, where there are a lot of male and female caretakers who get the same pay, I didn't have a claim,' she says. 'I told them I had only been doing this job for 9 months.' All her former colleagues who worked on vacant properties received payouts under a settlement with the council. She went to Stefan Cross, who succeeded in securing £15,000 last year. 'I was over the moon. It meant I could do something for myself which I could never have afforded before. I did up my house, got new windows, decking out the back and garden at the front. I also gave my daughter and my son some money.'

The GMB currently has 17,000 equal pay cases on its books in local government alone. 'A council might employ 5000 people and we negotiate a new equality-proof pay and grading structure, which means phasing out any levels of unequal pay men are having and increasing women's pay towards a proper level as well as a lump sum for past losses,' says Strutton. Equal pay legislation was introduced in 1975, but it was the Cleveland dinner ladies' case in 1997 that brought 1500 school dinner ladies a £5m payout and began the recent trend in settlements (see panel). Strutton calls the interest of 'no win, no fee' lawyers led by Cross, a former union lawyer who represented the Cleveland dinner ladies, a 'symptom rather than a cause' of a bigger problem. 'The way equal pay case law has been going has been to emphasise individual rights at the expense of the collective,' he says. 'Case law has been almost encouraging individuals to challenge collective approaches. That's what the lawyers have latched on to and recent tribunal decisions have helped to reinforce that. We believe that if this is about delivering 'equal pay' then the only way of doing that is on a collective basis. Individual litigation can never achieve that.' He insists that there is no evidence suggesting that private practice lawyers secure better deals then union lawyers. He also warns that women workers could end up losing a third of any compensation as well as having to pay £100-a-month fees during the life of their case. The general legal rule that 'costs follow the event' does not apply in employment tribunals – in other words, you are liable for your own costs. However, lawyers can run 'no win, no fee' deals where you do not pay if you lose, but if you win your lawyer will take a straight percentage cut, plus VAT. 'That isn't in the interests of women or equal pay,' Strutton says. 'It's in the interests of lawyers lining their pockets. It's obviously much better value for any individual to go with their union at no extra cost.' However, Mullins is not convinced. 'I'd sooner get 75% of something rather than 25% of nothing,' she says.

Kitchen drama

'The ruling came out in 1997, but we only found out we had a claim 12 months ago,' said Tina Kelly, a deputy cook at Kings Heath Primary School, Birmingham.

Equal pay and sex discrimination legislation has been in force since 1975 but it wasn't until just over a decade ago that unions won between £200 and £1300 compensation for more than 2000 dinner ladies working for Cleveland county council. Kelly, together with six kitchen staff (all women), is part of a 250-strong group action with equal pay claims against Birmingham council. They are all being represented by law firm Carvers on a 'no win, no fee' basis. The firm gets 10% of any compensation plus VAT, but nothing if they fail. 'I'm with the GMB but I haven't heard from them,' Kelly says. 'I'm not being funny, but a lot of [union reps] are council workers anyway and stand to lose money. A lot are in higher-paid jobs, so their pay scales come down because we all have to be equal. But we aren't asking for something that isn't ours and if they had paid up 11 years ago we wouldn't be asking now.'

So why haven't workers like Kelly been told about their equal pay rights by their union? 'We've had loads of mass meetings in Birmingham, but the message doesn't always get through,' says the GMB's Brian Strutton. What have the unions been doing since Cleveland? 'We've been negotiating equal pay. If councils haven't agreed, that's usually because they do not have any money, but that doesn't stop us pressing. The answer as to why not enough has happened is very simple: there's no money.'

(*Source: The Observer*, Sunday, 12 August 2007)

Questions

1. Discuss why the unions seem to have struggled to deal with equal pay issues.
2. How far can an individualistic approach to the problem of equal pay help to tackle the problem? What is the alternative?
3. What are the disadvantages in lawyers, as opposed to unions, taking up equal pay cases?

7.6 TRADE UNIONS AND DIVERSITY MANAGEMENT

This section explores how the relatively new diversity approach that so many work organisations have adopted has impacted on trade unions and their equality bargaining. Having said that unions now work more comfortably with the idea of workforce diversity and the need for them to tackle equality and diversity issues, it is quite clear that the more recent diversity paradigm poses challenges for trade unions. We have argued elsewhere (Kirton and Greene, 2006) that there are three key features of the diversity approach, which are likely to cause concern for unions, at least in theory, in pursuing equality objectives:

1. **The economic rationale for diversity**

   As we have seen in Chapter 5, traditionally, 'equal opportunities' reflect a moral concern for social justice, which in policy terms involves organisations implementing measures to eliminate discrimination and disadvantage in the workplace. This obviously resonates with the trade union 'sword of justice' orientation, and therefore, trade unions are generally supportive of employer-led equality policies, even if they seek to improve them by bargaining around equality issues. However, from a management point of view, this social justice rationale is one of the main criticisms of 'equal opportunities' and in contrast, the business case of diversity responds more to employer concerns. Although advocates of the diversity approach do not propose abandoning the moral principles of 'equal opportunities' altogether, it is suggested that 'managing diversity' is a new way forward (Kandola and Fullerton, 1998). The cornerstone of diversity is that it will deliver benefits to the organisation (Maxwell et al., 2001). The proponents of diversity approaches usually emphasize four main advantages to business: taking advantage of diversity in the labour market, maximizing employee potential, managing across borders and cultures, creating business opportunities and enhancing creativity (Cornelius et al., 2001). Unions, however, are likely to have more sympathy with critics of diversity (Dickens, 1999; Kaler, 2001) who argue that the business case is selective, partial and contingent and therefore a less robust way of tackling inequalities. Unions are also likely to be concerned about the implicit commodification of labour as a resource for organisational objectives.

2. The focus on the individual

The diversity discourse emphasizes individual difference, rather than social group difference. This is problematic for unions for several reasons. Firstly and fundamentally, a greater emphasis on individual difference might mean less policy focus on systemic discrimination and disadvantage. For example, within the diversity approach there is less emphasis on standardized procedures to eliminate discrimination (such as job evaluation) and more on individualized techniques such as performance appraisal and performance pay. In contrast, unions see strong collective agreements on pay and conditions as the vehicle for eliminating discrimination and disadvantage. Another unwelcome policy implication is that the diversity approach might mean the abandonment of positive action measures, such as recruitment initiatives or training courses targeting specific under-represented groups. Unions now favour the principle of positive action as they see it as a way of redressing historic disadvantage of particular social groups.

3. The positioning of diversity as a top-down, managerial activity

The diversity management literature typically emphasizes organisational vision, top management commitment and communication. Where employee involvement appears in models of diversity it is usually in individualized forms, such as suggestion schemes or attitude surveys; unions are usually invisible (Kandola and Fullerton, 1998). Even the more critical literature says little about the possible role of representative, organized forms of employee involvement, nor is their absence generally remarked upon. Therefore, we argue that, theoretically at least, the diversity approach threatens to marginalize the union role. This stands in contrast to the widely held ideal model of 'equal opportunities' practice, where the role of trade unions is seen as a vital piece of the 'jigsaw' making up the campaign for equality in the workplace (Dickens, 1997). This has echoes of the debate about the marginal role of unions within a Human Resources Management (HRM) framework (see Chapter 9). The fact that organisations held up as exemplars of diversity are predominantly non-union (Kandola and Fullerton, 1998; Liff, 1999) reflects this position.

However, this does not mean that unionized organisations have not adopted diversity. Rather it indicates that like its sister concept, HRM, it is an approach which theoretically fits best with non-union organisations. The shift towards a management-led equality paradigm is especially salient and ironic in the present context when there is renewed legitimacy accorded to unions by the polity at national and European levels and some evidence of a strengthening platform for collective bargaining (Colling and Dickens, 2001).

In summary, these three key features of the diversity approach have been identified theoretically to cause concern for unions because they are likely to impact on the content and processes of equality bargaining and threaten joint regulation of this important dimension of the employment relationship. Our research (Kirton and Greene, 2006) confirms that with regard to the first major feature of diversity – the economic rationale – trade unions are suspicious of the business-driven motives of the diversity approach. We found unions sceptical about whether a diversity approach would yield the stated outcome of valuing all individuals regardless of difference or whether it might prove in practice to be detrimental to tackling discrimination and inequalities. However, some union officers in our study believed that it was possible to talk the language of the business case for diversity, whilst continuing to push 'old' equality issues, because it can be argued that discrimination and harassment are bad for business. In this way the union officers in our study were advocating use of the diversity approach as a rhetorical device to resist and to challenge management-led policy, but at the same time they recognised the 'false dilemma' arguably involved in the social justice/business case divide (Liff and Dickens, 2000). The second major feature of diversity – the focus on the individual – raised a number of potential problems from the point of view of the union officers in our research. Arguably unionized organisations are managed differently from non-union ones, not least because of the existence of collective bargaining and other joint consultative machinery in unionized contexts. Unions have a preference for standardized treatment of employees through a common set of terms and conditions for the bargaining unit and a dislike of individualized employment practices. Therefore, it is no surprise to find unions suspicious of the individualist diversity approach, which threatens to position employees as individuals rather than as members of social groups. This view accords with the academic critique of diversity discussed in Chapter 5, where it is argued that diversity and equality policy can be framed either through a lens of individual difference or through one of social group difference. The individual difference lens is utilized to anchor diversity objectives within a business case rationale. In contrast, traditionally, the social group difference lens has been used to highlight and address discrimination and inequalities in organisations. It is not surprising then to find that trade union equality officers prefer to view diversity through the lens of social group difference. It is evident from our research that trade union equality officers believe they have a different understanding of management of the 'real' issues to be tackled by equality and diversity policies. For example, one of the longstanding 'equal opportunities' concerns of trade unions has been the concentration of certain social groups in the lowest pay and status positions in organisations – women and BME employees, for example. Although it might be argued that 'equal opportunities' has not been able fundamentally to redress this situation, unions generally perceive the diversity approach as a retrograde step in advancing the equality project. In the context of 'managing diversity' in New Zealand, Humphries and Grice (1995: 19) have argued that the diversity approach 'may diffuse the emancipatory potential of the historical evidence that unbridled capitalist systems will not provide fair access to employment for all who have been made to depend on it'. We have found that this is a view that unions are likely to have much sympathy with, for although unions themselves are not uncritical of 'equal opportunities', they continue to regard it as the most emancipatory of the approaches available to them in the context of a capitalist employment system.

Finally, with regard to diversity as a top-down managerial activity, contemporary diversity policy and practice is situated within a changed employment relations context, where unions generally have less influence and have greater difficulty in mobilizing support for collective action, arguably rendering them more dependent on maintaining a cooperative relationship with management. Therefore, the unions' role as an industrial relations actor has necessarily changed. Although the diversity approach might theoretically pose a threat to union involvement, as our research with trade unions has indicated, it is possible to work critically with diversity and pursue equality objectives within a diversity paradigm (Sinclair, 2000). Unions are pragmatic organisations and many union officers are always keen to identify new ways of promoting their equality agenda and if this means talking diversity with work organisations, many will be prepared to do so.

7.7 UNIONS AND INTERNAL ACTION ON EQUALITY AND DIVERSITY

There is a saying that unions are 'male, pale and stale', meaning that women and BME workers are under-represented in decision-making structures and that consequently the unions are out of touch with members' concerns. The degree to which unions can expect to meet with success in equality and diversity bargaining and in handling discrimination cases, when internally unions' decision-making structures and union officers and negotiators remain unrepresentative of the diversity of membership, is something which has increasingly come under scrutiny. It is to this topic that we now turn.

As democratic membership organisations, trade unions are governed by their membership by means of formal, local and national representative structures. Trade unions also employ a cadre of paid officials to carry out union business at both local and national levels. Through representative union structures, women, black members and other diverse social groups are, in theory, able to influence workplace bargaining and national union policies. In practice, because male members dominate unions numerically, their interests tend to prevail and be the ones that get onto bargaining agendas. This is at least in part because men also monopolise union positions of power, with white men dominating the governing bodies and decision-making structures of most unions (Kirton and Greene, 2002). The unrepresentative nature of union leadership is therefore thought to constrain unions' abilities to promote equality and diversity in employment (Cockburn, 1991; Kirton and Greene, 2002). Discussing unions' failure to adequately address women's equality issues, Colling and Dickens suggested about 20 years ago that the 'absence of women at the table has to be part of the explanation for the absence of women on the table' (1989: 32). The belief was, and still is, that members of 'minority' groups are in a better position to identify the needs and concerns of their group than 'outsiders' are. For example, female trade unionists are especially well placed to understand the particular problems faced by women workers and to identify gendered dimensions to traditional bargaining issues (e.g. Munro, 1999; McBride, 2001; Kirton and Healy, 1999). This principle of 'like understanding like' can also be applied to other groups of union members, for example, that black trade unionists are well placed to understand the concerns and experiences of black workers. It is therefore important for unions internally to be diverse so that a diverse range of needs and concerns can be brought to the bargaining table. For some years, unions have been striving to reflect membership diversity in the ranks of their national and local officers and negotiators by introducing a number of internal equality measures. Since Colling and Dickens (*ibid*) made their comment, the unions have come a long way and women and other 'minorities' are now much better represented in union decision-making structures. Nevertheless, it is widely thought that it is necessary for unions to sustain the effort.

Broadly following Trebilcock's (1991) categorisation of union efforts to achieve equality, we now examine the nature of the unions' internal equality initiatives. The first step that many trade unions, encouraged by the TUC, took was the adoption of an equality policy statement. Although this was a symbolic first step, policy statements, in themselves, do nothing more than declare a commitment to equality. Structural and organisational changes usually proved necessary to *deliver* equality. Unions did not adopt structural and organisational changes in a uniform way, nor did all the unions give equal priority to tackling inequalities. Women's equality has been pursued more vigorously by unions than equality for other under-represented groups such as disabled and lesbian and gay members, probably because women are such a significant source of union members. However, more recently the unions seem to have turned their attention to other under-represented groups, including BME and lesbian and gay members (TUC, 2007).

There are seven strategies used to a greater or lesser extent by individual trade unions in order to tackle internal inequalities: (i) equality conferences, (ii) equality committees, (iii) equality officers, (iv) trade union courses, (v) reserved seats on governing bodies, (vi) electoral reform and (vii) new approaches to conducting union business.

7.7.1 Equality conferences

Some unions hold annual equality conferences with a broad agenda containing a range of equality issues. Others hold conferences dedicated to particular groups including women, disabled members, lesbian and gay members and BME members. The latest TUC Equality Audit finds that 33% of unions hold regular women's conferences, 42% hold regular black member conferences, 27% hold disabled member conferences and 35% hold lesbian and gay member conferences (TUC, 2007). Equality conferences serve the twin purposes of raising awareness and exploring equality issues and of providing a forum in which delegates from under-represented groups can gain experience of trade union processes and procedures. In some cases, equality conferences are empowered to pass motions or resolutions, which influence the central governing body of the union.

7.7.2 Equality committees

Equality committees provide regular forums, at a regional and/or national level, in which equality issues are discussed. The TUC's latest Equality Audit (TUC, 2007) shows that 60% of unions have equality committees. Such committees usually have access to financial resources, which can be utilised for campaigning, educational and other activities. They also represent a place where under-represented groups can gain experience of trade union affairs. Critics argue that there is a danger, however, of equality issues being confined to a separate, powerless sphere. This can be avoided if there is a direct relationship between equality committees and unions' 'mainstream' decision-making structures (Healy and Kirton, 2000). In some instances, equality committees have been pivotal in calling for some of the internal equality strategies discussed here.

7.7.3 Equality officers

Equality officers are often members of the national unions' paid staff with an expertise in equality and diversity issues. They provide administrative support and expertise to the equality committees and generally work to raise the profile of equality and diversity issues within the union. The latest TUC Equality Audit shows that the majority of unions have a national officer whose main responsibility is for equality. The report also shows that 15% of unions have dedicated women's equality, race equality and disability equality officers, and 13% have a dedicated lesbian and gay equality officer (TUC, 2007). As discussed above, some unions also have 'lay' (elected volunteers) equality reps at workplace level who provide support and representation for members who experience discrimination or harassment.

7.7.4 Trade union courses

Trade union courses contribute to the development of union representatives and leaders. Around 70% of trade unions provide equality and diversity training courses for officers, representatives and members (TUC, 2007). The TUC and many individual unions also provide courses aimed at improving the participation in union affairs of under-represented groups. For example, women-only and black member-only training courses are offered by a number of unions. A more recent innovation is online courses on a range of equality issues developed by the TUC and some individual unions.

7.7.5 Reserved seats

A minority of UK trade unions has taken the more radical step of introducing reserved seats on governing bodies (usually for women and/or BME workers). Reserved seats are an example of a radical equality initiative (Kirton and Greene, 2002). The aim is to intervene in the democratic process to shape outcomes by recasting the composition of union government. In Jewson and Mason's (1992) terms, reserved seats seek to redistribute rewards by attempting to guarantee certain groups a role in union decision-making. (Chapter 5 explains and discusses in greater depth Jewson and Mason's conception of liberal and radical approaches to equality.) Reserved seats are controversial because they challenge liberal conceptions of fairness and justice, which place the emphasis on ensuring that 'the rules of the competition are not discriminatory' (Jewson and Mason, 1992: 221), rather than reshaping outcomes. For this reason, reserved seats have not proved popular with trade unionists – only 16% of trade unions have reserved seats for women and 20% have reserved seats for black members on their executive boards (TUC, 2007). There is the risk that those who occupy reserved seats will be treated as token figures without any real legitimacy (Trebilcock, 1991). For this reason reserved seats are not always popular with those they are designed to benefit – under-represented groups.

7.7.6 **Electoral reform**

The strategy of 'proportionality' is a complex electoral reform strategy adopted by some unions in order to increase women leaders. The idea is that women must be represented in union governing bodies in the same proportion as in the membership. This innovation is in recognition of women's increasing share of union membership and continued under-representation in union decision-making. One of the larger UK unions, the public sector UNISON, has adopted the parallel strategy of 'fair representation', which aims to ensure a broad balance of members in union leadership, including BME, disabled and lesbian and gay (McBride, 2001). Achieving fair representation is a more imprecise, complex and on-going process than proportionality (Colgan, 1999). Within UNISON, 'self-organisation' is a key ingredient to achieving the objectives of both strategies. 'Self-organisation' is the term used to describe forums in which under-represented groups (such as women, disabled, lesbian and gay and BME members) meet to share concerns and establish their own priorities. These forums are less formal and structured than unions' equality committees. In particular, participation is open to any member who self-identifies with the group, rather than to members elected to represent a particular constituency. The concerns and priorities the group identifies are then fed into mainstream union governing bodies. Self-organisation is a strategy adopted by a minority of other unions, but it is most highly developed in UNISON. Support for self-organisation among under-represented groups is widespread (Colgan, 1999).

7.7.7 **New approaches to conducting union business**

Most trade unions have made changes in the ways in which they have traditionally conducted their business in order to tackle the criticism that their *modus operandi* was masculine biased. The aim is to facilitate the participation of under-represented groups. The changes especially relate to removing the barriers to women's participation and include addressing childcare needs, arranging transport to and from meetings and adjusting the timing and location of union meetings. More recently, efforts have been made by many unions to facilitate the participation of disabled members, including disabled access at meetings and conferences, communication aids for members with hearing impairments, documents in more accessible formats, etc.

Key learning points

- Union decision-making structures are generally under-representative of membership diversity.
- Unions have developed various strategies in order to promote internal equality. These include introducing equality conferences, equality committees, equality officers, trade union education, reserved seats on governing bodies, electoral reform and new approaches to conducting union business.

7.8 CONCLUSION

From the above discussion, it can be seen that the union role in equality and diversity is broad based. Unions seek both to enforce and to build upon employees' legal rights. Collective bargaining has the potential to promote equality and diversity because it can widen the focus from individual cases of discrimination to achieving equality for the entire workforce. However, equality and diversity issues can easily slip off the bargaining agenda in a hostile economic or organisational climate and if union negotiators have little or no practical interest in them. Further, in order to realise their potential to act as equality and diversity agents, unions will need to strengthen their influence by increasing their membership. The recruitment of women members is critical, since forecasts of job growth are in the professional and associate professional occupations in which female unionization is highest. However, this optimistic outlook must be balanced against the likelihood that much of this growth will occur in sectors with very low rates of unionization such as hotels and catering, which poses an organizing challenge for unions.

Union decision-making structures are mostly unrepresentative of membership diversity and this is thought to constrain the effectiveness of collective bargaining as a means to promote equality and diversity. Unions are bureaucratic organisations and as such, the pace of change is slow. The unions' strategies and practices described in this chapter have met with varying degrees of success in terms of creating a more representative leadership; therefore the equality project within trade unions is still not completed. This is especially important for trade unions today, as it is a widely held belief that 'issues of internal equality [the position of women and BME workers and the representation of their interests within unions] are connected to issues of external equality' (Dickens, 1997: 288).

REVIEW AND DISCUSSION QUESTIONS

1. Why do you think it is important for unions to monitor the demographic composition of their memberships?

2. In what ways do the social, economic and political climates unions are faced with, influence the realisation of union objectives?

3. What are the main factors that promote or inhibit equality and diversity bargaining?

4. How can the under-representation of women and BME workers in union decision-making structures be explained?

FURTHER READING

Colgan, F., Ledwith, S., 2002.

This is an international volume containing articles exploring contemporary trade union strategies and policies in relation to diversity.

Dickens, L., 1997.

This is a short, but insightful article, summarising the strategies of the state, employers and trade unions in relation to equality.

Greene, A.M., Kirton, G., 2009.

This is a book presenting original evidence on the state of diversity management in the UK. The perspectives of different stakeholders are explored.

REFERENCES

Bercusson, B., Dickens, L., 1996. Equal Opportunities and Collective Bargaining in Europe: Defining the Issues. European Commission, Brussels.

Blyton, P., Turnball, P., 1998. The Dynamics of Employee Relations. Macmillan, Basingstoke.

Cockburn, C., 1991. In the Way of Women. Macmillan, Basingstoke.

Colgan, F., 1999. Moving forward in UNISON. In: Hunt, G. (Ed.), Labouring for Rights: a Global Perspective on Union Response to Sexual Diversity. Temple University Press, Ontario.

Colling, T., Dickens, L., 1989. Equality Bargaining – Why Not? Equal Opportunities Commission, Manchester.

Colling, T., Dickens, L., 1998. Selling the case for gender equality: deregulation and equality bargaining. British Journal of Industrial Relations 36 (3), 389–411.

Colling, T., Dickens, L., 2001. Gender equality and trade unions: a new basis for mobilisation. In: Noon, M., Ogbonna, E. (Eds.), Equality, Diversity and Disadvantage in Employment. Palgrave, Basingstoke, pp. 136-155.

Cornelius, N., Gooch, L., Todd, S., 2001. Managing difference fairly: an integrated 'partnership' approach. In: Noon, M., Ogbonna, E. (Eds.), Equality, Diversity and Disadvantage in Employment. Palgrave, Basingstoke.

Cunnison, S., Stageman, J., 1995. Feminising the Unions. Avebury, Aldershot.

Dickens, L., 1997. Gender, race and employment equality in Britain: inadequate strategies and the role of industrial relations actors. Industrial Relations Journal 28 (4), 282-289.

Dickens, L., 1999. Beyond the business case: a three-pronged approach to equality action. Human Resource Management Journal 9 (1), 9-19.

Dickens, L., Townley, B., Winchester, D., 1988. Tackling Sex Discrimination Through Collective Bargaining. Equal Opportunities Commission, Manchester.

Greene, A.M., Kirton, G., 2009. Diversity Management in the UK: Organisational and Stakeholder Experiences. Routledge, London.

Healy, G., Kirton, G., 2000. Women, power and trade union government in the UK. British Journal of Industrial Relations 38 (3), 343-360.

Humphries, M., Grice, S., 1995. Equal employment opportunity and the management of diversity. Journal of Organisational Change Management 8 (5), 17-32.

Jewson, N., Mason, D., 1992. The theory and practice of equal opportunities policies: liberal and radical approaches. In: Braham, P., Rattansi, A., Skellington, R. (Eds.), Racism and Antiracism. Open University Press, Milton Keynes.

Kaler, J., 2001. Diversity, equality, morality. In: Noon, M., Ogbonna, E. (Eds.), Diversity, Equality and Disadvantage in Employment. Palgrave, Basingstoke, pp. 51-64.

Kandola, R., Fullerton, J., 1998. Managing the Mosaic: Diversity in Action. Institute of Personnel and Development, London.

Kirton, G., Healy, G., 1999. Transforming union women - the role of women trade union officials in union renewal. Industrial Relations Journal 30 (1), 31-45.

Kirton, G., Greene, A.M., 2002. The dynamics of positive action in UK trade unions: the case of women and black members. Industrial Relations Journal 33 (2), 157-172.

Kirton, G., Greene, A.M., 2006. The discourse of diversity in unionised contexts: views from trade union equality officers. Personnel Review 35 (4), 431-448.

Labour Research, 1994. Same Sex - Different Deal. Labour Research Department, London.

Lee, G., 1987. Black members and their unions. In: Lee, G., Loveridge, R. (Eds.), The Manufacture of Disadvantage. Open University Press, Milton Keynes.

Liff, S., 1999. Diversity and equal opportunities: room for a constructive compromise? Human Resource Management Journal 9 (1), 65-75.

Liff, S., Dickens, L., 2000. Ethics and equality: reconciling false dilemmas. In: Winstanley, E., Woodall, J. (Eds.), Ethical Issues in Contemporary Human Resource Management. Macmillan, Basingstoke, pp. 85-101.

McBride, A., 2001. Gender Democracy in Trade Unions. Ashgate, Aldershot.

Maxwell, G., Blair, S., McDougall, M., 2001. Edging towards managing diversity in practice. Employee Relations 23 (5), 468-482.

Mercer, S., Notley, R., 2008. Trade Union Membership 2007. Department for Business, Enterprise and Regulatory Reform. London.

Metcalf, D., 2000. Fighting for Equality. CentrePiece, www.centrepiece-magazine/summer00/metcalf.htm.

Munro, A., 1999. Women, Work and Trade Unions, Mansell, London.

Noon, M., Hoque, K., 2001. Ethnic minorities and equal treatment: the impact of gender, equal opportunities policies and trade unions. National Institute Economic Review. 176.

Phizacklea, A., Miles, R., 1987. The British trade union movement and racism. In: Lee, G., Loveridge, R. (Eds.), The Manufacture of Disadvantage. Open University Press, Milton Keynes.

Rees, T., 1992. Women and the Labour Market. Routledge, London.

Sinclair, A., 2000. Women within diversity: risks and possibilities. Women in Management Review 15 (5/6), 237-245.

Trebilcock, A., 1991. Strategies for strengthening women's participation in trade union leadership. International Labour Review 130 (4), 407-426.

TUC, 2007. TUC Equality Audit 2007. Trades Union Congress, London.

TUC, 2009. TUC Equality Reps Project Report. Trades Union Congress, London.

Walby, S., 1997. Gender Transformations. Routledge, London.

Equality and diversity policy and practice in organisations

8

Aim

To explore equality and diversity policy and practice in organisations.

Objectives

- To consider the social justice and business case orientations of organisational policy approaches.
- To examine the nature and content of organisational equality and diversity policy and practice.
- To explore the role of key organisational actors in promoting equality and diversity.

8.1 INTRODUCTION

The development of formal equality policies in UK organisations dates back to the late 1970s and was strongly influenced by the anti-sex and race discrimination legislation of the period. The legislation of the 1970s was pivotal in drawing attention to inequalities in employment and in placing equality issues on the policy agenda of employers (Liff, 1995), but the legislation is essentially liberal and as such, fairly minimalist in nature despite some more recent changes (see discussion in Chapters 5 and 6). By minimalist, we mean that the legislation focuses on issues of equal access to and equal treatment in employment, avoiding the more sensitive political issues involved in the radical approach of 'redistributing rewards' or in shaping labour market outcomes. Following from this, organisational policies have traditionally tended to reflect liberal and mini-malist legal requirements and have, thus, generally been concerned to tackle inequality by the implementation of formal rules and procedures to be applied in a uniform way to all employees, irrespective of gender, race, disability and so on. This policy approach, usually known as 'equal opportunity' (EO), seeks to ensure that the employer stays within the law, but does little to actually *promote* equality or diversity.

Within EO policy, organisations typically produced a statement setting out their intention to be or become an 'equal opportunity employer'. Some employers did no more than this (Liff, 1995), whilst others developed a policy with clearly articulated aims and objectives. Whatever form they took, EO policies became widely criticised for their failure to deliver equality of outcome. In Chapter 4, we explored organisational culture, which can help reveal why liberal, bureaucratic EO policies had limited impact on outcomes. It is now widely accepted that formal equality and diversity policies are unreliable indicators of the *actual* practices, beliefs and values towards equality and diversity issues within organisations. Most UK organisations now use the term diversity within their policy title; for example 'diversity policy', 'managing diversity policy' and 'equality and diversity policy' are some of the newer labels that have replaced EO (Greene and Kirton, 2009). The main focus of this chapter is to examine present and emerging developments in employer equality and diversity policy approaches. The term EO policy is used here to mean the traditional approach to equality policy-making taken by most employers from the late 1970s onwards. The term diversity management (DM) policy is used to refer to the more recent and still emergent policy approach.

This chapter begins by examining the orientation of organisational policies; we then examine the form and content of equality and diversity policies. Finally, this chapter considers the role of key organisational actors in the equality and diversity project.

8.2 EQUALITY AND DIVERSITY POLICY ORIENTATIONS

As stated above, traditional EO policies were historically strongly influenced by the necessity to comply with the sex and race legislation of the 1970s. However, moving beyond the narrow imperative of the legal requirements, it is possible to identify two broad policy orientations, the *social justice case* and the *business case* for equality and diversity. Theoretically, the social justice case is most strongly associated with traditional EO policies, whilst the business case is associated with the more recent DM policies. In practice, organisations often develop policies containing a mix of elements stemming from the two different orientations and those responsible for equality in organisations have always attempted to some extent to couch their arguments in the language of the benefits to business.

What does the shift from EO to DM mean for policy and practice? Does the change in language signal a substantive change in policy orientation? EO is concerned with developing non-discriminatory employment practices and procedures and tackling discrimination and harassment. In contrast DM is generally seen as proactively capitalising on the different skills, qualities and viewpoints that a diverse workforce has to offer. EO emphasises the social justice case, whilst DM shifts the focus to the business case. Exhibit 8.1 provides examples of organisational statements of diversity, which reflect the shift towards the language of diversity and the business case. The social justice case and the business case are now explained in more detail with regard to the implications for the orientation of organisational policies.

8.2.1 The social justice case

From the social justice perspective, employment inequalities are unjust and unfair and employers have a social duty to develop policy and practice to address discrimination and disadvantage. Lack of workforce diversity is generally seen as evidence of discriminatory procedures and practices, which need to be tackled by various policy measures,

---

Exhibit 8.1: Examples of organisational diversity statements

Organisation	*Diversity statement*
British Telecom (BT) http://www.btplc.com/ careercentre/WhyjoinBT/ Morethanjustanemployer/ Diversityandequality/ Diversityandequality.htm	We are an equal opportunities employer. Our policies clearly state that everyone should have the same opportunities for employment and promotion based on their ability, qualifications and suitability for the work in question.
	In this, we're ahead of current legislation. We make sure that no job applicant or employee receives less favourable treatment because of their race, sex, religion/ belief, disability, marital or civil partnership status, age, sexual orientation, gender identity, gender expression or caring responsibilities.
	Where possible we will also take positive measures to recruit people from under-represented minority groups. In short, we value you for who you are, and what you can bring us.
JPMorgan Chase http://www.jpmorganchase. com/cm/cs?pagename= Chase/Href&urlname=jpmc/ community/diversity	Diversity is a cornerstone of our global corporate culture. *How we define diversity*
	Diversity is about all of us. It is the combination of unique qualities, abilities, traits, background and style that each person brings to the world. Here at JPMorgan Chase, it is the basis for a workplace culture where we respect one another as individuals – and value the different perspectives each person brings to the table.
HSBC Bank http://www.ukpersonal. hsbc.co.uk/hsbc/ diversity/our-diversity-strategy	To operate successfully, HSBC Bank plc, a principal member of the HSBC Group needs to understand the local communities and spread that understanding around the world. We know that employing diverse people makes us more adaptable to new situations. This is not simply about gender, ethnicity, disability, religion or age; it is about respecting individuals and treating everyone, customers and colleagues, with dignity.
GlaxoSmithKline http://www.gsk.com/about/ diversity.htm	Understanding the role of diversity within our company means that we need to be aware of the contribution that can be made by everyone with whom we do business. This includes our employees, customers and other stakeholders. For employees, we must create an environment that allows them to do their best work by being themselves. By encouraging diversity, we can recruit and retain the best people; respond to our customers' needs in a way that builds their confidence in our company and our products; and work effectively with other organisations

such as implementing formal, standardised recruitment and selection procedures. The equality project is therefore primarily an ethical and moral one and is perceived as an end in itself, regardless of whether there are any direct or immediate gains to the organisation. Workforce diversity is also perceived as a good thing because achieving socially balanced communities is an important social goal. This is not to say that there is no interest in business benefits, but this is not the primary emphasis. At a policy level, the social justice case places an emphasis on the 'good employer' and on 'best practice' (Dickens, 1999). This approach is strongly associated with the public sector and its overall aim to act as a good employer in order to promote good practice more widely among organisations. The good employer model influenced public sector equality policy during the 1980s in response to the legislation of the late 1970s. Employers typically developed formal EO policies, often containing a mix of liberal and radical policy instruments (see Chapter 5), designed to eliminate discrimination and promote equality. However, the social justice case traditionally found little purchase in the profit-oriented private sector and even came under pressure in the public sector where funding constraints compelled many organisations to imitate some of the management practices of the private sector. Therefore in both the public and private sectors, the business case for equality and diversity became increasingly used to justify policy developments.

8.2.2 **The business case**

During the late 1980s and 1990s, business case arguments increasingly came to the fore as the driving force behind EO policies and at the same time many organisations started to talk about diversity instead of equality. The business case is now firmly associated with DM as opposed to traditional EO policies. This shift in language and thinking has occurred against a background of increasing national and multinational competition facing many UK business organisations and the perceived need to find ways to enhance competitive edge. The workforce began to be posited as the primary source of competitive advantage and achieving and valuing workforce diversity as the route to organisational success (e.g. Kandola and Fullerton, 1998).

Instead of asking what can be done to tackle employment discrimination, the question within the business case centres on how workforce diversity can contribute to organisational goals. The cornerstone of the business case for equality and diversity is that valuing workforce diversity delivers benefits to the organisation. By implication eliminating discriminatory recruitment and selection practices is necessary because an organisation cannot benefit from diversity if it does not manage to recruit and retain diverse workers in the first place. Neither can an organisation benefit from diversity if it does not recognise the added value workforce diversity brings to the organisation. However, these are not the primary emphases.

The proponents of diversity approaches usually emphasise four main advantages to business (Cornelius et al., 2001). First, *taking advantage of diversity in the labour market*. The principal concern is the changing make-up of the UK labour market, outlined in Chapter 2. It is argued that organisations can minimise the recruitment problems associated with demographic change by recognising and valuing workforce diversity. Second, *maximising employee potential*. Here organisations are urged to harness the skills and experience possessed by diverse groups in order to improve organisational performance. It is also believed that this would avoid low morale and poor performance caused by prejudice and discrimination, linking with the concerns of traditional EO. Third, *managing across borders and cultures*. This is often seen as particularly important for the global organisation, which, it is argued, needs to recruit and retain diverse employees in order to thrive. Fourth, *creating business opportunities and enhancing creativity*. The assumption here is that organisations could gain access to new customer markets by tapping the culturally specific experiences and insights of a diverse workforce.

Critics of the business case for equality and diversity (e.g. Dickens, 1994; Kaler, 2001; Noon, 2007) believe that if the organisational benefits to be gained from diversity are too narrow or short term, the result might be a partial rather than a comprehensive policy, i.e. one addressing only the most obvious and immediate business problems. For example, skills and labour shortages are not universal; they vary over time and space. Women and older workers might become important sources of employees when the economy is booming and young people are in short supply. Employers might be compelled to develop policies to attract these groups, including flexible work arrangements. These policies might then be abandoned once the problem was over-come or once an economic downturn took hold. Secondly, a narrow approach might lead organisations to value certain types of diversity over others, depending on the business and labour market contexts. For example, are there always business benefits to be gained from employing older people or lesbians and gay men, or does this depend on factors such as the products or services being offered? If there are no proven business benefits, as long as the organisation is complying with relevant legislation (i.e. not actually discriminating), should it worry if these groups are under-represented in the organisation as a whole or at certain levels of management? A narrow business case would suggest not. The point is that the business case, as reflected in the above four benefits, cannot consistently promote equality for all and value equally all dimensions of workforce diversity; some organisations can be successful without valuing or even having diversity.

The alternative is to create a broader vision for the business case and to consider a fifth advantage to business – *conducting ethical business/providing service equality*, which links the social justice and the business cases. This includes social, ethical and environmental issues, so that, even where short-term gains are not apparent, organi-sations would attach greater importance to valuing workforce diversity and promoting equality as a factor in corporate reputation, thus linking equality and diversity to the corporate social responsibility agenda (Dickens, 1994). The central idea of this fifth business case argument is that organisations need social legitimacy if they are to survive and flourish in the longer term. This would involve taking more of a stakeholder approach to diversity policy, which is most likely to arise from shareholder, consumer and employee pressure and be linked to the corporate social responsibility agenda. Broadening the equality and diversity agenda would render the business case 'carrot' more attractive to employers and enable a move away from a dichotomous view of business case and social justice arguments.

In the mid-1990s, Dickens (1994) argued that the business case provided an oppor-tunity to identify equality as a strategic goal, thus facilitating the 'mainstreaming' of equality issues. A mainstreaming approach aimed to ensure that equality objectives were injected into the overall policies and activities of the organisation. Similar ideas are seen in the discourse of diversity where the aim is for DM to be 'owned' by all managers, rather than remaining the preserve of the human resource department, as was typically the case in the traditional EO approach (Dickens, 1994). The business case for equality and diversity has now become pervasive at least as rhetoric, particularly in larger organisations (Maxwell et al., 2000; Subeliani and Tsogas, 2005; Hoque and Noon, 2004).

Exhibit 8.2: Employer campaign organisations' statements

The Employers' Forum on Age

http://www.efa-agediversity.org.uk/

The business case for age diversity is founded on plain common sense. It can help companies adapt successfully to new markets, and keep them aligned with evolving legislation and social trends. Age diversity also counters the threat from a shrinking, ageing workforce.

Employers' Forum on Disability

http://www.efd.org.uk/

Employers' Forum on Disability is the world's leading employers' organisation focused on disability as it affects business. Our mission is to enable companies to become disability-confident by making it easier to recruit and retain disabled employees and to serve disabled customers.

Opportunity Past- Future and Now

http://www.opportunitynow.org.uk/about_us/opportunity_past.html

Opportunity Now is the only membership organisation representing employers who want to transform their workplaces by ensuring inclusiveness for women, supporting their potential to be as economically active as men. We work to build and communicate the business case for this, to share and inspire best practice and to give employers and their people the tools to drive change.

Race for Opportunity (RfO)

http://www.bitc.org.uk/workplace/diversity_and_inclusion/race/rfo.html

RfO is committed to improving employment opportunities for ethnic minorities across the UK. It is the only race diversity campaign that has access to and influence over the leaders of the UK's best-known organisations.

The campaign aims to:

- raise awareness of the barriers preventing the black and minority ethnic (BME) community from making progress in the workplace;
- communicate the need to speed up progress on the introduction of policies that further better representation of ethnic minorities;
- highlight the responsibility and role of leaders in delivering race diversity; and
- make clear the economic and business argument for organisations investing in race diversity.

Activity 8.1

The business case for equality and diversity

Study Exhibits 8.1 and 8.2. Answer the following questions.

1. Discuss the examples of organisational diversity statements set out in Exhibit 8.1. Would you say that these statements reflect the social justice case, the business case or both? Based on your reading of the critique in this chapter and in Chapter 5, identify the potential strengths and weaknesses of the policy orientations of the different companies.

2. Looking at the employer campaign organisations' statements in Exhibit 8.2, what messages do you think are conveyed? If you were a company director which, if any, of these organisations would you want your company to join and why?

Key learning points

- There are two main approaches underpinning organisational equality and diversity policies – the social justice and the business case. Within the social justice case both equality and diversity can be viewed as goals worth pursuing in themselves. In contrast, a business case orientation requires that policies be justified on grounds of benefits to business.

- Business case arguments are highly contingent and therefore a fragile basis for legitimating an equality and diversity agenda.

- There is an emergent argument tying together the business and social justice cases within a broader definition of commercial interests linked to corporate social responsibility.

8.3 ORGANISATIONAL POLICIES

The majority of UK organisations (at least large ones) now have a formal equality and diversity policy. As stated earlier the public sector originally led the way in the development of equality policy and there are indications that the public sector is still ahead of the private. Formal equality and diversity policies are now almost universal in the public sector (at 98% of public sector workplaces) (Kersley et al., 2005) and there is clear evidence that EO policies are less likely to constitute an 'empty shell' (where formal paper commitment is not supported by practical policies) in the public sector as compared to the private (Hoque and Noon, 2004). In comparison, the picture in the private sector is more mixed and dependent on company size. Overall, two-thirds of UK private sector workplaces have equality and diversity policies, but large workplaces (1000 employees or more) are significantly more likely to have a policy than small (100 employees or fewer) (94% as against 46%: Kersley et al., 2005: 238). However, there remains a substantial mismatch between an organisation's possession of an equality and diversity policy and organisational action in translating the policy into practice (Dickens, 2006: 446; Hoque and Noon, 2004). It seems though that the emergence and ascendancy of the business case, linked to government initiated changes in public sector employment and service delivery policies in the late 1980s and 1990s (Dickens, 1999), means that there is now greater convergence in public and private sector equality and diversity policy approaches. Thus, it is *not* the case that all public sector employers proactively pursue equality and diversity strategies, whilst all private sector employers take a minimalist approach.

As the selection of organisational diversity statements shown in Exhibit 8.1 suggests, organisations now tend to emphasise the business case for equality and diversity, although many do anchor this in a broader vision of business aims. It is also clear that many organisations see DM as having evolved from traditional EO policy, rather than standing alone as something entirely new. Exhibit 8.6 presents a case study of one large organisation, which reflects a mix of business case and social justice arguments in its policy approach.

This section considers the nature and content of equality and diversity policies in UK organisations at the present time. As stated above, the business case orientation has risen to the fore in both the public and private sectors and equality and diversity policies often reflect this, resulting in a mix of traditional equality initiatives sitting alongside business case-oriented diversity initiatives. In the UK, unlike in the US context, employers appear to understand diversity as an equality strategy that complements and supplements, rather than substitutes for traditional EO policies. This is a view espoused from the early days of DM by the Chartered Institute of Personnel and Development (CIPD), in its 'Position Paper' (IPD, 1996), which stated that '*the management of diversity complements established approaches to equal opportunities*'. Some organisations appear to be simply adopting the *language* of diversity, rather than making any substantive changes to policy. Building on traditional EO means that the organisation can develop a policy to enable differences between and among groups of employees to be recognised, at the same time as treating them equitably (Liff, 1999).

8.3.1 Classifying organisational policy approaches

This section classifies organisations according to orientations towards equality and diversity policy, linking to the social justice and business cases. Many organisations do no more than produce and publicise a statement of intent, whilst others develop and implement a formal and sometimes comprehensive policy. There is, therefore, a low correspondence between policy and practice and equality and diversity statements are sometimes used purely as 'window-dressing'. Exhibit 8.3 adapts Healy's (1993) earlier typology of four types of EO organisation adding the more recent developments in diversity policy. Exhibit 8.3 can be viewed as a continuum of organisational approaches to equality and diversity which move from reproducing inequality, to tackling discrimination, through to actively promoting equality and diversity. It is in the 'comprehensive proactive organisation' that we can expect to see the greatest variety of practical policy measures and where we can expect the policy to be more than an 'empty shell'.

Exhibit 8.3 – Types of equality and diversity organisation

1. *The negative organisation.* A negative organisation will not have a traditional EO policy or a diversity policy and it may not comply with the law. It will not claim to be an equal opportunity employer or to value diversity. It may practice, consciously or unconsciously, discrimination. It will not perceive itself to be an organisation standing to benefit from diversity. It will not see the merits of either the social justice or business case for equality and diversity.

2. *The minimalist/partial organisation.* This organisation will declare itself to be an equal opportunity employer and will probably follow management fashion and now claim to value diversity. However, in practice, equality and diversity will have a low profile and a narrow business case orientation. It might not have a written equality and diversity policy and therefore it will not have developed comprehensive measures designed to overcome discrimination and to promote equality and diversity. Neither senior nor line-managers will take any interest in equality and diversity issues.

3. *The compliant organisation.* This organisation has a narrow business case orientation towards equality and diversity, but it does fulfil its legal obligations through a formal policy, probably developed and implemented by HR practitioners. The emphasis is likely to be on recruitment, and procedures will adopt 'good practice' as advocated by the statutory agencies such as ACAS. Line-managers might resent and object to HR 'interference'. Paradoxically, this organisation may have switched to the individualist language of diversity in order to downplay social group-based disadvantage and discrimination.

4. *The comprehensive proactive organisation.* The proactive organisation will emphasise the business case for equality and diversity, but will broaden the agenda to encompass elements of the social justice case. Therefore, it will comply with the law, it will aim to develop and implement 'best practice' measures and it will also monitor the outcomes of policy and practice, in order to assess their impact. It might link equality and diversity to the corporate social responsibility agenda. Positive action initiatives might be a feature of policy here to ensure that the agenda moves beyond tackling discrimination towards promoting equality and valuing diversity. It is likely that a senior member of the organisation will be championing equality and diversity and equality and diversity might be linked to the performance objectives of individuals and the organisation.

Activity 8.2

EO and diversity policy and practice

1. Visit the web sites of a range of well-known private and public sector organisations and examine the case study in Exhibit 8.6. What do the organisations you have selected say about diversity and equality? Identify the policy orientation of the organisations – do they use social justice or business case rationales or both?

2. What kinds of policy measures do the organisations use and are these consistent with the overall policy orientation you have identified?
3. Can you identify any difference between the policy orientation and policy measures of public compared with private sector organisations?
4. Can you situate the organisations within the typology presented in Exhibit 8.3?

8.3.2 Key equality and diversity policy issues

In its guidance booklet for employers, *Delivering equality and diversity*, ACAS (undated) advises employers to take action where it is needed to address inequality or promote diversity. ACAS identifies eight key equality issues that an equality policy should cover: (i) recruitment and selection; (ii) training and development; (iii) promotion; (iv) discipline and grievances; (v) equal pay; (vi) bullying and harassment; (vii) adapting working practices; and (viii) flexible working. This section briefly considers each of these key equality issues – the good practice advice offered by ACAS together with brief comments.

8.3.2.1 *Recruitment and selection*

ACAS Good practice advice

- A good job description should be concise and straightforward and include the title of the job, the aim of the job, the main tasks and who the employee will work with.

- A person specification should link to the job description and give the skills, experience and knowledge a person needs.

- Be explicit with use of language – remember that terms like 'mature person' or 'young graduate' in your job adverts may be discriminatory.

- Application forms should ask whether a candidate has a disability as employers may need to make special arrangements for the interview.

- To avoid prejudice or bias more than one person should carry out the sift. Review the process at the end of the sift to check points have been awarded on the evidence alone.

- At interview do not ask questions of a personal nature – e.g. about marital status, sexual orientation or gender identity.

As reflected in the ACAS advice to employers, good practice in recruitment and selection is generally taken to mean the development of formalised, standard procedures, which are both transparent and justifiable. For example, drawing up a straightforward and concise job description and a person specification based on it (showing the skills and experience the person needs) should enable the objective requirements of the job to be more easily identified by both candidates and recruiters and force a selection decision based on a person's suitability, rather than acceptability, (see discussion in Chapter 3). Adherence to rigorous procedures can also challenge and even halt the perpetuation of negative stereotypes and myths. For example, a person specification should expose the fact that because a job has always been done by a man, does not mean it is necessary to have a man in that position; or the fact that a disabled person has never been employed does not mean that a disabled person could not do the job.

ACAS also encourages employers to make it clear in job adverts that applications from all sections of the community are welcomed. Related to this, formalisation of recruitment and selection usually means moving away from reliance on informal, 'word-of-mouth' methods, where family and friends of existing employees are appointed. The word-of-mouth recruitment method is often still favoured by many small companies and by those operating within local labour markets, because of its lower cost. However, where certain groups of people, BME workers or women, for example, are under-represented in an organisation, it is likely that it will simply perpetuate under-representation. In addition, job adverts should be carefully written so as to avoid deterring certain social groups from applying and to avoid the impression that particular 'types' of candidates will be favoured. ACAS provides some examples of phrases that should be avoided. For example, 'needs to be physically fit' could be taken to mean someone younger or non-disabled. A better and more accurate description of what the job entails should be provided, for example, 'needs to reach and bend to pick items from shelves'. Similarly, 'needs to give clear information to clients by phone' is better than 'needs a good command of spoken English' because the latter might be read as meaning someone whose first language is English or even someone who is English.

8.3.2.2 *Training and development*
ACAS Good practice advice

- All staff should have the same access to training – regardless of whether they are part-time or full-time.

- Be flexible about your training – residential training may not suit those with caring responsibilities or those who work from home.

One of the main messages of an equality and diversity policy should be that training and development is available equally to all staff. The ACAS advice highlights the way that organisations' training policies often make tacit assumptions about people's availability for training based on the male career norm (full-time work with no outside commitments). Training courses can be used as a way of implementing the equality and diversity policy by communicating the aims and objectives, by raising awareness of equality and diversity issues and by instructing managers and other employees of their roles and duties in relation to the policy. For example, managers involved in recruitment and selection and in staff appraisal are often required to undergo equality and diversity training to ensure that they adopt non-discriminatory approaches. Equality and diversity awareness training may also be used in an attempt to improve all employees' attitudes and behaviour towards diverse social groups both within the employment and customer service contexts.

Some organisations develop specially targeted training programmes to break down employment segregation and to achieve a more diverse and inclusive workforce. This type of initiative can sit well within both traditional EO policies with a social justice orientation and DM policies with a business case orientation. This kind of training is a form of positive action, an equality strategy that is not universally popular among employers in the UK. What is striking is that articles about equality initiatives in both the academic and practitioner journals tend to use the same few companies as examples, suggesting that the strategies adopted in the private sector, beyond a fairly limited list of exemplar employers, are generally less proactive. Nevertheless, it is important to highlight exemplars of good practice in order to provide encouragement and inspiration to key actors in other organisations.

8.3.2.3 *Promotion*
ACAS Good practice advice

- Promotion opportunities should be advertised to all staff.

- Ask the same questions to internal and external candidates – it may be discriminatory not to.

Offering internal career opportunities from a business case perspective can be a means of retaining employees and avoiding the high costs associated with excessive staff turnover, but also a way of developing existing talent and skills. As the ACAS advice suggests, individuals should not be hand-picked or groomed for specific promotions; it is far fairer to open up opportunities to all staff. Also as the ACAS advice implies, internal candidates should be neither advantaged nor disadvantaged and both internal and external candidates should be put through the same recruitment and selection process. From a social justice perspective, this helps to ensure procedural justice as well as helping to achieve fairer outcomes.

8.3.2.4 *Discipline and grievances*
ACAS Good practice advice

- The organisation's equality policy should state that any breaches of the policy will be dealt with through the disciplinary procedure.

It is clearly important that employees have confidence that any equality and diversity-related complaints or grievances will be dealt with seriously in the normal manner. Equally though, extra sensitivity is undoubtedly necessary when handling grievances of this kind.

8.3.2.5 *Equal pay*
ACAS Good practice advice

- An equal pay audit may help to make sure that men and women are getting equal pay.

- Employees are entitled to know how their pay is made up - for example, how are bonuses earned?

- The Equal Pay Act covers the right of women to equal pay with men for equal work, both for full-time and part-time employees.

As discussed in Chapter 2, the gender pay gap is a persistent issue that has proved resistant to policy interventions, including the legislation mentioned in the ACAS good practice advice. Equal pay audits were recommended in 2001 by the government-commissioned Kingsmill Report on women's pay and employment. However, the evidence shows that by early 2006, only about one-third of large organisations had completed an equal pay review; far fewer in the private compared with the public sector (Glover and Kirton, 2006). Thus, it seems that many employers ignore good practice advice and need a stronger push if they are to tackle the gender pay gap. New legal requirements for the public sector are outlined in Chapter 6.

8.3.2.6 *Bullying and harassment*
ACAS Good practice advice

- The organisation should have a clear management commitment to prevent unacceptable behaviour at work.

- The policy should explain that:

  – Harassment occurs when 'someone engages in unwanted conduct which has the purpose or effect of violating someone else's dignity or creating an intimidating, hostile, degrading, humiliating or offensive environment'.

  – Harassment may include offensive jokes, personal insults, persistent criticism, unwanted physical contact or 'freezing' someone out.

  – Harassment and bullying at work can cause fear, stress, anxiety and physical sickness amongst employees. It may also put a heavy strain on personal and family life. It can lead to increased absenteeism, an apparent lack of commitment, poor performance and even resignation.

  – It is not the intention of the perpetrator which defines a particular type of harassment but the effect it has on the recipient.

As can be seen, harassment can take many different forms and it can also impact in multiple ways on an individual. Harassment is based on non-acceptance of difference and can affect any of the 'minority' or marginalised social groups that we focus on in this book. With regard to policy, it is obviously a contentious issue, particularly in view of the fact that, as ACAS states, 'the intention of the perpetrator' is not what defines harassment. Awareness training is one of the possible means of increasing understanding about harassment that organisations might use.

8.3.2.7 *Adapting working practices*
ACAS Good practice advice

- The Disability Discrimination Act requires organisations to make 'reasonable adjustments' to the working environment to give employees or potential employees with disabilities equal opportunities. If there are employees with disabilities, they should be asked about changes that might help them. This might mean:

– providing an adequate, ergonomic chair,

– providing a power-assisted piece of equipment or

– changing hours to ease travel to and from work.

- Reasonable adjustments also include re-deploying an employee to a different type of work if necessary.

- Many employers respond sensitively to the religion or beliefs of their employees and provide prayer rooms, time off to observe religious festivals, flexible dress policies, etc.

As indicated by the ACAS advice, adapting working practices is particularly relevant to disability and a range of practical measures can be taken to facilitate the employment of disabled people. The ACAS advice under this key equality issue also highlights how working practices can be adapted to respond to minority religions.

8.3.2.8 *Flexible working*

ACAS Good practice advice

- Consider different forms of flexible working – such as job sharing, part-time working, flexible hours, homeworking and annualized hours. Can they help maximize available labour and improve customer service?

- A trial period might be a good way of testing if a form of flexible working is right for the organisation and its employees.

- Where parents of children and carers of adults are entitled to apply for flexible working, employers are obliged to give serious consideration to these requests.

Family-friendly working practices are aimed primarily at facilitating women's participation in employment and are fairly widespread in both the public and private sectors. Examples include enhanced maternity leave, career break schemes, flexible hours of work and job share schemes. The label 'work–life balance' is now more commonly used, signalling that these types of arrangements are available to all employees (not just women) and that everyone can benefit (in line with a diversity approach). Based on a survey of 2000 human resource managers (Taylor, 2003), Exhibit 8.4 indicates fairly limited provision of more expensive flexible working arrangements. Organisations with a broad and progressive equality/diversity policy may also offer flexible working practices aimed at other social groups. For example, offering BME workers arrangements for time off for religious observance (other than traditional Christian festivals) or extended holiday leave for visiting family overseas. In the case of disabled people, policies might include extended disability leave and transfer to part-time work or lighter/different duties.

Exhibit 8.4: Spread of work–life balance provisions

- 47% of managers said that their organisations' working time arrangements were sensitive to the needs of women with school-age children.
- 3% of organisations provided childcare.
- 40% provided some maternity pay above the statutory minimum.
- 8% said they offered financial assistance with childcare costs.
- Over two-thirds of organisations did not allow any paid parental leave beyond the statutory minimum.
- 67% did not offer any opportunities for career breaks.
- 22% offered term-time working contracts.
- 44% of organisations had a policy of allowing employees to change from full-time to part-time hours.

Source: Taylor, R (2003)

8.3.3 Equality and diversity audits

It has long been recognised that equality policy does not always translate into practice. One of the 'best practice' recommendations of traditional EO policies was to carry out monitoring and auditing. Taking a closer look regularly and systematically at the organisation's procedures, practices and outcomes enables an evaluation of whether or not the objectives of the policy are being achieved. All the major bodies concerned with employment equality and diversity (e.g. ACAS, CIPD, EHRC) recommend monitoring. Equality and diversity audits can provide the evidence required to justify and to plan any further action and initiatives. Monitoring and auditing should not simply be a bureaucratic, 'numbers' exercise. Within the business case policy orientation it makes good business sense for organisations to know what their resources are and where they are, in order to link equality and diversity policy with business objectives. As Noon (1993) pointed out *'In an increasingly competitive environment, where according to a plethora of human resource management literature, people are deemed to be an organisation's "most valued asset", can companies afford not to be making high quality decisions with regard to their personnel? Arguably, a thorough monitoring policy, covering gender, ethnic grouping, disability and age, may become a competitive advantage in the future'*. Within the social justice orientation, an equality and diversity audit can help an organisation identify any problems of discriminatory and unfair practice and under-representation.

Exhibit 8.5 shows the type of questions that an equality and diversity audit asks and the kinds of information it collects. The findings of the audit can be used to determine what effects the policy is having and to develop new measures to advance an equality and diversity agenda. An audit covers some sensitive areas, sickness absence, for example, therefore it is important that the confidence and trust of all employees is gained.

Exhibit 8.5: Monitoring equality and diversity

Monitoring involves:

1. Gathering individual personal information on the diversity of potential recruits and existing employees;
2. Comparing and analyzing this against:
   - Other groups of employees in the organisation
   - Job seekers in the local community
   - The broader national labour market

Monitoring questions:

Organisations need to monitor employees at every stage of their employment life: from recruitment right through to retirement.

- Who applies to work for the organisation?
- Who gets to interview and who is finally recruited?
- Who gets promoted?
- Who receives training and in what work areas?
- Who takes out grievances at work?
- Who gets disciplined and what for?
- Who is absent or sick and for what reasons?
- Who gets dismissed?
- Who leaves the organisation?

(*Source*: ACAS – *Delivering Equality and Diversity*)

Key learning points

- There are four types of equality and diversity organisation – the negative organisation, the minimalist/partial organisation, the compliant organisation and the comprehensive/proactive organisation.
- ACAS identifies eight key equality issues that an equality policy should cover: (i) recruitment and selection; (ii) training and development; (iii) promotion; (iv) discipline and grievances; (v) equal pay; (vi) bullying and harassment; (vii) adapting working practices; and (viii) flexible working.
- Equality audits are a means of collecting information on different segments of the workforce to assist in evaluating the success of policy measures and in the planning of new interventions.

8.4 CRITICAL APPRAISAL OF POLICY AND PRACTICE

8.4.1 Tensions within policy orientations

The brief examination of the content of equality and diversity policies shows that some policy initiatives involve treating all employees the same, for example a consistent, standardised approach to recruitment and selection. Others involve treating different groups of employees differently, in recognition of disadvantage, discrimination or life-style difference. For example, flexible practices to accommodate women's family responsibilities, disabled workers' needs and minority religious beliefs are recommended as good practice. (This links to the concepts of 'sameness' and 'difference' discussed in Chapter 5.) Therefore it is not always clear what the overall policy aim is, i.e. to ensure that everyone is treated equally, to achieve equality of outcome or to recognise and value difference?

It might be argued that ensuring that everyone is treated equally is a worthwhile aim in itself and certainly it is considered good employment practice. However, it does not guarantee fair and equal outcomes and does not always recognise difference. On the other hand, flexible practices are often equated with preferential treatment and often perceived as unfair. Liff and Cameron (1997) noted that earlier studies also recorded high levels of opposition to any form of positive action, because policy action on specific social groups is seen to violate the more favoured principle of treating all individuals the same. This can create tensions and conflict within organisations (Sinclair, 2000; Kossek et al., 2003). For example, in the US context, the group-based discourse of equality gave way to that of individual-based diversity, partly because of a 'backlash' from white men, who complained that progressive equality laws had led to their experiencing employment discrimination and disadvantage (Edwards, 1995). Some organisations may seek to avoid the risk of inter-group conflict by adopting the more inclusive language of diversity and by emphasising the needs of the individual and the business benefits of valuing diversity. This shifts policy away from the moral ground of the social justice case towards the utility of diversity and the business case. Some of the actual policy measures may remain the same within both traditional EO policies and the newer DM policies. However, what is important for policy-makers who fear resistance or conflict is that the underlying rationale for policy changes sits more comfortably within a liberal, individualistic, business-driven orientation, resonant with current management thinking in the search for competitive edge. This approach takes the political and moral sting out of equality policy and endows it with a common sense meaning, i.e. it makes business sense; therefore no more needs to be said. Thus, diversity is appealing to some organisations because it does not lay claim to what may look to many people like the 'specious moral high ground' of righting wrongs and promoting justice (Edwards, 1995: 177).

8.4.2 Limitations of policy measures

There are also problems with some of the detailed prescriptions and common policy measures associated particularly with traditional EO policies. For example, the belief that the formalisation of recruitment and selection procedures will eradicate discrimination rests on the spurious assumption that there will always be a 'best person' for the job and that rational, unbiased procedures can reliably detect whom that person is. In reality, it is more likely that countless applicants could perform any particular job equally well, especially lower-skill jobs. So, if there is no immediately obvious single best person, how is the selection decision made? The reality is that recruitment decisions are often made on the basis of which candidate the recruiter believes will fit in. The belief that gendered, racialised and subjective human beings can construct entirely objective criteria and then translate them into practice is naive. Collinson et al.'s (1990) detailed study of insurance sales showed how gendered judgements are made in recruitment and selection. For example, when evaluating male candidates, involvement in sport was a definite advantage; in contrast, selectors viewed a female's sporting achievements as indicative of a 'very narrow existence' (1990: 147). Behaviour described as 'pushy' when exhibited by a female candidate, was described as 'showing initiative' when a male candidate was involved (1990: 101). These examples from Collinson et al.'s case studies highlight the way that certain personal characteristics are often viewed as appropriate to one gender, but not the other. In short, managers often find it difficult to disassociate characteristics such as leadership from the socially constructed concept of masculinity (Liff, 1995). These problems remain unresolved by the formalisation of procedures, so that there is room for bias, prejudice and discrimination even in an 'equality and diversity proofed' recruitment and selection policies.

Further, even if we assume that a formalised recruitment policy eliminates discrimination and allows all levels of the organisation to become more diverse, will this be welcomed, or might some employees resent the changes? For example, workforce diversity might not increase creativity; instead it might create divisions and disagreements in work teams and arouse conflict in the organisation (Kirton, 2008). From a business case perspective, if people are not used to working with diversity, performance might suffer, at least in the short term, as they learn to adapt to the new environment (Kirton, 2002). The fact that increasing workforce diversity makes the whole organisational context more competitive means that some groups lose their privileged position and this is bound to provoke tensions, which managers might prefer to avoid by keeping the work group relatively homogenous.

There are also tensions and contradictions within the area of equality and diversity training. On the one hand there is a strong case for diversity awareness training because it can shift discriminatory attitudes and break down the widespread ignorance of issues such as disability, racism, sexism, ageism and sexual orientation. However, controversy surrounds some of the *methods* employed by equality and diversity training, rather than the *aim*. In the past, critics argued that 'racism awareness training' induced 'white guilt' and led to defensive behaviour, particularly by white males (Shapiro, 1999). This kind of training is also seen by some as stirring up conflict where there is none and of personalising racism, making white participants feel guilty, rather than seeing it as an institutional problem. Furthermore, whether diversity training does actually change attitudes and behaviour is debated. Nevertheless, in some organisations, awareness training is still used in one form or another and is often explicitly linked to specific organisational procedures and practices and used as a means of encouraging behavioural change. For example, training often focuses on selection procedures, in particular interviewing, and encourages participants to reflexively challenge their own biases and prejudices, as well as encouraging strict adherence to the formalised measures designed to eliminate discrimination. There is some evidence suggesting that well-designed equality and diversity training can contribute to the achievement of a number of objectives, including conveying to participants the rationale for equality and diversity initiatives and creating a greater awareness of participants' own stereotypes (Liff, 1997). One of the other main concerns about equality and diversity training is whether attendance should be compulsory for all employees or for all employees in a specific area of activity, such as recruitment, or should it be voluntary? Making it compulsory risks resistance and hostility and it could then do more harm than good. On the other hand the voluntary approach probably means that people most in need of the training do not attend. Where resistance and anger are encountered, they must be confronted as part of the training process, but this is a sensitive area for trainers to handle (Sinclair, 2000).

Dilemmas and controversies also surround the positive action training programmes targeted at under-represented groups, which may be no more popular with those they are designed to benefit than with other organisational members. Being positioned as disadvantaged and in need of help can be a stigmatising and lonely experience. Positive action defies the merit principle in which most people believe and there may always be an air of doubt as to whether the outcome was deserved (Liff and Dale, 1994). This can engender negative attitudes and behaviours among the dominant group towards the under-represented group; e.g. 'she was only promoted because they wanted a woman manager'. Nevertheless, some organisations, especially those associated with the national campaigns 'Opportunity Now' and 'Race for Opportunity', have reported successes with targeted training interventions. Without special initiatives of these kinds to improve the position of under-represented groups, the pace of change is likely to be very slow, even where recruitment policy and practice are genuinely non-discriminatory. However, the subjective experiences of those who have 'benefited' from this type of training is an interesting area of enquiry, at present under-researched, which might shed light upon the social processes and relations involved in positive action.

Flexible working practices designed to facilitate the employment of women are also controversial and double-edged. Family friendly or work–life balance provisions are often viewed as a *concession for those who cannot conform to "normal" working patterns* (Lewis, 1997: 15), usually women. Women who take advantage of these arrangements are often constructed as being uncommitted to the organisation and to paid work or as being unable to compete with men without assistance. The alternative approach is for organisations to think about ways in which *they* need to change to adapt to a changing workforce, rather than the converse. In this vein there has been a shift in work–life balance discourse to attempt to make flexible practices more inclusive by extending the debate beyond women's needs, to include fathers and families. For example, the idea that men might wish to spend more time caring for children, or that men and women without children might wish to take time out of employment for personal development and might therefore be able to benefit from flexible working practices. This is the approach now adopted by the British government, the Trades Union Congress (TUC) and many employers under the more gender-neutral umbrella of 'work–life balance' (as opposed to 'family friendly'). However, there is a danger that 'work–life balance' policies, by treating all employees the same and by downplaying female disadvantage, might lead to the dilution of the equality and diversity agenda, rather than to its transformation (Liff and Cameron, 1997). Traditional equality issues may become subsumed under business imperatives and repackaged as individual lifestyle concerns. Also, it is doubtful that a 'work–life balance' approach could have a deeply transformative effect unless men were to take up the 'benefits' in such large numbers as to force a rethink of traditional gender stereotypes and traditional career structures.

It was suggested above that equality and diversity audits are an essential ingredient of a good equality and diversity policy. An audit should regularly and systematically evaluate and review policy and practice. It is important that the audit is not simply used to legitimate existing policy and practice, but also to identify areas where further action is needed. Data collection needs to move beyond a simple 'head count' approach (i.e. finding out where different groups of employees are), and needs to capture the qualitative, subjective experiences of diverse employees. Liff and Cameron (1997: 42–43) cautioned that the results of auditing are open to conventional interpretation. For example, there are few women in management positions, because women do not apply or do not possess the appropriate qualifications, or because they prioritise their family commitments. This approach does little to unpack the reasons for the 'choices' employees appear to be making and absolves the organisation of any responsibility for patterns of under-representation. Another consideration is that employees may be suspicious of some aspects of auditing, for example, questions on sexual orientation or disability. Lesbians and gay men who disclose their sexual orientation may fear victimisation. Similarly, some disabled people are unwilling to disclose information about disability (Cunningham and James, 2001). It is important to think about how the information gathered will be stored, who will have access to it and how it will be used. The collection of sensitive information must be justified on the basis that it will result in action to tackle the barriers and obstacles to equality and valuing diversity.

Key learning points

- It is often unclear whether equality and diversity policies seek to treat people the same or differently.
- There are cognitive difficulties inherent in the process of constructing 'fair and objective' decision-making criteria, which arise from human beings' subjectivist positions and perceptions.
- Some 'positive action' measures risk alienating and arousing hostility among dominant groups.
- Equality and diversity audits are an essential ingredient of a proactive policy, but the audit should capture the experiences and perceptions of employees, rather than simply be about numbers.

8.4.3 The role of key organisational actors

Traditionally, responsibility for the formulation and implementation of equality policy has resided with human resource or equality managers. Within the context of the 'flattening' of organisational hierarchies and the devolution of some human resources responsibilities to line-managers, it is also now necessary to consider the role of line-managers in implementing equality and diversity policy, even where human resource and equality and diversity managers remain the guardians of the policy.

8.4.3.1 *Equality and diversity managers*

In an article exploring the costs and opportunities of doing diversity work in the 2000s, Kirton and Greene (2009) explain in detail the changed role of equality and diversity practitioners. They argue that during the 'EO era', many larger public and some private sector organisations employed specialist equality officers and a small number, usually in the public sector, had entire 'equality units' whose work included monitoring organisational policies and management practices, recommending changes to existing policies, developing new policy initiatives and providing training on equality issues. Most equality officers came from leftist community/political activist backgrounds and were often feminist women and/or BME people, who brought with them personal experiences of discrimination and harassment. They were generally viewed as progressive, politicised people who identified with particular disadvantaged social groups and had a clear social justice agenda. It was their personal experiences (rather than professional training or qualifications) that gave them the credibility, the authority and, arguably, the expertise to lead EO policy (see Cockburn, 1991; Jewson and Mason, 1986). Cockburn (1991: 235) argued earlier that equality officers were 'a relatively new kind of employee, inserted to be an interface between a particular constituency of interests and the management system'. However, EO in mainstream organisations proved to be an area of intense contestation, often arousing hostility, conflict and backlash. Therefore to make equality initiatives more palatable, EO officers pushed not only the social justice case for equality, but also the business case and they also forged alliances with senior white men in order to increase the acceptability and credibility of policy initiatives (Cockburn, 1991).

The specialist equality and diversity role certainly still exists and if anything the number of organisations with a 'diversity manager' seems to have increased, particularly in the private sector where there is now often someone senior (Johnstone, 2002). Is this simply a title change reflecting a new fashionable language or does the title change signify a changed role? It is argued that diversity managers have a key role in managing expectations and that they should adopt certain basic principles to accomplish this, including using 'the same rationale, language and format as the strategic plan', linking 'the diversity action plan to issues which are important to managers', demonstrating 'robust, intelligent diversity measurement' and ensuring common understanding of diversity among managers to 'secure ownership and commitment' (Johnstone, 2002: 53–54). While these 'principles' also undoubtedly influenced the strategies and practices of equality officers, disadvantaged social groups were the primary constituency of EO (Cockburn, 1991; Jewson and Mason, 1986). In contrast, we can see from these 'principles' that managers are positioned as the primary constituency of DM (Zanoni and Janssens, 2003).

The idea of business managers being the primary DM constituency is also reflected in the fact that in some organisations diversity managers are involved in both HR and business (service delivery and customer-facing) issues (Greene and Kirton, 2009). Yet in some ways, involving diversity practitioners in business issues has echoes of the rather older notion of equality 'mainstreaming' (the integration of EO into all organisational policies) (Rees, 1998). However, what comes through the diversity discourse now is not so much a question of mainstreaming equality in order to address the *rights* of diverse groups of employees and consumers, as embedding diversity in order to improve business/organisational success (Cornelius et al., 2000). This shift in emphasis means that diversity managers might be expected to have a broader business and management background, rather than a background in equality activism or HR (as required for equality officers). They might need less of an understanding of the institutional structures and processes that produce social group-based inequalities and a greater grasp of individual psychology and how to get the best out of people. Personal experiences of discrimination and harassment or being a member of a 'minority' group also seem less important attributes for diversity practitioners. Finally, a stronger affiliation with a business agenda rather than with a social justice one and with management rather than with disadvantaged social groups might be expected. However, Lorbiecki (2001) positions what she calls 'diversity vanguards' as 'outsiders-within', because she found them to be people who felt compelled to speak out against discrimination and yet who also had to uphold the organisation's business objectives, suggesting an inherent tension in the role. Similarly, Kirton et al. (2007) argue that diversity practitioners sometimes need to temper any radical ideals and objectives they might have in order to be taken seriously by management.

8.4.3.2 *Line-Managers*

Kirton and Greene (2009) regard it as significant that within DM there is an increased role for managers (Cornelius et al., 2000). Senior managers are regarded as pivotal in lending top-level commitment to DM (Gilbert et al., 1999) and middle managers are seen to play a critical role in implementing the policy on a day-to-day basis (Cornelius et al., 2000). Senior managers (e.g. chief executive officers) are often seen as catalysts of change and the 'success' of DM is often attributed to their involvement and leadership, particularly in the management literature (Gilbert et al., 1999; Gilbert and Ivancevich, 2000; Thomas, 2004). The rather optimistic assumption is made that the senior individual's widely communicated commitment to diversity filters down to individual managers, creates a climate of acceptance of diversity and modifies management and employee behaviour (Gilbert and Ivancevich, 2000). Flowing from this, a new type of diversity practitioner has emerged – the 'diversity champion' – operational managers, sometimes very senior (e.g. board of directors, CEO), who are expected to give credibility to the policy and to model desired management behaviours (Johnstone, 2002; Thomas, 2004). There is also a belief that line-managers have greater authority to determine what diversity policy should be about as they more fully understand the challenges facing other managers and the organisation.

The recent debates about the role of line-managers emerged from the shift towards 'human resource management' (discussed in Chapter 9). However, line-managers have always played a role in equality policy implementation, even if only by virtue of the fact that they are often involved in recruitment and selection and performance appraisal. Further, dependent upon the degree of autonomy they have, line-managers have always been able to ignore or actively subvert equality policy (Woodall et al., 1997), especially as human resource practitioners are often weak in organisational terms. The behaviour and actions of line-managers contribute to explaining why traditional EO policies have so frequently failed to establish equal treatment, let alone to significantly recast outcomes (Liff and Cameron, 1997). In other words, part of the problem lies with key actors' lack of commitment to and interest in the principles of equality, especially within the social justice orientation and its moral emphasis. Collinson et al.'s (1990) in-depth case studies mentioned above explore the 'power structures' and dynamics of the social relations and practices within organisations and labour markets. They place the emphasis on human agency (1990: 11), arguing that human beings retain a relative autonomy and a capacity to act in a manner of their choosing, regardless of what formal procedures tell them to do. By virtue of their position in organisations, line-managers can either reinforce or challenge traditional patterns of disadvantage. Collinson et al.'s evidence found that line-managers generally acted in ways that reinforced inequalities.

What are line-managers' objectives and how can equality and diversity managers secure their commitment to equality objectives? It goes without saying that line-managers' principal concerns lie with business objectives. Accordingly, a crucial element of the business case policy orientation is to transfer responsibility for equality and diversity from human resource to line-management in order to make equality and diversity a business issue (Cornelius et al., 2000; Liff and Cameron, 1997). The alignment of equality and diversity goals with broader business goals should, the argument goes, ensure that line-managers become committed to their implementation and interested in the outcomes. There is, however, a lack of empirical evidence supporting this proposition. As we have discussed earlier, the business case for equality and diversity is partial and contingent and in some circumstances business needs could point managers away from equality and diversity practice. For example, in the long term a diverse workforce might improve service delivery, but in the short term diversity might create divisions and disagreements in work teams and arouse conflict, which would prevent the organisation from performing effectively. Managers might decide to avoid conflict by avoiding diversity. As another example, Woodall et al.'s (1997) study found that organisational restructuring had negative implications for equality programmes, because of the added pressures line-managers were placed under during and after a period of change. Many organisations in the public and private sectors have undergone considerable change over the last 10 years and any new responsibilities placed on managers can be seen as another burden.

However, even without evidence to support the claim that a transfer of responsibility to line-managers engenders a sense of ownership of equality and diversity policy, it remains an important goal, because of the important role line-managers play in day-to-day policy implementation. For example, in recruitment and selection there are many opportunities for line-managers to exercise bias and prejudice, whether consciously or unconsciously and thereby to perpetuate the very myths and stereotypes that equality and diversity policy seeks to challenge. Indeed, Noon's (1993) study involving speculative application by two bogus candidates, Evans and Patel, to the UK's top 100 companies, revealed that companies with no EO policy were more likely to practice blatant discrimination, but that even companies with an EO policy did treat the white candidate more favourably. Line-managers also have the opportunity to exercise bias and prejudice when selecting employees for training and promotion, even if there are highly formalised procedures. Take, for example, performance appraisal, a process usually carried out by line-managers and one that often opens the door to training and promotion opportunities, as well as to performance or merit pay. Despite the rhetoric that equality and diversity policy should be 'owned' by the people who are able to translate it into practice, there is abundant evidence that managers continue to make decisions on the basis of stereotypes. Managers also tend to favour candidates in their own image, and often hold strongly sex-typed views of job requirements (Liff and Wacjman, 1996). Given that certain groups of employees are under-represented in management, particularly women, BME and disabled people, this has obvious worrying implications. The popular negative stereotypes of older workers and gay men and lesbians are also an issue here. In the context of gender equality, Woodall et al. (1997) argued that it is doubtful whether line-managers can be left with responsibility for managing women's careers.

What the above discussion highlights is the potentially negative consequences of transferring responsibility for the implementation of equality and diversity policy to line-managers without finding some way of rewarding them for their commitment (Liff and Dale, 1994). One answer is to tie equality and diversity aims to managers' performance targets and appraisals. Some organisations have stressed the importance of top-level commitment, believing that equality or diversity 'champions' can act as catalysts of change (Greene and Kirton, 2009). Although this is a worthwhile aim, in itself it does not resolve the problem of how to embed equality and diversity policy within everyday organisational practice.

Key learning points

- Many large organisations have equality and diversity managers responsible for developing policy, often within a business case orientation.
- Line-managers play an important role in either challenging or reproducing inequalities. It is essential to consider how the commitment of line-managers to equality and diversity goals can be won.

Exhibit 8.6: Example Case Study

Goldman Sachs International: Diversity Task Force

In 2006, Goldman Sachs formed its second global Diversity Task Force comprising 34 Managing Directors. Fifty-one focus groups were held and extensive interviews were carried out with senior management to shape the foundation of a five-year diversity plan.

Goldman Sachs' belief in diversity as a business imperative has constantly driven commitment to achieve meaningful progress in this area. The first Diversity Task Force (DTF) was created in 2001 to assess the status of the firm's diversity progress and to make concrete recommendations to drive behavioural changes to advance diversity and inclusion at the firm.

Comprising 34 Managing Directors representing each division and region of the firm, the second DTF convened from April to July 2006. The main aim of the task force was to help shape the next generation of programmes and ensure that Goldman Sachs continued to build an inclusive environment. Much focus was put on ethnicity, multiculturalism, religion and sexual orientation. The recommendations made have provided the foundation of our next five-year diversity plan.

While Goldman Sachs has made important strides in diversity, progressing the agenda demands a renewed sense of obligation and energy. Since the first task force, the Office of Global Leadership and Diversity has been established, they have launched the People Survey which is an important tool for them to assess employees' satisfaction and further support has been provided to the affinity networks.

The DTF represented the significant commitment and long-term effort needed to address the strategic priority that the firm places on this business imperative.

Impact

- Methodology has been developed to evaluate the diversity performance of senior business leaders
- A Diversity and Inclusion training curriculum that explores the entire spectrum of diversity topics has been launched
- Senior leaders are also proactively interweaving diversity agendas into their divisional addresses

(*Source*: http://www.bitc.org.uk/resources/case_studies/goldman_sachs.html)

8.5 CONCLUSION

This chapter has examined organisational approaches to equality and diversity policy, exploring social justice and business case orientations. Diversity policy is still developing in the British context, but is most strongly associated with the business case, although many organisations have broadened the agenda to encompass elements of the social justice case. Some writers have argued that when a link is forged between equality and diversity and business objectives, there is evidence of increased resources devoted to equality, as well as raised awareness of equality issues within the organisation (Shapiro, 1999). Others have expressed doubt as to whether the business case alone can ever be powerful enough to effect fundamental change (e.g. Dickens, 1994; Lewis, 1997). Diversity policy is usually complementary to traditional EO policy, rather than a totally separate or new approach. Many of the initiatives placed by organisations and some writers under the diversity umbrella would not be out of place within a traditional EO policy, for example monitoring and auditing (Cornelius et al., 2000; Liff and Wajcman, 1996). It is also clear that line-managers have an increasingly prominent role in equality and diversity, but that they can either reinforce or challenge discriminatory practices and outcomes. The multiple constraints and pressures faced by line-managers may mean that it is difficult to persuade them to commit to equality and diversity objectives (Cornelius et al., 2000; Greene and Kirton, 2009). Chapter 9 continues the discussion of developments in the practice of human resource management and equality and diversity.

REVIEW AND DISCUSSION QUESTIONS

1. How easy is it to distinguish between the equality and diversity policy measures associated with a social justice orientation and those associated with a business case orientation? Provide some examples.

2. In what circumstances might a specific policy measure be justified either by a social justice or by a business case orientation, or by both? As an example, start with management training targeted at BME employees.

3. Discuss the extent to which the formalisation of procedures can ever deliver equality of outcome.

4. Identify the possible uses for information gathered by an equality and diversity audit.

FURTHER READING

Davidson, M., Fielden, S. (Eds.), 2003. Individual Diversity and Psychology in Organisations. John Wiley, Chichester.

This volume is a collection of essays on a range of diversity issues, including empirical research and theoretical pieces.

Greene, A.M., Kirton, G. 2009. Diversity Management in the UK. Organisational and Stakeholder Experiences. Routledge, London.

This book is based on original research in the UK private and public sectors. It explores employee, trade union, line-manager and diversity practitioner experiences.

Noon, M., Ogbonna, E. (Eds.), 2001. Equality, Diversity and Disadvantage in Employment. Palgrave, Basingstoke.

This volume is an edited collection of essays on a range of diversity issues. It contains both empirical and theoretical pieces.

REFERENCES

ACAS, undated. Delivering Equality and Diversity. ACAS, London.

Cockburn, C., 1991. In the Way of Women. Macmillan, Basingstoke.

Collinson, D., Knights, D., Collinson, M., 1990. Managing to Discriminate. Routledge, London.

Cornelius, N., Gooch, L., Todd, S., 2000. Managers leading diversity for business excellence. Journal of General Management 25 (3), 67-78.

Cornelius, N., Gooch, L., Todd, S., 2001. Managing difference fairly: an integrated 'partnership' approach. In: Noon, M., Ogbonna, E. (Eds.), Equality, Diversity and Disadvantage in Employment. Palgrave, Basingstoke.

Cunningham, I., James, T., 2001. Managing diversity and disability legislation: catalysts for eradicating discrimination in the workplace?'. In: Noon, M., Ogbonna, E. (Eds.), Equality, Diversity and Disadvantage in Employment. Palgrave, Basingstoke.

Dickens, L., 1994. The business case for women's equality. Is the carrot better than the stick? Employee Relations 16 (8), 5-18.

Dickens, L., 1999. Beyond the business case: a three-pronged approach to equality action. Human Resource Management Journal 9 (1), 9-19.

Dickens, L., 2006. Equality and work–life balance: what's happening at the workplace. Industrial Law Journal 35 (4), 445-449.

Edwards, J., 1995. When Race Counts. The Morality of Racial Preference in Britain and America. Routledge, London.

Gilbert, J., Stead, B.A., Ivancevich, J., 1999. Diversity management: a new organisational paradigm. Journal of Business Ethics 21, 61-76.

Gilbert, J., Ivancevich, J., 2000. Valuing diversity: a tale of two organisations. Academy of Management Executive 14 (1), 93-105.

Glover, J., Kirton, G., 2006. Women, Employment and Organisations. Routledge, Abingdon.

Greene, A.M., Kirton, G., 2009. Diversity Management in the UK. Organisational and Stakeholder Experiences. Routledge, London.

Healy, G., 1993. Business and discrimination. In: Stacey, R. (Ed.), Strategic Thinking and the Management of Change. Kogan Page, London.

Hoque, K., Noon, M., 2004. Equal opportunities policy and practice in britain: evaluating the 'Empty Shell' hypothesis. Work. Employment & Society 18 (3), 481-506.

IPD, 1996. Managing Diversity. An IPD Position Paper, Institute of Personnel and Development, London.

Jewson, N., Mason, D., 1986. The theory and practice of equal opportunities policies: liberal and radical approaches. Sociological Review 34 (2), 307-334.

Johnstone, S. (Ed.), 2002. Managing Diversity in the Workplace. Eclipse/IRS, London.

Kaler, J., 2001. Diversity, equality, morality. In: Noon, M., Ogbonna, E. (Eds.), Equality, Diversity and Disadvantage in Employment. Palgrave, Basingstoke.

Kandola, R., Fullerton, J., 1998. Managing the Mosaic: Diversity in Action. Institute of Personnel and Development, London.

Kersley, B., Alpin, C., Forth, J., Bryson, A., Bewley, H., Dix, G., Oxenbridge, S., 2005. First Findings from the 2004 Workplace Employment Relations Survey. Department of Trade and Industry, London.

Kirton, G., 2002. What is diversity? In: Johnstone, S. (Ed.), Managing Diversity in the Workplace. IRS, London.

Kirton, G., Greene, A.M., Dean, D., 2007. British diversity professionals as change agents radicals, tempered radicals or liberal reformers? International Journal of Human Resource Management 18 (11), 1979-1994.

Kirton, G., 2008. Managing multi-culturally in organisations in a diverse society. In: Clegg, S., Cooper, C. (Eds.), Handbook of Macro Organisational Behaviour. Sage, London/Thousand Oaks, pp. 309-322.

Kirton, G., Greene, A.M., 2009. The costs and opportunities of doing diversity work in mainstream organisations. Human Resource Management Journal 19 (2), 159-175.

Kossek, E., Markel, K., McHugh, P., 2003. Increasing diversity as an HRM change strategy. Journal of Organisational Change 16 (3), 328-352.

Lewis, S., 1997. Family friendly employment policies: a route to changing organisational culture or playing about at the margins? Gender. Work and Organisation 4 (1), 13-23.

Liff, S., Dale, K., 1994. Formal opportunity, informal barriers: black women managers within a local authority. Work, Employment and Society 8 (2), 177-198.

Liff, S., 1995. Equal opportunities: continuing discrimination in a context of formal equality. In: Edwards, P. (Ed.), Industrial Relations. Blackwell, Oxford.

Liff, S., Wacjman, J., 1996. 'Sameness' and 'difference' revisited: which way forward for equal opportunity initiatives? Journal of Management Studies 33 (1), 79-94.

Liff, S., 1997. Two routes to managing diversity: individual differences or social group characteristics. Employee Relations 19 (1), 11-26.

Liff, S., Cameron, I., 1997. Changing equality cultures to move beyond 'women's problems'. Gender, Work and Organisation 4 (1), 35-46.

Liff, S., 1999. Diversity and equal opportunities: room for a constructive compromise? Human Resource Management Journal 9 (1), 65-75.

Lorbiecki, A., 2001. Openings and Burdens for Women and Minority Ethnics Being Diversity Vanguards in Britain. Gender, Work and Organisation. Keele University, UK.

Maxwell, G., Blair, S., McDougall, M., 2001. Edging towards managing diversity in practice. Employee Relations 23 (5), 468-482.

Noon, M., 1993. Racial discrimination in speculative application: evidence from the UK's top 100 firms. Human Resource Management Journal 3 (4), 35-47.

Noon, M., 2007. The fatal flaws of diversity and the business case for ethnic minorities. Work, Employment and Society 21 (4), 773-784.

Rees, T., 1998. Mainstreaming Equality in the European Union. Routledge, London.

Shapiro, G., 1999. Quality and equality: building a virtuous circle. Human Resource Management Journal 9 (1), 76-86.

Sinclair, A., 2000. Women within diversity: risks and possibilities. Women in Management Review 15 (5/6), 237-245.

Subeliani, D., Tsogas, G., 2005. Managing diversity in the Netherlands: a case study of Rabobank. International Journal of Human Resource Management 16 (5), 831–851.

Taylor, R., 2003. Managing Workplace Change. Economic and Social Research Council, London.

Thomas, D., 2004. Diversity as strategy. Harvard Business Review (September), 98–108.

Woodall, J., Edwards, C., Welchman, R., 1997. Organisational restructuring and the achievement of an equal opportunity culture. Gender, Work and Organisation 4 (1), 2–12.

Zanoni, P., Janssens, M., 2003. Deconstructing difference: the rhetoric of human resource managers' diversity discourses. Organisation Studies 25 (1), 55–74.

Human resource management and diversity

9

Aim

To provide an evaluation of the theory of human resource management in terms of what it means for equality and diversity policy and practice.

Objectives

- To show why human resource management (HRM) is salient to a discussion of equality and diversity approaches.
- To present the main normative models and theories of HRM, looking at the impact on the equality and diversity agenda within organisations.
- To critically appraise the capacity of HRM to advance equality and diversity.

9.1 INTRODUCTION

HRM has been a popular management concept since the early 1990s, and its continued popularity is evidenced by the proliferation of texts and the number of university courses bearing the title. However, equality and diversity issues are often absent from the debate, with the theory, policy and practice of HRM tending to assume a 'generic' universal employee (Dickens, 1998; Benschop, 2001). This gap is significant because the human resources (HR) function is most likely to hold the main responsibility for equality and diversity policies. However, there are interesting debates about the extent to which the HR function can be the main driver of progressive equality and diversity change (Gooch and Blackburn, 2002; Cattaneo et al., 1994; Gooch and Ledwith, 1996). Also, many writers agree that there is considerable 'fit' between the theory of HRM and diversity management (DM). Indeed, Miller stated that *'Managing diversity can arguably be classed as the HRM approach to equality initiatives in the workplace'* (1996: 206). Looking through editions of the Chartered Institute of Personnel and Development's (CIPD) journal *People Management* indicates that more than a decade later, equality and diversity issues have become a central part of HRM practice. Indeed the CIPD proclaims, *'Managing diversity is central to good people management in the view of the CIPD'* (CIPD, 2004). Further, the shift to DM reflects the shift in thought about people management more generally. Webb pointed to the 'fit' between the theory of HRM and DM, seeing the move towards diversity approaches as capturing *'the wider political shift from collective models of industrial relations, state regulation and associated bureaucratic control procedures to deregulation, free market competition and notions of human resource management based on maximising the contribution of the individual'* (1997: 164).

Thus, the scene is set for a discussion of what the theory and practice of HRM offer the organisational equality and diversity project. This chapter begins by briefly presenting the most widely known normative models of HRM. This will highlight the similarities between HRM and DM and will critically appraise HRM as a force for challenging inequalities. We suggest later some key texts which offer a more extensive discussion of HRM. Specific HRM policy areas will also be analysed in more detail, drawing on Guest's (1987) model, in order to frame an analysis of what the theory of HRM has to offer the equality and diversity project. Potential advantages and benefits for equality and diversity will be discussed, as well as a critique of the theory of HRM, pointing to weaknesses of both theory and practice in advancing the position of disadvantaged groups of workers.

9.2 A BRIEF EXPLANATION OF HRM

Like DM, the theory of HRM originated in the US, building on theories of motivation and of human behaviour (Guest, 1987; Sisson and Marginson, 2003). HRM moves away from general management theories that prescribe policies and management styles which should be applied to *all* employees to take account of the *individual*. The theory of HRM is predicated on the notion that some workers will seek out and respond to work environments that provide challenging work, above average pay and conditions, increased levels of autonomy and opportunities for learning and training. Thus, HRM is based on the assumption that managers need to foster the kind of motivation within the workplace that would attract and retain the 'right' kinds of employees either through appropriate management style or by careful recruitment and selection (Guest, 1987: 511).

HRM is also essentially based on a 'business case' approach to people management (see Chapters 5 and 8). Increased competition in national and global arenas forced managers to reconsider the management of all resources within the organisation. While traditional approaches to managing people were built on bureaucratic power structures, money-based incentives and Taylorist-style work organisation, HRM emphasises the role of the individual, motivated worker, focusing on fostering a sense of involvement in, and commitment to, the organisation. The shift in people management from control to commitment strategies is felt to lead to increased productivity and greater success in meeting organisational objectives, thus making the organisation more competitive through more effective management of HR (Guest, 1987; Storey, 1989, 1992). The link between this and the business case for valuing diversity is clear. For example, it is assumed that the organisation will benefit from making people feel comfortable and motivated at work so that they can be more effective; that mixed work teams give competitive advantage; that drawing on a diverse range of skills and viewpoints will enhance the potential to understand a wider range of customer needs (Cornelius, 2002; Kirton, 2002). The need for many multi-national organisations to manage cross-cultural teams in international settings is also highlighted (Iles and Kaur Hayers, 1997). All of this fits into the remit of the HR function and underscores the need for effective people planning.

9.2.1 **A normative HRM model**

Defining HRM in theoretical terms is not, however, an easy task. A good starting point is what has been widely viewed as the 'original' conception of HRM from Michael Beer and his colleagues at the Harvard Business School in the early 1980s. At the centre of Beer et al.'s model is the view that HR should be seen as being as important (if not more important) to the success of the business as any other organisational resource. Therefore, it follows that effective management of HR is directly linked to business success. Beer et al. place an emphasis on HRM policies such as employee influence, HR flow, reward systems and work systems, which should be designed to promote the development of flexible, adaptable and highly committed employees. Most significantly, however, there is an emphasis on the need for HR policies to be integrated within the overall organisational business strategy. This has echoes of the mainstreaming approach to equality, except that here the concern is that all HRM policies (including equality and diversity) should be integrated into all business decision-making.

In addition, equality and diversity issues are an explicit element of the model. Beer et al. (1984) highlight the positive long-term consequences that HRM could have for individuals and for society. Managers are advised to track the long-term trends in the labour market in order to be able to identify potential opportunities and difficulties in acquiring skills in the future. As part of this, equality and diversity issues are highlighted and managers are advised to take account of the increased participation of women and minority ethnic groups in the labour force, as well as the ageing population. In addition, managers should recognise the changing values and aspirations of the workforce by offering education and training (Beer et al., 1984: 31). While the primacy of managers and their role is clear in this conception of HRM, it also explicitly recognises the importance of different stakeholder interests, potentially offering space for equality and diversity issues to be raised as organisational concerns by employees, trade unions or other pressure groups. The view taken is that in order to be successful, management needs to mobilise the support of various stakeholders including shareholders, employees, unions, government, customers and community groups.

There are other features of the theory of HRM which DM shares (see also Chapter 5). Most significant of these for discussion later in this chapter is the individualistic focus of HRM. HRM is directed towards the individual employee; the task of the HR function is seen as the need to harness individual commitment and talents. This stands in contrast to collectivist approaches to people management that saw employees as members of occupational groupings to which standard terms and conditions could be applied, usually negotiated with the relevant trade unions. In contrast, the theory of HRM is usually viewed as denying a role for trade unions (Guest, 1987) and indeed exemplars of HRM practice have commonly been non-union firms such as Marks and Spencer or IBM (Turnbull and Wass, 1997). However, there has been much debate about whether or not in practice union exclusion has been an aim of HRM or indeed whether the presence of unions actually encourages more practices associated with HRM (Kessler and Purcell, 2003; Guest and Conway, 1999).

In addition, like DM, HRM highlights the role of management in initiating action and mobilising support for policies. Indeed Dale (1997) stated that a specific parallel could be drawn between DM and HRM, where HRM is regarded as the discovery of personnel management by chief executives, and 'managing diversity' is regarded as the capturing of the territory of equal opportunities by managers. The idea of senior level leadership and management commitment is central in many DM textbooks and practitioner guides (see Kandola and Fullerton, 1998; Cornelius et al., 2001).

Overall then, there are many similarities between HRM and DM. Characteristics integral to DM echo those of some versions of HRM, notably the strategic integration of people as a resource to be managed towards the achievement of business goals, and the valuing of workforce diversity as a direct contribution to the success of an organisation. The HRM emphasis on the role of individuals and their involvement and commitment also has resonance with DM.

9.2.2 'Hard' and 'Soft' versions of HRM

Another feature of HRM relevant to our discussion of links with equality and diversity is the existence of 'hard' and 'soft' models of HRM (see Storey, 1992). Beer et al.'s model is widely seen as 'soft' HRM because employees are positioned as highly valued assets. Within 'soft' HRM, policies are directed towards skills development and high levels of commitment, adaptability and competence (Hollinshead et al., 1999) – the emphasis is on the *human*. It is probably this version of HRM that has most potential for progressive equality and diversity initiatives. However, at the time Beer et al.'s model was published, so too was a different version that has been characterised as 'hard' HRM (Frombrun et al., 1984). Here, principles of cost effectiveness hold primacy and HR are seen as a business expense just like any other organisational resource – the emphasis is on the *resource*. In the 'hard' version, HRM policies are primarily directed towards meeting organisational objectives rather than the development of employees (see Storey, 1992; Legge, 1995 for a more extensive discussion). As will be discussed in greater detail later, there is some parallel here between 'short' and 'long' agendas of equality, where 'hard' HRM would be viewed as following a 'short agenda' and 'soft' HRM a 'long agenda'.

Key learning points

- The theory of HRM is based on the premise that paying attention to HR and making use of appropriate HRM policies to engender increased commitment and satisfaction of employees would be directly linked to competitive advantage.
- There are strong links between the theory of HRM and the theory of DM. These include the link between the need for HRM policies to be integrated within the overall business strategy and 'mainstreaming' approaches to equality; the need to mobilise the support of diverse stakeholders within an organisation to be successful and considering the interests of a diverse workforce; and the individualistic focus of HRM and the DM focus on individual differences.
- A distinction has been made between 'hard' and 'soft' forms of HRM. It is the 'soft' version which seems to offer the most potential for progressive equality and diversity policies, with its focus on employees as valued assets and the premium placed on engendering high levels of employee commitment.

9.3 KEY DIMENSIONS OF HRM AND EQUALITY AND DIVERSITY

Guest's (1987) article provides a useful summary of the evolution of the theory and practice of HRM and its relevance to the British context. It is useful here to outline the main dimensions of Guest's theory because it provides a useful way of tapping into the constituent parts of the theory of HRM, allowing us to appraise each dimension with reference to its utility for promoting equality and diversity in the workplace. The overlap between these dimensions and the characteristics of the Harvard model will be apparent. Guest (1987) views HRM as encompassing four main dimensions or goals: strategic integration, employee commitment, flexibility and quality, each of which will be discussed below as they relate to equality and diversity.

9.3.1 Strategic integration

The first dimension of Guest's theory of HRM is strategic integration. HRM is characterised as having a concern with organisational performance as its long-term primary strategic goal (Wilson, 2007). To achieve this, the HR function and HRM policies and practices must be fully integrated into the organisation's strategic planning process. There is a need for both vertical integration (of HRM with other strategic functions and business concerns, for example sales, production and so on) and horizontal integration (ensuring that HRM policies form a coherent entity, for example, that payment systems and work organisation complement each other). Additionally, there should be integration of the HRM strategy into the responsibilities of line-managers. The idea here is that the HR function devolves tasks and activities, such that line-managers are directly empowered to take responsibility for managing people (mainstreaming people management) rather than responsibility only residing within the HR function (see Cornelius et al., 2001). Finally, employees should be fully integrated within the organisation by fostering a strong sense of company identity.

It should be clear from this that an attempt to make effective management of HR a concern throughout the organisation offers potential equality benefits. At the very least, employees are recognised as an important asset to the organisation which should be nurtured. Indeed, despite her overall pessimism with regard to the ability of new managerial approaches to deliver equality, Webb (1997: 167) argued that in the era of HRM there is at least a greater awareness than formerly of how to achieve effective organisational change towards equality (even if the evidence is limited). This includes the need for senior level commitment and resources and the need for regular monitoring of progress (a key feature of DM – see Kandola and Fullerton, 1998).

However, there are critiques of this dimension of HRM in terms of its potential to advance the equality and diversity project. First, how effectively can HRM issues be 'strategically integrated' into mainstream business strategy? There is little point debating the potential for equality and diversity of a strategically integrated HRM policy if strategic integration cannot occur in the first place. The initial criticism is the assumption that managers can be rational and strategic. Many of the prescriptions of HRM rest on free market-based assumptions where management has the key role in initiating action and mobilising support for policies. Within the theory of HRM, there is emphasis on the need to change corporate cultures. Within the corporate culture literature (and connecting to HRM), it becomes the role of the idealised 'symbolic manager' to take the lead in shaping the culture. However, there is much discussion about whether managers are able to be 'strategic'. The general picture is that there is great variation in managerial activities and much of managerial work is reactive, rather than strategic (Hales, 1986), meaning that the notion of the manager as primarily a strategist may be misconceived. Managers often have a pragmatic approach to their work because they have differential access to information and resources, depending on their position in the hierarchy and the culture of the organisation. Thus, individual managers are often limited in their ability to make strategic decisions. Purcell and Hutchinson (2007) argue that it is not the quality of HR practices per se that is important, but the behaviour of line-managers in translating and delivering those HR practices. They found that employees who were dissatisfied with the way HR policies were applied had more negative attitudes about the organisation and organisational performance was weaker. It is suggested therefore that the design of HR policies should include consideration of how line-managers can apply them (Purcell and Hutchinson, 2007: 17).

Another factor is that managers are a heterogeneous group and may be highly divided across functional, spatial or hierarchical lines. Armstrong (1986) stated that managerial control lies in the knowledge and techniques possessed by professional groups. Such groups are in competition for key positions and resources within the organisation. Different managerial professions (for example accountants, marketing managers) aim to maintain their positions of influence in the organisation by retaining a monopoly of, and excluding others from, such techniques and knowledge. For example, an implicit part of the strategic integration or 'mainstreaming' of HRM is the idea that HR specialists should 'give away' some of their power and responsibility as professionals to other management functions (Gooch and Blackburn, 2002; Cornelius et al., 2001). Further, Guest (1987: 519) discusses the difficulty of line-managers accepting what they might see as an abdication of responsibility by HR specialists – why should other managers do HR specialists' job for them? Gooch and Blackburn (2002: 145) summarise research that suggests that line-managers are selective about which aspects of HRM they choose to be involved with (Brewster and Hegewich, 1994). They tend to choose aspects that involve the setting of short-term business targets. In contrast, effective equality and diversity policies would need a long-term, 'long agenda' approach. Thus, issues of inter-professional competition and disagreements surrounding who should take responsibility for HR matters may prove to be obstacles to the strategic integration of HRM (and by extension of equality and diversity issues), even if managers are able to act strategically in the first place. In terms of the reality of line-management practice, while certain surveys indicate that line-management roles are expanding and taking on more people management tasks, traditional day-to-day operational responsibilities remain the norm, with broader HRM responsibilities being the exception rather than the rule (Hales, 2005).

Nevertheless, another associated problem is that the primacy of management appears contradictory to the simultaneously held view within the HRM model of the importance of other stakeholder interests. Hollinshead and Leat (1995: 22) point out that often the interests of, for example, employees as stakeholders are conceptualised as the need for forms of employee participation that would gain increased commitment, not that would allow any real sharing of decision-making. Thus, what relative standing do the different stakeholders have and whose voices are heard, given the unequal nature of the employment relationship and its domination by white, male hegemonic power? (See discussion in Chapter 4.)

Another debate relates to the contingent nature of strategic integration. The effectiveness of integration depends on the role of the HR function within the organisation, which often does not hold equal power in comparison, for example, to marketing, production, finance or sales (Cattaneo et al., 1994). Evidence from the late 1990s clearly showed a marked decline in the presence of the HR function on company boards of directors (Cully et al., 1999). Gooch and Ledwith (1996) provided a detailed analysis of the way in which equality issues become constrained and controlled when they are anchored within the powerless HR function. More recently, a CIPD survey (Brown, 2003) indicates that only two-thirds of organisations have a defined HRM strategy. Furthermore, in terms of stakeholder voice in strategy, less than half involved line-managers (who would be expected to implement it) and less than 10% involved employees.

Cattaneo et al. (1994) identified four different levels of strategic integration depending on the place held by the HR function. The first level is an 'ad hoc' strategy, where the HR function holds a place of low prestige. Here, any gains for equality and diversity rely on committed individuals, who make a concerted effort to ensure that equality and diversity remain on the organisational agenda, even if the structures and systems are not encouraging. The 'traditional' strategy relies solely on the business case argument, where the pursuit of equality and diversity initiatives derives from defensive responses to external pressures (for example, legislation or market competition). It involves mainly a 'numbers game', where the aim is to increase the amount of employees from disadvantaged groups. The 'results oriented' strategy is also related to the business case, and is similar to a 'hard' HRM approach, where the bottom-line concerns of profit remain the prime concern. The latter two forms of strategic integration have limited ability to deliver greater equality, even if they deliver workforce diversity, because they ultimately defend the status quo and do not challenge the existing organisational culture (which has been discussed in Chapters 4 and 5 as a factor perpetuating segregation and discrimination).

The last form, the 'transformational' strategy relates more to the ideal of strategic integration within the HRM model, where equality is seen as a strategic imperative in its own right and where equality and diversity issues form part of a continual development of, challenge to, and adaptation of organisational culture and processes. Thus, there are 'short' (ad hoc, traditional and results-oriented strategies) and 'long' (transformational strategies) agendas of strategic integration (Cockburn, 1991; Rees, 1998).

One issue is that the business case tends to support only the short equality agenda, which militates against being able to strategically integrate HRM policies, including equality policies. Hoque and Noon (2004) demonstrate that while most companies have formal equality policies in place, these tend to be 'empty shells', with only 50% of workplaces adopting any back-up policies, and 16% having no support policies at all. This is seen as crucial to effective equality outcomes, and in line with HRM rhetoric. Policies would need to be part of an integrated and coherent system. Kossek et al.'s (2003) research endorses the need for horizontally integrated support policies for diversity initiatives. In their study, aims to increase workforce diversity through hiring policy may have negative consequences for group/team cohesion, and will lead to detriment for the minority groups recruited whether women, minority ethnic workers, disabled workers, etc., if this policy is not supported by additional HRM policies. Such policies would need to ensure that sufficient numbers of 'minority' individuals were recruited to avoid their isolation and that they were provided with the resources (training, information) to allow them to enter work groups on an equal footing.

9.3.2 Commitment

Linked to the need to integrate employees into the organisation is the concern with developing in individual employees a feeling of commitment to the organisation. The assumption is that committed employees will be more satisfied, more productive and more adaptable, thus leading to improved organisational performance (Guest, 1987: 513). Beer et al. comment that organisational commitment is important, leading to *'more loyalty and better performance for the organisation...self-worth, dignity, psychological involvement, and identity for the individual'* (1985: 20). This last comment has resonance with DM, with the emphasis on the need to nurture the individual worker and focus on job design and intrinsic conditions of work which will allow individuals to achieve greater satisfaction from their work.

What implications does the emphasis on the individual employee feeling 'included' in the organisation have for equality and diversity? To engender such a feeling might involve ensuring that individual (and differing) needs are taken into account, that unfair discrimination is challenged, and that employees have equal opportunities in terms of pay, promotion and training. This would point to a range of possible policies including careful recruitment and selection, good job design and sensitive management of organisational culture (Guest, 1987: 514). The focus on commitment to the organisation also links to DM with its individualistic ethos where commitment to other organisations such as professional bodies or trade unions or identification with social groups on the basis of class, gender, or ethnicity is de-emphasised.

The first problem with this dimension of the HRM model is that HRM focuses primarily on organisational commitment. Committed employees are seen as those who have internalised the corporate vision, perhaps even at the expense of their own interests (Legge, 2007). The issue of employee commitment is actually far more complex. There are many other 'commitments' which might play a part within an organisational context; for example, employees might feel commitment to their profession, trade union or family. The competing loyalties demanded by these multiple commitments are downplayed within the theory of HRM. What are the equality implications of prioritising organisational commitment? HRM is essentially a unitarist theory (see Edwards, 2003: 10 for a general discussion) within which conflicts and competing interests are often seen as deviant. This means that individual employees' differing identities and loyalties are often viewed negatively rather than valued. It is likely that other loyalties and responsibilities beyond the organisation (such as domestic responsibilities) would not necessarily be accommodated and valued if they were seen to conflict with organisational objectives and goals. The likelihood is that only people who can meet the dominant norm (of the white, male, full-time employee) would benefit from the goal of commitment within the theory of HRM, because they would be the ones seen as most committed to the organisation.

Commitment within HRM is essentially individualistic. It involves the commitment of the individual employee to the organisation. This has implications for equality issues because it excludes the possibility of collective action. A unitarist approach has little room for trade unions and indeed the theory of HRM has been positioned by many as involving an implicit attack on the role of trade unions within organisations. In comparison, Colling and Dickens (1998: see also Dickens, 1999) highlighted the importance of unions and collective bargaining in maintaining a focus on equality issues within organisations. They discussed how the equality agenda declined in the firm they studied, when new market imperatives led to restructuring which marginalised the role of the union and in turn narrowed the collective bargaining agenda. The equality agenda is easily marginalised with a move from joint regulation of employment conditions to managerial prerogative. This was also a feeling expressed by trade union officers in our research, where a typical comment was:

> *'There's a suspicion that managing diversity is all about individuals...rather than the commonality of disadvantage that some groups can experience...the concept that we still cling to...is overcoming disadvantage and getting rid of discrimination [which] is not something that employers feel comfortable with'.*
> **(Kirton and Greene, 2006)**

This quote illustrates, from a trade union point of view, the problems which were discussed in Chapter 5, associated with the individualistic focus of the diversity approach, which we argue are also applicable to the individualistic focus of HRM. Emphasising individual commitment to the organisation weakens the ties between people through common experience of other commitments and identities. This can have negative implications, denying the similarity between people's experiences in the workplace and the importance of the collective. If we also consider that the ideal HRM approach has no place for trade unions or other representative bodies, then this leaves the individual employee very isolated. Thus within HRM practice: *'the position of individual employees is in fact quite precarious, with a high degree of dependency on the benevolence of employers'* (Hollinshead and Leat, 1995: 24).

9.3.3 Flexibility

The ability of managers to implement an (integrated) strategy requires a capacity to adapt and respond to pressures from both inside and outside of the organisation. According to this, the organisation must avoid rigid bureaucratic structures and more significantly for a discussion of equality and diversity issues, must avoid the development of powerful interest groups which might lead to divisions and demarcations (job boundaries) between groups of employees, and break down the commitment to the organisation (Guest, 1987: 514). Additionally, there is a requirement for employees to be both temporally and numerically flexible (hours of work and type of contract) and functionally flexible (types of task) in order that a multi-skilled workforce can be developed which can adapt and respond to changes in production and demand and therefore gain competitive edge (Walsh, 1990). Thus, within the business case for HRM, one of the solutions to the challenges facing organisations lies in the flexibility and adaptability of labour.

On the one hand, the move towards flexibility holds potential benefits for promoting equality in the workplace (Dickens, 1997). For example, acceptance and encourage-ment of flexible working arrangements could be a challenge to the dominant norm of the long hours culture and full-time employee. This would potentially have particular advantages for women, facilitating their integration into the labour market (Dickens, 1997: 283). Widespread encouragement of temporal and numerical flexibility could allow a re-conceptualisation of what is seen as 'standard' working time, avoiding the negative categorisation of part-time and temporary workers as 'atypical' or 'non-standard' (equalling less committed). This re-conceptualisation might in turn facilitate a more equal distribution of paid and unpaid labour between men and women, and lead to a breakdown in the pay and status differential between full-time and part-time work. Finally, encouragement of functional flexibility could potentially challenge existing employment segregation, where job territories are racialised and gendered.

However, the opportunities for these kinds of positive equality outcomes from flexibility policies do not appear to have been realised. Indeed much research indicates the adverse implications of flexibility policies on employment equality (Dickens, 1997; Purcell, 1997; Walby, 1997). Numerical flexibility has not been used by organisations as an equality strategy; instead part-time work has been increasingly 'ghettoised' as low-paid, low-grade jobs, further perpetuating gender and race segregation (Dickens, 1997: 284; Stanworth, 2000). Inequalities in pay, employment rights and opportunities for promotion and training are seen as the price which women and minority ethnic workers are expected to pay for flexible jobs. Even the trend for family and work–life balance policies has not attempted to challenge the prevailing trend for childcare to be seen as a female responsibility. While the 'family-friendly' lobby stresses that these issues are of concern to all employees, the evidence of the introduction and implementation of work–life balance policies suggests that this is still seen as a women's issue (Purcell, 1997; see additional discussion in Chapter 10).

Thus, flexible work arrangements tend to operate to the disadvantage of the women and men employed on this basis, evidenced by poorer pay and conditions, and limited access to training and promotion (Stanworth, 2000; Fagan and Burchell, 2002). As Walby comments, '*the strategy of numerical flexibility…is one which provides employment opportunities…albeit under worse conditions of service*' (1997: 74). Furthermore, flexible work arrangements are usually only initiated when they meet organisational needs – that is flexibility on employers' terms: '*flexibility by workers to suit operational needs, and not flexibility for workers or families*' (Dickens, 1997: 284). Again, this does not reflect a transformational approach as the status quo of the segregated labour market is not challenged. All the evidence suggests that the encouragement of flexibility by employers usually reflects a business case orientation rather than a social justice one. The most important reasons employers usually see for having flexible working arrangements include being able to respond to variations in trade, to reduce labour costs and developments in new technology. Only a few organisations regard equality issues as a factor in moving towards increased flexibility.

With regard to the practice of functional flexibility, most of the evidence points to approaches centred on job enlargement (adding more similar tasks) and work intensi-fication (expecting more in less time), rather than the multi-skilling approach which could potentially break down traditional gendered and racialised employment segre-gation (by adding skills to allow upward progression). While eroding demarcations might be attractive to managers (particularly demarcations that foster employee or trade union solidarity), multi-skilling will not necessarily be a key issue for them. The quali-tative benefits of training are often regarded as secondary to meeting immediate organisational objectives and offering higher wages to recruit skilled workers from outside might often be preferred to training up existing employees. Most so-called multi-skilling initiatives involve the addition of lower level tasks, rather than up-skilling. Where attempts have been made to break down traditional job demarcations, the focus has been on breaking down segregation <u>within</u> rather than <u>across</u> boundaries (Dickens, 1997: 284). This means, for example, that the opportunity for someone to move out of low-graded, low-skill work is severely restricted. In summary, functional flexibility rarely offers any real challenge to the status quo that excludes disadvantaged workers from higher-quality jobs.

Atkinson's (1986) model of the 'flexible firm' demonstrates how flexibility policies are implicated in the perpetuation of a segregated labour market. This model identifies a core group of full-time, functionally flexible employees, who will receive relatively good terms and conditions and opportunities for training and development. At the same time managers will also actively pursue a policy of hiring peripheral groups of numerically flexible employees who will have a more precarious and disposable status. Critical commentators argue that the core workforce is often predominantly white and male, whilst the peripheral workforce often comprises 'minority' workers (Legge, 2007). Walby (1997) concludes that if employers are seeking to increase numerical flexibility, the evidence indicates that they are likely to create categories of employment which will be filled by less protected workers. Within this, critics of Atkinson's flexible firm have observed that the tendency has been towards increasing the use of the peripheral workforce rather than on nurturing the development of the core (Sisson and Marginson, 2003).

Thus, flexibility policies side step equality issues and the rights embedded in equality legislation by increasingly employing workers on contracts with less legal protection. Chapter 6 discusses the role of the more recent legislation that has sought to address this problem by extending employment rights to workers with 'atypical' hours. On balance the evidence seems to indicate that much HRM practice does not use flexibility in a way that promotes equality and therefore, arguably, there is a need for increased regulation to protect more vulnerable workers. With legislation now in place providing a right to request flexible working, equality issues have been more prominent in employer decisions on flexibility. However, the legislation only offers the right to *request* flexible working. The features and reports on the Trades Union Congress (TUC) Working Life web site (http://www.tuc.org.uk/work_life) are testament to the difficulties faced by employees in persuading employers to think about new ways their jobs could be carried out.

9.3.4 Quality

This dimension of HRM refers to the quality of employees, quality of performance and quality of HR policies. Thus, it brings together many inter-related elements and connects the other three dimensions of Guest's model. The idea is that considerable attention should be placed on recruitment, selection, rewards, training, appraisal and goal setting so that high-quality staff are attracted and retained (Guest, 1987: 515). High-quality staff in HRM terms means people who are committed to the organisation, strategically integrated, and flexible and adaptable. In assessing the role that the quality dimension of HRM could play in promoting equality, arguments discussed earlier can be reiterated. For example, there are undoubtedly potential benefits for employees to come from the recognition that HR are important and should be developed and nurtured. In terms of organisational benefits, if the organisation has a reputation for high-quality treatment of the workforce, this will have a positive impact on future recruitment of staff and on customer choice. This argument links to the business case for diversity and the ways in which a focus on developing and retaining quality staff can aid organisational competitiveness.

However, while the organisational benefits of attracting and retaining high-quality employees seem unquestionable, there are problems with the conception of 'quality employees'. Let us refer back to a statement made earlier about the evolution of HRM – that HRM is predicated on the notion that some workers will seek out and respond to work environments that provide challenging work, high levels of autonomy and opportunities for learning and training. On the one hand, this implies that organisations seek to recruit a particular type of 'quality' employee through methods that will attract this type of employee. On the other hand, HRM is insular in that many of the policies and practices deal with issues internal to the organisation; consequently, if there are to be any equality benefits from HRM, these will tend to be for people already within the organisation. Thus reflecting the critique of DM, HRM may only help employees already within the organisation rather than seek to challenge disadvantage outside of the workplace (Miller, 1996).

The significant point is that HRM policies are usually incapable of tackling the wider societal structures and systems which perpetuate disadvantage in the labour market. To begin with there is rarely any acknowledgement within HRM policies that the gendered, aged, sexualised and racialised roles within the labour market reflect wider social inequalities. Instead, the theory of HRM tends to emphasise employee choice and agency – that is, people seeking out and obtaining the roles they aspire to. In contrast, we have previously discussed the ways in which people are 'socialised' into 'gender appropriate' roles at work, meaning that the notion of 'choice' becomes restricted (Chapters 3 and 4). All of this suggests that HRM initiatives may not benefit all workers. Some studies indicate employee resistance to so-called enriched jobs (multi-skilled, increased autonomy) because they often mean extra work without increased pay and the addition of unwanted extra responsibility (Corbett, 1994; Maher, 1971). The belief that all workers want an enriched job (of the HRM 'quality' type) makes generalised assumptions about personal characteristics and work motivation, which are seen as invariant across people. In addition, such a view ignores the fact that people's choices are constrained by external factors such as domestic roles and responsibilities. For example, women's 'choice' to work part-time usually derives from time management concerns to fit work around care responsibilities, preventing them from seeking out better pay and conditions that usually come with full-time jobs (Glover and Kirton, 2006).

Secondly, the statement that 'quality' employees will seek out 'quality' jobs and will be attracted by 'quality' HR practices belies this insular view of disadvantage in the labour market. It may not be a question so much of whether people *seek* out or are *attracted by* 'quality' jobs, but more of whether disadvantaged workers will *get* 'quality' jobs if they do seek them out or whether they will be barred by stereotypes within 'acceptability' criteria identified so often in recruitment and selection exercises. Organisational and wider societal values continue to be gendered, sexualised and racialised. Therefore, we argue that it is people who can most easily meet the dominant norm of the 'quality' employee, (namely the full-time, under 40, white, heterosexual, male, non-disabled employee) who will benefit most from HRM policies within this framework.

Key learning points

- The main dimensions of HRM in Guest's (1987) model are strategic integration, commitment, flexibility and quality. These dimensions offer potential advances for equality in the workplace. However, the theory and practice of this model also demonstrate significant barriers to the fulfilment of this potential.
- The need to mainstream HRM issues within wider organisational strategy could provide a positive justification for progressive equality and diversity policies. However, the potential benefits are often not realised because of competing demands on managers, issues of inter-professional competition and the relatively low status of the HR function.
- The emphasis placed on highly committed, satisfied and motivated employees can provide a business case for equality and diversity policies. However, potential benefits are often not realised due to competing commitments which lessen the success of HRM initiatives together with the individualistic nature of commitment expected within HRM.
- Flexibility policies within HRM offer opportunities to make real challenges to employment segregation. However, in practice, functional and numerical flexibility policies tend to be more detrimental to many groups of workers, placing many in vulnerable, insecure employment.
- HRM policies, with their focus on the internal organisation, often ignore the wider societal systems and structures which perpetuate disadvantage.

9.4 EQUALITY AND DIVERSITY – WEAKNESSES OF HRM

9.4.1 Gap between rhetoric and reality

First, any potential benefits that the theory of HRM may seem to offer for the promotion of equality and diversity seem undermined by the lack of evidence that distinctive HRM even exists in practice (Guest, 1987; Hollinshead and Leat, 1995; Legge, 1989). Research supporting the claims of strategically integrated HRM is scarce and largely anecdotal, with much of the evidence relating to 'excellent' companies. These firms are usually foreign-owned, and on 'greenfield' sites and are not considered to be typical of British firms. An analysis of the take-up of 15 HRM practices revealed that just 14% of firms had more than half of these practices in place (TUC, 2001). Even in the 'best case scenarios' where there is an HR specialist and an integrated employee development policy, only 6 of the 15 practices are in place in the majority of UK workplaces (Sisson and Marginson, 2003). Research indicates that while the rhetoric of HRM is often 'soft' (which as stated would have most potential for the promotion of equality), the more frequent reality is of 'hard' HRM (Truss et al., 1997; Legge, 2007) in which DM will not figure very strongly. Kessler and Purcell summarise the developments in approaches to managing people and employee relations: '*evidence suggests that management are driven more by a cost-minimization and opportunistic approach to employees, reflecting more than anything a traditional style*' (2003: 335). This obviously does not bode well for the advancement of equality and diversity agendas or for realising some of the potential benefits for employees found within the theory of HRM. Further, if, as Wilson (2007) puts it, DM is viewed in isolation from other strategic HR decisions, then the 'human' could end up being missing from HRM, which would undoubtedly be detrimental for equality and diversity.

9.4.2 Dangers of the business case

This takes us to consideration of the dangers of the business case. In line with the business case, many of the prescriptions which underlie Beer et al.'s influential model of HRM rest on free market-based assumptions, where firms need to be flexible and responsive to the market (Hollinshead and Leat, 1995). According to this, HRM policies should be designed and implemented with the prevailing contextual factors in mind (a 'best fit' approach – Sisson and Marginson, 2003). Thus the practice of HRM is contingent on the particular organisation and the internal and external influences and challenges faced by it. As discussed earlier with regard to flexibility, matching HRM policy to business strategy generally calls for labour costs to be minimised rather than for employees to be treated as a valuable resource. For example, in their eight case study firms, Truss et al. (1997) identified training policies which demonstrated the significant gap between HRM rhetoric and reality. Training was tailored to meet specific organisational objectives rather than to create a 'quality', multi-skilled workforce. Training and development initiatives were seen as necessary investments in human capital only insofar as they improved bottom-line competitive advantage. In none of the firms, did HR concerns take precedence over other strategic business considerations.

As is also reflected in DM, the bias within the HRM paradigm is to put organisational needs before those of disadvantaged workers. Under these terms, the potential for HRM to promote equality and diversity will be limited (Miller, 1996). Colling and Dickens (1998) pointed to the fact that the business case for HRM emphasises the most easy to tackle areas of the equality agenda – cleaning up recruitment and selection procedures and concentrating on external image, rather than the more difficult issues of power inequalities, low pay, part-time rights and so on. While commentators highlight the ways in which the business case could be expanded to include social justice concerns (see discussion in Chapter 8), generally the business case simply maintains the status quo, with the emphasis on tailoring employees to the needs of the organisation, rather than the other way around. In addition, the business case orientation of HRM leads to workforce diversity only being valued if it results in market advantage; there is no conception of a wider social justice concern for equality and diversity (Webb, 1997; Liff, 1996). HRM policy and practice are based on organisational contingencies, not wider social problems which still need to be regulated by law even within an HRM framework.

Another related problem is that the business case approach to HRM is typically focused on the short term, particularly in the British context where the priority is often to satisfy immediate performance goals demanded by shareholders and other investors (Newell and Scarborough, 2002; Guest, 1987). In contrast, equality and diversity initiatives which aim for transformation in organisational culture require a long-term strategy (Colling and Dickens, 1998). The contradictions within the HRM model are revealed again as from an equality and diversity perspective the goal of strategic integration would undoubtedly require a longer-term approach. The business case focus on short-term organisational objectives will in practice only result in 'tinkering' and 'tailoring' approaches to equality (Rees, 1998) – the short, rather than the long agenda (Cockburn, 1991; Richards, 2001). The primacy of the (short term) business case within

HRM can also serve to reinforce employment segregation and inequalities. For example, Biswas and Cassell (1996) investigated HRM initiatives within the hotel industry and identified requirements for particular workforce characteristics as forming part of the business case within HRM strategy. The 'quality' of employees required by the industry's specific business objectives encouraged the perpetuation of 'acceptability' stereotypes in recruitment. For example, being 'attractive' was seen as a necessary requirement for women in the role of receptionist. The equality implications are clear for 'faces that do not fit', possibly excluding disabled, older, or minority ethnic workers.

Thus, it can be argued that HRM initiatives will tend to help only certain groups of disadvantaged workers. For example, Miller (1996) argued that the business case for HRM and DM helps people at the 'glass ceiling', rather than people at the 'sticky floor'. The objective within the business case for DM tends to be based around a 'numbers game', increasing the proportions of certain previously under-represented groups of worker (the short agenda), rather than seeking to challenge the organisational and societal norms and values (the long agenda) that excluded them in the first place. The earlier discussion about flexibility focused on how this 'numbers game' could increase the proportions of numerically flexible and vulnerable workers without addressing equality issues. In summary, the theory and practice of HRM has most to offer 'high fliers' at the upper levels of the hierarchy (for example increasing the numbers of women and minority ethnic managers) rather than meeting the needs of the workforce at the lower levels. For example, so-called 'family-friendly' policies (that go beyond legal requirements) are often restricted to the higher grades in the organisation and so only benefit people who are less disadvantaged to begin with (Colling and Dickens, 1998; Liff and Dickens, 2000).

9.4.3 Valuing women's difference

In the 1970s, Schein identified managerial sex-typing as a major barrier to the advancement of women in the US, with her main finding being that *'think manager, think male'* was the predominant view held by both men and women (for a summary of these studies see Schein, 2001). This perception was found, through replicating the study in different national settings, to be a global phenomenon. A similar study some 20 years later found that while the perception was no longer held by women in the 1990s, it was still held by men. According to these findings, to succeed in management, women would have to take on masculine behaviours and characteristics (Wacjman, 1999). In comparison, what is known as the 'feminine-in-management' thesis aims to emphasise that in the new era of globalisation, women's unique 'feminine skills' can make important contributions to organisational management in the competitive and demanding external context (e.g. Maddock, 1999; Webb, 1997; Calas and Smircich, 1993; Rosener, 1990). Women's 'special contribution' is considered particularly important in the context of flatter organisational structures and the dismantlement of traditional hierarchies that is supposed to go hand in hand with HRM strategies such as team working and flexible working (Davies and Thomas, 2000). The argument goes that these supposed changes may offer up new opportunities for female managers and herald increased female representation in management through the utilization of and search for 'feminine' skills such as communication and co-operation, interest in affiliation and attachment and female views of power as being transforming and liberating rather than controlling (Calas and Smircich,

1993; Hatcher, 2003). The possession of 'feminine' skills may make women managers more 'suitable' for the flexible, non-hierarchical structures, team working and high-trust employment relationships that have become the new organisational norm (fitting with the HRM goals of commitment and flexibility) (Rosener, 1990).

However, there are serious problems with these arguments. Let us think back to the discussion in Chapter 5, where we discussed how an emphasis on the differences between individuals and groups could reinforce stereotypes and employment segregation and therefore do nothing for the promotion of equality. Focusing on women's 'unique' skills implies essentialist claims about female characteristics (Davies and Thomas, 2000); that is the idea that *all* women naturally have certain skills, talents and dispositions. Added to this is the fact that the feminine-in-management thesis is a business case model where diversity is only valued if it offers the employer more efficient, committed labour. Thus, '*the appropriation of "women's difference" discourse by management writers is merely another episode in a long history of economic reasoning that ends up valuing women out of economic necessity*' (Calas and Smircich, 1993: 75). This leads also to the danger that negative essentialist notions of women as passive or weak may also be used to justify gender segregation and their exclusion from certain types of work. In this case women are viewed as inferior because of their difference (Davies and Thomas, 2000: 1129). Moreover, the 'feminine' skills found within the feminine-in-management thesis encourage the fulfilment of a public version of womanhood defined by patriarchy (Webb, 1997). The focus is on a stereotype of woman as caring, nurturing and co-operative. This approach does nothing to challenge the existing gender divisions between paid and unpaid labour (e.g. why women do most of the household chores) and only supports and naturalises the existence of gender-segregated jobs. It does not challenge the wider causes of female disadvantage, and women who are successful have to give in to the dominant expectations in a '*self-interested pursuit of market opportunities*' (Webb, 1997: 166). It is chiefly middle-class, highly qualified, white women who have made the most gains from these widely held beliefs and stereotypes of women.

Key learning points

- There is a lack of evidence that the theory of HRM is translated into organisational practice, particularly the 'soft' version which offers most space for progressive equality and diversity initiatives.
- The primacy of the business case within HRM means that there is often no wider social justice concern attached to equality and diversity. The business case results in a short, rather than long, agenda.
- HRM initiatives tend to help people who need less assistance in the first place, for example those who are highly qualified and at middle-level management. The theory of HRM seems to have more to offer people who can most easily meet the dominant norm of the white, male, full-time worker.
- The feminine-in management thesis provides an example of the potentially detrimental consequences of the celebration of difference within HRM (and DM) where stereotypes and employment segregation can be further perpetuated rather than challenged.

9.5 CONCLUSION

Sadly, despite the fact that HR practitioners are usually seen as the guardians of good employment practice, this chapter offers a relatively negative appraisal of the potential that HRM theory and practice have for the pursuit of equality and diversity. This is not to deny the potential advantages that the theory of HRM could have for promoting equality and diversity. Strengths include the recognition within HRM of the importance of paying attention to the ways in which individual employees are managed and highlighting the importance of HR for organisational effectiveness. However, the evidence shows that the practice of HRM does not seem to match up to the ideals of the theory. This chapter has briefly discussed the gap between the rhetoric and reality of HRM (Legge, 1989, 1995; Truss et al., 1997) and the issues of power and resources which can undermine the positive potential that HRM may have for equality and diversity, particularly where the business case is used to justify HRM policy and practice. However, there are also fundamental weaknesses inherent to the theory of HRM that cannot be escaped. In particular, the individualistic focus and business case assumptions militate against the development of a long, transformational equality and diversity agenda.

Activity 9:1

Developing and implementing equality and diversity policy at ServiceCo

ServiceCo is a multi-divisional company with a central HRM function. Diversity issues became part of ServiceCo's formal policy agenda around 2004. A launch campaign for the equality and diversity policy took place in mid-2004 with the intention of rolling it out to all areas of the business from 2005 through 2006. The female Head of Employee Relations (ER) within the HR department explained how she had come to take over responsibility for equality and diversity from a senior management colleague:

I volunteered to pick up the equality banner from one of my colleagues who was dropping it because he'd got some other pressing issues to deal with from a work perspective. So I stuck my hand in there and that's how I got equality.

It should be noted that this woman took on diversity responsibilities in addition to her other ER and HR duties. Whilst this is not an unusual practice – recent research by the CIPD found that 53% of those with responsibility for diversity in their organisation reported that they were not contracted to work exclusively on diversity (CIPD, 2006: 8) – it does beg the question about the extent of the resources the company was prepared to invest in equality and diversity. From this point, reporting to the Group HR Director, the Head of ER together with two assistants in the HR office developed the company's equality and diversity policy. The Head of ER – who had had no background or training in these issues – said that she and her assistants focused on what they could learn from 'best practice' advice from ACAS, from ServiceCo employment lawyers and from relevant web sites:

> We got examples from past lives and all sorts of stuff. So anywhere we could grab bits of information from, obviously the Internet is abound with this stuff. So primarily that's where we were coming from, in terms of putting a policy together… And we just swamped ourselves with information and then went into a darkened room and wrote a policy.

The policy developed in a fairly ad hoc fashion and notably with little stakeholder involvement. No formal input was requested from the recognized trade unions, from line-management or non-management staff, despite the existence of employee involvement mechanisms such as consultative Staff Forums.

According to the Head of ER, there were a number of 'drivers' for the development of this policy. One was awareness of the costs of falling foul of anti-discrimination law (there had been some high-profile and costly cases taken against the company in the recent past) and a perception that nowadays employees were both more aware of their rights and more ready to take action through Employment Tribunals. Other important drivers included the desire to be an 'employer of choice' in a tight labour market for skilled workers; extensive work with the public sector and that sector's expectation of equality and diversity policies; and the increasing importance to City investors of equality and diversity measures as indicating a 'sustainable organisation'. The Head of ER also, however, expressed the opinion that this was 'the right thing to do'.

After drafting the policy on the basis of a self-taught approach, it was sent to other senior HR directors within the company for feedback. This was a process that, according to the ER manager, was carried out 'quite quickly, because everyone was particularly mindful that what we'd got at that time was not particularly robust'.

The DM policy

About a year after the company's DM policy development project started, the Head of ER decided to change the policy title from solely 'diversity' to include 'equality'. She said that this was because she had discovered that people in the company understood the idea of equality but had no understanding of 'diversity'. This amendment was therefore based on helping understanding and so presumably acceptance within the organisation – it did not reflect a paradigm change. The final version of the document was labeled the Equal Opportunities and Diversity Policy. Its main aims were stated as follows:

- At ServiceCo we operate and make every effort to ensure that a working environment exists where all employees are treated with courtesy, dignity and respect irrespective of gender, race, colour or sexual orientation.
- All efforts are geared to eliminating all bias and unlawful discrimination in relation to job applicants, employees, our business partners and members of the public.
- To complement ServiceCo's 'core values' of 'openness, collaboration and mutual dependency'.

The objectives were to:

1. Match the diversity of our society.
2. Create a working environment free from discrimination, harassment, victimisation and bullying.
3. Ensure that all employees are aware of the Group Equal Opportunities and Diversity Policy and provide any necessary ongoing training to enable them to meet their responsibilities.
4. Strive to become an organisation that will recognize, value and understand diversity and provide its employees with genuine opportunities to improve and reach their full potential.

Responsibility for DM policy implementation was not placed directly with HR in ServiceCo, but was supposed to be given to Heads of the different business groups and then 'cascaded' down through the organisational hierarchy. Nobody on the ServiceCo executive board had any formal association with the development of the DM policy. The person designated responsible for employee-focused issues was not a member of the executive board. Nevertheless, the Head of ER made it clear that her task was to 'sell' the policy company-wide, particularly to senior managers. She did not seem to seek to use her resources to push through any radical organisational change, but seemed to regard modification to existing structures as sufficient. There was a significant level of unionization at ServiceCo, but the unions were not perceived as potential partners in developing and implementing DM or even useful communication conduits for management practices relating to equality and diversity issues. There was certainly no consideration of unions affecting ServiceCo's cost/benefit analysis of equality and diversity issues.

Most ServiceCo managers seemed to have positive perceptions of what they knew of the equality and diversity policy and there were very few criticisms. However, awareness of policy objectives and initiatives became more limited further down the managerial hierarchy, to the point where supervisors and line-managers with direct responsibility for non-managerial employees were almost completely unaware of any specific initiatives. Some managers saw the DM policy as simply *labeling* existing managerial practices that they had carried out for years and had thought of simply as managing people, trying to treat people fairly and, as one line-manager put it, 'staff welfare, HR-side issues'.

(*Source*: Edited extract from Greene and Kirton (2009))

Questions

1. Would you say that ServiceCo's approach to equality and diversity fits into a 'soft' or 'hard' model of HRM?
2. Would you characterise ServiceCo's approach to equality and diversity as strategic?
3. Discuss the role of line-managers and other stakeholders in ServiceCo's equality and diversity policy.
4. How far is the business case a justification for ServiceCo's work on equality and diversity? What are the implications of this for a discussion of how HRM can advance equality?

REVIEW AND DISCUSSION QUESTIONS

1. What benefits do you think there would be in ensuring equality and diversity within an HRM framework? Think about how equality and diversity issues might fit into an HRM business strategy.

2. Think about the conceptual fit between HRM and equality and diversity approaches discussed in Chapter 5. To what extent and how are HRM and DM theoretically compatible?

3. What segments of the workforce benefit most and why from the theory and practice of HRM?

4. Discuss the difference between 'hard' and 'soft' versions of HRM and the potential that each offers for equality and diversity in the workplace. Think about 'soft' and 'hard' elements of the four dimensions of HRM discussed earlier.

FURTHER READING

Bolton, S., Houlihan, M., 2007. Searching for the Human in Human Resource Management. Palgrave Macmillan, Basingstoke.

An edited collection exploring aspects of the human relationships embedded in the practice of HRM.

Guest, D. 1987. Human resource management and industrial relations. Journal of Management Studies, 24 (5), 503-521.

A key article for the HRM model in Britain that summarises the evolution of the theory of HRM and its distinctiveness from personnel management.

Winstanley, D. Woodall, L. 2000. Ethical Issues in Contemporary Human Resource Management. Macmillan, London.

A collection analysing contemporary HRM practices through the use of business ethics concepts. Issues of equality and inequality issues are implicit in most of the articles.

REFERENCES

Armstrong, P., 1986. Management control strategies and interprofessional competition. In: Knights, D., Wilmott, H. (Eds.), Managing the Labour Process. Gower, Aldershot.

Atkinson, J., 1986. Four stages of adjustment to the demographic downturn. Personnel Management August, 26-29.

Beer, M., Spector, B., Lawrence, P., Quinn-Mills, D., Walton, R., 1984. Managing Human Assets. Free Press, New York.

Beer, M., Spector, B., Lawrence, P., Quinn-Mills, D., Walton, R., 1985. A General Manager's Perspective. Free Press, Glencoe, Illinois. HRM.

Benschop, Y., 2001. Pride, prejudice and performance: relations between HRM, diversity and performance. International Journal of Human Resource Management 12 (7), 1166-1181.

Biswas, R., Cassell, C., 1996. Strategic HRM and the gendered division of labour in the hotel industry. A case study. Personnel Review 25 (2), 19-34.

Brewster, C., Hegewich, A., 1994. Policy and Practice in European Human Resource Management. Routledge, London.

Brown, D., 2003. Orchestral manoeuvres in the dark. People Management 15th May, 25.

Calas, M., Smircich, L., 1993. Dangerous liaisons: the 'feminine-in management' meets globalisation. Business Horizons March/April, 73–83.

Cassell, C., 1996. A fatal attraction? Strategic HRM and the business case for women's progression at work. Personnel Review 25 (5), 51–66.

Cattaneo, R., Reavley, M., Templer, A., 1994. Women in management as a strategic HR initiative. Women in Management Review 9 (2), 23–28.

CIPD, 2004. 'Diversity: Stacking up the Evidence'. Available from: <http://www.cipd.co.uk/subjects/dvsequl/general/diversity.htm?IsSrchRes=1>.

CIPD, 2006. Diversity in Business: How Much Progress Have Employers Made? First Findings, Survey Report. Chartered Institute of Personnel and Development (CIPD), London.

Cockburn, C., 1991. In the Way of Women: Men's Resistance to Sex Equality in Organisations. Macmillan, Basingstoke.

Colling, T., Dickens, L., 1998. Selling the case for gender equality: deregulation and equality bargaining. British Journal of Industrial Relations 36 (3), 389–411.

Corbett, J.M., 1994. Critical Cases in Organisational Behaviour. Macmillan, London.

Cornelius, N., Gooch, L., Todd, S., 2001. Managing difference fairly: an integrated partnership approach. In: Noon, M., Ogbonna, E. (Eds.), Equality, Diversity and Disadvantage in Employment. Palgrave, Basingstoke.

Cornelius, N. (Ed.), 2002. Building Workplace Equality: Ethics, Diversity and Inclusion. Thomson.

Cully, M., Woodland, S., O'Reilly, A., Dix, G., 1999. Britain at Work. Routledge, London.

Dale, K., 1997. Book review article. Industrial Relations Journal 28 (1), 92–93.

Davies, A., Thomas, R., 2000. Gender and human resource management: a critical review. International Journal of Human Resource Management 11 (6), 1125–1136.

Deal, T., Kennedy, A., 1982. Corporate Cultures. Addison-Wesley, Reading, Massachusetts.

Dickens, L., 1997. Gender, Race and Employment Equality in Britain: inadequate strategies and the role of industrial relations actors. Industrial Relations Journal 28 (4), 282–289.

Dickens, L., 1998. What HRM means for gender equality. Human Resource Management Journal 8 (1), 23–40.

Dickens, L., 1998. Gender, race and employment equality in Britain: inadequate strategies and the role of industrial relations actors. Industrial Relations Journal 28 (4), 282–289.

Dickens, L., 1999. Beyond the business case: a three-pronged approach to equality action. Human Resource Management Journal 9 (1), 9–19.

Edwards, P., 2003. The employment relationship and the field of industrial relations. In: Edwards, P. (Ed.), Industrial Relations: Theory and Practice in Britain. Blackwell, Oxford, pp. 1–36.

Fagan, C., Burchell, B., 2002. Gender, Jobs and Working Conditions in the European Union. European Foundation for the Improvement of Living and Working Conditions, Brussels.

Frombrun, C.J., Tichy, N.M., Devanna, M.A. (Eds.), 1984. Strategic Human Resource Management. John Wiley, New York.

Glover, J., Kirton, G., 2006. Women, Employment and Organisations. Routledge, Abingdon.

Gooch, L., Ledwith, S., 1996. Women in personnel management re-visioning of a handmaiden's role? In: Ledwith, S., Colgan, F. (Eds.), Women in Organisations. Macmillan, London.

Gooch, L., Blackburn, A., 2002. Managing people-equality, diversity and human resource management: issues for line managers'. In: Cornelius, N. (Ed.), Building Workplace Equality: Ethics, Diversity and Inclusion. Thomson, London.

Greene, A.M., Kirton, G., 2002. Trade unions and managing diversity. In: Paper Presented at the 18th EGOS (European Group of Organisation Studies) Colloquium, July, 2002, Barcelona.

Greene, A.M., Kirton, G., 2009. Diversity Management in the UK. Organisational and Stakeholder Experiences. Routledge, London.

Guest, D., 1987. Human resource management and industrial relations. Journal of Management Studies 24 (5), 503-521.

Guest, D., Conway, N., 1999. Peering into the black hole: the downside of the new employment relations in the UK. British Journal of Industrial Relations 37 (3), 367-389.

Hales, C., 1986. What do managers do? A critical review of the evidence. Journal of Management Studies 23 (1), 88-116.

Hales, C., 2005. Rooted in supervision, branching into management: continuity and change in the role of first-line manager. Journal of Management Studies 42 (3), 471-506.

Hatcher, C., 2003. Refashioning a passionate manager: gender at work. Gender, Work and Organisation 10 (4), 391-412.

Hollinshead, G., Leat, M., 1995. Human Resource Management: An International and Comparative Perspective. Financial Times Management, London.

Hollinshead, G., Nicholls, T., Tailby, S., 1999. Employee Relations. Financial Times Management London.

Hoque, K., Noon, M., 2004. Equal Opportunities Policy and Practice in Britain: Evaluating the "Empty Shell" Hypothesis. Work, Employment and society 18 (3), 481-506.

Iles, P., Kaur Hayers, P., 1997. Managing diversity in transnational project teams: a tentative model and case study. Journal of Managerial Psychology 12 (2), 95-117.

Kandola, R., Fullerton, J., 1998. Managing the Mosaic: Diversity in Action. Institute of Personnel and Development, London.

Kessler, I., Purcell, J., 2003. Individualism and collectivism in industrial relations. In: Edwards, P. (Ed.), Industrial Relations: Theory and Practice in Britain. Blackwell.

Kirton, G., 2002. What is diversity? In: Johnstone, S. (Ed.), Managing Diversity in the Workplace. Eclipse, London, pp. 1-22.

Kirton, G., Greene, A.M., 2006. The discourse of diversity in unionised contexts: views from trade union equality officers. Personnel Review 35 (4), 431-448.

Kossek, E., Markel, K., McHugh, P., 2003. Increasing diversity as an HRM change strategy. Journal of Organisational Change Management 16 (3), 328-352.

Legge, K., 1989. Human resource management: a critical analysis. In: Storey, J. (Ed.), New Perspectives in Human Resource Management. Routledge, London.

Legge, K., 1995. HRM Rhetorics and Realities. Macmillan, Basingstoke.

Legge, K., 2007. Putting the missing H into HRM: the case of the flexible organisation. In: Bolton, S., Houlihan, M. (Eds.), Searching for the Human in Human Resource Management. Palgrave Macmillan, Basingstoke, pp. 115-136.

Liff, S., 1996. Two routes to managing diversity: individual differences or social group characteristics. Employee Relations 19 (1), 11-26.

Liff, S., Dickens, L., 2000. Ethics and equality: reconciling false dilemmas. In: Winstanley, D., Woodall, L. (Eds.), Ethical Issues in Contemporary Human Resource Management. Macmillan, London.

Maddock, S., 1999. Challenging Women: Gender, Culture and Organisation. Sage, London.

Maher, J., 1971. New Perspectives in Job Enrichment. Litton Educational, Syracuse.

Miller, D., 1996. Equality management: towards a materialist approach. Gender, Work and Organisation 3 (4), 202-214.

Newell, H., Scarborough, H. (Eds.), 2002. HRM in Context: a Case Study Approach. Palgrave, Hampshire.

Purcell, K., 1997. The Implications of Employment Flexibility for Equal Opportunities. Presented at the BUIRA Conference, Bath, 4-6 July.

Purcell, J., Hutchinson, S., 2007. Front-line managers as agents in the HRM-performance causal chain: theory, analysis and evidence. Human Resource Management Journal 17 (1), 3-20.

Rees, T., 1998. Mainstreaming Equality in the European Union: Education, Training and Labour Market Policies. Routledge, London.

Richards, W., 2001. Evaluating equal opportunities initiatives: the case for a 'transformative' agenda. In: Noon, M., Ogbonna, E. (Eds.), Equality, Diversity and Disadvantage in Employment. Palgrave, Basingstoke.

Rosener, J., 1990. Ways women lead. Harvard Business Review. Nov/Dec, 119-125.

Schein, V., 2001. A global look at psychological barriers to women's progress in management. Journal of Social Issues 57 (4), 675-688.

Sisson, K., Marginson, P., 2003. Management: Systems, Structures and Strategy. In: Edwards, P. (Ed.), Industrial Relations: Theory and Practice in Britain. Blackwell.

Stanworth, C., 2000. Flexible working patterns. In: Winstanley, D., Woodall, L. (Eds.), Ethical Issues In Contemporary Human Resource Management. Macmillan, London.

Storey, J., 1989. New Perspectives in Human Resource Management. Routledge, London.

Storey, J., 1992. Developments in the Management of Human Resources. Routledge, London.

Truss, C., Gratton, L., Hope-Hailey, V., McGovern, P., Stiles, P., 1997. Soft and hard models of human resource management: a reappraisal. Journal of Management Studies 34 (1), 5-73.

Turnbull, P., Wass, V., 1997. Marxist management: sophisticated human relations in a high street store. Industrial Relations Journal 29 (2), 98-111.

TUC 2002. The Low Road. TUC Briefing Document at http://www.tuc.org.uk/em_research/tuc-5459-f0.cfm#_edn12.

Wacjman, J., 1999. Managing Like a Man: Women and Men in Corporate Management. Allen & Unwin St Leonards.

Walby, S., 1997. Flexibility and the Changing Sexual Division of Labour'. Gender Transformations. Routledge, London, Chapter 3, pp. 66-79.

Walsh, T.J., 1990. Flexible labour utilisation in the private service sector. Work, Employment and Society 4 (14), 350-375.

Webb, J., 1997. The politics of equal opportunity. Gender, Work and Organisation 4 (3), 159-169.

White, B., Cox, C., Cooper, C.L., 1992. Women's Career Development: a Study of High Fliers. Blackwell, Oxford.

Wilson, F., 2007. Searching for the human in the HR practice of diversity. In: Bolton, S., Houlihan, M. (Eds.), Searching for the Human in Human Resource Management. Palgrave Macmillan, Basingstoke, pp. 155-170.

Equality and diversity policy in a European context

10

Aim

To place the discussion of equality and diversity policy within a European context.

Objectives

- To explore the role of the state and social policy in encouraging progress on employment equality and diversity.
- To discuss the role that wider social attitudes play in perpetuating discriminatory practices in the labour market.
- To discuss the role of trade unions in promoting equality and diversity.

10.1 INTRODUCTION

This book is largely set within the UK context, however, it is important to consider policy within other European countries. The UK is a Member State of the European Union (EU) and as discussed in Chapter 6, the directives, recommendations, action plans and rulings of the European Court of Justice (ECJ) have driven substantial parts of UK equality legislation. In Chapter 2, an overview of labour market trends and patterns across the EU was presented. In this chapter we add information about the wider context of these trends, examining the different social and employment policy approaches adopted by governments, identifying a variety of models and their implications for the advancement of equality in the labour market. We also explore the role of wider social attitudes towards black and minority ethnic (BME) workers and women in the labour market. Finally, we consider the roles of trade unions as key stakeholders in the European labour market. We therefore draw on the discussions in some of the earlier chapters, but within a European context. Some countries have very different policy approaches to the UK, the examination of which allows us to broaden our perspectives on equality and diversity, and to consider whether there are examples of more positive or more negative equality outcomes. Are there policy models which could be successfully implemented within the UK context, and equally, does UK policy offer any lessons or examples for other European countries?

There is not the space here to do any more than present a very brief sketch of the social policy context of different European countries. More information is available on

Table 10.1 Members of the European Union

EU-15	New Member States	Candidate Countries	European Free Trade Association (EFTA) Members
Austria	Bulgaria	Croatia	Norway
Belgium	Cyprus	Turkey	Switzerland
Denmark	Czech Republic		
Finland	Estonia		
France	Hungary		
Germany	Latvia		
Greece	Lithuania		
Ireland	Malta		
Italy	Poland		
Luxembourg	Romania		
Netherlands	Slovakia		
Portugal	Slovenia		
Spain			
Sweden			
United Kingdom			

some countries compared with others; in particular there is less research and information for the 12 newer EU members. Countries also vary in terms of their collection of data on different social groups. For example, there is often very little concrete information on lesbian and gay workers. The discussion that follows reflects these imbalances. The EU member states are shown in Table 10.1. For the purposes of analysis European employment policies and data are often grouped as follows: continental countries (e.g. Austria, Belgium and France); Ireland and the UK; central and eastern European countries (e.g. Hungary, Latvia); southern European countries (e.g. Cyprus, Italy, Malta); Scandinavian countries and the Netherlands; and European Free Trade Association (EFTA) countries. Similarities in immigration and welfare regimes are found among the countries within these different groups.

10.2 THE ROLE OF THE STATE

10.2.1 Policies impacting on race/ethnic equality

The immigration and citizenship policies of different EU countries have played a significant role in producing the unequal employment outcomes of BME groups that we see today (outlined in Chapter 2). In particular, immigration and citizenship policies have implications for eligibility for various social benefits, legal protection in employment and even access to job opportunities. While there has been some convergence in policy across the EU over the last two decades, the rules and practices of different countries still vary (Wrench et al., 2003). This is particularly the case since the more recent expansion of the EU. There is an ongoing project to develop an EU-wide common immigration policy and an EU framework for the integration of immigrants (EC, 2008). For the purposes of this discussion, an im(migrant) is defined as an individual who resides in a country other than the one where they were born. This is known as a 'country of birth' approach, rather than a nationality-based one. It provides a more complete picture of immigrants' experiences because different countries have different rules relating to naturalization (EC, 2008).

In Chapter 2, the importance of the history of immigration within any particular national context was highlighted. Countries with a long history of mass immigration are concerned not simply with those born outside the country of residence, but also with the employment prospects and experiences of the descendants of immigrants. Table 10.2 presents a classification of public policy approaches to immigration and citizenship

---

Table 10.2 Social Policy Approaches on Citizenship and Immigration

Differential Exclusion
Immigrants are seen as guest workers without full social and political rights. Citizenship is defined by descent with proof of descendants having been citizens required. Naturalization is possible for non-nationals but requires the renunciation of other citizenships and evidence of meeting the criteria for the national way of life and affiliation to the country. Civil society is suspicious of ethno-pluralism.
Examples of countries categorised: Germany, Austria, Switzerland and Belgium.

Assimilation
Immigrants are awarded full rights but are expected to assimilate to cultural norms. Citizenship is defined by a mixture of birth in the country, descent and residence. Unlike the differential exclusion model, citizenship is to a territorial community rather than one based on descent. Dual nationality is not encouraged.
Examples of countries categorised: France, Denmark and the UK (in the 1960s).

Pluralism/Multi-culturalism
Immigrants have full rights but maintain some cultural differences. Citizenship is based on a mixture of descent, birth and residence. Dual nationality is allowed. Unlike the two models above, different group identities are officially recognised. The accommodation of different ethnic cultures and norms is encouraged although requires a basic loyalty to the nation.
Examples of countries categorised: The Netherlands and Sweden.

Pragmatist Pluralism
Immigrants have full rights and maintain some cultural differences. However, there is a lack of a defined policy perspective. A civic nation (rather than an ethnic nation as with the differential exclusion model) in which the emphasis is placed on the accommodation of different groups. This is like the pluralist model but has come about in a de facto way rather than legally defined. Citizenship is officially based on birth but naturalization is available under certain conditions and dual nationality is allowed.
Examples of countries categorised: the UK since the 1970s.

Sources: Drawn from Wrench (1998), Castles (1995) and Bryant (1997).

in European countries. The classification was developed prior to the enlargement of the EU in 2004 and 2006; it therefore only classifies the EU-15 countries. The approaches outlined are influenced by each country's historical immigration context.

It is important to remember that this classification creates ideal types that do not necessarily reflect actual approaches in all areas of social policy. Indeed in the case of Germany, there has been a more recent shift towards multi-cultural policies in education. In the UK for more than a decade there has been a mix of assimilationist and pluralist approaches to policy-making (Wrench, 1998). However, elements of these ideal types are translated into, or have a strong influence on, social policies (Bryant, 1997; Wrench, 1997). In particular, Wrench (2002) explores how national understandings of ethnicity, race and nationality (as partly reflected in immigration and citizenship policies) are central to understanding different countries' policy approaches to ethnic diversity. Looking back to Chapter 5, a central component of the diversity approach is the recognition and celebration of diversity. However, in some parts of Europe, the very idea of highlighting ethnic diversity might be seen as undesirable (Wrench, 2002). Within the French context for example, the prevalence of an assimilationist perspective means that the very word 'diversity' provokes controversy (Wrench, 2002). The idea that a group might have civic or political recognition on the basis of its cultural or ethnic traits seemingly stands in opposition to the notion of an integrated, universalist French culture (Bourdieu and Wacquant, 1999 cited in Wrench, 2002). At the level of practice this means that in some countries it is considered unacceptable to conduct ethnic monitoring. In contrast, in the UK a question on ethnic background is included within the official Census and this is seen as an important tool for developing policies to tackle ethnic inequalities. In France, recording 'racial' or ethnic origin in official registration would run counter to social and legal norms (Wrench, 2002). Consequently, in France, this means that any initiatives encouraging the recruitment of BME workers tend to be as an indirect consequence of policies linked to broader equal rights for *all* citizens and workers, rather than in the specific form of anti-racism or anti-discrimination policies. Therefore, many equality initiatives common to the UK would run counter to the French philosophy of universalistic treatment (Wrench, 2002). In contrast, in the Netherlands the situation is quite different. Here a pluralist approach influences a policy of support for separate institutional social provision (for example separate trade unions, schools, universities, political parties) for different religious groups (Bryant, 1997).

A clear relationship between immigration and citizenship policies and the employment outcomes of BME workers has been shown. Differences in the underlying ideologies of different nation states in Europe have implications for the extent to which BME workers are accommodated at the workplace (Bryant, 1997: 170; Wrench, 2002). Migrants who enter a country for the purposes of work face considerable variation in the work permit restrictions placed on them. In some countries work permits are issued only for a specific employer and job, a policy that prevents migrants from seeking better work once they have arrived. The more restrictive the conditions, in general the poorer are the employment outcomes (EC, 2008). There are indications that naturalization has a positive effect on labour market outcomes. For example, Turkish migrants in Austria, Belgium, Denmark, Sweden and the UK fare better if they have become naturalized citizens of the country of residence. Immigrants who do not naturalize within the first 10–15 years are especially likely to remain in low-skilled and low-paid employment (EC, 2008).

Table 10.3 Categories of Worker in the EU

Group 1. Citizens living and working within their own country

Group 2. Citizens of an EU Member State who work in another country in the Union (EU denizens)

Group 3. Third country nationals (non-EU) who have full rights to residency and work in a Member State (non-EU denizens)

Group 4. Third country nationals (non-EU) who have leave to stay on the basis of a revocable work permit for a fixed period of time

Group 5. Undocumented or illegal workers

Source: Wrench (1998: 3).

In Table 10.3, a categorisation of workers in the EU is presented. It is clear that the status of each of these groups is influenced by the immigration and citizenship policies of the different countries. For example, the differential exclusion model found in Switzerland translates into regarding immigrant workers simply as a way to meet short- to medium-term economic needs within the labour market (a purely 'business case' rationale – see discussion in Chapter 5). Switzerland's labour market is shaped by its 'guest worker' policy (a mixture of group 3 and 4 workers in Table 10.3) where being in employment is necessary in order for immigrants to gain residential status. The exact status of 'guest workers', however, depends on the category of work permit held; indeed many on shorter-term work permits are only allowed to stay for a maximum of nine months in any one year and there are restrictions on family and spouses joining them. Given the restrictive citizenship laws in Switzerland, 'guest workers' are predominantly made up of BME workers. In Austria, the 'guest worker' status means that, similarly, rights to residence are in the hands of the authorities, and the working lives of guest workers are severely constrained. This includes, for example, a legal bar on guest workers being elected as members of works councils (Gachter, 1997 in Wrench, 2002). Restrictions on the amount of workers allowed to hold temporary work permits in Austria forces more workers into the realm of illegality (Group 5 in Table 10.3), with the result that many immigrant BME workers have to accept the lowest paid and lowest status jobs to try and ensure that they gain a permit, thus reinforcing employment segregation by ethnicity (Wrench, 1998). Fekete (1997) pointed to the inherent racism within 'guest worker' policies, the greater use of which in the 1990s arose from the push towards more flexible working in the EU. For example, while Germany relied heavily on 'guest workers' (gastarbeiter) during the period of labour shortages in the post-1945 reconstruction, the 1990s saw a number of incidences where the government attempted to take residency rights away from some groups of immigrant workers. For example in 1994, the German government revoked residence permits for Vietnamese workers who immediately became part of Wrench's (1998) category of illegal workers. However, more recently, Germany began relaxing its immigration laws in recognition of severe skills shortages in an attempt to attract some 20,000 IT workers from developing countries (*Guardian*, November 6, 2001). Other EU countries too have seen discriminatory changes in citizenship and residency policy. For example, the French Pasqua laws, introduced in 1993, reversed measures that had allowed foreign workers to renew their permits at regular intervals and that had allowed citizenship after a certain number of years. Thousands of previously legal workers were rendered illegal. Similar examples can be found in the Koppelingswet Law in the Netherlands and the Vande Lanotte Act in Belgium in 1996 (Sivariandam, 1997).

The proportion of illegal workers in the European workforce is considerable. For example, the illegal, informal sector is estimated to account for 23% of the workforce in Spain and 29 % in Greece (Wrench et al., 2003). Estimates from the late 1990s indicated that of around 500,000 construction workers in Germany, one in four were illegal workers (Fekete, 1997: 8). Fekete (1997) concluded that what many governments at that time in Europe desired was a *'work tourist'* rather than guest worker. In other words, the labour was desired but not the labourer. It is such patterns which led to the term 'Fortress Europe', denoting the barriers and disadvantages faced by many immigrant BME groups in Europe.

There are two main issues to consider here. First, recognition that state policy can be actively involved in supporting discrimination against and disadvantage for many immigrant BME workers that can have long-term implications for the descendants of immigrants. Second, drawing on theoretical discussions in Chapter 5, we need to question whether a diversity approach, as opposed to an equality approach, is appropriate for dealing with the disadvantage faced by these most vulnerable of workers:

> *'In countries where a major proportion of immigrants are found in category 5 [illegal workers]...then diversity management is even less appropriate as an anti-discrimination measure. To talk about 'ethnic monitoring', 'positive action' or 'valuing diversity' in an environment where immigrants are legally constrained into taking jobs others don't want, in worse conditions and at lower pay, or where large numbers of undocumented workers would suffer intense exploitation, would be entirely inappropriate'*

(Wrench, 2002: 79)

Another factor that makes the discussion of immigration and citizenship policies significant is that there is a direct impact on the kinds of equality policies that can be conceived of. It is difficult to see the utility of encouraging voluntary equality and diversity measures at the organisational level, if one of the major barriers to employment is the legal status of workers to begin with (Wrench, 1998). However, there are also examples of policy approaches which appear to offer more chance of equality of treatment. For example, the multi-cultural model of Sweden has been held up as almost unique, offering the most comprehensive set of rights to foreign workers and therefore by association to BME workers (Blos et al., 1997). This involves the explicit rejection of granting residence permits on the basis only of economic grounds (such as in the Swiss example above), instead emphasising the long-term integration of 'foreigners' admitted to the country for other non-economic reasons (for example asylum) (Blos et al., 1997). 'Foreigners' can enjoy the same legal privileges as Swedish citizens and the overall ethos is a quest to create social equality amongst ethnic groups, respecting cultures and providing resources for ethnic diversity to flourish (Alund and Schierup, 1993). Interestingly, Sweden stands out in Europe as having a lower wage gap between majority group and BME workers.

At the organisational level, there are examples of policies aiming to increase the recruitment of BME workers irrespective of legal status, state policy and prevailing political discourse. Wrench (1997) provides 25 case studies of good practice from the

> **Table 10.4** Common Features of Immigration Policies Across the EU
>
> 1. Acceptance of foreigners to visit for a short period of time for business purposes
> 2. Rules allowing spouses and close relatives of citizens to enter the country on a permanent basis
> 3. The possibility for individuals who claim social and political persecution in their country to apply for asylum
> 4. Mechanisms for individuals to enter largely for the purpose of employment
> 5. Naturalization rules enabling foreign citizens to acquire national citizenship

Source: EC (2008).

EU-15 (see also Wrench, 1998: 36–60). One example is a shopping centre in France that managed to introduce an initiative of disproportionate benefit to BME workers, without it running counter to the French state policy of universalistic treatment. Retailers were asked to give preference to applicants from local districts, which being an urban area of Marseilles included a high percentage of BME workers. The initiative did not challenge the French philosophy of equal treatment for all because it was not explicitly targeted at BME workers. In effect it was a strong positive action policy which was uncontroversial because paradoxically it was framed not as positive action for BME groups, but for local people (Wrench, 1998: 52).

At present, countries' immigration policies vary enormously leading to inconsistencies and a lack of coordination at EU level. Nevertheless, there are some common features of immigration policies across the EU set out in Table 10.4. There is also an ongoing project to develop a common immigration policy and an EU framework for the integration of immigrants. Employment is recognised as a key part of the integration process. There is a recently adopted proposal for a framework directive laying down a common set of rights for non-EU migrants legally residing in member states (EC, 2008).

Key learning points

- Immigration and citizenship policies have a significant effect on employment opportunities and outcomes among BME groups.
- The immigration and citizenship policies of some countries could be identified as indirectly racist. Immigrant workers, especially those who are working illegally, face the most vulnerable and unprotected employment conditions.
- The multi-cultural model is identified as providing the most opportunities for equality of treatment and opportunity for BME workers in Europe.
- There is currently an agenda at EU level to move towards a common framework for immigration and citizenship.

10.2.2 Policies impacting on gender equality

In order to drive gender equality forward, the European Commission has devised a 'roadmap' (http://europa.eu/) for equality between women and men with six priority areas that are the focus of action 2006–2010:

1. **Equal economic independence for women and men**
   EU states must strengthen efforts to combat gender discrimination in employment; the gender pay gap is regarded as too wide; women's pension rights need to be improved; and multiple discrimination against BME women needs to be tackled.

2. **Reconciliation of private and professional life**
   There is concern that the fact that far more women than men make use of flexible working arrangements means that there is a negative impact on women's position in the workplace; better childcare facilities are needed in order to avoid wasting human capital; and measures should be taken to encourage more men to take up family responsibilities.

3. **Equal representation in decision-making**
   Women's persistent under-representation in public life is a democratic deficit.

4. **Eradication of all forms of gender-based violence**
   This includes the trafficking of women.

5. **Elimination of gender stereotypes**
   Gender stereotypes are seen to contribute to both horizontal and vertical gender segregation.

6. **Promotion of gender equality in external and development policies**
   This priority takes gender equality beyond the boundaries of the EU.

All of these priority areas impact on women's employment. However, the remainder of this section focuses on policies relating to care responsibilities. Chapter 2 highlighted the significant impact that caring and domestic responsibilities have on women's career patterns in Europe. The lack of universal state-sponsored childcare and eldercare facilities is widely seen as a significant factor contributing to gender segregation and women's concentration in lower-paid, lower-status and part-time employment.

The welfare system is where policy-making on care responsibilities occurs. There are several different classifications of European welfare systems (e.g. Esping-Anderson, 1990; Langan and Ostner, 1990). Table 10.5 draws on these to categorise the welfare systems of the EU-15. Langan and Ostner's (1990) analysis identifies the different implications that different welfare systems have for the support of women in the labour market. None of the models offer any real challenge to the traditional gender division of domestic responsibilities, but some facilitate greater gender equality than others. For example, in giving welfare benefits and rights as a universal individual right, the Scandinavian model takes the emphasis away from the traditional family, however the welfare regime is still gendered; it does not challenge the traditional gender division of domestic responsibilities. The Conservative and Latin Rim models also support the traditional family structure and traditional gendered roles. The UK model, in seeing men and women as economic free agents and in avoiding special treatment, creates inequalities by continuing to reinforce traditional gender norms. However, it offers little

---

Table 10.5 Classification of European Welfare Systems

Scandinavian/Social Democrat: Labour market policies should be at the heart of the welfare state based on universal notions of individual citizenship. The focus is the individual rights of workers so that the costs of raising a family should be made a state concern in order to maximise individual capacity within the labour market (Denmark, Finland, Sweden, Norway).

Conservative/Institutional: Traditional corporatist model based on provision of social policy by the state only where the family is unable to provide. The state takes the role of financial compensator, where the cost of raising a family cannot be borne by the family itself (Germany, Austria, France, Italy).

Anglo-Saxon/Liberal: Belief in the self-regulatory capacity of the free market. No one group needs special treatment or services. Those who cannot enter the labour market will be offered means-tested state support. (UK).

Latin Rim: Rudimentary state welfare support for the non-working population, but rights to welfare are not necessarily guaranteed. Supported by the welfare tradition of the Catholic Church (Spain, Portugal, Greece, Italy).

---

state support or help for gendered roles (i.e. minimal childcare and eldercare provision) unlike the state in the Scandinavian countries.

The prevailing model in each country influences the extent to which work–life balance policies are supported. Policy measures could include support for childcare and eldercare, parental and other family leave, flexible working (part-time, flexitime, job sharing, home and teleworking, etc.) and monetary benefits or tax rebates (Euro-Foundation, 2002). The European Council has emphasised the need to move away from informal, unpaid care (such as in the Anglo-Saxon, Conservative and Latin Rim welfare models) towards formalised state and private provision of facilities and resources (towards the Scandinavian model). Another major area of concern here is the fact that women make up the overwhelming majority of workers in the care sector, which is recognised as being poorly paid, offering few prospects for career development. The exceptions to the system of informal, unpaid care are those countries with an integrated system of services for young children under compulsory school age, particularly the Scandinavian countries.

The highest female employment rates (especially for women with young children) in Europe are found in the Nordic countries where childcare and family leave provision are the most developed. Overall, Denmark stands out in terms of quality and quantity of services. This includes paid family care leave (even for the unemployed), statutory minimum maternity leave, paternity leave, pre-school nursery and after school services. This is predominantly provided by the public sector and there are very few private facilities. The link between family-friendly provision and women's labour market participation is clear when the fact that roughly equal numbers of mothers in Denmark work compared to women without children is taken into account. In addition, the number of Danish women working part-time is considerably less than in the UK. 'Childcare issues' was the main reason cited in an EU-wide survey by 41% of respondents for working part-time (Bielenski et al., 2002).

There is a trend towards providing more publicly funded childcare for example, in Austria, Germany, the Netherlands and Spain, countries which did not traditionally provide a high level of publicly funded services (EC, 1998). However, despite positive examples in Sweden and Denmark, state-supported care provision is low everywhere else. Indeed while female employment has increased throughout Europe, there does not seem to have been a corresponding increase in state provision of care services, which forces women into part-time, temporary and generally low-paid, low-status occupations.

It should be noted that Danish women with children still tend to work part-time. However, as Bielenski et al. (2002) point out, for the Nordic countries, this derives from a different context of 'choice'. In countries like the UK or Germany, women with childcare responsibilities often have a choice between not working or part-time work. In the Nordic countries, the choice is between full-time and part-time work, where the part-time option is often only a temporary measure. In addition, there is far less disparity between full-time and part-time pay rates in Sweden, Denmark and Norway (Bielenski et al., 2002). Generally therefore, women in the Nordic countries have more genuinely free choices about their working lives.

It should also be noted that there is an imbalance between care provisions for children and those for dependent adults, especially older people. There have been developments though; for example, more than a decade ago Finland, Austria and France introduced financial benefits devoted specifically to eldercare (EC, 1998: 11). The Scandinavian countries (and the Netherlands) again stand out as having the greatest provision and older peoples' rights to services are laid down in legislation. This is in comparison to the other Member States where there are no clear entitlements to a minimum level of service. Given that the ageing of the population is occurring at the fastest rate in the Southern European countries, it is of particular concern that these countries have the lowest public provision of either institutional or home-based eldercare.

With regard to monetary benefits and tax rebates for care, only a small number of countries offer such provisions (EC, 1998) and where they exist, they tend to reinforce a female-centred model of care. Such a policy is typified by Austria, where leave provisions, part-time work and financial compensations allow women, but not men, to stay at home for care purposes. Similarly, gendered provisions are found in Germany, Greece, Belgium and France, the last of which sees benefit given to parents at the birth of their second child (Allocation Parentale d'Education). This has been directly related to a decline in the activity rates of <u>mothers</u> of two or more children (EC, 1998: 10). In addition, with regard to eldercare, in most EU countries, the trend is in favour of home-based care and away from institutionalization (EC, 1998: 12). Given the existing imbalance in the gender responsibility for care and domestic work, this trend does not bode well for facilitating women's employment participation. Once again policy can be criticised for doing little to progress gender equality in employment.

In addition, taxation systems can militate against increased female employment participation. Taxation systems differ to the extent that they consider individual or household income. For example, while Sweden has a completely individualised tax system, in Luxembourg the system of compulsory joint taxation results in the penalization of spouses (usually the female) who want to return to work after a break for caring (Villota and Ferrari, 2001). Finally, linking back to earlier discussion, the situation of migrant workers in gaining access to care services should also be considered. Given the citizenship and immigration policies of many European countries, such resources and facilities will only be available to workers who are citizens, reinforcing once again the double disadvantage faced by migrant women.

Key learning points

- Different models of family state policy can be identified which have different implications for the gender division of domestic labour and care services. The predominant pattern in each of the models however supports a system of female-centred care.
- The UK compares negatively with family care provision and policy in many other European countries. However, despite outstanding examples such as that of Denmark, with its integrated system of state-supported services and provisions, women are still primarily responsible for care and the need to manage the interface between work and family life across Europe.
- The trend is towards further accommodation of women's care roles rather than challenging the traditional gender division of household labour.

Activity 10.1

Time off after childbirth 'to be shared more fairly between men and women'

For two generations, the fight for time off work after the birth of a child has focused exclusively on rights for women. But today a call comes from an unlikely source that turns this on its head. The Equality and Human Rights Commission says that the scales have tipped too far in favour of mothers, and Britain now has the most unequal parental leave arrangements in Europe. It warns that well-meaning reforms, which will soon mean mothers having a full year of paid leave, have had the unintended consequence of discrimination against women as employers weigh up the costs of taking them on during childbearing years. The rules mean that fathers are squeezed out of the early months of the child's life as they head back to work after two weeks' paternity leave.

This month a study by the Hire Scores recruitment agency suggested that the commission may be right. It found that half of British businesses admitted that the age of prospective female employees was a factor in deciding whom to hire, and 80% would ask them what their plans were for a family if it were not illegal. The commission proposes a radical overhaul of the current system to be introduced in three stages over 10 years. Statutory maternity leave would be cut from the current nine months, back to six months. That would just about comply with World Health Organisation guidelines on breastfeeding, but be paid at a more generous 90% of salary rather than £117.18 statutory allowance. Thereafter, mothers and fathers would have equal rights to taking time off work to care for their children. First, both would be entitled to four months of paid parental leave. If the leave is not used up by either, it would be lost. They would then have an additional four months paid at a lower rate to divide between them.

The commission argues that the total time off currently available of 80 weeks is actually unchanged. That is the amount of time both parents are allowed when paternity leave, a year of maternity leave and unpaid parental leave for emergencies are added up. The plans redistribute the time more fairly. Low-income parents, who make less use of the current maternity and paternity leave allowance, would be far more likely to make use of the new rights, it argues. Although policy chiefs at the commission argue that nothing is being taken away from women, the reality is that few families are going to be able to take the full 80 weeks of leave. It is likely that the more time fathers take off, the less time mothers would take.

A poll conducted for the report, *Working Better*, found reasonable although not overwhelming support for the changes among new parents. More than half (54%) of new fathers with children under one said they felt that they spent too little time with their children. More than half of parents (53%) said that current childcare arrangements were made by necessity rather than choice. The report, which is timed to feed into the manifesto drafting by the main political parties, is the final contribution to the parental leave debate from Nicola Brewer, chief executive of the commission, who first voiced her concern that things had gone too far last year.

How we compare

Britain Nine months' maternity leave, set to increase to one year. 90% pay for the first six weeks, thereafter low flat rate or unpaid. Two weeks' paid paternity leave by 2010 could increase to 26 weeks at low pay rate, taken at different time to mother.

France Four months' maternity leave: six weeks before birth and ten afterwards.

Sweden Four hundred eighty days, of which 390 days are paid at 80% and 90 days at a flat rate. The leave must be shared between both parents, with the maximum claim for one parent being 420 days.

Germany One year maximum parental leave from work, two months for second parent. Up to 67% of earnings paid.

Norway Fifty-four weeks of highly paid parental leave, of which nine weeks are reserved for the mother and six weeks for the father. Initial two weeks of 'daddy leave' on full pay.

Greece Sixteen weeks' paid maternity leave: eight weeks before, eight afterwards.

Switzerland Ninety-eight days' paid maternity leave after the birth of a child at 80% pay.

(*Sources*: European Jobs Mobility Portal, Equality Commission)

(*Source*: *The Times*, March 30 2009)

Questions

1. Compare the maternity and paternity leave provisions of the various European countries above. Which do you think new parents would favour? Which do you think do the most for gender equality?
2. Consider the arguments made by the UK Equality and Human Rights Commission that things have gone too far in favour of mothers. Do you agree that the new provisions are a set back for women's equality?

10.2.3 Policies impacting on age equality

All EU countries are trying to develop provisions to cope with demographic changes as the costs of supporting inactive elderly people increase and the implications of an ageing workforce, with significant skill shortages projected, are considered. Most countries have aimed to make retirement ages higher and to make pensions more flexible; indeed there has been a clear trend away from encouraging the exit of older workers through early retirement, to one where retention of older workers is increasingly favoured (EIRO, 2000).

However, there are clear differences between approaches to retirement and pensions and legislative protection against age discrimination in different countries. As Chapter 6 discussed, EU-wide legislation on equal treatment outlawing age discrimination has been in place since 2006. Before this, most EU states did not have specific legislation on age, although often some aspects of age discrimination were covered within state constitutions or labour codes (EIRO, 2000). In some cases this was through a general anti-discrimination clause which theoretically included age, or a specific age-related clause. Examples of specific legislation included Germany and Austria, which both had longer standing legislation requiring employers to report any planned redundancies of older workers in order to ensure against discrimination. These two countries also had explicit protection for older workers though their labour codes. In France, workers aged 50–54, if made redundant, were excluded from the state pension and employers were forced to bear the cost. Companies in Sweden and France had to make payments to the unemployment insurance fund if they dismissed long-serving employees aged over 50 (EIRO, 2000). With regard to measures to recruit and retain older workers, wage subsidies were available for employers recruiting older workers in Germany, Austria, France and Luxembourg (EIRO, 2000). Ireland had the most fully developed legislative approach within the 1998 Employment Equality Act. Overall, however, Europe lagged behind Japan which has the strongest tradition of measures for older people, where 85% of people aged 55–64 work (Moore et al., 1994), and the US with the most long-standing and wide-ranging legislative provisions (since 1967) and a range of agencies for advice, guidance and support to older people.

While there is no doubt that older workers may experience disadvantage in the labour market, it could be argued that older workers enjoy greater social and employment protection than younger workers. Older workers often enjoy seniority- or service-related pay and benefits and are generally less likely to be made unemployed (although once unemployed, older workers experience greater difficulty in finding a job). In the debate on reform of the welfare system in Italy in the 1990s, for example, it was claimed that it was mainly young people who suffered from unemployment and atypical work, whereas older workers benefited from secure employment, seniority rules and a generous pension system (EIRO, 2000). Young and older workers are covered by the new EU legislation (see Chapter 6).

It remains difficult, however, to assess the possible and actual effects of anti-age discrimination legislation, because discrimination is only a contributory factor to the low level of older people's employment participation. For example, health problems, the firm's economic performance, and the pension and retirement rules of the various governments also come into play. Rix (1993) found that the long-standing US anti-discrimination legislation had little effect on employer practices or on attitudes towards older workers. Individual choice also has to be considered. People do not always want to work beyond their 50s, let alone past official retirement age. Early exit from employment is generally welcomed by employee groups as a human right, especially by trade unions. For example, in the Netherlands, trade unions tried to stop the government abolishing early retirement arrangements (Moore et al., 1994). Early retirement has become entrenched within society, partly because of the expectations of employees (older and younger alike) who often see it as a reward for long service and of employers who often see it as a less painful way of managing workforce contraction (EIRO, 2000).

Key learning points

- All EU countries are developing policies to cope with the ageing population. A policy shift from encouraging the early exit of older workers through the 1980s towards recognition of the need to retain older workers can be identified.
- The issue of individual choice to retire early and opposition by some stakeholders against increasing retirement ages might be a possible impediment to current policy initiatives.

10.2.4 Policies impacting on disability equality

'Disability spending' – the amount countries spend on disability benefits – can be measured as a percentage of total benefits made available or as a percentage of Gross Domestic Product (GDP). There are enormous variations across the EU. For example, Sweden – a high spender on disability benefits – spends 4.3% of GDP, compared with 0.8% in Ireland. As a percentage of total benefits, disability spending is as little as 5.1% in Ireland and over 10% in the highest spending countries – Luxembourg, the Nordic countries, Poland, the Netherlands and Portugal.

But disability spending is not the only issue pertaining to the effectiveness of disability policies. The difficulties in monitoring the disabled population were high-lighted more than a decade ago by a Joint Employment Report by the Social Partners, with national policy action being severely hampered by the lack of data on the scale, nature and needs of disabled people in the labour market (EIRO, 2001). Moreover, a significant criticism of public policy in all European countries is the way in which disabled people continue to be excluded from mainstream society. A more recent agenda at European level has been to reduce the barriers preventing disabled people from participating fully in all aspects of society (EIRO, 2001). In 1999 the social partners issued a specific 'call to action' in the labour market sphere in a Joint Declaration on the Employment of People with Disabilities (see http://europa.eu.int/comm/employment_social/soc-dial/social/news/declaration_en.htm). Also, 2003 was proclaimed as the European Year of Disabled People with the aim of providing a focus for new policy developments in the Member States (see http://europe.osha.eu.int/good_practice/person/disability/).

Traditionally, EU state policies tended to be made on the basis of a 'charity ethic' rather than policy being discussed, decided and initiated by disabled people themselves. The most common way for disabled people to be involved in policy development would be through their representative organisations, usually Non-Governmental Organisations (NGOs). However, there is huge variety in the degree of involvement of disability NGOs in developing and implementing policies, as well as differing levels of collaboration between NGOs and the social partners. For example, NGOs were involved in the preparation of disability legislation in the Netherlands and Spain, but there is less information about levels of collaboration with social partners. In contrast, policy-making and legislative developments are almost exclusively dominated by government and/or social partners in Austria and Portugal, with little NGO involvement. Formal arrangements for active collaboration are found in many more countries (Denmark, France, Germany, Ireland, Italy, Norway, Spain), but only the UK stands out as an example of really productive collaboration (EIRO, 2001). Largely because of the comparative strength of the disabled movement in the UK, such policies as the *Access to Work* scheme in the UK have aimed to give disabled workers direct control over decisions about the best way to meet their needs in employment. This is in comparison to much European policy-making which has taken place without the involvement of disabled workers themselves (Hurst, 1995).

Discrimination at work on the grounds of disability is explicitly prohibited by national constitutions in five of the EU-15 countries. In addition, specific legislation prohibiting discrimination has been introduced in France, Spain, Sweden, UK, Denmark and Ireland. Disabled workers are also protected against dismissal by law in Austria, France, Germany, Spain, Sweden and the UK. In Austria, the dismissal of a disabled employee requires approval by a regional disability committee, after discussion with the relevant Works Council (EIRO, 2001). In addition, many countries operate systems of subsidies for the employment and training of disabled people (EIRO, 2001). This includes funding for non-medical helpers or personal assistants, and for necessary adaptations (such as to buildings, equipment, etc.). However, this specific type of anti-discrimination legislation and subsidy has been criticised for achieving much more for people already in work, rather than encouraging further recruitment of disabled people (EuroFoundation, 1998: 83). Disability legislation is widely seen as lacking enforcement measures and there is little attempt to ensure that all aspects of society are accessible to disabled people. This obviously negatively affects the employment chances of disabled people.

Across Europe, there has been a general shift in state disability policy from a medical model (focusing on the disability as residing in the person) to a social model (focusing on the disability as residing in society's attitudes towards the person) (EC, 1997: 111). There has also been a shift away from quota systems requiring firms to employ a minimum proportion or number of disabled workers. While such systems still exist in some Member States, it has been recognised since the mid-1980s that they have failed to deliver real gains; indeed quota systems have been abandoned in the UK, and restricted in other countries (EC, 1997: 112; Thornton and Lunt, 1995: 9). Explanations for this policy shift range from the negative 'backlash' effects of quotas as a form of positive discrimination (see discussion in Chapter 5, also Hurst, 1995: 531) to the way in which the systems were operated. For example the now abandoned UK system of quotas was regarded as '*uniquely odd in its conception*' (Thornton and Lunt, 1995: 11) for having no enforcement of penalties for non-compliance and for relying on the number of people officially registered as disabled when the trend was towards a decline in disability registration due to the stigmatization it was felt to bring. Ireland and Portugal also have quota systems that have no legal enforcement. However, quota systems are still enforced through legislation in nine of the EU-15 countries, with Austria, Luxembourg and Spain reportedly fining employers who do not employ the required number of disabled people (EIRO, 2001). Fines for non-compliance were replaced in Germany, France and The Netherlands by voluntary contributions to special funds supporting disabled causes, thus encouraging the social responsibility of firms (Lunt and Thornton, 1993).

Moving onto welfare packages in the UK and Ireland, the system of state benefits is seen as a major barrier to employment for disabled people. If a disabled person earns too much or works too many hours, they might be disqualified from state benefits, yet they might not earn enough to live off. Therefore, taking up paid work depends on the complete package of pay and benefits available, which can mean that short part-time hours of work might be the only feasible option (EuroFoundation, 1998: 76). This can explain the high level of inactivity by choice referred to in Chapter 2, at least for the UK and Ireland, whereas in other countries, the social security system does not discourage paid work for disabled people in the same way.

However, the fact that the European labour market is segregated by disability and that economic inactivity and unemployment among disabled people are widespread, indicates that the various disability policies are failing to deliver real gains. For example, there has long been evidence that subsidies for employing disabled workers are not taken up very often and that their appropriateness is questioned by employers (EuroFoundation, 1998: 79). Research also found that employers were often unaware of or were unconcerned about other publicly funded aid and adaptation schemes such as grants to improve access and training (EuroFoundation, 1998). It should also be remembered that there are restrictions on eligibility for protection under the legislation and within the variety of state-sponsored schemes. First, in many countries, eligibility is restricted to legal citizens or denizens, highlighting once more the disadvantaged position of millions of guest workers, especially illegal workers. As discussed earlier, this means that BME disabled workers experience multiple disadvantage. Second, much of the legislation is not applied to small- and medium-sized enterprises, with less than 500 employees (accounting for two-thirds of EU employment). This led to concern about the position of disabled workers within smaller workplaces, and prompted the production by the EC of the report on *The employment of people with disabilities in small and medium sized enterprises* (Euro-Foundation, 1998).

Individuals who have worked prior to becoming disabled, but who have been off work long enough to qualify for disability benefits are considered to be a group at major risk of labour market exclusion. As such, this group is the subject of more recent increasing interest in the EU at policy level (Wynne et al., 2006). A number of services have been identified that would assist this group in obtaining paid work: guidance and counselling services; information and advice services; advocacy services; case management services; psychological supports; vocational assessment; job matching; job coaching; pre-vocational training; vocational rehabilitation; specialised vocational education/training; and assistance in accessing grants. Combined, these service elements are said to constitute, theoretically, a comprehensive and effective disability support system. However, although most EU countries report that their systems contain most of the service elements listed, in many countries the services are available on a limited basis only and are not always easily accessible or effective. In Austria and

Slovenia, for example, no elements are easy to access. In contrast, in Norway and Denmark, most service elements are easy to access (Wynne et al., 2006).

Key learning points

- Disability spending varies across the EU. EU state policies can be criticised for failing to take into consideration the views of disabled people themselves.
- There has been a lack of integrated attempts to ensure that all aspects of society are accessible to disabled people with obvious negative consequences for employment opportunities.
- State policies can have a detrimental effect on the labour market participation of disabled people. Disability services are patchy across the EU in their availability, accessibility and effectiveness.

10.3 WIDER SOCIAL ATTITUDES

Employment discrimination and disadvantage occur against a backcloth of wider social attitudes that impact on both employment patterns and opportunities and on social policy developments. This section explores wider social attitudes in relation to race and ethnicity and gender.

10.3.1 Racism and xenophobia

A particularly worrying trend is the current resurgence of racist and extreme nationalist movements that seem to be gaining popular support in a number of European countries. Over the last two decades or so, right wing political parties have gained an increased share of the electoral vote, approaching or exceeding 10% of the national parliamentary vote in roughly half of the politics of Western Europe (Swank and Betz, 2003). The 'Front National' in France is perhaps one of the most conspicuous of racist groups, but there are similar political groups in other EU countries such as the British Nationalist Party (BNP), Italy's Northern League, the German People's Union, and Austria's Freedom Party (FPO). The FPO won second place in the 1999 general election and a place in government, while the Swiss People's Party (SVP) won a seat in Cabinet on an anti-immigration, xenophobic platform, where extreme racism was part of the election campaign with campaign posters showing a caricature of a black face and the slogan 'The Swiss Are Becoming Negroes' (*Observer*, Feb 22, 2004). More recently in the UK, the BNP won two seats in the European Parliament.

In addition, Deland (1997) (see also Swank and Betz, 2003) pointed to the rise in the 1990s of many small extreme right groups all over Europe, for example the Research Group for Studies of the European Civilization in France, the Salisbury Group in the UK, Vesta Nueva in Italy, the Young Forum in Germany. Even in Scandinavia, countries held up as models of egalitarian values, there are similar trends, for example, the Norwegian People's Movement Against Immigration, the Danish League and the Swedish Homestead Party. These smaller groups base their arguments not on biological differences which often provoke immediate criticism and rejection, but on cultural differences, arguing about the impossibility of cultural integration, the threat posed to national cultures by diversity and the need to separate ethnic groups.

It is difficult to say how widespread racist and xenophobic attitudes are among the general public of different European countries. In a recent survey nearly half of respondents said that discrimination on the basis of ethnic origin was more widespread than five years ago (EC, 2008). Wrench (2002) argues that a 'cultural racism' that views Danes as culturally superior has become a deep-rooted aspect of Danish public debate and the November 2001 election was fought in a climate of anti-immigration rhetoric. Wrench (2002) reports a survey of 1200 private sector employers carried out by the Danish Ministry of Labour in 2000, 25% of whom said that they would not hire an immigrant. In Italy, divisions between the rich North and poorer South are emphasised, with direct campaigns against immigrants in Northern cities (Fekete, 1999: 193). Such attitudes have also begun to filter through into public discourse in Sweden (Pred, 1997; Deland, 1997). Relating to the earlier discussion of immigration and citizenship policies, a shift away from Swedish multi-cultural and pluralist ideologies could have significant negative implications for BME groups in these countries. In Central and Eastern European countries, it is often Roma people who face considerable hostility. For example, in Hungary, research investigating the practices of the corporate sector showed that only around one-third of companies investigated did not discriminate at all, and more than half of the companies discriminated against Roma as employees or job seekers. In Romania, a survey conducted in Bucharest showed that young Roma face real barriers when trying to enter the labour market (FRA, 2007). On the other hand, in another survey 65% of respondents said that people of different ethnic origins than the majority population enrich the country's culture. Further, around half of respondents thought that not enough effort was being made in their country to fight discrimination (EC, 2008).

Wider social attitudes undoubtedly have an influence on developments in legislation and state policy, where the EU level recommendation is that in order to achieve greater inclusion, there must be changes in both the legal status of migrant workers, as well as a greater attempt to change social attitudes towards race and ethnicity. On the one hand, as was argued earlier, changing state policy and citizenship rights will not guarantee equal treatment if social attitudes towards BME groups are negative or even hostile. On the other hand, nor will more inclusive recruitment by employers provide equality, if migrant workers are denied residence rights and free movement. Legal citizenship may be of limited value if there are structural and cultural impediments, including discrimination and racist attitudes, to the exercise of such rights (Bryant, 1997). Wrench (1998) takes a similar line in his argument that making citizenship easier will not necessarily help the millions of workers not covered by EU legislation, particularly the most vulnerable 'group 5' workers. Clearly wider social attitudes can have highly detrimental effects if BME workers, regardless of legal status or background, are classified by other people as 'foreign' or 'immigrant': the case of 'Fortress Europe' once again. There is a programme of work in place to tackle racism and xenophobia in Europe. The EU has declared that it is 'committed to the absolute condemnation of all forms of racism and xenophobia by making full use of its powers and safeguarding fundamental rights, non-discrimination and equal opportunities for all' (FRA, 2007: 135).

Key learning point

- A current resurgence of racist movements can be identified across Europe. Widespread racist attitudes impede the employment opportunities of BME workers. However, the EU agenda is to develop policies to counter the spread of such attitudes.

Activity 10.2

Far-right parties in the European Parliament

Following the European elections in June 2009, there has been considerable debate about the increased presence of far-right parties in the European Parliament. Below is a summary of such parties and their policies.

British National Party, UK (number of MEPs: 2) No black members allowed, wants to outlaw mixed-race relationships, 'racism' is part of human nature. Stop immigration, deport foreign criminals and introduce voluntary repatriation by paying legal immigrants to leave. Withdraw from EU, keep the pound.

Front National, France (3) End non-European immigration and stop payments to help family members to join migrants. Reintroduce the French franc. Give French people priority for jobs, social support and housing. Restore border controls and the death penalty. Renegotiate EU as a band of nation states, or hold referendum on leaving.

Vlaams Belang (Flemish Interest), Belgium (2) Wants an independent Flemish state within the EU and tight rules on immigration. Foreigners who want to settle in Flanders should pass language and cultural tests in their own country first. Asylum-seekers should be sent to countries near their home country rather than accepted in Europe.

Jobbik (The Movement for a Better Hungary), Hungary (3) Wants the establishment of local gendarmerie in Hungary to protect the population against crime, and a special police unit for Gypsy crime. Has its own militia, the Hungarian Guard, of several thousand uniformed volunteers who have campaigned against 'Roma criminality'. Its motto: 'Hungary belongs to the Hungarians'.

Ataka (Attack), Bulgaria (2) Wants to outlaw the use of other languages in Bulgaria, opposes privatisation and foreign ownership. Volan Siderov, its leader, has campaigned against Turkish membership of the EU, saying: 'If we sit and don't work like Bulgarian patriots, one day they will conquer us indeed. They will annex whole regions.' Motto: 'Let's bring Bulgaria back to Bulgarians'.

Liga Nord (Northern League), Italy (9) Favours immigration from non-Muslim countries and supported legislation to make it a crime to be an illegal immigrant in Italy. Its leader, Umberto Bossi, has said that migrants heading for Italy should be 'blown out of the water'.

Danish People's Party, Denmark (2) Strict policies to restrict immigrants and refugees. Opposes 'islamisation' and Turkey's EU membership. Also against the euro and greater EU powers. Motto: 'Give us Denmark back'.

Freedom Party, Netherlands (4) Wants to end immigration from non-Western countries, prevent new mosques being opened and opposes Turkey joining the EU. Its leader, Geert Wilders, is banned from Britain for his anti-Islamic rhetoric, likening the Koran to Hitler's Mein Kampf.

Freedom Party, Austria (2) Anti-Islamic and opposed to Turkey joining the EU. Opposes EU controls over Austria and any increase in the country's contribution to EU budget.

Greater Romanian Party, Romania (2) Wants to recreate the Kingdom of Romania to unite ethnic Romanians by taking land from Moldova and Ukraine. Strong rhetorical attacks on the Hungarian minority in Romania.

Slovak National Party, Slovakia (1) Anti-Gypsy and homophobic, also hostile to the country's Hungarian minority.

(*Source*: *Times Online*, June 18 2009)

Questions

1. Consider the impact that the increased representation of far-right parties in the European parliament might have on wider social attitudes.
2. Thinking about the socio-economic context, what do you think gives rise to the increased popularity of far-right politics?

10.3.2 The continuing gender regime

The traditional male breadwinner/female carer model is widely regarded as a major contributor to women's employment disadvantage. However, there are signs that attachment to this model is breaking down. As far back as the mid-1990s, Van der Lippe and Roelofs (1995) found that while overall, women still spent more time than men on domestic activities, across all of the European countries studied women were devoting less time to domestic duties including childcare. Bielenski et al.'s (2002) more recent study (involving 20,000 respondents across 16 European countries) looked at working time preferences in 16 European countries and found that only 15% of people had a preference for the typical male breadwinner, female carer model. It is clear that the present distribution of employment does not match men's or women's preferences. Overall, men and women now seemingly seek a more equal sharing of paid and unpaid work.

However, the prevalent 'long hours culture' is seen as a significant contributing factor to gender segregation, but it appears that there is also change in attitudes across Europe towards working hours. Generally, the number of hours worked is not in line with people's preferences, with 50% of men and 42% of women wishing to reduce their hours (Bielenski et al., 2002). Generally there was opposition to both the very long hours (over 40 hours per week), which men often work and the very short hours (less than 20 hours per week) that women often work.

On the other hand, there is also considerable evidence of the continuation of the traditional gender regime. Attitudinal changes do not necessarily result in changes in personal practices. While only 15% of people claim to prefer the male breadwinner model, 35% of respondents actually lived out this model (Bielenski et al., 2002). Studies have also found that if one parent has to give up work to care for a child, it is almost always the woman (Van der Lippe and Roelofs, 1995). Similarly with regard to the balance between work and family life, the implicit assumption is that if some adaptation and flexibility is required, the onus is on the family to adjust to the workplace rather than the other way round, and within families, on the woman to adjust. Even in the Scandinavian countries, women still take primary responsibility for domestic tasks, with women doing 38% more work in the home than men in Sweden, and 43% more in Norway (Villota and Ferrari, 2001). While Danish women spend the least time on childcare, this is not because the load is shared with Danish men, but because greater use is made of state childcare facilities. A clear illustration of this is the take-up of paternity leave which few Danish men make use of, even if their failure to use it results in its loss or in financial penalties. Men's low take-up of paternity leave undermines the objective of gender equality, since it means that it is still mainly women who take time off to fulfil parental responsibilities. Indeed, as Leira (1994) pointed out, the dual earner model (both partners in paid work) does not necessarily mean a dual carer model (both partners taking on caring responsibilities).

Moreover, while preferences may be for shorter working hours and increased flexible working, only 18% of respondents indicated that they could afford to move away from the norm of full-time working. Partly, this was explained by the lower pay that part-time work typically attracts; indeed it is notable that the highest rates of people saying they could afford to move to more flexible working were found in Denmark and the Netherlands where average hourly part-time pay rates are higher. In addition, as discussed earlier, the taxation system can militate against dual earning couples (Villota and Ferrari, 2001). However, an explanation is also found in perceptions of employer opposition. Fifty-nine percent of full-time workers state that their employer would not be agreeable to flexible working (ranging from as many as 71% in Austria to 44% in France). Fifty-eight percent state it would be impossible to do their job part-time, and 47% state they would have problems in their career progress if they worked part-time (Bielenski et al., 2002).

In summary, on the one hand there appears little change to the prevalent view that domestic work is women's work. Legislation and public policy initiatives appear to have done little to change this attitude. New patterns of female participation require a specific social infrastructure to allow paid and unpaid work to be combined (Plantenga, 1995). However, at the present time, only the Scandinavian countries come close to reflecting this model. In any case, should the aim be to increase women's uninterrupted career paths, ultimately meeting the dominant norm of work? Or, would the more radical aim be to work towards alternative forms of working, including broken career paths and part-time work, where household work would also be valued?

Key learning points

- There is evidence that women are spending less time on domestic duties and more time in the labour market. However, overall the gender division of labour has altered very little, with people's behaviour largely supporting the existing gender regime.
- We need to question whether the trend towards increased childcare provision and other measures designed to allow women to juggle work and family is a positive development. These policies support the traditional gender regime rather than leading to a radical transformation in gender roles.

10.4 TRADE UNIONS AND EQUALITY IN EUROPE

Chapter 7 discussed the important role that trade unions can play in promoting equality in the workplace. The role that unions play, however, varies between countries, depending on factors such as membership density, collective bargaining coverage (see Table 10.6) and established structures of social dialogue between government, employers and unions. In some countries employer–union relations are underpinned by legislation, while in others unions are more dependent on employer acceptance of their

Table 10.6 Collective Bargaining Coverage for Pay and Conditions in 2001

Country	Collective Bargaining Coverage %
Austria	98
France	90–95
Belgium	90+
Sweden	90+
Finland	90
Italy	90
Netherlands	88
Portugal	87
Denmark	83
Spain	81
Germany	67
Luxembourg	58
UK	36

Source: EIRO (2003).

legitimacy. For example, across the EU there are countries such as France, Germany and Greece, where the law plays a more important role in regulating conditions of employment. Meanwhile in other member states – notably the Nordic countries, Italy and the UK – collective bargaining is also important. Unions in different countries have different approaches to and different records on tackling equality issues. However, according to a European-wide survey, 34 of the 44 responding unions stated that they provided information to negotiators on equality and diversity issues, while 33 organisations stated that they included equality and diversity issues in collective bargaining (Pillinger, 2008). For example, many European trade unions are actively involved in bargaining around equal pay and the gender pay gap. In Finland a national collective agreement in 2000–2001 introduced a positive action measure in the form of 'equality allowances' – an industry level subsidy paid in proportion to the number of women in the sector in order to directly improve women's wages (EIRO, 2002). Many European trade unions also bargain over race issues. For example, after the Social Partners made a joint declaration of anti-racism in 1995, a number of agreements flowed from this (ETUC, 2003). For instance, at national level, 11 union confederations (out of 24, covering 17 countries) have guidelines on collective bargaining, which cover issues of specific concern to BME workers. While it should be noted that general statements on equality and on equal access to training, promotion and other workplace benefits are the most frequently included elements in the guidelines, some union confederations report progress on more specific issues such as agreed changes in working time to accommodate religious practices. Mahon (2002) reports how Swedish unions were instrumental in gaining agreements enshrining the principle of equal pay for migrant workers in comparison to Nordic workers doing the same jobs. Mahon (*ibid*) also provides an example of local agreements where employers met the total costs of language courses for migrant workers to aid their integration into the Swedish labour market. Wrench (2002: 86) details how the largest Danish union HK (representing commercial and clerical employees) has adopted an ambitious ethnic equality programme which includes ensuring that local and national collective agreements specifically promote ethnic equality. On sexual orientation the history of trade union bargaining is generally more recent. A recent report found that the unions in some European countries have a long history of campaigning for lesbian, gay, bi-sexual, transgender (LGBT) rights in the workplace, while others have only just recently begun to deal with the issues. Some of the new member states of the EU are at a very early stage in addressing LGBT issues and have experienced difficulties in getting issues raised on trade union agendas. According to the report, all unions were at an early stage in developing actions on the rights of transgender workers (Pillinger, 2008).

Many European trade unions also lobby governments for greater legal rights. In Italy, unions have campaigned actively on sexual harassment, enhanced maternity benefit, and in 2000, a union-promoted law on parental leave was passed (Beccalli and Meardi, 2002: 120). Trade unions have also become increasingly involved in EU consultation and policy-making as part of the 'Social Dialogue'. This involves on the one hand, unions across Europe coming together as a 'united' body within the European Trades Union Congress (ETUC), and on the other, the ETUC consulting with other social partners including employer federations and the European Commission. Cockburn's research indicated how meeting at the European level had highlighted to national trade unions the differences in working conditions between countries and consequently motivated campaigns for improved European legislation and European collective agreements (1995: 217). The involvement of the ETUC within the social dialogue was key in pushing for a declaration on measures to combat racism and xenophobia, encouragement of anti-racist action in all the 22 countries where the ETUC had affiliates in 1994 and in the launch of the 1997 European Year Against Racism (EIRR, 1997). Joint actions such as this reflect the realization that unions throughout Europe need to mobilise against racist violence.

Finally, trade unions also work in coalition or alliance with community and social movement groups (civil rights groups, environmental groups, NGOs, charities, etc.). Indeed Ledwith and Colgan (2002: 20) see 'coalition' as one of their six trade union equality strategies. Coalitions are seen as key to moving beyond sectoral- and workplace-based interests towards wider social change and a framework of social rights. This can also be a way of making links with communities that are currently under-represented in the unions. For instance, a number of Italian unions set up special services to help workers apply for residence permits and social housing, which aid the integration of migrant workers into the labour market (EIRO, 2003).

However, union equality bargaining agendas are still typically short, rather than long, focusing more on anti-discrimination and on accommodation of difference, rather than demanding fundamental social change. Part of the explanation for this lies in the fact that union officers throughout Europe are predominantly white males. However, there are a number of women's structures within the ETUC, just as there are within the UK Trades Union Congress (TUC), which aim to draw more women into decision-making processes. The UK TUC is actually better than most national trade union confederations in respect of women's representation (Greene and Kirton, 2006). However, few women fill senior, negotiating roles and the structures at European level remain male dominated. Where women are involved, it is usually in very specific 'women's issues'. BME trade unionists are also under-represented at European level. In addition, as is the case when evaluating state policies, there is a need to recognise that trade union action has to be conducted within the context of a wider public discourse and national culture, as well as within different legal contexts that provide different levels of protection for different groups in the labour market, as discussed earlier in this chapter. Therefore, there may be different national interpretations in the trade unions of what equality is and what the most appropriate policy approaches are. As an example, collective agreements based on a principle of equal (same) treatment, may actually work against more radical bargaining agendas that would aim to achieve more fundamental social change. In Germany, unions fought during the 1970s and 1980s to ensure that migrant workers were covered by the same regulations as German workers (equal pay, equal rights to representation, etc.). The consequence was that no positive action measures could be countenanced, including some anti-discrimination measures, because this would be seen to contradict the policy of equal treatment (Wrench, 2003: 19). Therefore, the fact that migrant workers tended to work in different occupations and under different (worse) conditions was not acknowledged and action could not be taken to improve the situation (Rathsel, 1999). Commentators have argued that even where unions do tackle equality issues, the agenda is not always progressive. Bargaining agreements may often act to support existing stereotypes, particularly gender. For example, Kravaritou's comparative European study (EIRO, 1997) showed how collective agreements remained male-oriented and perpetuated a masculine norm. For example, agreements focused on enabling women to cope with their dual role, rather than making more radical challenges, such as campaigning for a radical reorganisation of work and the redistribution of caring and domestic roles.

Key learning points

- National trade unions are becoming increasingly involved in 'European' matters, through the formation of the ETUC and through discussion and consultation with social partners as part of the 'Social dialogue'.
- While there are examples of the ETUC encouraging trade union action on equality, European trade union structures remain white, male dominated.
- Equality issues need to be mainstreamed within collective bargaining agendas in order to gain the most effect. At present the European trade union equality agenda is based on liberal rather than radical aims.

Activity 10.3

Strikes over foreign workers spread to Sellafield as Mandelson ups stakes

Lord Mandelson today raised the stakes in the row over foreign workers by declaring that 'no laws were broken' by the company which brought over Italian and Portuguese employees. As a new wave of wildcat strikes hit Britain, the Business Secretary appeared to pre-empt the findings of Acas, the conciliation service, which has been asked by government to determine if any laws were broken at the Total refinery in Lincolnshire. The Government's stance appears to have inflamed workers at energy and construction sites around Britain. Amongst the walkouts this morning include:

- Hundreds of contract workers at Sellafield nuclear site, which the management said they expected to last a day.
- Around 700 contractors at the Grangemouth oil refinery in central Scotland, who took unofficial action on Friday, walked out again today. They also decided they would return to work tomorrow.
- Two hundred workers at Fiddlers Ferry power station in Widnes, Cheshire, also walked out in support this morning.
- The Longannet power station in Scotland was also hit.
- Contract workers at the Heysham nuclear power station in Lancashire and a site at Staythorpe near Newark in Nottinghamshire also joined the strikes.

Speaking on the BBC, Lord Mandelson rebutted union allegations that employment laws were broken and Portuguese and Italians were being paid less than the going rate, adding Acas 'would confirm' this later today.

The peer also defended the company, saying the contract at the centre of the dispute was originally awarded to a British firm but it did not fulfil it so it was given to an Italian company which then drew on its own workforce.

His stance is likely to escalate the row with the unions, who are angry at the ability of companies to bring in foreign workers for below the union-negotiated going rate at construction and energy plants around the country. The row caught national attention on Friday after an unofficial walkout by workers at the Total's Lindsey refinery in Lincolnshire over the arrival of the foreign workers which sparked copycat protests across Britain. Yesterday saw the government in disarray over the issue, with ministers forced into an embarrassing U-turn yesterday after Alan Johnson, the Health Secretary, suggested that the Government was preparing to bow to union demands to push for measures in Europe to protect British jobs.

Unions want a new EU directive to overturn a ruling by the ECJ in 2007 that made it easier for companies to circumvent pay deals by hiring foreigners on lower wages by making it harder for unions to strike. They believe that Gordon Brown could be forced to take action after promising 'British jobs for British workers' in his 2007 Labour conference speech. Lord Mandelson suggested this morning that Mr Johnson had not been in full possession of the facts when he did the interview on the Marr programme yesterday.

At the Total refinery, more than 1000 workers agreed to allow union officials to start talks with management. Kenny Ward, from Unite, told the crowd: 'The fight started here at Lindsey – the fight against discrimination, the fight against victimisation and the fight to put bread on your table for your children'. Gordon Brown said, 'It is indefensible. If the Prime Minister will not defend the working man, if Parliament will not defend the working man, then the union will defend the working man. The people in Europe need to sit up and judges who twist and interpret the law to the advantage of the employer need to have a rethink. The politicians need to sit down and sort this problem out.'

(*Source*: *Times Online*, February 2 2009)

Questions

1. During a period of recession, should 'British jobs' be reserved for 'British workers'? In this context, what does 'British' mean?
2. Do you think the unions are being racist or xenophobic in taking this line?
3. What challenges does this kind of union action pose for a government trying to project itself as pro-equality?

10.5 CONCLUSION

This chapter has explored the wider social and policy context of employment in Europe. The chapter has shown that approaches to citizenship and immigration are not uniform across Europe. There are also differing welfare systems and different levels of welfare service provision. The Scandinavian countries are highlighted as having the most progressive and egalitarian of welfare systems, where women have the most chance of coming closest to gaining equality within the labour market (although the shortcomings of even these systems have been discussed).

We have also discussed wider social attitudes that are reflected in workplace discrimination and inequalities. Across the EU we can identify a worrying rise of racist groups and the continuation of a traditional gender regime which impede the equality project. However, such developments will have greater or lesser effect depending on their intersection with state policy. For example, extreme right wing political groups might pose more threat to the position of BME workers where the immigration and citizenship policies also discriminate against them. It is clear that a variety of factors (including state welfare provisions, dominant political discourses, social and employment policy regimes and history of immigration) in different national contexts result in different equality issues being prioritised. This indicates that the different European countries attach different value to tackling the different dimensions of diversity or equality strands.

The chapter outlined trade union action on equality issues, both in the wider social and political sphere through campaigning activities and through workplace collective bargaining. Some of this action has made positive gains for disadvantaged workers, however, much more needs to be done. For a variety of reasons in the social, political and legal contexts (e.g. structural support for collective bargaining, different bargaining levels, fears of backlash towards positive action, prevalence of traditional gender relations), union campaigns and collective agreements are often conservative in nature. More progressive policies are necessary to challenge and transform the status quo. In many respects, the overall picture across Europe indicates slow progress towards greater equality.

REVIEW AND DISCUSSION QUESTIONS

1. Consider where you think the UK equality record stands in relation to other countries in Europe.

2. Consider the position of illegal workers, both from the point of view of state and EU policies and of wider social attitudes. Consider the statement that their treatment stands as: '*the super-exploitation of migrants suffering conditions which would not be tolerated by native workers but which they are not in a position to reject*' (Wrench, 1998: 11). Are there models or countries which provide more opportunities for equality for migrant workers than others?

3. What are the implications of the maintenance of the existing gender division of paid and household work? Does state and EU policy contribute to support for the status quo? Which models or countries offer the greatest prospect of gender equality?

FURTHER READING

EC, 2007. Report on Racism and Xenophobia in the Member States of the European Union. European Commission, Brussels.

Following introduction of the EU level Race Equality Directive, this report looks at the implementation of the directive and the initial evidence on how the legislation is applied by courts and tribunals,

EC, 2007. Discrimination in the European Union. Special Eurobarometer. European Commission, Luxembourg.

This report presents findings of a survey investigating public experiences of and attitudes to discrimination across the equality strands.

EC, 2008. Employment in Europe 2008. European Commission, Luxembourg.

This report presents survey findings and information on a variety of trends and patterns in European labour markets.

Ledwith, S., Colgan, F., 2002. Gender, Diversity and Trade Unions: International Perspectives. Routledge.

This book is an international collection of articles that explores the policies and practices of trade unions.

REFERENCES

Alund, A., Schierup, C., 1993. The thorny road to Europe: Swedish immigrant policy in transition. In: Wrench, J., Solomos, J. (Eds.), Racism and Migration in Western Europe. Berg Publishers (Chapter 7).

Beccalli, B., Meardi, G., 2002. Italian labour's changing and singular ambiguities. In: Colgan, F., Ledwith, S. (Eds.), Gender, Diversity and Trade Unions, International Perspectives. Routledge, London, pp. 113-131.

Bielenski, H., Bosch, G., Wagner, A., 2002. Working Time Preferences in 16 European Countries. European Foundation for the Improvement of Living and Working Conditions, Brussels.

Blos, M., Fischer, P., Straubhaar, T., 1997. The impact of migration policy on labour market performance of migrants: a comparative case study. New Community 23 (4), 511-533.

Bourdieu, P., Wacquant, L, 1999. On the cunning of imperialist reason. Theory, Culture and Society 16 (1), 41-58.

Bryant, C.A., 1997. Citizenship, national identity and the accommodation of difference: reflections on the German, French, Dutch and British cases. New Community 23 (2), 157-172.

Cockburn, C., 1995. Redrawing the boundaries: trade unions, women and Europe. In: Itzin, C., Newman, J. (Eds.), Gender Culture and Organisational Change. Routledge, London.

Deland, M., 1997. The cultural racism of Sweden. Race and Class 39 (1), 51-60.

EC, 1997. The Employment Situation of People with Disabilities: Employment in Europe. European Commission, Luxembourg.

EC, 1998. Reconciliation Between Work and Family Life in Europe, Employment and Social Affairs. European Commission, Luxembourg.

EC, 2007. Discrimination in the European Union. Special Eurobarometer. European Commission, Luxembourg.

EC, 2008. Employment in Europe 2008. European Commission, Luxembourg.

EIRO, 1997. Equal Opportunities and Collective Bargaining in the EU. Available from: <http://www.eiro.eurofound.ie/1997/04/study/Tn9704201S.html>.

EIRO, 2000. Industrial Relations and the Ageing Workforce: A Review of Measures to Combat Age Discrimination in Employment. Available from: <http://www.eiro.eurofound.ie/2000/01/study/index.htm>.

EIRO, 2001. Workers with Disability: Law, Bargaining and the Social Partners, European Industrial Relations Observatory. Available from: <http://www.eiro.eurofound.ie/2001/02/study/index.htm>.

EIRO, 2002. Gender Pay Equity: A Comparative Study. January 2002. Available from: <http://www.eiro.eurofound.ie/2002/01/study/TN0201101S.html>.

EIRO, 2003, EIRO Observer Bulletin May Issue. European Industrial Relations Observatory. Available from: <http://www.eiro.eurofound.ie/pdf/eo03-3.pdf>.

EIRR, March, 1997. European Year Against Racism. European Industrial Relations Review 278.

Esping-Anderson, G., 1990. The Three Worlds of Welfare Capitalism. Polity Press, Oxford. 2003. Migrant and Ethnic Minority Workers: Challenging Trade Unions. Labour Research Department and ETUC. ETUC.

EuroFoundation, 1998. The Employment of People with Disabilities in Small and Medium-Sized Enterprises. European Foundation for the Improvement of Living and Working Conditions, Dublin.

EuroFoundation, 2002. Reconciliation of Work and Family Life and Collective Bargaining: An Analysis of EIRO Articles. European Foundation for the Improvement of Living and Working Conditions, Brussels.

Fekete, L., 1997. Blackening the economy: the path to convergence. Race and Class 39, 11-17.

Fekete, L., 1999. Popular racism in Europe. Race and Class 40 (2/3), 189-198.

FRA, 2007. Report on Racism and Xenophobia in the Member States of the EU. FRA - European Union Agency for Fundamental Rights, Vienna.

Gachter, A., 1997. Case studies of good practice for the prevention of racial discrimination and xenophobia and the promotion of equal treatment at the workplace: Austria. European Foundation for the Improvement of Living and Working Conditions, Brussels.

Greene, A.M., Kirton, G., 2006. Trade unions and diversity. In: Konrad, A., Prasad, P., Pringle, J. (Eds.), Handbook of Workplace Diversity. Sage, London, pp. 489-510.

Hurst, R., 1995. Choice and empowerment - lessons from Europe. Disability and Society 10 (4), 529-535.

Langan, M., Ostner, I., 1990. Gender and welfare: towards a comparative framework. In: Paper Presented to the 1990 Social Policy Conference, Bath.

Ledwith, S., Colgan, F., 2002. Tackling gender, diversity and trade union democracy: a worldwide project? In: Colgan, F., Ledwith, S. (Eds.), Gender, Diversity and Trade Unions. International Perspectives. Routledge, pp. 1-27.

Leira, A., 1994. The woman-friendly welfare state: the case of Norway and Sweden. In: Lewis J. (Ed.), Women and Social Policies in Europe: Work, Family and the State.

Lunt, N., Thornton, P., 1993. Employment practices for disabled people: a review of legislation and services in fifteen countries. In: Research Series, Vol. 16. Employment Department, Sheffield.

Mahon, R., 2002. Sweden's LO. Learning to embrace the differences within? In: Colgan, F., Ledwith, S. (Eds.), Gender, Diversity and Trade Unions. International Perspectives. Routledge, pp. 48-72.

Moore, M., Tilson, T., Whitting, G., 1994. An international overview of employment policies and practices towards older workers. Research Series, Vol. 29. Employment Department.

Pillinger, J., 2008. Extending Equality: Trade Union Actions to Organise and Promote Equal Rights, Respect and Dignity for Workers Regardless of Their Sexual Orientation and Gender Identity. European Trade Union Confederation, Brussels.

Plantenga, J., 1995. Labour market participation of women in the EU. In: Doorne-Huiskes, A.V., VanHopf, J., Roelofs (Eds.), Women and the European Labour Market. Open University, The Netherlands (Chapter 1).

Pred, A., 1997. Somebody else, somewhere else: racisms, racialized spaces and the popular geographical imagination in Sweden. Antipode 29 (4), 383-416.

Rathzel, N., 1999. Workers of migrant origin in Germany: forms of discrimination in the labour market and the workplace. In: Wrench, J., Rea, A., Oali, N. (Eds.), Migrants, Ethnic Minorities and the Labour Market: Integration and Exclusion in Europe. Macmillan.

Rix, S., 1993. Older workers in the United States: conditions of work and transitions to retirement. In: Paper Presented to the International Congress of Gerontology, July.

Roelofs, E., 1995. The European equal opportunities policy. In: Doorne-Huiskes, A.V., Van Hopf, J., Roelofs, R. (Eds.), Women and the European Labour Market. Open University, The Netherlands (Chapter 8).

Sivariandam, A., 1997. Introduction. Race and Class 39 (1), 1.

Swank, D., Betz, H., 2003. Globalization, the welfare state and right-wing populism in Western Europe. Socio-Economic Review 1, 215–245.

Thornton P., Lunt N., 1995. Employment for disabled people: social obligation or individual responsibility? Social Policy Research Unit Report 2.

Van der Lippe, T., d Roelofs, E., 1995. Sharing domestic work. In: Doorne-Huiskes, A.V., Van Hopf, J., Roelofs, R. (Eds.), Women and the European Labour Market. Open University, The Netherlands (Chapter 6).

Villota, P., Ferrari, I., 2001. The Impact of the Tax/Benefit System on Women's Work. Madrid. Available from: <http://europa.eu.int/comm/employment_social/equ_opp/women_work.pdf>.

Wrench, J., 1997. European Compendium of Good Practice for the Prevention of Racism in the Workplace. Office for Official Publications of the European Communities, Luxembourg.

Wrench, J., 1998. The EU. Ethnic Minorities and Migrants in the Workplace. Kogan Page, London.

Wrench, J., 2002. Diversity Management, Discrimination and Ethnic Minorities in Europe: Clarification, Critiques and Research Agendas. CEUS, Norrkoping. ThemES No. 19.

Wrench, J., 2003. Breakthroughs and Blind Spots: Trade Union Responses to Immigrants and Ethnic Minorities in Denmark and the UK. University of Southern Denmark, Esbjerg.

Wrench, J., Jandl, M., Kraler, A., Stepien, A., 2003. Migrants, Minorities and Employment: Exclusion, Discrimination and Anti-discrimination in the 15 Member States of the EU. European Monitoring Centre on Racism and Xenaphobia (EUMC), Brussels, October.

Wynne, R., McAnaney, D., O'Kelly, C., Fleming, P., 2006. Employment Guidance Services for People with Disabilities. European Foundation for the Improvement of Living and Working Conditions, Dublin.

The future of equality and diversity

Aim

To provide a summary of themes addressed in this book and to offer some thoughts on the future direction of equality and diversity policy and practices.

Objectives

- To highlight and identify key themes and issues dealt with in Chapters 1–10.
- To explore the prospects for a 'diversity' paradigm eclipsing the present 'equality' paradigm.

11.1 INTRODUCTION

In Chapter 1, we set out our objectives for this book. The primary aim of this book was to fill the gap identified within the field of equality and diversity and to help readers to 'manage' the study of diversity in the employment context. One objective was to situate current and emerging equality and diversity debates and issues within the context of UK and European labour markets. This involved providing conceptual and theoretical underpinning and examining the social and economic contexts within which labour market activity takes place. Other objectives were to stimulate debate and critique of theory, policy and practice in the area of equality and diversity and to trace developments in equality and diversity approaches in order to identify possible future directions in the twenty-first century. In particular, our objective was to critically evaluate whether or not the shift to diversity approaches can be viewed as a positive development. This chapter attempts to summarise the key themes of the 10 chapters in this book and to indicate how these objectives have been met.

11.2 SUMMARY OF THEMES AND ISSUES

11.2.1 Continuing patterns of inequality

'Equality is evolving every day. It was not so long ago that signs in shops, pubs and restaurants said 'no dogs, no blacks, no Irish'. We have come

a long way since then but there is still a lot more to be done to combat the evil of racism.'

(Beverly Bernard, acting Chair, Commission for Racial Equality, EOR, 2003)

Perhaps the most prominent finding of the book is the continued patterns of inequality faced by many social groups within the UK and European labour markets. Whichever way the statistics are looked at, the labour market is still characterised by segregation, inequalities, disadvantage and discrimination, which disproportionately affect 'minority' groups (Chapter 2). These employment inequalities are reflective of wider social attitudes, institutions and structures.

There are countless examples of sexist, racist, ageist, disableist and homophobic discrimination within the policies and practices of organisations and governments. Chapters 4 and 8 highlighted how organisational structures and practices are gendered, racialised and sexualised. Chapters 6 and 10 highlighted the role of the state both as policy-maker and legislator in contributing to the unequal and discriminatory character of labour markets. Chapters 3 and 5 indicated how free-market theories that privilege notions of competition and supply and demand factors are insufficient to explain the continuing patterns of labour market inequalities. It is also necessary to consider the significance of wider social attitudes towards diverse social groups, including stereotyping and discriminatory practices at the organisational level (Chapters 4 and 8). The newspapers and television are full of incidents of employment-related discrimination and efforts to combat it. In the area of race equality for example, highly publicised events such as the Stephen Lawrence Inquiry and the widely publicised MacPherson Report that followed from it, exposed the extent to which racism is embedded within our society and its institutions. This has generated considerable debate and 'soul-searching' especially by public sector organisations in the UK. However, the prevalence of institutional racism continues to be a current issue, for example, the BBC documentary that uncovered virulent racial prejudice among police trainees (*Observer*, October 26, 2003).

11.2.1.1 *Continuation of the white, male norm*

'If Britain is to have achieved equality for women and men by 2013, it requires a step-change in the way we approach the whole issue of equality. We cannot address inequalities between the sexes without also taking into account the impact of other sources of inequality, including race, disability, age, sexual orientation and belief.'

(Julie Mellor, chair, Equal Opportunities Commission)

Chapter 5 traced the recent changes in thinking on equality issues and the shift towards conceptualising workforces as composed of diverse social groups ('difference' rather than 'sameness' approaches) with multiple and intersecting identities. Liberal approaches to equality focus on the need for formalisation of procedures to ensure equal treatment and include an emphasis on legislation. Chapter 6 pointed out the weaknesses of British equality law. Although the anti-sex and anti-race discrimination legislation is longstanding, it is too early as yet to gauge the impact of the more recent legislation on other equality strands including sexual orientation, religion or belief and age. Further, as discussed in Chapter 6, legislation outlawing discrimination on grounds of sexual orientation may seem to conflict with that outlawing discrimination on grounds of religious belief. Overall, the tenacity of the male norm, and we would say the white, male, non-disabled, heterosexual, 25–40 years norm, weakens the impact of the legislation.

This discussion reflects a key theme emerging from the book – the weaknesses of both equality and diversity approaches because both remain within a liberal and 'short' agenda. Overall, the evidence presented indicates that policy and practice at both national and organisational levels pose little challenge to the status quo – existing social attitudes and the existing norm of work, which as we have argued, is gendered, racialised and sexualised.

This raises the question of whether diversity approaches are a *new way forward* for equality within the UK labour market. Chapters 5 and 8 highlighted the shift towards diversity approaches, within which there is recognition of individual and group-based differences. The diversity paradigm also sees a need to view difference in a positive way and to include a broader range of people than in traditional liberal equality approaches. In addition, diversity rhetoric appears to encourage wider culture change, which might lead to more radical challenges to existing structures and attitudes. However, what is emphasised overall is that in practice, the move to diversity approaches often really represents little change from the liberal equality model, with many of the measures included under the diversity label, also being part of conventional equal opportunities policies (Kandola and Fullerton, 1994; Webb, 1997). In the UK in particular, as Chapter 8 discussed, employers have not really taken up diversity in the same way as in the US, so that diversity initiatives become more of a supplement to equal opportunities policies rather than posing a new and radical challenge to the organisational structures and cultures.

We also question whether diversity approaches can be seen as a way *forward*. Chapter 5 discussed the negative implications of the emphasis on 'difference', which can serve to reinforce stereotypes and lead to ignoring similarities between individuals and groups. Further, the diversity approach tends to place the emphasis on the individual, a development which many commentators see as detrimental (Dickens, 1997). As Chapter 9 discussed, this reflects the similarity between human resource management (HRM) and diversity approaches. The unitarist and individualist focus of HRM can be seen as a challenge to the role of collective groups such as trade unions, which as Chapters 7 and 10 highlighted, have an important role to play in encouraging policies and initiatives which enhance the pursuit of equality issues at workplace and societal levels.

The link between diversity and HRM also raises the issue of the business case, as discussed in Chapter 8. Our overall argument is that the business case is not a fruitful basis on which to frame policies, encouraging only a 'short' (equality) agenda and only a minimal or compliance approach to equality, rather than encouraging the development of comprehensive, proactive policies where a strong sense of social justice will also underpin initiatives and practices. As Chapter 8 goes on to debate, the diversity approach may actually encourage the avoidance of more radical and 'long' equality agendas because what might be seen as 'preferential' treatment will be at odds with a diversity approach (Liff, 1995).

Overall this seems fairly depressing reading. However, such a critical perspective is valuable, we feel, in order to combat the overly optimistic viewpoints contained in some textbooks and practitioner texts. It is certainly important to recognise that many social groups within the labour market are far from achieving equality. For example, the 'you *can* have it all' literature, which perpetuates the 'superwoman' image of female success within the male norm of work, we feel, is detrimental to the position of women in the labour market. Women who are most able to be 'superwomen' are predominantly in better paid, higher status, and usually professional jobs, but are held up as examples to all other women who are trying to juggle work and family responsibilities. As Chapter 9 discussed, liberal equality approaches tend to help only a small segment of people facing disadvantage, arguably people who are in a considerably better position to begin with (Dickens, 1997; Webb, 1997). Such views significantly underplay the role of identity constructions and unequal power structures, which are discussed in the chapters of this book.

On the other hand it is certain that there have been improvements over the last 30 years or so in the employment opportunities of many of the groups that we have considered within this book. Workforce diversity is commonly recognised, incidents of discrimination often cause public outrage, and legislation continues to improve (if only in a limited way) the protection and increases the rights of a diverse workforce. While the overall picture is of continued patterns of inequality, there are plenty of examples of 'good' practice and more progressive models and policies discussed within this book. Despite a context of inequality and disadvantage, it is important that people are not simply seen purely as victims of the structures and cultures in which their work careers take place. As stated in Chapter 1, individuals are also makers of their own histories and some individuals can and do overcome socially constructed barriers and obstacles typically encountered by their social group.

Also, there is evidence in the earlier chapters of organisational and government models and practices which do attempt to challenge (in a more radical or 'long' agenda sense) socially constructed barriers and obstacles. For example, Chapter 10 offered some alternative models of state policy and provision, which potentially allow more opportunities for equality within the labour market, such as in the Scandinavian countries. Chapter 8 provided examples of organisations where a comprehensive, proactive approach to equality and diversity policy is taken. Such evidence can soften the pessimistic tone of the summary of equality and diversity issues within the UK.

However, it is important that continued patterns of inequality are recognised in order that they can be tackled. Without doubt there is still much work to be done in advancing equality within employment, particularly at the level of the 'sticky floor', as well as at the 'glass ceiling' which has received more public and organisational policy attention. The question now is how can we move forward? What does the evidence presented in this book indicate about the models, policies and practices which appear to offer the most potential for advancing equality and valuing workforce diversity?

11.2.2 **Possible ways forward**

'Because litigation is expensive, uncertain, and stressful for the individual litigant, the balance has shifted in favour of persuasion and promotion, concentrating on systems and practices and avoiding confrontation. The real question is what impact the plethora of equal opportunity policies actually has on the level of discrimination.'

(Geoffrey Bindman, senior partner in Bindman and Partners Solicitors, EOR, 2003)

As stated in Chapter 1, our objectives in writing this book do not include making recommendations or drawing prescriptive conclusions from our discussions. However, the evidence and debates discussed do highlight models, approaches and practices, which appear to either impede or facilitate progression along the road to equality for different groups in the labour market. We are not suggesting a blueprint for future practice, but are suggesting elements which we feel should play an important part in policy and practice. Four themes emerge as important in potentially facilitating this progress: first, the need to maintain a group focus within equality and diversity policies and to encourage diverse social groups to organize their own support networks. Second, there is a need to broaden the business case for equality beyond short-term consider-ations. Third, the need to integrate 'sameness' and 'difference' approaches, rather than seeing equality and diversity as opposed and contradictory. Fourth, the need for a signif-icantly revised view of what paid work means, and its centrality in our lives.

11.2.2.1 *Group focus*

The discussions in many chapters of this book highlight the importance of a group focus in equality and diversity policy and practice. We suggest that the individualistic focus of mainstream diversity management is not a productive basis on which to frame policies. While we acknowledge that categorising individuals in reference to their social groups might be in some ways constraining, we also argue that individuals can never entirely escape their socially constructed positioning, and this needs to be recognised as a fundamental contributing factor to patterns of inequality experienced.

Thus, we highlight the potentially detrimental effects of equality and diversity approaches that emphasise the individual. Chapter 6 indicated the weaknesses of equality law in the UK, which places the onus on the individual having to fight their case, or uphold their individual rights, unlike the 'class action' approach of the US. To us, this seems only to further victimise the individual, focusing on their own experi-ences and failure to succeed within the unequal and discriminatory structures, rather than recognising the structures as part of the essential problem. Given the financial resources that are needed to fight legal cases, this approach will tend to benefit only a minority of people. We emphasise the importance of collective groups, because it is collective groups, such as trade unions, which can provide essential resources to the individuals concerned.

More significant than resource issues, however, collective groups provide essential support for those facing disadvantage in the labour market. Chapter 4 highlighted the importance of organisational networks to people facing discriminatory structures and practices. The value of role models as symbols of what is possible for 'minority groups', was also underlined. Chapter 7 showed the important role that trade unions can play in pushing for equality issues as part of the bargaining agenda. In contrast, an emphasis on differences between *individuals* (characteristic of diversity management) weakens the ties that people have through common experience, leaving people feeling alone and isolated in their equality struggles. It is these ties that provide the necessary support for individuals and groups to push from the bottom-up for action (Cockburn, 1989). In Dickens' (1997) ideal model of Equal Opportunities (EO) practice, the role of trade unions for example is seen as vital in the campaign for equality in the workplace. Such an emphasis on collective social groupings needs to be maintained within diversity approaches.

11.2.2.2 **Broadening the agenda of the business case**

'Equal opportunities and business success go hand in hand. You simply cannot have one without the other. The organisations that do best in a world where people's skills are increasingly important will be those that put equality and diversity at the heart of their strategy'.

(Patricia Hewitt, Secretary of State for Trade and Industry and Minister for Women, EOR, 2003)

In a 2004 lecture held at Warwick Business School, Renate Hornung-Draus (Director of European and International Affairs at the German Employers' Confederation) talked about the role of national and European employers' associations in the twenty-first century. When asked by an audience member, what the role of employers' associations was in mainstreaming equality, her answer was that this was largely a wider societal rather than organisational concern and that the internal context of organisations should be the concern of the HR department. The view that inequality is caused by wider societal attitudes and structures and consequently something that organisations have no control over, or input into, is a common one. For example, the excuse often given for there being no black and minority ethnic senior managers is that 'they' simply do not apply. Or similarly, that there are no women engineers because women do not choose engineering degrees. However, we would argue that this is little more than a feeble excuse; organisations have to take some responsibility for the part they play in upholding employment segregation. An agenda to work towards changing wider social attitudes has to be part of a broadened business case.

One of the themes emerging from our discussions is the potentially detrimental effects of a purely business case approach to equality and diversity (Chapters 5, 8 and 9). We must recognise that the 'bottom line' is what most organisations will be concerned with; they are after all, business organisations. However, we suggest that a more fruitful way forward, following Dickens (1994; see also Liff and Dickens, 2000), is to conceive of a broader definition of business case interests. Organisations need to link their business case for equality and diversity to wider issues of social justice and corporate social responsibility. As discussed in Chapter 8, consumer, shareholder and employee pressure may be the catalyst for this broader agenda. This also connects to our discussion of wider social structures and of public policies that offer the most potential for tackling labour market inequalities (Chapter 10). Public policies in Scandinavia, for example, are based more around social justice rather than only economic necessity.

11.2.2.3 **Integrating equality and diversity approaches**

Is 'diversity' a *new way forward*? It is clear that some commentators certainly do not agree:

Diversity training is really a PR exercise, a way of projecting a positive public image. 'Diversity' has become a brand, a kind of Benetton shorthand for cool, liberal modernity. And any organisation that wants to brush up its image signs up. When the BBC wanted to shake off its fuddy-duddy image, it replaced its big globe balloon logo with shots of wheelchair-bound dreadlocked basketball players and Indian classical dancers. When the Arts Council wanted to become more relevant it launched its Year of Diversity. When Ford Motor Company was revealed to be 'whiting out' black faces on its posters, it instituted a glossy, multi-million-pound diversity programme.

(Guardian, 29 October 2003.)

The quote above by Kenan Malik appeared in a national newspaper article on the day that his television documentary '*Segregated Britain, Disunited Kingdom*' was aired on Channel 4. His position is clearly that diversity is simply the new management fad. More than this, it may have negative consequences. Concerning race in British society, Malik contends that the diversity discourse take the attention away from the realities of discrimination experienced by 'minority' groups, whilst also dividing communities more effectively than racism by legitimising a myriad of cultural differences, which end up isolating and dividing groups of people.

These are debates that we have discussed, however, even engaging with this question of whether the diversity approach is something better, it does not appear particularly useful, and may actually be counter-productive. Why should we think of new policies and approaches as necessarily eclipsing the old? Not only is this often detrimental, but it is also quite obvious that this does not happen in reality. Just as HRM techniques are built on traditional industrial relations and management practices, the older, liberal equality tradition lives on in today's diversity management policy and practice, even if it has been partly superseded in theory. Moreover we argue that it would actually be more practical and useful to integrate equality *and* diversity, liberal *and* radical approaches. All have weaknesses and strengths as have been discussed in depth in the earlier chapters. This may be an idealistic aspiration, but why could the strengths of both not be integrated, so that they were seen as a complement to each other (Liff, 1999)? The diversity approach for example, suffers from its individualistic focus, but also is much more forward-looking than liberal equality in its view of difference as positive and as something that should be valued. Dickens (1997), for example, suggested that collective equality bargaining by trade unions could underpin and generalise employer's equality initiatives, while the law could generalise and underpin both of these. It is important that in taking up aspects of the diversity approach, the support and protection offered by legislation and formalised procedures are not lost, or are still fought for. There is still much more progress that could be made in the legislative and procedural arena (Rees, 1998; Liff, 1996). The diversity approach offers challenges to organisational cultures, but it needs to be underpinned by increased legal protection and rights and by positive action policies. This would all help to ensure that the diversity of the labour market is reflected in organisational workforces to begin with (Miller, 1996).

11.2.2.4 *A new model of work*

Finally, we believe that changes in the patterns of disadvantage in the labour market can only come through radical revision of what is considered to be the norm of work. The existing norm, based around the white, male, full-time, non-disabled, young(ish) and heterosexual worker, offers little chance for facilitating a labour market which values diversity, rather than one that simply attempts to accommodate and assimilate difference. Developing a new model of work would involve the need for radical changes in wider social attitudes, better state provisions in areas such as childcare and eldercare and more inclusive organisational structures and practices (Liff and Wajcman, 1996).

This book has examined changes in wider social attitudes, and while on the one hand, there is, for example, increasing evidence of more egalitarian attitudes towards gender roles, and acceptance that discrimination should be outlawed, on the other hand, there is also evidence of the rise of racism within Europe, the tenacity of the traditional gender regime and continued incidents of discrimination. Changing wider social attitudes is obviously not simple and is unlikely to happen rapidly. However, we should not necessarily feel that attitudes will never change. For example, a recent survey of experiences, perceptions and attitudes to discrimination in the European Union explored the extent of diversity in respondents' social circles. The report argued that this is important when considering the issue of discrimination.

The findings were that over half of all Europeans have friends or acquaintances who are of a different religion or have different beliefs to them (61%), who are disabled (55%) or of a different ethnic origin to them (55%). It was found to be comparatively rarer for respondents to have homosexual friends or acquaintances (34%) or to have Roma friends (14%). The report contends that cultural attitudes towards diversity play a factor, particularly with regard to homosexuality. Sixty-nine percent of Dutch respondents said that they have homosexual friends, whilst just three percent of Romanians said the same (EC, 2008).

Existing policies at national and organisational levels still appear to uphold the dominant norm of work, and this has been repeated as a fundamental criticism of policy and practice throughout this book. Chapters 8 and 10 engaged with the way in which organisational policies and state policies interact with wider social attitudes, so that neither can be sufficient in order to bring about fundamental change. However, it is important that policies and practices do not simply uphold and continue to perpetuate dominant and inherently discriminatory structures. So for example, the UK Employment Relations Act, introduced in 1999, included recommendations and legislation supplying family-friendly provisions such as childcare support, parental leave and domestic leave. However, this legislation was met with disappointment by trade unions and other interest groups because in practice it continued to uphold the mother as the primary carer, despite bearing the label 'parental leave'.

As Liff and Wacjman (1996) suggest, a new norm has to recognise the overlapping and multiple identities ascribed to and achieved by individuals. The 'long hours culture' is one of the most tenacious norms of work and is detrimental for both women and men seeking to achieve work–life balance. The existing norm supports a notion that the employee's commitment to the job should always take primacy over alternative commitments such as caring responsibilities. While part-time and other forms of more flexible work are on the increase and are being encouraged by employers and the government, this does not necessarily achieve equality, especially when flexible workers face lower-paid, lower-status and less-protected jobs. Chapter 8 discussed the detrimental effects of work as defined by this hegemonic norm on the five social groups. Changes in the status, pay and protection of flexible work arrangements would be a significant and progressive step towards equality.

However, once again the interaction between attitudes and policy and practice is highlighted. While social attitudes continue to accept and perpetuate the dominant norm, state and organisational attempts to challenge it are limited in their effects. One example is the failure of the Swedish welfare model to lead to a more equal gender division of domestic responsibilities even though the opportunities for this exist within the policies and provisions available to women and men. Change at only one level will not be sufficient to achieve transformation in the patterns of disadvantage. There needs a combined effort at state, organisational and societal levels; some might say that this is an impossible venture. However, without such fundamental change, the equality project will continue to be piecemeal and limited and there will be relatively little alteration in labour market patterns in future. Nevertheless, this should not cause total despondency, the utility of inquiry and critique such as in this book is to inspire alternative conceptualisations and models of good practice.

REFERENCES

Cockburn, C., 1989. Equal opportunities: the long and short agenda. Industrial Relations Journal Autumn, 213–225.

Dickens, L., 1997. Gender, race and employment equality in Britain: inadequate strategies and the role of industrial relations actors. Industrial Relations Journal 28 (4), 282–289.

EC, 2008. Discrimination in the European Union: Perceptions, Experiences and Attitudes. Special Eurobarometer. European Commission, Luxembourg.

EOR, 2003. Agenda: future world of equal opportunities. Equal Opportunities Review, No. 113.

Kandola, R., Fullerton, J., 1994. Managing the Mosaic: Diversity in Action. Institute of Personnel and Development (IPD), London.

Liff, S., 1995. Equal opportunities: continuing discrimination in a context of formal equality. In: Edwards, P. (Ed.), Industrial Relations. Oxford, Blackwell.

Liff, S., 1996. Two routes to managing diversity: individual differences or social group characteristics. Employee Relations 19 (1), 11–26.

Liff, S., Wajcman, J., 1996. 'Sameness' and 'difference' revisited: which way forward for equal opportunity initiatives? Journal of Management Studies 33 (1), 79–95.

Liff, S., 1999. Diversity and equal opportunities: room for a constructive compromise? Human Resource Management Journal 9 (1), 65–75.

Liff, S., Dickens, L., 2000. Ethics and equality: reconciling false dilemmas. In: Winstanley, D., Woodall, L. (Eds.), Ethical Issues in Contemporary Human Resource Management. Macmillan, London.

Miller, D., 1996. Equality management: towards a materialist approach. Gender, Work and Organisation 3 (4), 202–214.

Observer, 2003. Inside the ranks of racism. Sunday, October 26.

Rees, T., 1998. Mainstreaming Equality in the European Union. Routledge, London.

The Guardian, 2003. The dirty D-word by Kenan Malik.

Webb, J., 1997. The politics of equal opportunity. Gender, Work and Organisation 4 (3), 159–167.

Glossary of Terms and Abbreviations

ACAS: Advisory, Conciliation and Arbitration Service.

Acceptability criteria: Term most often used in the recruitment and selection context and refers to subjective criteria that may often have stereotyped or prejudicial underpinnings, including whether or not a person will 'fit in' to the social networks and relationships of the organization.

Business case: A justification of equality/diversity initiatives based upon economic rationality.

CAC: Central Arbitration Committee.

CIPD: Chartered Institute of Personnel and Development, the professional body for those involved within the field of human resource management. It produces various guides and resources for human resource practitioners, which encourage good employment practice.

Class action: US system which permits individuals who have been affected by identical discrimination to be given the same remedy as the person who was successful in a previous case.

Codes of practice: Government guidance providing recommendations on employment practice, which are not legally binding. May be used as evidence at employment tribunal.

Collective bargaining: The method of determining working conditions and terms of employment through negotiations between an employer and a trade union. A **collective agreement** is the outcome of such negotiations.

Concrete ceiling: The term used to describe the seemingly impenetrable barriers preventing the progress of people from minority ethnic groups.

CRE: Commission for Racial Equality set up by the Race Relations Act 1976. Its duties were to work towards the elimination of race discrimination, to promote equality and good relations between people of different racial groups. It issues various guides for employers on good practice. Now replaced by the Equality and Human Rights Commission (EHRC).

DDA: Disability Discrimination Act 1995.

Demand-side: An economic term. Demand-side factors are those that influence employers' requirements for labour.

DfES: Department for education and skills.

Domestic sphere/domestic labour: Terms used to denote unpaid work in the home and family responsibilities.

Downward occupational mobility: The term used to describe the tendency for women to enter lower status employment following a break for childbirth/care.

DRC: Disability Rights Commission, now replaced by the Equality and Human Rights Commission (EHRC).

EAT: Employment Appeal Tribunal.

EC: European Commission.

ECHR: European Court of Human Rights.

ECJ: European Court of Justice.

Economic activity rate: The proportion of the workforce that is either in employment or registered as unemployed.

EEC: European Economic Community.

EHRC: Equality and Human Rights Commission. The Commission's role is to promote human rights and fairness for all. It provides advice and guidance to individuals, employers and the government. It works to implement effective legislation and to raise public awareness of rights. It is an amalgamation of the former CRE, DRC and EOC.

EIRR: European Industrial Relations Review.

Employment tribunal: Employees can complain to the employment tribunal when they suspect that a statutory employment law has been breached by an employer. The tribunal system operates like an informal court of law.

EO: Equal Opportunities.

EOC: Equal Opportunities Commission set up by the Sex Discrimination Act 1975. Its aim is to work towards the elimination of sex discrimination and promote equality between the sexes. It issues various guides for employers, encouraging good practice. Now replaced by the Equality and Human Rights Commission (EHRC).

EOPs: Equal Opportunities Policies.

Equality bargaining: Collective agreements on equality issues.

ETUC: European Trades Union Congress.

EU: European Union.

Family-friendly policy: Employment policies facilitating the balancing of work and parental/caring responsibilities.

Feminine-in-management: A thesis emphasizing women's unique management skills, also termed as 'women in management'.

Gender pay gap: The term frequently used to describe the earnings disparity between women and men. If the 'gap' is 20%, then women earn 80% of men's average earnings.

Glass ceiling: The term refers to invisible barriers preventing women from advancing to higher levels within organizations.

GOR: Genuine Occupational Requirement.

HR: Human Resources

HRA: Human Rights Act 1998.

HRM: Human Resource Management.

Human capital: The term used to describe the skills, education, training, abilities and experience possessed by individuals.

Immigrant worker: Non-nationals who intend to reside permanently in the country of migration.

Indirect labour costs: Costs other than direct remuneration associated with the employment of labour, for example maternity/parental leave and training.

Institutional racism: The term used to describe the existence of policy and administrative processes within social institutions, which result in the adverse treatment of minority ethnic people.

Mainstreaming: The inclusion of equality issues in every part of business strategy and policy.

Migrant worker: Non-nationals moving from country to country, predominantly for work.

Occupational segregation: The tendency for certain social groups to be disproportionately situated in certain occupations or status positions.

ONS: Office for National Statistics.

OPCS: Office for Population and Census Surveys.

Patriarchy: Has been defined as 'a system of social structures and practices in which men dominate, oppress and exploit women' (S. Walby [1990]. *Theorizing Patriarchy*, Blackwell, p. 20).

Positive action: Refers to efforts to remove obstacles to the free operation of the labour market. The aim is to promote free and equal competition among individuals.

Positive discrimination: Involves the deliberate manipulation of employment practices with the intention of achieving a proportional distribution of disadvantaged social groups within the workforce.

Public sphere: A term used to denote paid work in the labour market.

RRA: Race Relations Act 1976.

SDA: Sex Discrimination Act 1975.

Social Chapter: Seeks to pursue Europe-wide regulation of the labour market, including working conditions, dialogue between management and labour and protection of workers.

Social identity: The process of achieved or ascribed categorization, which occurs within societal relations.

Social justice case: Justification of equality/diversity initiatives based upon ethical or moral rationality.

Stakeholder: One of many participants (individual or group based) with a vested interest in the organization (e.g. employer, management, trade union, employee, customer, supplier, government).

Statistical discrimination: Discrimination against groups of workers, relating to perceived characteristics of that particular group.

Suitability criteria: Term most often used in the recruitment and selection context and refers to more objective criteria based around skills, qualifications and experience.

Supply-side: An economic term. Supply-side factors are those that shape the nature of the labour supply, that is the workforce, including demographic and skill variables and personal preferences.

Third country nationals: Migrant and immigrant workers who are nationals of non-EU countries.

TUC: Trades Union Congress, the coordinating body of Britain's trade union movement.

Union recognition: An employer may 'recognize' a trade union either as the representative of employees who are members (in cases of grievance or discipline, for example) and/or for the purposes of collective bargaining.

UNISON: One of the UK's largest trade unions. Membership is located in the public services.

WERS: Workplace Employee Relations Survey (formerly **WIRS:** Workplace Industrial Relations Survey).

Work–life balance: Employment policies facilitating the balancing of work and life outside of work (implicitly extends beyond parenting/caring responsibilities).

Index